Sepher Raziel

Liber Salomonis

ספר רזיאל

Sourceworks of Ceremonial Magic Series

Volume VI – Sepher Raziel: Liber Salomonis

In the same series:

Volume I – The Practical Angel Magic of John Dee's Enochian Tables - ISBN 978-0-9547639-0-9

Volume II – The Keys to the Gateway of Magic: Summoning the Solomonic Archangels & Demonic Princes – ISBN 978-0-9547639-1-6

Volume III – The Goetia of Dr Rudd: The Angels & Demons of *Liber Malorum Spirituum seu Goetia* – ISBN 978-0-9547639-2-3

Volume IV – The Veritable Key of Solomon– ISBN 978-0-9547639-8-5 (leather) also available as 978-0-7378-1453-0 (cloth hardback)

Volume V – The Grimoire of Saint Cyprian: Clavis Inferni - ISBN 978-0-9557387-1-5 (cloth) – ISBN 978-0-9557387-4-6 (limited leather)

Volume VI – *Sepher Raziel: Liber Salomonis* – ISBN 978-0-9557387-3-9 (cloth) – ISBN 978-0-9557387-5-3 (limited leather)

Volume VII - *Liber Lunæ & Sepher ha-Levanah* - ISBN 978-0-9557387-2-1 (cloth) - ISBN 978-0-9557387-3-8 (limited leather)

Volume VIII - The Magical Treatise of Solomon, or *Hygromanteia* - ISBN 978-0-9568285-0-7 (cloth) - ISBN 978-0-9568285-1-4 (limited leather)

For further details of forthcoming volumes in this series edited from classic magical manuscripts see www.GoldenHoard.com

Books and Online Essays by Don Karr

Approaching the Kabbalah of Maat - Teitan
Liber Lunae [with Calanit Nachshon] – Golden Hoard
Notes on the Study of Later Kabbalah in English - online
Notes on the Study of Merkavah Mysticism and Hekhalot Literature in English - online
The Study of Christian Cabala in English - online

Selected Books on the Western Esoteric Tradition by Stephen Skinner

Complete Magician's Tables – Golden Hoard & Llewellyn
Dr John Dee's Spiritual Diaries (1583-1608) a revised edition of "A True & Faithful Relation of what passed…between Dr John Dee…and some Spirits" - GHP
Geomancy in Theory & Practice – Golden Hoard
Goetia of Dr Rudd: Liber Malorum Spirituum [with David Rankine] – Golden Hoard
Grimoire of Saint Cyprian: Clavis Inferni [with David Rankine] – Golden Hoard
Key to the Latin of Dr John Dee's Spiritual Diaries (1583–1608) – Golden Hoard
Keys to the Gateway of Magic [with David Rankine] – Golden Hoard
Millennium Prophecies: Apocalypse 2000 - Carlton
Nostradamus [with Francis King] – Carlton
Oracle of Geomancy – Warner Destiny & Prism
Practical Angel Magic of Dee's Enochian Tables [with David Rankine] – Golden Hoard
Sacred Geometry – Gaia/Hamlyn
Search for Abraxas [with Nevill Drury] – Spearman & Salamander
Sepher Raziel: Liber Salomonis [with Don Karr] – Golden Hoard
Techniques of High Magic [with Francis King] – Inner Traditions
Terrestrial Astrology: Divination by Geomancy – RKP
Veritable Key of Solomon [with David Rankine] – Golden Hoard & Llewellyn

On Feng Shui by Stephen Skinner

Feng Shui Before & After - Haldane Mason
Feng Shui for Modern Living aka *Feng Shui for Everyday Living* - Cico
Feng Shui History – Golden Hoard
Feng Shui Style - Periplus
Feng Shui the Traditional Oriental Way - Haldane Mason
Feng Shui: the Living Earth Manual - Tuttle
Flying Star Feng Shui - Tuttle
Guide to the Feng Shui Compass – Golden Hoard
K.I.S.S. Guide to Feng Shui (Keep it Simple Series) – Penguin/DK
Living Earth Manual of Feng Shui - Penguin/Arkana
Practical Makeovers Using Feng Shui - Tuttle

Sepher Raziel

also known as

Liber Salomonis

a 1564 English Grimoire

from Sloane MS 3826

manuscript transcribed, annotated and introduced

by Don Karr

foreword and modern English version

by Stephen Skinner

GOLDEN HOARD PRESS

2017

Published by Golden Hoard Press Pte Ltd
Robinson Road PO Box 1073
Singapore 902123

www.GoldenHoard.com

Second Expanded Edition

© 2010, 2013 Don Karr (Introduction, transcription, bibliography and annotations) &
        Stephen Skinner (Foreword and modern English text of Sloane MS 3826)

© 2017 Second Expanded Edition

All rights reserved. No part of this publication may be reproduced or utilized in any form or by any means, electronic or mechanical, including printing, photocopying, uploading to the web, recording, or by any information storage and retrieval system, or used in another book, without specific written permission from both authors, except for short fully credited extracts or quotes used for scholastic or review purposes.

ISBN: 978-1912212026 paperback edition

Printed by CreateSpace

Sepher Raziel

also known as

Liber Salomonis

a 1564 English Grimoire
from Sloane MS 3826

manuscript transcribed, annotated and introduced
by Don Karr

foreword and modern English version
by Stephen Skinner

GOLDEN HOARD PRESS
2017

Published by Golden Hoard Press Pte Ltd
Robinson Road PO Box 1073
Singapore 902123

www.GoldenHoard.com

Second Expanded Edition

© 2010, 2013 Don Karr (Introduction, transcription, bibliography and annotations) & Stephen Skinner (Foreword and modern English text of Sloane MS 3826)

© 2017 Second Expanded Edition

All rights reserved. No part of this publication may be reproduced or utilized in any form or by any means, electronic or mechanical, including printing, photocopying, uploading to the web, recording, or by any information storage and retrieval system, or used in another book, without specific written permission from both authors, except for short fully credited extracts or quotes used for scholastic or review purposes.

ISBN: 978-1912212026 paperback edition

Printed by CreateSpace

Acknowledgements

The cover image of a scribe working in a scriptorium is that of Jean Miélot (d. 1472) canon of Lille who transcribed many interesting and magical works, including the *Secret of Secrets*. The pages from Sloane MSS 3826, 3846, 3847, 3853 have been reproduced with the kind permission of the British Library, for which we are duly grateful. Our thanks to Sears Jayne of Brown University who originally provided the microfilm of *Cephar Raziel* in 1978.

Bibliographic Note

Note that despite similar names, the English grimoire *Sepher Raziel: Liber Salomonis* is quite different in content from the Hebrew *Sepher Raziel ha-Melakh* as edited by Steve Savedow in *Sepher Rezial Hemelach: The Book of the Angel Rezial*, Weiser, York Beach, 2000. The only thing they appear to have in common is the same source of angelic inspiration, and a few short passages. They represent two completely different 'Raziel' traditions.

Contents

Acknowledgements & Bibliographic Note	7
Contents	9
List of Figures	11
Foreword – Stephen Skinner	13
The Study of Solomonic Magic in English – Don Karr	25
Introduction to the Manuscript – Don Karr	68
Sepher Raziel (transcription by Don Karr)	71
1. *Clavis* of astronomy and of the stars (ff 5ᵛ-11ᵛ)	78
2. *Ala*, the virtues of some stones, of herbs, and of beasts (ff 12ʳ-27ʳ)	88
3. *Tractatus Thymiamatus* of suffumigations (ff 27ʳ-34ʳ)	113
4. The *Treatise of Times* of the day and of the night (ff 34ʳ-46ʳ)	124
5. The *Treatise of Cleaness and of Abstinence* (ff 46ʳ-51ʳ)	143
6. *Samaim* which nameth all the heavens and her angels (ff 51ᵛ-53ᵛ)	151
7. The *Book of Virtues and Miracles* (ff 53ᵛ-57ᵛ)	155
Sepher Raziel – Liber Salomonis (modern text – Stephen Skinner)	163
Preface & Introduction	165
The Seven Treatises	167
The Parchment, the Pen and the Ink	169
1. *Liber Clavis,* the Book of the Key of Astronomy and of the Stars	172
Attribution of the 7 Planets to the 12 Zodiacal Signs	174
The Nature of the 12 Zodiacal Signs	175
The Nature of the 7 Planets	175
The Aspects	179
The Houses	181
2. *Ala*, the Virtues of some Stones, Herbs, Beasts, and Words	183
De Prima *Ala* – Stones	184
De Secundus *Ala* – Herbs	190

De Tertia *Ala* – Beasts, Birds and Fish	197
De Quartus *Ala* – Words	204
3. *Tractatus Thymiamatus* of Suffumigations	207
Perfumes of the Days	208
Method of Using the Thymiamata	209
The Perfumes of the Zodiac	214
4. *Treatise of Times* of the Day and of the Night	217
The Planets in the 7 Heavens	218
The 12 Hebrew Months	218
The First Work & Sacrifice	221
The Angels of the 12 Hebrew Months	223
The Angels of the 7 Days of the Week	226
The Names of the Hours of the Night	228
The Names of the Heavens in the 4 Seasons	229
Names of the Angels of the 4 Elements	229
The Proper Names of the Planets in the 4 Seasons	231
5. *Treatise of Purity and of Abstinence*	233
The Ark of the Covenant	236
6. *Samaim* which Names all the Heavens and their Angels	240
7. *Book of Virtues and Miracles* and properties of the Ark of Magic	244
The Seven Semiforas	244
The Semiforas of Moses	246
Appendix 1 – Incense Nomenclature	249
Appendix 2 – Selected Table of Angels	252
Bibliography	258
Manuscripts of *Sepher Raziel*	259
Printed Sources of Solomonic Magic & Works of Related Interest	266
Solomonic Magic on the Internet	284
Index	285

List of Figures

1	First page from the present text *Liber Salomonis* or *Sephar Raziel*, Sloane MS 3826, f.2.	12
2	First page from the English text *Liber Salomonis* or *Cephar Raziel*, Sloane MS 3846, f.129.	24
3	First page from the Latin text *Librum Razielis* or *Cephar Raziel*, Sloane MS 3847 f.161.	43
4	First page from of the Latin text *Sephar Rasiel*, Sloane MS 3853, f. 46.[1]	44
5	Page from the 1701 Hebrew edition of *Sepher Raziel ha-Melakh*.	139
6	Title page from the *Sepher Raziel ha-Melakh*.	140

---

[1] Original folio 41. Note the different spelling of the titles in each manuscript, although they all embody the same basic text in either Latin or English. These differences have been deliberately preserved, here and in the introduction, and should not be construed as careless editing. Note that the two older Latin texts do not have '*Liber Salomonis*' in their titles, suggesting that this was added by the English scribe to the original *Sephar Raziel* title.

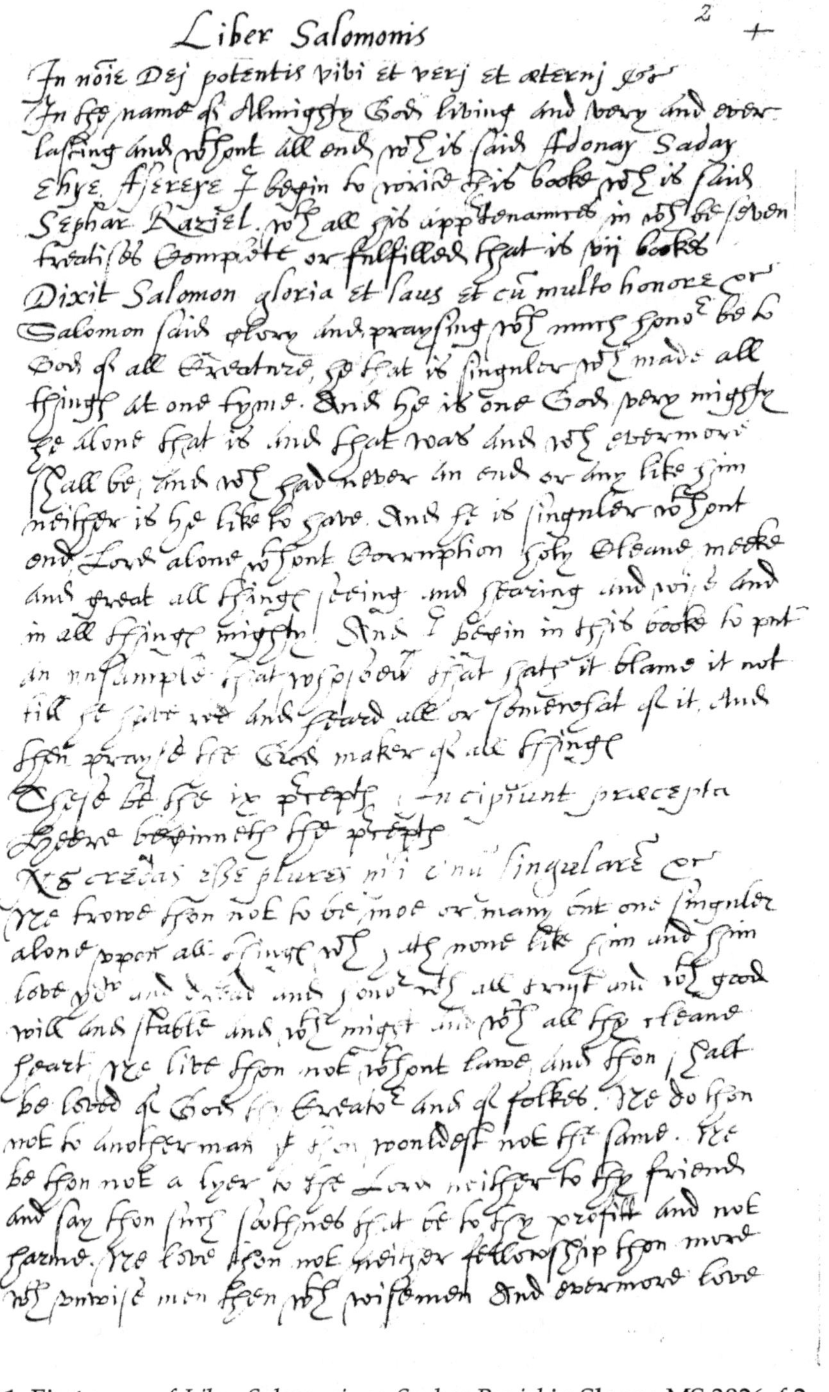

Figure 1: First page of *Liber Salomonis* or *Sephar Raziel* in Sloane MS 3826, f.2. c. 1564. Note the alternate title at the beginning of the fifth line.

Foreword

Legendary Origins

The name of the Angel (or Archangel) Raziel means "secrets of God" and is therefore a most appropriate pseudepigraphical author for a book on magic. According to the *Jewish Encyclopedia,* Raziel's mission is as the "transmitter of secrets." Various spellings of his name include Raziel, Ratziel, Razial, Ratzial, Retziel, Reziel, and Rezial. The spelling of Sepher/Cephar, will also vary.

The legend of the ספר רזיאל the *Sepher Raziel*, or 'Book of Raziel', states that the book was originally inscribed on a sapphire stone.[1] A copy was given to Seraph, then Metatron, then Adam. It is said that the angels (specifically the Cherubim) were upset that such knowledge was given to Adam, and so they descended to earth to steal the book back from him. This is an interesting echo of the idea that both angels, and their fallen brethren the demons, are unhappy that books of magic, containing formulae that can constrain them, have been made available to man. To ensure that the book would not be found again, the angels tossed it deep into the ocean. However, according to Jewish tradition, God ordered the archangel Raphael (or Rahab, according to some sources) to retrieve it, who then gave it to Noah to protect him during the flood. Eventually, after a number of adventures, it was given to King Solomon by a Babylonian prince (who is mentioned in the present manuscript on folio 2v). So much for the legend.

Hebrew Sources – the various Raziel Traditions

Because of this legend, the angel Raziel became a popular reference, and has generated a number of different pseudepigraphical books or Raziel traditions, which may be quite independent of each other:[2]

    a) *Sepher Raziel ha-Melakh,*[3] with sections drawn from Rabbi Eleazar of Worms (1160-1237) *Sepher ha-Razim* and *Sepher ha-Shem.*

    b) *Sepher Raziel* (divided into chapters according to the Seven Heavens).

    c) The 13th century rabbinical *Sepher Raziel,* with content from Rabbi Eleazar.

    d) *Cephar Raziel* (containing Seven Treatises) - the present volume.

Let us look at each of these separate *Sepher Raziel* books and traditions in turn:

---

[1] This is reminiscent of the Smaragdine Tablets of Hermes Trismegistus, inscribed on an emerald tablet. Sapphire is the stone most often mentioned in connection with the floors of Jewish heavens.

[2] Further research is needed to establish the exact family relationships between these groups of books and manuscripts.

[3] First published in Hebrew in 1701, translated into English 2000.

Sepher Raziel

a) *Sepher Raziel ha-Melakh*

The Hebrew *Sepher Raziel ha-Melakh* was published in 1701 in Amsterdam,[1] and later reprinted nearly 40 times, probably because of the popular belief that the presence of the book in a house protected it from fire. This book has been translated into English by Steve Savedow as *Sepher Rezial Hemelach*, 'The Book of the Angel Rezial.'[2] The present Raziel text and the one published by Steve Savedow are *not* closely related. The anonymous author of *Sepher Raziel ha-Melakh* acknowledges the fact that there are other Raziel books/traditions, although he claims (immodestly and probably incorrectly) to be their source:

> "There are two [*Raziel*] books from other countries. I see mine is the original of all of them. They have all been copied from my book... Also included [in my *Sepher Raziel ha-Melakh*] is the smaller work of Eleazar [of Worms],[3] son of Rabbi Judah who received the work of Merkabah [chariot] from the pious Rabbi Judah."[4]

The Foreword explains that this book is in turn divided into 5 Parts:

　　i) *Sepher ha-Malbush*, the 'Book of the Vestment', gives the names of the seasons and of the *Malachim* (angels) ruling in every season, and every month, and every day. The names of the Heavens and Earth also change according to the season.[5] This section also lists "every spirit and angel ministering over every sign of the zodiac, and the angels of the seven planets in every season, and days of the week."[6] Book One page 7 of this Part has two paragraphs on the sacrifice of turtledoves, which are repeated in the present manuscript (37v-38r). Also pages 11-28 have a very similar structure to the present manuscript (44r-46v), but the names attributed are different.

　　ii) *Sepher Raziel ha-Gadol*, or 'Book of the Raziel the Great' is in 4 Parts and relates to *Merkavah* (chariot) mysticism. It draws a lot of its contents from the *Sepher Yetzirah*. Part 3 and 4 are concerned with the Kabbalah of *Genesis*, and the structure of the Universe. They have nothing in common with the present text.

　　iii) *Sepher ha-Shem*, or 'Book of the Holy Name' or Shem ha-Mephorash. This treats of 72 three letter divine names, but does not relate to the present

---

[1] Published by Moses Mendes Coutinho.
[2] Steve Savedow, *Sepher Rezial Hemelach*, York Beach: Samuel Weiser, Inc., 2000. Savedow's transliteration is rather non-standard, transliterating (for example) 'IHVH' as 'IHOH'; 'ha-Malbush' as 'Hamelbosh'; and 'ha-Razim' as 'Hereziem.' See Figures 5 and 6.
[3] A reference to *Sepher ha-Razim* by Eleazar.
[4] Translated by Savedow (2000), page iv.
[5] See the present text ff. 34r-46r. This idea resurfaces in Peter de Abano's *Heptameron* where the words in the magician's protective circle change according to the season and the day, a key concept.
[6] Savedow (2000), page x.

iv) *Sepher ha-Razim,* or 'Book of Mysteries' or 'Book of Magical Secrets.' *Part 1*: It seems much more likely that this section was taken *from* Eleazar of Worms' *Sepher ha-Razim*, rather than the other way around, as claimed by the anonymous author.[1] Anyway, only a subset of *Sepher ha-Razim* is incorporated here into *Sepher Raziel ha-Melakh*, and a much more cohesive, complete and useful version of the *Sepher ha-Razim* is that edited by Morgan.[2]

Part 2: of Savedow's *Sepher ha-Razim* contains background Jewish cosmology.

Part 3: typically deals with the physiology and dimensions of god, drawing material from *Shi'ur Qomah*. Neither forms part of the present manuscript.

v) *Sepher ha-Mazloth* or 'Book of the Signs of the Zodiac' includes various charms, and the use of the 22-letter, and the 42-letter name of god. The illustrations which appear in this book, especially in this last section, do not appear in any of the other *Sepher Raziels*, but are often used as illustrations by writers on Jewish magic, like Joshua Trachtenberg, Gustav Davidson and David Goldstein. See Figure 5 and 6.

b) Sepher Raziel (divided according to the Seven Heavens)

The sections in this particular group of *Sepher Raziel* manuscripts are divided up into chapters by the seven Jewish Heavens. This tradition is preserved in Italian manuscripts such as Alnwick MS 585 and Alnwick MS 596.

c) The 13th century Rabbinical Sepher Raziel

Perhaps the best Hebrew version of the Rabbinical *Sepher Raziel* is found in Additional MS 15299, a 13th century manuscript, beautifully executed in very clear Hebrew on large parchment folios. This particular manuscript was owned by Prince Augustus Frederick, the Duke of Sussex (1773-1843) who was the son of King George III. The Duke was also one of the early Grand Masters of Freemasonry, President of the Royal Society, and supportive of the cause of the Jews in England.

After the Duke's death the manuscript was bought by the British Museum in 1844. The second half of that manuscript (ff.133-153) also contains a commentary

---

[1] The text of *Sepher ha-Razim* in *Sepher Raziel ha-Melakh* is in fact rather scrambled. For example a section on page 211 is repeated word for word again on page 253. There are also missing sections, so for example, on pages 208-210 the sequence repeats the 'third host of Malachim' twice, and then jumps (via the 12 Princes and days of the week) to the 'sixth host' of the Malachim. This may be the fault of the original Hebrew of 1701, rather than the translator.

[2] Michael Morgan, *Sepher ha-Razim: the* Book of Mysteries, Chico California: Scholars Press, 1983.

Sepher Raziel

explaining the magical (rather than philosophical) uses of the *Sepher Yetzirah* by Rabbi Eleazar of Worms, material later thought relevant to Golem making.

Probably as a result of that inclusion, Rabbi Louis Ginzberg, in *Legends of the Jews*,[1] attributed the whole of *Sepher Raziel* to Rabbi Eleazar of Worms (1160-1237), otherwise known as Rabbi Eleazar of Germiza, or Rabbi Eleazar ben Judah ben Kalonymus of Worms. He maintained that Eleazar had preserved some of the wisdom of the Geonic period [2] in this book. This assertion was repeated by Joshua Trachtenberg.[3] This attribution is however probably only partly true; as one book by Eleazar called *Sodei Razya* (סודי רזיא 'Secret of Secrets') became part of the *Sepher Raziel ha-Gadol* published in *Sepher Raziel ha-Melakh* in 1701. The *Sepher ha-Shem* ('Book of the Name') on the 22-letter Name of god is also attributed to him, and has had some input into the *Sepher Raziel*. This version of the *Sepher Raziel* was probably compiled in the thirteenth century. We have no indication that the *Sepher Raziel* which Ginzberg and Trachtenberg refer to is related to the present manuscript.

It remains for further research to identify to what extent Rabbi Eleazar was responsible for each of the different Raziel traditions.

d) Cephar Raziel (containing Seven Treatises)

The present text is divided into seven Treatises. It is quite different in structure and content to the preceding three types of *Sepher Raziel*. It does however have an amount of Hebrew content, and even uses the Hebrew word for heavens, *Samaim*, as the title of one of its seven constituent Treatises. Repeated references to purity and chastity, and the description of the sacrifice of turtledoves, suggest Jewish roots. Having said that, the few examples of Hebrew writing in the present manuscript are execrable, and so it is certain that the English scribe did not know Hebrew. One Latin version from which the English version may have been translated, on the other hand, has quite competent Hebrew orthography. This suggests that the roots of the present manuscript were probably a Hebrew original, filtered through a Latin intermediary, to the present Middle English version. We will now just concentrate upon this last version of *Sepher Raziel* (in seven Treatises), which exists in at least seven manuscripts (see Bibliography).

Sloane MS 3826

The present manuscript of *Sepher Raziel* is in English. It has been translated from

---

[1] In Vol. I, pages 90-93 and Vol. V, pages 117,110, 1909-1938.
[2] Jewish mystical and interpretive material from the period 589-1038 CE.
[3] Trachtenberg, *Jewish Magic and Superstition*, Philadelphia: University of Pennsylvania, 2004, page 315.

Liber Salomonis

Latin, and is written in a sixteenth century hand, which is superficially like that of Edward Kelley. See Figure 1. Each subsection begins with an opening Latin tag line, which was designed to facilitate reference back to the Latin original.

Sloane MS 3846

Another very similar English copy of *Sepher Raziel*, Sloane MS 3846, which is precisely dated November 1564, gives us some additional clues.[1] See Figure 2. Because the manuscripts are very close in style and content, we have presumed to date the present manuscript to the same year, on the grounds that often several copies of the same grimoire were made at the same time, though these two manuscripts were not executed by the same scribe. Even if we are a few years out, this is still the oldest manuscript so far published in the *Sourceworks of Ceremonial Magic* series.

Sloane MS 3846 is bound up with a number of other extracts from writers like Cornelius Agrippa, a number of magical recipes, spells, workings with the skrying crystal, invocations, sigils, angelic calls, methods for cutting the magical wand, and other interesting items. One bound-in slip identifies the suffumigations (incenses) used for individual planetary angels:

> "Mercury – Askariel – Mastic
> Venus – Uriel – Costus
> Luna – Anael – Aloes
> Saturn – Galban[um]?
> Jupiter – Crocus
> Mars – Piper Nigrum [black pepper]
> Sol – Red Sanders [red sandalwood]"

Another fascinating item in Elias Ashmole's handwriting occurs on f.102v of Sloane MS 3846 where a blob of red wax has been impressed with a seal ring, which is then described in detail:

> "A Ring made by Dr ~~Napier~~ Forman[2] in Silver. On the signet part were these Characters. On the outside verge of the Signet was engraved ARIEL & ANAEL.[3] On the circumference of the Ring, was engraved these words on the outside DIE ET PHORA [Venus] IN [Taurus] 1598.[4] This ring was given to me by Tho[mas] Napier Esq[uire] son of Sir Rich[ard] Napier."

---

[1] The actual title is *Liber Salomonis* or *Sephar Raziel* [*sic*].
[2] The manuscript has been corrected by Ashmole from 'Dr Napier' to 'Dr [Simon] Forman.'
[3] The two angels which were most significant for Shakespeare and Dr John Dee respectively.
[4] The ring was therefore made and consecrated between 5th March and 7th July 1598.

Further on in the same volume is an 'Invocation of Oberion [1] concerning Phisick [medicine]' [f. 102v-106]. It is very usefully and clearly divided into the correct *portio* of a properly conducted evocation: Consecratio Dei, Invocatio, Constrictio, Ligatio, and Licentia. It is not often that this sequence is so clearly delineated.

The later half of Sloane MS 3846 contains material which is parallel to the contents of the present manuscript, Sloane MS 3826, which is catalogued as follows:

Liber Salomonis	fo. 139 [f.129] [2]
The Rule of the Book of Consecration, or the manner of working	fo. 168b [f.158]
Liber Lunae	fo.182 [f.172v]
Adellardus Bathoniensis [3]	fo. 192 [f.181]

The items, *The Rule of the Book of Consecration*, and *Liber Lunae* also occur at the end of Sloane MS 3826, strengthening the argument that both manuscripts were probably derived from the same source, and are similarly dated.

Owners of Sloane MS 3846

It is not easy to determine the 16th century owners of Sloane MS 3826, but from the mid 17th century onwards it 'travelled' with Sloane MS 3846, from owner to owner, so it is enlightening to examine the owners of both manuscripts. One early attempt at beginning a transcription of *Cephar Raziel* is preserved in an Ashmole fragment dated 1564.[4] Sloane MS 3846 states that it was also written in the same year by William Parry [5] of Clifford's Inn and is clearly dated 2nd November 1564. The note reads:

> "The booke, entituled *Cephar Raziel*, contain'g seuen treatises, was written by William Parry of Clyffords Inne by Josuy[?], le barre [a barrister] in London borne at North of in the County of Flynt & at the charges of John Gwyne [6] of Llandlos [Llanidloes] in the County of Mountgomericke Esquire [Montgomeryshire] in the year of our Lord god a thousand five hunderd three score & four et Anno

---

[1] This spirit name is the probable source of the fairy Oberon found in Shakespeare's *Tempest*.
[2] The 'fo.' number is the seventeenth century folio number shown in the contents listing at the front of the manuscript, while the 'f.' number is the current re-numbered folio.
[3] Adelard of Bath (c. 1080-c. 1152) translated many works on astrology and mathematics.
[4] Bodleian Ashmole MS 1790 f.116-116v.
[5] One of the more colourful Parrys of this period was the Welsh Dr William Parry, who after several attempts on the life of Queen Elizabeth I, who forgave him, was finally sent to the gallows in 1585. However, as this Parry signed himself "of Clifford's Inn" it is most likely that he was not the traitor, but instead a lawyer. This is no surprise as a number of senior lawyers were to be found amongst the angel magicians of the seventeenth century.
[6] Probably meaning at the expense of John Gwyne.

Liber Salomonis

Elizabetha dei gra[tia] Angeliæ &c. Reginæ sexton.

Londinij 2º Nouembris 1564. William Parry."[1]

Above this is an inscription indicating yet another early owner:

"Ego Scribener Eruditio[?]...Haec ex Lomporo[?] Scripsit, Westrum[?] 27 Julii 1570. Haec litera John Gioin astin[?] Magister mihi transcript ut pz."

And later on folio 182, in the Adellardus item, it is more clearly written:

"J Gioyn of Pormall. 1575. borded 1570 at Mr Stewards. Booke delivered to Howell ap Mathew 1º Martii [March] 1568. my broet[her] in glostershire now…at one Mr W A Vaughan a lawyer…"

Here we have other people, possibly all lawyers, through whose hands the manuscript may have passed between 1570 and 1575: John Gioin of Pormall, Mr Stewards, Howell ap Mathew and Mr W A Vaughan.

Another undated owner of these, or other magical books, William Walmesbury, is identified on folio 126 of Sloane MS 3846.

"Mr Willia[m] Warmesbury Register of Worcester [2] hath these booke[s] in vellum.
1. The characters & vertues of yᵉ Psalmes in 8º [octavo].
2. A Booke of [Magical] Experiments in 4tº [quarto] written in redd & blacke.
These bookes were left with Mr Freeman, a Physician, of Paxford neere Camden, who [later] dyinge left them with his owne Bookes to Mr Warmesbury."

The handwriting suggests a date circa 1600. The interesting thing about this owner is that, as Registrar of Worcester, he would have been well placed to know the subsequent owners of this manuscript, all of whom had links with Worcester.[3]

An interesting side-light on the importance of *Sepher Raziel* was thrown by the influential alchemist Andreas Libavius (1555-1616), who in 1615 speculated that one of the *Sepher Raziels* was the founding document for the Rosicrucian

---

[1] Folio 128. A John Gwyne was for a while mayor of Llanidloes, supporting the above interpolations. On 17ᵗʰ January 1598, John Dee's messenger (Edmond Arnold) went to Llandlos to deliver a letter, possibly to the same John Gwyne. This Gwyne might also be the author of a number of alchemic manuscripts in the Bodleian Library by one 'John Gwynne.'

[2] Yet another resident of Worcester owning what was possibly the vellum originals of the present manuscript. This is yet further proof of a continuum of members of the legal profession and aristocrats living in, or connected with Worcester, who were engaged in the practice of angel magic.

[3] More detail will be found about the Worcester group of angel magicians in Skinner & Rankine, *Practical Angel Magic of John Dee's Enochian Tables,* London: Golden Hoard, 2004, pages 21-22, 43-47.

cosmology of angelic spheres.[1] It is therefore likely that a copy (but probably not this copy) of one of the *Sepher Raziels* passed through his hands. Over a century later, the mystic Emanuel Swedenborg (1688-1772) was also reported to have been influenced by *Sepher Raziel* in his opinion about angels. But to return to the historical appearances of this manuscript.

Around 1630, Sir Richard Napier (1607-1676) wrote in a letter to his uncle Richard Napier (1559-1634) that:[2]

> "I found in the Archives in our pub[lic] Library [the Bodleian], a Booke of Solomons called *Cephar Raziel*, which is in Latin as I finde, [called] *Angelus Magnus Secreti Creatoris*, & in the Hebrew *Cephar Raziel*, in which is contained 7 Treatises, the first is said [called] *Clavis*...[3] This booke is a little folio about three quire of paper.[4] I hope in tyme to purchase [procure] a coppy of it by my own hande, though it be worthier of a more honest pen, for I am persuaded that it is Liber est Magnae, virtutis, & magni sunti[?]. I doubt not to transcribe it in a short time, & to be so happy as to present you with my Coppy; were it possible that I could get that booke to my owne study, I would copy it out in 2 weekes, yet as it is, I have made a faire way to goe into the Library privately where I please & use to sit from 6 of the clocke in the morning to 5 at night... I have made the Second Keeper of the Library my friend & servant, who promised me his key at all tymes to go in privately."[5]

Napier asked his uncle to "make me a paper booke of Royall [size] paper"[6] so he could use it to transcribe *Cephar Raziel*. He signed his letter "Your most observant Sonn and thankful debtour [?], Richard Napier.[7] It is likely that this copy made by Napier was eventually left to Elias Ashmole (1617-1692), who was to a large extent responsible for preserving the works of Dr John Dee.

Another owner, or at least the writer of a note bound in Sloane MS 3846, was Henry Swibers [?] of Crookham in 1672.

From then onwards we can trace the wanderings of both manuscripts in greater detail. Both Sloane MS 3826 and Sloane MS 3846 belonged to Baron Somers of Evesham (1651-1716) who was Chancellor of England. In fact the

---

[1] In his *Examen Philosophia Nova*, Leipzig, 1615. See Åkerman (1999), page 16.
[2] Richard Napier was greatly interested in magic, and a pupil of the astrologer Simon Forman, and inherited Forman's copy of another famous grimoire, the *Picatrix*. He became rector of Great Linford, Buckinghamshire in 1589.
[3] Here follows a copy of the opening paragraphs outlining the contents of the present manuscript.
[4] In the Middle Ages a quire was a manuscript section of 16 pages. Therefore Napier is asking for 48 pages. This would accommodate Sloane MS 3846. Modern usage is 24/25 pages per quire.
[5] In Bodleian Ashmole MS 1730, ff.168-16v.
[6] 20 x 25 inches.
[7] Sir Richard Napier was also the godson of his uncle.

contents list of both manuscript volumes is in the hand of Lord Somer's library cataloguer. Lord Somers in turn passed both manuscripts to his brother-in-law Sir Joseph Jekyll (1663-1738), who was a prominent lawyer and Master of the Rolls (an antique title given to the second most senior judge in England). Both Somers and Jekyll were intensely interested in magic, and had a number of key manuscripts on practical angel magic.

On Sir Joseph Jekylls's death, his books and manuscripts were sold by the auctioneer Mr Cocks of Covent Garden, London (at St Paul's Coffee House).[1]

On 26th February 1738 both manuscripts were sold to the same buyer, Sir Hans Sloane (1660-1753), who bought at least 21 manuscript volumes at this sale. Sloane's collection later became the basis of the manuscript collections of the British Museum, which was later separated from the old Russell Street premises of the British Museum, removed to St. Pancras, and re-named the British Library, which is where the manuscripts reside today.

Although the early owners of Sloane MS 3846, before Lord Somers, do not necessarily tell us anything about Sloane MS 3826, they do indicate who was familiar with, read, and may have practiced, the magical methods outlined in *Sepher Raziel*.

Latin Sources

The earliest Latin version appears to date from before 1259 for in that year Alfonso X (1221-1284) ordered a translation of *Liber Razielis* from Latin into Castilian. This Alfonsine *Liber Razielis* was also divided into seven books, like the present text, and may have been its earliest source.[2]

A separate *Sepher Raziel* was translated out of Hebrew into Latin for the Roman prelate Cardinal Egidio da Viterbo (1465-1532), who collected Kabbalistic manuscripts, with the help of the Jewish scholar and humanist Elias Levita (1469-1549).

Sloane MS 3847 (f. 161-188v) is a beautifully written Latin version of *Sepher Raziel*. It was closely associated with Sloane MS 3846, and 'travelled' with it from one owner to another for most of its life. It was also auctioned at Jekyll's sale, and had the very next lot number (373). See Figure 3. It could be partially the origin of Sloane MS 3846, and therefore is well placed to answer queries about illegible words in the English translation. It has a number of Latin margin tags which make it easier to follow, and its Hebrew is much better than that of the English copy, however it only encompasses the first three chapters.

---

[1] Sloane MS 3826 was lot 396, and Sloane MS 3846 was lot 372 in the sale catalogue.
[2] Bibliotheca Vaticana MS Reg. Latin 1300.

Sepher Raziel

This Latin version is actually entitled *Librum Razielis* or *Cephar Raziel* and is bound at the back of a fascinating collection of magical manuscripts. The manuscripts that it is bound with include several books that are actually referred to within *Sepher Raziel* itself, so it is well worthwhile listing them in detail:[1]

> The work of Solomon the wise called his *Clavicle* revealed by King Ptolomeus the Greacian [sic]...Truly copyed verbu[m] pro verbo [word for word] by H: G: in anno χρο 1572 in mense Aprielis circa octano [8th April 1572]. fo. 1 [f.2].[2]
>
> Opus mirabile *de Quatuor Annulus Solomonis.* fo. 65b [f.66v].[3]
>
> What Stones and Herbs are appropiated [sic] unto the 15 Stars accordinge to John Gower in his booke intitled, *de Confessione Amantis,* the wh[ic]he he Dedicated unto King Henry the eight[h].[4] fo. 84 [f.83].[5]
>
> *Liber Hermetis* tractans de 15 Stellis et de 15 Lapidibus et de 15 Herbis et de 15 harum rerum figures sic incipiense. fo. 85 [f.84].[6]
>
> Dictum Thebit. fo. 100b [f.99v].
>
> *Liber Imaginum* Zebel [Sahl ibn Bishr] alias Zoel. fo. 102 [f.101].
>
> Hebreorum Machubales...Decem principalia Nomina Divina... fo. 115 [f.113].[7]
>
> Divers [various] Spells. fo. 125 [120r]
>
> *Liber Razaelis.* fo. 166 – 193 [161-188v]. [A Latin version of the present text.]

Another Latin version, Sloane MS 3853 (see Figure 4), has just a few pages related to '*Sephar Rasiel*' (f. 46-49v). The initial letter of '*Sephar*' could easily be read as a 'C' or an 'S', and this may well have contributed to the spelling of '*Cephar*' in later manuscripts. These pages are followed by some very interesting circle diagrams, which probably did not form part of *Sephar Rasiel*. The rest of the manuscript, much of it in Latin, is devoted to extracts from *The Sworn Book of Honorius* and some of Roger Bacon's magical works.

John of Morigny's *Liber Visionum* is several times explicitly mentioned in the present text, and its techniques may contribute to some parts of *Sepher Raziel* or

---

[1] The descriptions listed on the contents page have been amplified by reference to the actual items themselves.
[2] In each case the first 'fo.' folio reference is what is listed by Lord Sommer's librarian at the front of the manuscript, whilst the 'f.' folio reference is the current re-numbered folio of the item.
[3] The fact that a copy of the *De Quatuor Annulus Solomonis* ('Of the Four Rings of Solomon') is included within the same binding, helps to support the Solomonic nature of the present manuscript.
[4] Gower lived 1330-1408, so the dedicatee was Henry IV, not Henry VIII.
[5] The Second Treatise on the four *Ala* in *Sepher Raziel* contains similar material.
[6] This book is quoted in *Sepher Raziel*.
[7] Attribution of the Divine names to the planets, angels and Tree of Life, in Latin.

to the author's methods of discovering correspondences.[1]

Structure and Origins of the Manuscript

There are other clues as to the manuscript's origins. One of these is its division into 7 books, which is emphasised several times at the beginning of the manuscript. This structure includes separate books on astronomy/ astrology; plants and animals; perfumes; times and days; and angel lists, each organised as a separate book. This is more like the structure of the Byzantine Greek *Magical Treatise of Solomon* than later European grimoires, and therefore the present manuscript may owe some of its contents to Byzantine Greek, as well as Hebrew roots.

Another small clue is afforded by the number of incenses beginning with 'a' whose names have Spanish roots. This suggests that the earliest Latin version of this manuscript might have been the Latin copy of the *Liber Razielis* that was extant in the Spanish court of Alphonso X (1221-1284), but that remains to be investigated.

It seems likely that both Sloane MS 3826 and MS 3846 were translated or copied from an unknown intermediate Latin manuscript. If Sloane MS 3847 had been a complete Latin version, then that manuscript might have been the immediate source of both of these, especially as its stone and plant names are less garbled. Sloane MS 3853, an even older Latin version, is also incomplete.

Note that Appendix 1 has more complete identification of the various incenses and plants mentioned in the text than do the footnotes.

However the construction of a complete *stemma* requires a full survey of each of the *Sepher Raziel* traditions and an analysis of the connections between them.

- Stephen Skinner
London & Singapore, June 2010

---

[1] Claire Fanger [ed.], *Conjuring Spirits: Texts and Traditions of Medieval Ritual Magic*, University Park: Pennsylvania State University Press, 1998, pages 163-265.

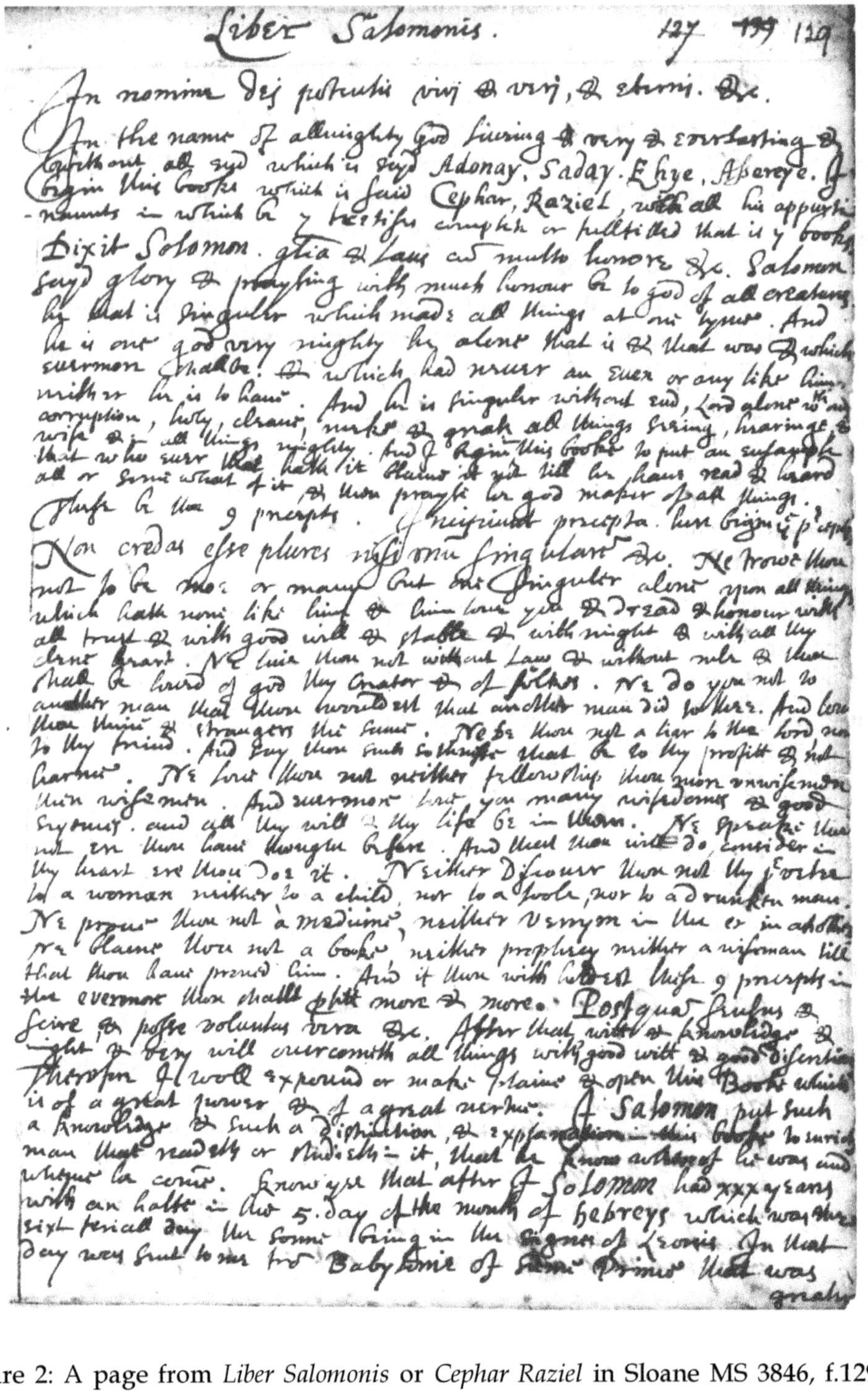
Liber Salomonis. 127 ~~1??~~ 129

In nomine dei potentis vivi & veri, & eterni. &c.

In the name of allmighty god liuing & very & everlasting & without all end which is sayd Adonay. Saday. Ehye. Asserye. I begin this booke which is said Cephar, Raziel, with all his appurtenaunts in which be y testifies complete or fulfilled that is y booke.

Dixit Solomon. glia & laus cu multo honore &c. Salomon sayd glory & praysing with much honour be to god of all creatures

Figure 2: A page from *Liber Salomonis* or *Cephar Raziel* in Sloane MS 3846, f.129. 1564.

The Study of Solomonic Magic in English
Don Karr

IT IS IMPOSSIBLE to neatly circumscribe a canon of magic texts as being safely of the "Solomonic cycle." By arbitrary and rather unscientific means, one might do so by simply including those works which, by tradition or artifice, bear Solomon's name or derive from works which do. Even here, we find at least three classes of material:
1. medieval grimoires, such as *The Key of Solomon*
2. Byzantine Greek texts of the *Magical Treatise of Solomon*, or *Hygromanteia*[1]
3. magical works from late antiquity through the early Middle Ages, such as *The Testament of Solomon* and *Sepher Razim*[2]

---

[1] *Hygromanteia* is a 5th- or 6th-century Greek astrological/magical text also known as Solomon's *Epistle to Rehoboam*. For a full treatment and an English translation of the *Hygromanteia*, see Ioannis Marathakis' *Magical Treatise of Solomon or Hygromanteia* [SOURCEWORKS OF CEREMONIAL MAGIC, Volume 8], foreword by Stephen Skinner (Singapore: Golden Hoard Press, 2011).

A translation of *Hygromanteia* appears as APPENDIX 1 of Pablo A. Torijano's *Solomon the Esoteric King: From King to Magus, Development of a Tradition* [SUPPLEMENTS TO THE JOURNAL FOR THE STUDY OF JUDAISM] (Leiden: Brill, 2002). See also Torijano's more recent work, "The Hygromancy of Solomon: A new translation and introduction," in *Old Testament Pseudepigrapha: More Noncanonical Scriptures*, Volume 1, edited by Richard Bauckham, James R. Davila, and Alexander Panayotov (Grand Rapids: William B. Eerdmans Publishing, 2013), pages 305-325.

Two works trace likely source material for the traditions under discussion:
(1) Stephen Skinner's *Techniques of Graeco-Egyptian Magic* (Singapore: Golden Hoard Press, 2014), which sheds light on—makes sense of—the magical papyri published in Hanz Dieter Betz' *Greek Magical Papyri in Translation, Including the Demotic Spells*, Volume One: Texts (2nd edition, Chicago: University of Chicago Press, 1992).
(2) Skinner's *Techniques of Solomonic Magic* (Singapore: Golden Hoard Press, 2015), which is described at some length below.

Hygromanteia is often brought into the discussion in the former work and looms quite large in the latter as a source for the medieval Solomonic grimoire tradition.

[2] For English translations of *The Testament of Solomon*, see (listed chronologically)
- Conybeare, F. C. "The Testament of Solomon," in *Jewish Quarterly Review*, no. XI (London: 1899)—digital edition by Joseph H. Peterson (1997) at TWILIT GROTTO/ESOTERIC ARCHIVES > http://www.esotericarchives.com/solomon/testamen.htm.
- McCown, C. C. *The Testament of Solomon* (Leipzig: J. C. Hinrichs, 1922).
- Shah, Sayed Idries. "The Catalogue of Demons" = CHAPTER 11 of *The Secret Lore of Magic* (Secaucus: Citadel Press, 1972).
- Duling, D. C. "Testament of Solomon," in *The Old Testament Pseudepigrapha* (= *OTP*), edited by J. H. Charlesworth (Garden City: Doubleday, 1983).

Sepher Raziel

Attribution to Solomon already complicates several biblical texts[1] and apocrypha.[2] Solomon is the hero of many ancient tales in the East; still his legend figures into late traditions of the Freemasons.[3] Rumors which suggest that the wise king left secret books of magic seem never to have died — nor to have slumbered — since ancient times.[4]

In order to make short work of closing the category of Solomonic magical works, we shall follow E[liza] M[arian] Butler[5] and focus on #

Duling's introduction in *The Old Testament Pseudepigrapha* deals with Solomonic attribution and legend in the older material. He mentions M. Seligsohn's article, "Solomon—Apocryphal Works" (in *The Jewish Encyclopedia*, vol. 11, page 447—online at http://www.jewishencyclopedia.com/articles/13842-solomon) as listing forty-nine Solomonic "scientific and magical books" in Arabic and Hebrew literature, and C. C. McCown's added comment (*Testament of Solomon*, page 100) that Seligsohn's list is by no means exhaustive.

On the *Testament's* background and dissemination: Sarah Iles Johnson, "The *Testament of Solomon* from Late Antiquity to the Renaissance," in *The Metamorphosis of Magic from Late Antiquity to the Early Modern Period*, edited by Jan N. Bremmer and Jan R. Veenstra (Leuven: Peeters, 2002).

For a critical summary of *Testament of Solomon* scholarship, refer to Todd E. Klutz, *Rewriting the TESTAMENT OF SOLOMON: Tradition, Conflict and Identity in a Late Antique Pseudepigraphon* (London – New York: T & T Clark International, 2005), and *idem*, "The Archer and the Cross: Chorographic Astrology and Literary Design in the *Testament of Solomon*," in *Magic in the Biblical World: From the Rod of Aaron to the Ring of Solomon*, edited by Todd E. Klutz (London – New York: T & T Clark International, 2003).

Sefer ha-Razim, a third- or fourth-century Hebrew text, claims in its preface to have been "more precious and more honorable and more difficult" than any other books in the possession of Solomon. See Michael A. Morgan's translation, *Sepher ha-Razim: The Book of the Mysteries* (Chico: Society of Biblical Literature/Scholars Press, 1983), and Philip S. Alexander's "*Sefer ha-Razim* and the Problem of Black Magic in Early Judaism," in *Magic in the Biblical World...* (ed. Klutz, 2003), cited immediately above. Further, find the list of *Sefer ha-Razim* references in my "Notes on the Study of *Merkabah* Mysticism and *Hekhalot* Literature," TRANSLATIONS & REFERENCES, § K, at http://www.digital-brilliance.com/contributed/Karr/Biblios/mmhie.pdf.

[1] Proverbs, Ecclesiastes, and Song of Songs.
[2] Wisdom of Solomon, Odes of Solomon, and the Psalms of Solomon.
[3] Albert Pike's *Morals and Dogma...* (Charleston: [L. H. Jenkins, Inc.], 1871) contains references to Solomon throughout. See Albert Gallatin Mackey, *The History of Freemasonry...*, in 7 volumes (New York – London: The Masonic History Company, 1898), CHAPTER XXIV, "The Temple Legend" (pp. 151-165); Arthur Edward Waite, *A New Encyclopaedia of Freemasonry...*, in 2 volumes (London: Rider & Co./Philadelphia: The David McKay Co., 1921), "Kabalistic Tradition and Masonry" (vol. 1, pp. 416-427), and "Solomon" (vol. 2, p. 421); *The Bible* and *King Solomon's Temple in Masonry* by John Wesley Kelchner, *illustrated* [also called "The Masonic Bible"] (Philadelphia: A. J. Holman Company, 1924).
[4] See Torijano, *Solomon the Esoteric King*, and Yaacov Shavit, "'He was Thoth in Everything': Why and When King Solomon Became Both *Magister omnium physicorum* and Master of Magic," in *Envisioning Judaism: Studies in Honor of Peter Schäfer on the Occasion of his Seventieth Birthday*, edited by Ra'anan S. Boustan, Klaus Herrmann, Reimund Leicht, Annette Y. Reed, and Giuseppe Veltri, with the collaboration of Alex Ramos, Volume 1 (Tübingen: Mohr Siebeck, 2013), pages 587-606.
[5] See Butler's *Ritual Magic* (Cambridge: Cambridge University Press, 1949) and its companion volumes, *The Fortunes of Faust* (1946) and *The Myth of the Magus* (1949), all reprinted in 1979 by

1, the late grimoires. The limitations of her work, however, must be acknowledged: Butler depended primarily on published works of the nineteenth and early twentieth centuries, including familiar works in English: Francis Barrett's *Magus* (1801), Montague Summers' *Witchcraft and Black Magic* (rpt. 1945), C. J. S. Thompson's *Mysteries and Secrets of Magic* (1927), Grillot de Givry's *Witchcraft, Magic and Alchemy* (1931), Arthur E. Waite's *Book of Black Magic and of Pacts* (1898) — even Aleister Crowley's *Magick in Theory and Practice* (1929) — along with works in other modern languages, in particular the collections of J. C. Horst (*Zauberbibliothek*, 1821-6) and J. Scheible (*Das Kloster*, 1846-1851).[1]

Cambridge University Press. *Ritual Magic* and *The Fortunes of Faust* have again been reprinted (1998) as volumes of Pennsylvania State University's MAGIC IN HISTORY SERIES, along with these other books (in chronological order):

- *Forbidden Rites* by Richard Kieckhefer (1997)
- *Conjuring Spirits* edited by Claire Fanger (1998)
- *The Bathhouse at Midnight: Magic in Russia* by W. F. Ryan (1999)
- a reprint of *Spiritual and Demonic Magic: From Ficino to Campanella* by D. P. Walker (2000, orig. 1958)
- *Icons of Power: Ritual Practices in Late Antiquity* by Naomi Janowitz (2002)
- *Battling Demons: Witchcraft, Heresy, and Reform in the Late Middle Ages* by Michael D. Bailey (2003)
- *Prayer, Magic, and the Stars in the Ancient and Late Antique World* edited by S. Noegel, J. Walker, and B. Wheeler (2003)
- *Binding Words: Textual Amulets in the Middle Ages* by Don C. Skemer (2006).
- *Strange Revelations: Magic, Poison, and Sacrilege in Louis XIV's France* by Lynn Wood Mollenauer (2006)
- *Unlocked Books: Manuscripts of Learned Magic in the Medieval Libraries of Central Europe* by Benedek Láng (2008)
- *Alchemical Belief: Occultism in the Religious Culture of Early Modern England* by Bruce Janacek (2011)
- *Invoking Angels: Theurgic Ideas and Practices, Thirteenth to Sixteenth Centuries*, edited by Claire Fanger (2012)
- *The Transformations of Magic: Illicit Learned Magic in the Later Middle Ages and Renaissance* by Frank Klaassen (2013)
- *Magic in the Cloister: Pious Motives, Illicit Interests, and Occult Approaches to the Medieval Universe* by Sophie Page (2013)
- *Rewriting Magic: An Exegesis of the Visionary Autobiography of a Fourteenth Century French Monk* by Claire Fanger (2015)

[1] Further regarding the limits of Butler's work, consider the following quote from *Ritual Magic*, page 135: "*Picatrix*, according to Mathers and other authorities, is an Italian edition of the *Clavicle*, strongly impregnated with black elements." This is an astounding mistake. *Picatrix*, or *Ghayat al-Hakim* [THE GOAL OF THE WISE], is an Arabic compendium of philosophy and magic from the tenth or eleventh century.

Sepher Raziel

The classes and selections of the "Solomonic cycle"[1] according to Butler are

1. The Clavicles (Keys)
   a. THE KEY OF SOLOMON
   b. *Lemegeton,* or LESSER KEY OF SOLOMON

2. The Grimoires
   a. *Grimorium Verum*
   b. TRUE BLACK MAGIC
   c. THE GRAND GRIMOIRE

3. Honorius
   a. The *Grimoire* of Honorius
   b. *Liber iuratus,* or SWORN BOOK of Honorius

To the list above, we have ventured to add[2]

---

[1] Compare the list of Solomonic texts presented in my outline (which is according to Butler) with that appearing in *The Black Arts* by Richard Cavendish (New York: G. P. Putnam's Sons, 1967), Appendix 1: "The Grimoires," page 371: 1. *Key of Solomon,* 2. *Lemegeton,* 3. *Testament of Solomon,* 4. *Grimoire of Honorius,* 5. *Grimorium Verum,* 6. *Grand Grimoire,* 7. *Red Dragon* ("a version of the *Grand Grimoire*"), 8. *True Black Magic,* 9. *Arbatel of Magic,* 10. *The Black Pullet,* 11. *Fourth Book* (pseudo-Agrippa), and 12. *Heptameron* (Peter de Abano).

[2] *The Keys to the Gateway of Magic: Summoning the Solomonic Archangels & Demon Princes*, by Stephen Skinner and David Rankine (London: Golden Hoard Press, 2005) offers transcriptions of *Janua Magica Reserata* (KEYS TO THE GATEWAY OF MAGIC), *Dr Rudd's Nine Hierarchies of Angels with their Invocations to Visible Appearance with the Nine Great Celestial Keys, or Angelical Invocations*, and *The Demon Princes* (from British Library Sloane MSS 3628, 3821, 3824, 3825, Harley MS 6482, and Rawlinson D. 1363). This material bears great similarity to the items described in this paper, and a case could certainly be made for wedging these texts into our canon. However, our additions to Butler's list contain specific internal references to Solomon, which the texts in *The Keys to the Gateway of Magic* do not—despite the subtitle of the book.

Within our additions, we find the following:
- *S&S* [paragraph 2]: "In the name of the highest, almighty Creator, I, King Solomon, hold to the interpretation of the name of (God) Semiphoras…"
- *Liber Salomonis* [2ʳ]: "*Dixit Salomon Gloria et laus et cu multo honore &c* / Salomon said glory and praysing wᵗʰ much honor be to God of all Creatures, he that is singular wᶜʰ made all things at one tyme."

The Keys to the Gateway of Magic is volume 2 of the Golden Hoard Press series SOURCEWORKS OF CEREMONIAL MAGIC:
- Volume 1. *Practical Angel Magic of Dr John Dee's Enochian Tables: Tabularum Bonam Angelorum Invocationes* (Skinner & Rankine, 2004)
- Volume 3. *The Goetia of Dr Rudd: Angels and Demons...* (Skinner & Rankine, 2007)—discussed below, § 1. b. *Lemegeton*
- Volume 4. *The Veritable Key of Solomon* (Skinner & Rankine, 2008)—discussed below, § 1. a. THE KEY OF SOLOMON
- Volume 5. *The Grimoire of St. Cyprian: Clavis Inferni*, Latin [sic] translation by Peter Forshaw (Skinner and Rankine, 2009)

4. *Semiphoras* and *Shemhamphoras Salomonis Regis*
5. *Liber Salomonis : Cephar Raziel*

While reference to the contents of some of these works is made, it is not the aim of this essay to offer summaries or analyses. Instead, the reader is referred to sources in which these works are translated into or described in English. My initial advice to anyone interested in pursuing this material is to go to Joseph Peterson's remarkable site, TWILIT GROTTO at www.esotericarchives.com, where most of the items discussed below, along with a wealth of other texts, are responsibly and tastefully presented—and can be viewed for free. If the omissions at the site frustrate the reader, for the cost of one typical printed grimoire, a CD can be ordered from TWILIT GROTTO containing "50+ complete books/31 complete grimoires"—a forgivably mild exaggeration. Further, whenever Peterson has ushered into print an edition of one of the Solomonic texts, it is usually the best version—and offered at a reasonable price.

▼

- Volume 6. *Sepher Raziel* (Don Karr & Stephen Skinner, 2010) this book — see below, § 5. LIBER SALOMONIS : CEPHAR RAZIEL
- Volume 7. *Liber Lunæ—Book of the Moon—Sepher ha-Levanah* (Don Karr, with translations by Calanit Nachshon, 2011; second edition [paperback], 2017)
- Volume 8. *The Magical Treatise of Solomon or Hygromanteia* (Ioannis Marathakis, 2011)

The first three volumes of this series feature the works and expansions of one Dr. Rudd, "a scholar-magician of the early seventeenth century who knew Dr. John Dee." This Dr. Rudd is also the supposed compiler of the material in MS Harley 6482, an edition of which was published by Adam McLean as *A Treatise on Angel Magic* (Edinburgh: MAGNUM OPUS SOURCEWORKS [# 15], 1982, and subsequently reprinted; see the bibliography below: "McLean").

A facsimile of Frederick Hockley's transcription of Rudd's MS, *Dr. Rudd's Nine Hierarchies of Angels—also Clavis Angelica*, edited and introduced by Alan Thorogood, has been published by Teitan Press (York Beach: 2013); it includes translations of John Dee's angelic keys and invocations for the angels over the Table of the Earth.

See Egil Asprem, "False, Lying Spirits and Angels of Light: Ambiguous Mediation in Dr Rudd's Seventeenth-Century Treatise on Angel Magic," in *Magic, Ritual, and Witchcraft*, Volume 3, Number 1 (Philadelphia: University of Pennsylvania Press, Winter 2008), pages 54-80.

Notice must be given here to Aaron Leitch's *Secrets of the Magical Grimoires: The Classical Texts of Magick Deciphered* (Woodbury: Llewellyn Publications, 2005). Leitch, a practitioner himself, has made a valiant effort to offer a single-source epitome of the "classic grimoires" with descriptions, tables, and excerpts clearly and logically presented through 400+ oversized pages. The book is in two parts: (1) "history and scholarship," and (2) "practical work," including experiments and how-to instructions.

In Part One [*Oculta Philosophia*], CHAPTER ONE, Leitch provides an efficient if not particularly nuanced historical background. He then offers an account of the major grimoires, describing 22 texts, including the Solomonic texts discussed below, plus *Picatrix*, *The Sacred Magic of Abramelin*, Agrippa's *De occulta philosophia*, the pseudo-Agrippan *Fourth Book*, *Heptameron*, John Dee's diaries, Barrett's *Magus*, etc. Unfortunately, the preamble to these descriptions is marred by some irksome errors. For example, on page 9, Leitch writes,

> The *Ethiopian Book of Enoch*, the *Hebrew Book of Enoch*, the *Pirkei Heichaloht* (sic), and even such canonical biblical texts such as Ezekiel and the Revelation of St. John are all centered upon—or connected to—the *Merkavah* tradition. The *Merkavah's* use of ritual drugs, its focus on talismans and seals, the summoning forth of angelic gatekeepers, and the gaining of mystical visions are elements that run throughout the grimoiric spells.

As an example of a work "centered upon...the *Merkavah* tradition," the *Ethiopian* (more correctly, *Ethiopic*) *Book of Enoch* is an odd choice to set next to the *Hebrew Book of Enoch* and *Pirkei Hekhalot*. Yet, with "or connected to" interjected, Leitch allows enough slosh room for its inclusion as well as that of the Revelation.

More serious is Leitch's putting drugs and *merkavah* together, apparently through reading—but not thoroughly—James R. Davila's accounts of shamanic techniques. In the article which Leitch cites (and in Davila's book *Descenders of the Chariot*, Leiden: Brill, 2001), the use of drugs is indeed mentioned as a shamanic technique, *and* comparison is made between shamans (generic) and *merkavah* mystics (specific). However, Davila states, "Nothing in the Hekhalot literature indicates that the descenders to the chariot made use of psychoactive drugs to induce their visionary experiences" ("The Hekhalot Literature and Shamanism"—the article that Leitch cites—at the web page Divine Mediator Figures in the Biblical World at http://www.st-andrews.ac.uk/~www_sd/mediators.html). Leitch does go on to give a fairer account of *merkavah* mysticism, again based on Davila, later in the book (Chapter Two: "Shamanism, Tribal to Medieval," pages 54-5), where there is no mention of drugs, and *hekhalot* is spelled more conventionally.

Leitch's approach to the grimoires is best expressed in Chapter Three, "The Art of Ecstasy: Way of the Prophet-Shaman," which begins,

> The altered mental state is the most essential and critical aspect of magickal practice.

A few pages before (page 71) Leitch states,

> Some of the material in the grimoires may be, in fact, outdated. However, my focus is not upon the content or intent of the spells but on the foundational occult philosophy upon which the magick itself is based. It is my hope that this book will outline the processes by which this kind of magic works, and allow the practitioner to experiment with gaining conversation with various entities.

Part Two [*Oculta Practique*] mixes Leitch's prose with tables and extracts from the grimoires on all the technical matters: times, tools, and talismans; purification and prayer; angels and spirits.

As a first or stand-alone book, *Secrets...* has much to recommend it. Leitch has reached beyond the old stand-bys (Mathers, Waite, Crowley, original and later Golden Dawn material, E. M. Butler) and utilized some recent scholarship (James R. Davila, Claire Fanger, Richard Kieckhefer, Robert Mathiesen), though perhaps not enough (Leitch does not draw on the work of Michael D. Bailey, Charles Burnett, Ioan Couliano, Valerie Flint, David Halperin, Deborah Harkness, Gösta Hedegård, Naomi Janowitz, Frank Klaassen, Christopher Lehrich, Rebecca Lesses, Marvin Meyer, or Robert Turner, to name a few who have dealt directly with the texts and topics in *Secrets...*; the "classic" works of Lynn Thorndike and Joshua Trachtenberg are also neglected. See my bibliography below: Works of Related Interest.) Nearly all of the texts and scholarly sources Leitch refers to are readily available (in English), thus, the book has little new to offer, save Leitch's synthesis and organization, which sets the "grimoiric" material out in the form that suggests a unified system—which it certainly is not.

Despite all of the times I furrowed and bristled while poring over Leitch's book, because of its range, readability, and spirit, I recommend *Secrets of the Magickal Grimoires*, especially to those who intend to do the stuff. For the practitioner, *Secrets...* could serve well as a hard-copy anchor to the mass of texts available on Internet sites, such as TWILIT GROTTO at www.esotericarchives.com, SACRED TEXTS at www.sacred-texts.com, and NORTON'S IMPERIUM > "Classics of Magick" at www.hermetic.com/browe-archive. Academics, however, would do better to go directly to Leitch's sources—and well beyond.[1]

Another significant—and sizable (848 pages)—general work on magic is Gary St. Michael Nottingham's *Foundations of Practical Sorcery*, "[a] seven-part set of magical treatises on Ceremonial Magic and the Occult Arte" (London: Avalonia, 2015), published simultaneously as seven paperbacks and as a single hardback, "Collected Works: Unabridged," containing the entire set.

The volumes of the paperback, or chapters of the hardback, are

    Volume I   - LIBER NOCTIS (*A Handbook of the Sorcerous Arte*)
    Volume II - ARS SALOMONIS (*Being of the Hidden Arte of Solomon the King*) "...working with the talismanic figures found in the Key of Solomon."
    Volume III - ARS GEOMANTICA (*Being an account and rendition of the Arte of Geomantic Divination and Magic*)
    Volume IV - ARS THEURGIA GOETIA (*Being an account and rendition of the arte and praxis of the conjuration of some of the spirits of*

---

[1] For the comments of an experienced "Solomonic magician," refer to Carroll "Poke" Runyon's three-star review of Leitch, "A Good Survey in Need of Some Important Corrections" at Amazon.com > § REVIEWS WRITTEN BY THABION "THABION": http://www.amazon.com/gp/cdp/member-reviews/A13AN1BZVI4K02/ref=cm_pdp_about_see_review/104-3689026-2823924. The same review with some minor variations appears in *The Seventh Ray, Book III: "The Green Ray,"* edited by Runyon (Silverado: Church of the Hermetic Sciences & the Ordo Templi Astartes, 2011), pages 202-203.

Solomon), "...working with the versatile spirits and wandering princes of the *Theurgia Goetia*, part of the seventeenth-century *Lemegeton*."

Volume V – Oᴛᴢ Cʜɪᴍ (*The Tree of Life*), which includes "the *Massa Aborum* (sic) *Vitae* (the Mass of the Tree of Life),[1] a previously unavailable rite based on the aspects of the Tree and used by the author's ritual group."

Volume VI – Aʀꜱ Sᴘᴇᴄᴜʟᴜᴍ (*Being an instruction on the arte of using mirrors and shewstones in magic*)

Volume VII – Lɪʙᴇʀ Tᴇʀʀɪʙɪʟɪꜱ (*Being an instruction on the seventy-two spirits of the Goetia*)

These volumes were previously published individually in the years 2004-2013 [2] by Verdelet Publishing (Craven Arms), along with Nottingham's other works, such as *Ars Spagyrica: Being an Account and Rendition of the Alchemical Arte of Spagyric* (2005) and *Charms, Charming and the Charmed: Welsh Witcraft* (sic) *and the Shropshire Border* (2009).

The blurb on the author in the Avalonia promotional email (March 1st, 2015) states,

> Gary's personal magical practices draw on his interest in the alchemical arte, the 17th-century astrologer William Lilly and the arte of horary astrology, grimoires and spirit conjuration, as well as ritual magic. When not peering at bubbling flasks or a shewstone, he can usually be found either reading about such matters, playing chess, or, with his background being in horticulture, in the garden.

Given the present context, that of an essay on the literature of Solomonic magic, our attention naturally turns to Nottingham's CHAPTERS/VOLUMES II, IV, and VII (all page references are to the hardback edition):

II. Aʀꜱ Sᴀʟᴍᴏɴɪꜱ (pages 177-257) is an extended consideration of S. Liddell MacGregor Mathers' version of the *Key of Solomon* (1888) informed a bit by more recent editions (*e.g.*, Rankine and

---

[1] Nottingham clearly intends *Arborum*. However, even if the missing "r" is restored, the title is still something like "wad of trees of life." *Massa* might be better rendered *Missa*.

[2] I. *Liber Noctis* (2004), II. *Ars Solomonis* (2009), III. *Ars Geomantica* (2009), IV. *Ars Theurgia Goetia* (2012), V. *Otz Chim* (2012), VI. *Ars Speculum* (2012), and VII. *Liber Terribilis* (2013).

Note the additional volume: *Ars Alchemica – Foundations of Practical Alchemy: Being a Prima* (sic) *in the Paracelsian Arte of Solve et Coagula* (London: Avalonia, 2016). They must mean "primer."

Skinner's *Veritable Key of Solomon* [2008]). Mathers' text is generously paraphrased, and all of the pentacles are reproduced.

IV. ARS THEURGIA GOETIA (pages 317-476) "is an interpretation of the seals of the second part of the Solomonic grimoire cycle," *i.e.*, the *Lemegeton*, "giving the full seals of the spirits for the first time." Nottingham's introduction to this chapter concludes,

> It will be noted that additional conjurations as laid down in the *Steganographia* [of Trithemius] are also included for the use in the conjuration of the spirit. (—page 322)

VII. LIBER TERRIBILIS (pages 635-822) offers instructions on summoning the seventy-two spirits of the *Goetia*, the first section of the *Lemegeton*. Nottingham has "also given what [he] consider[s] to be missing information that makes the working more likely to be successful" (—pages 643-644).

LIBER TERRIBILIS opens with an entry on the fruitful "conjuration of the Goetic spirit Seere" as conducted by the Nottingham and two of his friends, which shows that

> Whilst *Goetia* conjuration is an effective part of the magical corpus, it will sometimes have you living on the edge, as it can take you right down to the wire before it resolves the situation. Although it is a powerful form of magic it is demanding too and if you can stick the pace you will find it highly effective. (—pages 640-641)

Nottingham's account of magical practice is described as "personal," yet nothing here seems particularly original, which, considering the nature of the subject matter, is probably a plus. He is clearly comfortable with a range of methods, having had some forty years' experience, and he is surely conversant with the texts he presents. Regrettably, he utilizes a rather narrow band of secondary sources, mostly of the "how-to" sort, and overlooks the wealth of recent scholarly literature on his texts and topics which could have greatly enhanced his presentation of the material.

Nottingham occasionally skitters hastily over terms which carry complex implications. For instance, we read in OTZ CHIM, "The Kabbalah says that originally creation came out of nothing and that nothing concentrated itself to a point and became something" (page

484). There is clearly a lot wrong with this sentence, beginning with the cardinal sin of employing the facile "Kabbalah says...."[1]

At times, Nottingham goes against the covey. For instance, he says that he doesn't believe the Wiccan "law of three-fold return." In his opinion,

> ...it was invented by the founders of modern wiccan/witchcraft revival to encourage society to think that they, modern witches/wiccans, were nice people and those modern witches, or those who think they are, are a little misunderstood by society, but kindly folk just the same." (LIBER NOCTIS, page 125)

This quote is an example of Nottingham's rather inefficient prose; when making his more personal points, he tends to be a bit scattered and redundant. (Another example of this unchecked style is quoted above in the description of LIBER TERRIBILIS.)

Cross references among the chapters/volumes would have been helpful. In ARS THEURGIA GOETIA (page 461), Nottingham mentions his assumption

> that the reader is familiar with various occult practices from the corpus of Western Magical Traditions, such as the Lesser Banishing Ritual and the Pentagram, the Middle Pillar, and consecrating of the Magic Circle. This also implies that you have the various tools of the arte and are familiar with their use.

---

[1] Nottingham repeatedly begins paragraphs with "The Kabbalah considers...," "The Kabbalah makes clear...," "The Kabbalah teaches...," each followed by a dilute smattering of kabbalistic wisdom. While Nottingham quotes the *Zohar* with attribution (page 485), he does not provide the conventional volume and section numbers (in this case *Zohar* 2:76a), nor does he cite his source for the quote, namely Israel Regardie, *A Garden of Pomegranates* (St. Paul: Llewellyn, 1995), page 93.

This is not the place to reiterate the whole argument against references like "*kabbalah* says." Briefly, *kabbalah* is not a work, a specific source, or even a unified doctrine. Citing a specific text and, if possible, its author seems an obvious minimum requirement. Imagine if someone wrote, "English literature says...."

This issue is taken up in some of my papers:
- "Kabbalah Study: Jewish Mysticism in English," which is appended (pages 42-49) to "Notes on the Study of Early Kabbalah in English" at http://www.digital-brilliance.com/contributed/Karr/Biblios/ekie.pdf
- "Which—or Whose—Lurianic Kabbalah?" which constitutes the major portion (essay section: pages 9-21) of the paper "Notes on the Study of Later Kabbalah in English: The Safed Period and Lurianic Kabbalah" at http://www.digital-brilliance.com/contributed/Karr/Biblios/lkie.pdf.

Nottingham does not note here that all this is covered in CHAPTER/VOLUME I, LIBER NOCTIS, along with basic information on a wide array of practices: geomancy, sigils, "kameas," magical use of the Psalms, candle magic, etc. Whereas the Lesser Banishing Ritual of the Pentagram is spelled out in its proper place in a working described in ARS GEOMANTICA (pages 294-296), in the praxis described in ARS THEURGIA GOETIA, we simply read "Perform LBRP" (—page 462). This could be particularly frustrating to the reader of ARS THEURGIA GOETIA in the separate paperback edition.

Yet, with these shortcomings, Nottingham writes with a welcome offhand earnestness. In this, his approach to magic is never far from good common sense. Case in point: under the banner of the old "To Know, to Dare, to Will and to Keep Silent," he bids the practitioner, "Don't talk about what you're about" (—page 18). O, what following this advice would have spared so many magicians—not to mention the people around them.

All in all, *Foundations...* supplies an impressive amount of practical information from a knowledgeable and reasonable fellow. As a stand-alone source or as an anchor to a collection of grimoires, this book could serve well. For anyone who has confronted a magical text and thought, "Okay, now what?" *Foundations of Practical Sorcery* offers a broad and well-considered inroad providing all of the information needed for a range of operations.

▼   ▼   ▼

Techniques of Solomonic Magic by Stephen Skinner (Singapore: Golden Hoard Press, 2015) is introduced as part of Skinner's Ph.D. dissertation, others being *Techniques of Graeco-Egyptian Magic* (which has been published—Singapore: Golden Hoard Press, 2014), and two further works on the *practice* of Graeco-Egyptian and Solomonic magic, which are forthcoming. While the already-published titles present intertwined material, this review treats only *Techniques of Solomonic Magic* due to its focus on the subject at hand. No doubt, this work can stand alone.

Skinner, who is both an experienced practitioner and a judicious scholar, is very careful to define and delimit just what Solomonic method entails (most succinctly in his APPENDIX 6: "The Classic Solomonic Method"). In this, he preserves Solomonic method as "learned magic," as distinct from "folk magic or village magic," which would include the English "cunning man," the hoodoo "conjure man," and witchcraft (pages 20-21).

The title, *Techniques of Solomonic Magic*, might lead one to think that this is an instruction book, for the words "practice," "methods," and "techniques," are often used interchangeably. Skinner draws a distinction between "practice" and the other two terms, reserving for "practice" the performative (read "practical") aspects of his subject. In *Techniques of Solomonic Magic*, Skinner seeks to determine the historic trajectory of the "techniques" and "methods" of what has coalesced as Solomonic magic.

In composing this trajectory, Skinner has marshaled a broad array of recent scholarship. More importantly, he has done a vast amount of original research, basing his observations and comparisons directly on the pertinent texts, whether in printed editions or unique manuscripts, the vast majority of which Skinner viewed first-hand.

Skinner's research encompasses more than his years formally working towards his Ph.D. Indeed, his long and admirable career has in large part been involved with the grimoire tradition.[1] In a more concentrated way, the works published in Golden Hoard's important SOURCEWORKS OF CEREMONIAL MAGIC series, for which Skinner edited eight volumes and, of these, co-authored six, serve as a preamble to the production of Skinner's dissertation. In *Techniques of Solomonic Magic*, Skinner writes (page 27)

> As an accompaniment to this volume, I suggest you have to hand copies of some of the source texts: *The Magical Treatise of Solomon or Hygromanteia*[2] by Ioannis Marathakis; *The Veritable Key of Solomon* by

---

[1] Among Skinner's many books, note in particular *Techniques of High Magic: A Manual of Self-Initiation*, first published in 1976, now in its third revised edition (Singapore: Golden Hoard Press, 2016), and *The Fourth Book of Occult Philosophy*, first published in 1978 (London: Askin Publishers Ltd) and republished in 2005 (Berwick: Ibis Press).
[2] See pages 1-2, note 2 above.

myself and David Rankine; *The Key of Solomon* by MacGregor Mathers; *Sepher Raziel: Liber Salomonis* by Don Karr and Stephen Skinner; and *The Lesser Key of Solomon* by Joseph Peterson.

The first, second, and fourth books on this list are volumes in the SOURCEWORKS series. Mathers' edition of *The Key of Solomon*, first published in 1889, is, of course, the "classic" text. *The Lesser Key of Solomon*, also known as *The Lemegeton*, is the other major "proof text" of the Solomonic tradition; the edition recommended here was most ably prepared by Joseph Peterson (2001).

The value of *Techniques of Solomonic Magic* goes far beyond Skinner's conclusions about where the material in the *Key of Solomon* came from, for Skinner has presented his entire scholarly process, complete with charts (vast outlines of text groups and manuscripts), tables (comparing details of various texts), and illustrations, all for us to engage. Skinner admits, in so many words, that the book and, for that matter, his entire dissertation project remain works in progress. Case in point: after delivering evidence for his suggestion that *Apotelesmatikē Pragmateia* by Stephanos is "an early version or forerunner of the *Hygromanteia*" (page 69), he adds

> I would be happy to have this attribution refuted, but only if a better candidate for the authorship of the *Hygromanteia* can be discovered.

Skinner often acknowledges that further research may lead to different conclusions regarding various issues surrounding his primary thesis, but he presents, in overwhelming detail, his case quite convincingly. To me, of Skinner's nineteen conclusions, the following (ii and iii) are by far the most important (page 280):

ii) There is a clear line of transmission from the *Hygromanteia* to the *Clavicula Salomonis* which is identifiable down to the very detailed level of Solomonic method and specific pieces of equipment. Therefore there can be no doubt that the *Hygromanteia* is the forefather of the *Clavicula Salomonis*.

iii) There are two main exceptions to the above point:
   a) The scrying chapters in the *Hygromanteia* have not been passed on to the *Clavicula Salomonis*. These scrying methods are however found almost word-for-word in an 11th-century

Jewish source. Accordingly, the Jewish sources probably supplied these chapters to the *Hygromanteia*.

b) The pentacles chapters in the *Clavicula Salomonis* do not derive from the *Hygromanteia*, but probably come from the manuscript *Sepher ha-Otot*, or from a related Hebrew source.

Thus, the trend away from supposing that the Solomonic grimoires had Jewish origins is in part confirmed yet in part reversed through Skinner's discoveries and observations.[1]

Techniques of Solomonic Magic is not a magic instruction book. The description posted at the website of Llewellyn Worldwide — the North American distributor for Golden Hoard publications — accurately identifies the work as

> The most detailed analysis of the techniques of Solomonic magic from the seventh to the nineteenth century ever published. This volume explores the methods of Solomonic magic in Alexandria, tracing how the tradition passed through Byzantium (the *Hygromanteia*) to the Latin *Clavicula Salomonis* and its English incarnation as the *Key of Solomon*.[2]

We will have to wait to see what Skinner's sequel on the practice of Solomonic magic provides. But anyone who has collected grimoires in the Solomonic tradition can here, in the channels that Skinner has excavated, find an enormous amount of information about the province and composition of the oft-reproduced texts (*The Key of Solomon, The Lemegeton,* Agrippa's *Three Books of Occult Philosophy,* etc.)

---

[1] One small quibble: In his sub-chapter (3.2) on "The Input of Jewish Magic to the *Clavicula Salomonis*," Skinner speculates (page 40, note 5): "Interestingly the angel ambiguously referred to as the 'Lord God of Israel' is Zoharariel, which might better be read as 'Zohar Ariel.' An angel name possibly generated from the title of that great classic of the Kabbalah, the *Sepher ha-Zohar*."

This doesn't follow at all given that Zoharariel already appears in texts of the *merkavah* tradition (200-800 CE), most importantly *Hekhalot Rabbati* (§§ 96, 99, 102, 103, 110, 111, 119, 121, 197, 204, 232, and 251), but also *Hekhalot Zutarti* (§ 418, as one of the seven angels: Zoharariel, Uriel, Afael, Gabriel, Nuriel, Panael, and Serafiel), *Ma'aseh Merkava* (§ 581), and the Geniza Fragments (§ 121). § numbers follow Peter Schäfer *et al.*, *Synopse zur Hekhalot Literatur* (Tübingen: J. C. B. Mohr [Paul Siebeck], 1981).

The *Sefer ha-Zohar* was not written/redacted/manifest/circulated (take your pick) until around 1300.

[2] At http://www.llewellyn.com/product.php?ean=9780738748061. Also, see the description at the Golden Hoard Press website, http://www.goldenhoard.net/index.htm, for a lengthy, albeit "partial," list of contents.)

while learning that not all of the famous grimoires are "Solomonic," and acquaint themselves with less-known magic texts from antiquity and medieval times that contributed to Solomonic literature. Thus, Skinner's work bears less comparison with the books singled out above by Aaron Leitch and Gary St. Michael Nottingham than it does to, say, *Ritual Magic* by E. M. Butler and the more recent *Grimoires* by Owen Davies—among all of which I would surmise that Skinner's *Techniques of Solomonic Magic* will prove the most significant.

OTHER NOTEWORTHY RECENT PUBLICATIONS:

Readers should note Stephen Skinner's expansion of Aleister Crowley's *Liber 777*, namely, *The Complete Magician's Tables* (Singapore: Golden Hoard Press, 2006/St. Paul: Llewellyn Publications, 2007). The subtitle elaborates: *The most complete set of Magic, Kabbalistic, Angelic, Astrologic, Alchemic, Demonic, Geomantic, Grimoire, Gematria, I Ching, Tarot, Pagan Pantheon, Plant, Perfume and Character Correspondence in more than 777 tables*. The Crowley editions circulating have something fewer than 200 columns, whereas Skinner's 2006 volume has more than 800 columns, and Skinner's new expanded fifth edition (2015) has 840.

§ M, "Magic of the Grimoires—Angels, Demons and Spirits," connects with the topic at hand. § M offers tables drawn from

- *Testament of Solomon*
- *Liber Juratus, the Sworn Book of Honorius*
- Peter de Abano's *Heptameron*
- *Codex Latinus Monacensis*
- *Goetia* (*Lemegeton* Book I)
- *Theurgia Goetia* (*Lemegeton* Book II)
- *Ars Paulina* (*Lemegeton* Book III)
- *Ars Almadel* (*Lemegeton* Book IV)
- *Key of Solomon – Clavicula Salomonis*
- *Sacred Magic of Abramelin*
- Franz Bardon's *Practice of Magical Evocation*
- *Grimorium Verum*
- *Grand Grimoire*

Liber Salomonis

The oft-cited but frustratingly scarce works on the Hebrew MS called *Sepher Maphteah Shelomoh* (ca. 1700) by Hermann Gollancz have been reprinted in a single volume by Teitan Press (York Beach: 2008):

- *Maphteah Shelomo. Clavicula Salomonis: A Hebrew Manuscript newly discovered and now described.* (London: D. Nutt / Frankfurt a.M: J. Kauffmann, 1903)
- *Sepher Maphteah Shelomoh* (BOOK OF THE KEY OF SOLOMON). An exact facsimile of an original book of magic in Hebrew with illustrations now produced for the first time. (London – New York: Oxford University Press, 1914 — of which only 300 copies were printed)

The Teitan edition adds a seven-page foreword by Stephen Skinner, which states that "there is no doubt that this manuscript [i.e., *Sepher Maphteah Shelomoh*] is part of the Solomonic magical tradition," and "in a large measure derived from them, which is quite the reverse of the usual assumption" (—page viii). In a section sub-headed CONFIRMATION OF THE LATINIZED CONTENTS, Skinner (following Claudia Rohrbacher-Stricker) presents "proof that this text [i.e., *Sepher Maphteah Shelomoh*] is a translation from a Latin/Italian original, by a Hebrew translator" (—page xii).

Alas, the reprint is a limited edition of 358 copies.

Sepher Raziel

TEXTS OF SOLOMONIC MAGIC IN ENGLISH

BOOKS REFERRED TO FREQUENTLY:

- Butler, E. M. *Ritual Magic* (Cambridge: Cambridge University Press, 1949 and 1979; rpt University Park: Pennsylvania State University, 1998, as a volume of their MAGIC IN HISTORY SERIES).
- Fanger, Claire (ed.) *Conjuring Spirits: Texts and Traditions of Medieval Ritual Magic* (University Park: Pennsylvania State University Press, 1998); hereafter *Conjuring Spirits*.
- Fanger, Claire (ed.) *Invoking Angels: Theurgic Ideas and Practices, Thirteenth to Sixteenth Centuries* (University Park: The Pennsylvania State University Press, 2012); hereafter *Invoking Angels*.
- Nottingham, Gary St. Michael. *Foundations of Practical Sorcery* (London: Avalonia, 2015); hereafter Nottingham's *Foundations*.
- Shah, Idries. *Secret Lore of Magic* (New York: Citadel Press, 1958; rpt. 1972); hereafter *Secret Lore* or simply "Shah."
- Thompson C. J. S. *Mysteries and Secrets of Magic* (London: J. Lane the Bodley Head, 1927; rpt. New York: Causeway Books, 1973); hereafter Thompson's *Mysteries*.
- Waite, Arthur Edward. *The Book of Ceremonial Magic* (London: Rider, 1911; rpt. New York: Bell Publishing, 1969); hereafter *Ceremonial Magic* or simply "Waite." [1]

1. a. THE KEY OF SOLOMON

The best-known presentation of the KEY OF SOLOMON is Samuel Liddell MacGregor Mathers' *Key of Solomon the King* (London: Redway, 1888; rpt. New York – York Beach: Samuel Weiser Inc., 1974 and subsequently). Mathers compiled his edition from several MSS found in the British Library's Sloane, Harleian, Landsdowne, and King collections, attempting to weave from these an "ideal" text.[2]

The KEY is described in Butler's *Ritual Magic*, pages 47-64, and in Thompson's *Mysteries*, pages 229-240. Another fair presentation of the KEY appears in Shah's *Secret Lore*, pages 9-60. Not quite so good is Arthur Edward Waite's treatment in *Ceremonial Magic*, pages 58-64 (Bell edition).

---

[1] *Ceremonial Magic* is a revision of Waite's earlier *Book of Black Magic and of Pacts* (London: Redway, 1898; rpt. New York – York Beach: Samuel Weiser Inc., 1972 — and subsequently).

[2] Mathers' version of the KEY is included in the no-frills "pirate" collection, *The Clavicula Solomonis* (sic) by Magus Tsirk Susej—Jesus Krist backwards—(n.p.: Embassy of Lucifer, 2005); this edition has the text of the KEY and the LESSER KEY (see below 1.b, page 9)—with no introduction, notes, or mention of sources, MSS or printed editions.

The most extensive treatment of the KEY to date is Volume IV of the Golden Hoard Press series, SOURCEWORKS OF CEREMONIAL MAGIC: *The Veritable Key of Solomon* by Stephen Skinner and David Rankine (London – Singapore: Golden Hoard Press / Woodbury: Llewellyn Publications, 2008), which presents three KEY OF SOLOMON texts translated from the French by Paul Harry Barron:

> KEY 1. *The Keys of Rabbi Solomon* (Wellcome MS 4670 [1796])
> KEY 2. *La Clavicule ou La Clef de Salomon* (Wellcome MS 4669 Art. 1 [1796])
> KEY 3. *Traité Universal des Clavicucles de Salomon* (Wellcome MS 4669 Art. 2)[1]

these being "three different texts from those translated by S. L. MacGregor Mathers." The texts are introduced by a 60-page survey of the history and various "text-groups" of the KEY, supplemented by several appendices listing KEY MSS.[2]

A composite of material related to the KEY was assembled by Ebenezer Sibley (*or* Sibly) as *Clavis or Key to Unlock the Mysteries of Magic of Rabbi Solomon, translated from Hebrew into French and from French rendered into English with additions*, ca. 1800. Two reproduction editions have recently been published:

> (1) Ebenezer Sibly, *Solomon's Clavis, or Key to Unlock the Mysteries of Magic* (Leicestershire: Society of Esoteric Endeavor, 2008), which offers Sibly's manuscript, English translations primarily from various French magical sources unadorned, *i.e.*, "no modern introduction," with Sibly's preface.

---

[1] Additional material from Wellcome MS 4669 has been published as *A Collection of Magical Secrets, Taken from Peter de Abano, Cornelius Agrippa and from other Famous Occult Philosophers & A Treatise of Mixed Cabalah, Which comprises the Angelic Art Taken from Hebrew Sages*, translated from Wellcome MS 4669 by Paul Harry Barron from the original French manuscript dated 1796, with introduction and commentary by Stephen Skinner & David Rankine (London: Avalonia, 2009).

[2] In "The Key of Solomon: Toward a Typology of the Manuscripts" (in *Societas Magica Newsletter*, Issue 17, Spring 2007—online at http://www.societasmagica.org/), Robert Mathiesen "offer[s] some materials for an eventual typological study of these [*Key of Solomon*] texts," starting with an account of 122 MSS written in languages using the Latin alphabet, as opposed to those in Greek or Hebrew, then offering a provisional division of these into "Western text groups," *e.g.*, "Oldest (Western) Text [OT]," "Toz Graecus Text-Group [TG]," "Invocation of Angels Text-Group [IA]," and so on. Mathiesen adds some comments on "*A Hebrew Version of the* Key of Solomon," namely, *Mafteach Shelomoh*, and "*An Arabic Version...*" entitled *Al-Miftah al-Azam li-Sulayman al-Hakim*, and proffers some "Tentative Conclusions."

(2) Ebenezer Sibley, *The Clavis or Key to the Magic of Solomon...from a manuscript prepared by Frederick Hockley*, with introduction, notes, and commentary by Joseph Peterson (Lake Worth: Ibis Press, 2009).[1]

Along similar lines: *The Keys of Rabbi Solomon* "translated accurately from the Hebrew into English" by Edward Hunter, *circa* 1830 (The Hell Fire Club, 2016). As with Sibly's works, this is a hand-copied MS of a composite of Solomonic and other materials. Alas, the obscurity of the work is assured in that the publisher saw fit to release only lovely but high-priced limited editions (42 of calfskin, 250 of kidskin).

There is also *The Pentacles of Solomon* by S. Aldarnay (Hadean Press, 2012): "Author and illustrator S. Aldarnay presents each of the Pentacles given in the *Key of Solomon*, precisely redrawn and with explanations of the divine names, the names of spirits, as well as the vesicles in English, Latin and Hebrew, in an attempt to make the individual's use of the seals more effective." (—online description; I have not seen the book).[2]

Note the re-presentation of material from Mathers' version of the KEY in Nottingham's *Foundations* (described above, pages 7-9): Chapter/Volume II – ARS SALOMONIS (*Being of the Hidden Arte of Solomon the King*) "...working with the talismanic figures found in the Key of Solomon."

Refer also to Stephen Skinner's *Techniques of Solomonic Magic* (described above, pages 9-11), which traces the origins of the KEY's methods and contents.

Lastly, find Christopher Warnock's informative, albeit provocative, blog, "The Greater Key of Solomon is Wrong!" (April 16, 2012), at RENAISSANCE ASTROLOGY[3] Warnock concludes,

> Renaissance Astrology pentacles don't follow the *Greater Key* exactly and we do this because following the true full chart traditional astrological methodology provides a much more powerfully charged

---

[1] See Joscelyn Godwin, *The Theosophical Enlightenment* (Albany: State University of New York Press, 1994): on Sibly, pages 107*ff*; on Hockley, pages 170*ff*.
[2] http://www.shop.hadeanpress.com/
[3] http://renaissance-astrology.blogspot.com/2012/04/greater-key-of-solomon-is-wrong.html

talisman. We don't use the traditional metals because it simply isn't necessary for a powerful talisman.

1. b. *Lemegeton,* or LESSER KEY OF SOLOMON

The *Lemegeton* consists of five sections:
  i. *Goetia* – on binding evil spirits and their seals
  ii. *Theurgia-Goetia* [§§ I and II] – on both good and evil spirits
  iii. Pauline Art – on the good spirits of the planets and the 360 degrees of the zodiac
  iv. *Almadel* – good spirits of the quaternary of the altitudes
  v. Notary Art (OR *Ars Nova* – see discussions below regarding content)

Goetia is the best circulated of the *Lemegeton's* sections, having been published numerous times. The best-known version is the one transcribed by S. L. MacGregor Mathers in 1898, with an introductory essay entitled "Preliminary Definition of Magic." A few years later, Aleister Crowley published this same edition enhanced by his own introduction, preface, preliminary invocation, and other ornaments (Foyers: S[ociety for the] P[ropagation of] R[eligious] T[ruth] Ltd, 1904). In 1916, the pirating began—or continued—with an edition bearing the name L. W. de Laurence and the title *The Lesser Key of Solomon – Goetia: The Book of Evil Spirits* (Chicago: de Laurence, Scott and Co.), which is the Mathers-Crowley work unacknowledged; this edition is listed as still *in print*.

A larger version—in size, not in content—bearing Crowley's name was published in 1970 (New York: Ram Importer Inc.; subsequent editions from Equinox Ltd in 1976, Magickal Childe in 1989, and First Impressions in 1993) as *The Book of the Goetia of Solomon the King*; this is, for the most part, a dressed-up version of the "SPRT/de Laurence" edition.[1]

---

[1] See also *Aleister Crowley's Illustrated Goetia*, by Lon Milo DuQuette and Christopher Hyatt, illustrated by David P. Wilson (Tempe: New Falcon Publications, 1992). This work presents the list of spirits "from Crowley's original Goetia—which also includes many other prerequisites for evocation" along with material from *777*, where Crowley "attributed the Seventy-Two Spirits of the Goetia (in pairs, Day/Night) to the Decans of the Zodiac." (page 71) Each spirit is also given a full-page image drawn by "artist-clairvoyant David P. Wilson, who is also a talented and adept Goetic magician" (page

Goetia is described and quoted in Butler's *Ritual Magic* (pages 65-80); it is presented in both Shah (pages 179-211; 299-304) and Waite (pages 64-66; 184-235). Waite's "list of the seventy-two spirits ... along with their sigils" is reproduced in Christopher McIntosh's *Devil's Bookshelf* (Wellingborough: The Aquarian Press, 1985: pages 168-189).

Of the Arte Goetia by Colin Campbell (York Beach: Teitan Press, 2015) offers a manner of *Goetia* companion, which has been a long-standing desideratum. After singling out Joseph Peterson's "critical edition of the complete *Lesser Key of Solomon*"[1] (of which *Goetia* is the first section) as the text-source of record, Campbell's first chapter concludes with this statement of intention:

> This present work was composed with several aims in mind, the chief of which was to trace the emergence of *Goetia* into the English language manuscripts with which it is now closely identified. By comparing the known sources and influences, it is possible to observe the subtle and not-so-subtle changes; the errors, omissions, inclusions, and other alterations that together combine to create the text as we now know it. We can also use these comparisons to aid us in historical research into the origins of the work, as well as to identify the external influences that affected it (page 22).

At his website, COLIN CAMPBELL'S DE ARTE MAGICA,[2] Campbell writes

> Many are aware that the listing of spirits that is presented in *Goetia* is derived almost in its entirety from the earlier work *Pseudomonarchia Daemonum* (THE FALSE MONARCHY OF DEMONS) as given by Johann Wier (Wierus [or Weyer]) in his publication in protest of the witch hysteria in his native Germany, *De Praestigiis Daemonum* (OF THE ILLUSIONS OF SPIRITS)[3] [1563; *Pseudomonarchia Daemonum* was added as an appendix to *De Praestigiis Daemonum* in 1577]. ...

---

72). The text is supplemented by nine chapters which expand on Crowley's version of the *Goetia*, offering background, advice, and anecdotes.

[1] See my comment on Peterson's *Lesser Key...* below, page 21.

[2] http://campbell.hrmtc.com/2015/09/30/goetia-origins/ - accessed 10/10/15.

[3] Wier's work is available in English: *Witches, Devils, and Doctors in the Renaissance* (*DE PRÆSTIGIIS DÆMONUM*, 1583), introduction and notes by George Mora; translation by John Shea; preface by John Weber [MEDIEVAL AND RENAISSANCE TEXTS & STUDIES, volume 73] (Binghamton: State University of New York at Binghamton, 1991; rpt. Tempe: Arizona State University, 1998). Unfortunately, this volume does not include the appendix, *Pseudomonarchia Daemonum*.

This work [*i.e.*, Wier's], specifically with relation to its advocacy against persecution of suspected witches (typically, impoverished elderly women), was picked up in England by Reginald Scot, a lawyer, who argued in *The Discoverie of Witchcraft* (1584)[1], that not only were witches not actually able to do all the things of which they were accused, but that regardless they should be tried for the crime they were accused of committing rather than witchcraft itself. …

One of the aims of *Of the Arte Goetia* was to place these three sources—Wier, Scot, and the [*Goetia*] manuscripts—side by side so that one could see the evolution of each spirit's description. Once accomplished, it was easy to show where discrepancies arose.

From among the "manuscripts," Campbell uses the *Goetia* as it appears in Sloane MS. 3825 as his base text.

A catalogue of demons which is closely related to the *Goetia* is offered in *A Book of the Offices of Spirits – The Occult Virtue of Plants and Some Rare Magical Charms & Spells*, transcribed by Frederick Hockley from a Sixteenth-Century Manuscript on Magic and Necromancy by John Porter (1583), with an introduction by Colin D. Campbell (York Beach: Teitan Press, 2011). Campbell suggests that

> [g]iven the close relationship between the two manuscripts [*i.e.*, *The Offices of Spirits* and *Goetia*], it would seem reasonable to speculate that they have a common ancestor. If so, then *The Offices of Spirits* is probably the earlier of the two, as *Goetia* is considerably more organized and includes additional seals for each of its spirits.

Goetia and *Theurgia-Goetia* are given full treatment in Gary Nottingham's *Foundations* (described above, pages 7-9): (1) on *Goetia*, Chapter or Volume VII – LIBER TERRIBILIS (*Being an instruction on the seventy-two spirits of the Goetia*); (2) on *Theurgia-Goetia*, Chapter or Volume IV – ARS THEURGIA GOETIA (*Being an account and rendition of the arte and praxis of the conjuration of some of the spirits of Solomon*) "…working with the versatile spirits and wandering

---

[1] *The Discovery of Witchcraft* has long been available as one of the ubiquitous Dover paperbacks, which reprints the edition published by John Rodker in 1930. On the *goetic* spirits as derived from Wier, see BOOKE XV, CHAPTER II. Refer also to Philip C. Almond's *England's First Demonologist: Reginald Scot & 'The Discoverie of Witchcraft'* (London – New York: I. B. Taurus Co Ltd, 2011).

princes of the *Theurgia Goetia*, part of the seventeenth-century *Lemegeton*."

Waite considers the *Pauline Art* in *Ceremonial Magic* (pages 66-72), and Christopher McIntosh includes the conjuration of Samael from a MS of the *Pauline Art* "copied out by Frederick Hockley, the indefatigable nineteenth-century collector of occult documents," in *The Devil's Bookshelf* (pages 190-1).

Hockley's full transcription (1838) of both sections of the *Pauline Art* (1. on the spirits of the hours of the day, *and* 2. on the 360 angels of the zodiac) has been published under the title *The Pauline Art of Solomon* (York Beach: Teitan Press, 2016). Editor Alan Thorogood provides a history of the *Pauline Art*, fills in much of what Hockley edited out, and corrects errors that accumulated in the text. This edition includes a somewhat undersized facsimile of Hockley's manuscript.

Shah and Waite also treat [*The Art of*] *Almadel* (full text from Sloane 2731—*Secret Lore*, pages 169-178; excerpts—*Ceremonial Magic*, pages 72-77).[1] A full transcription of *The Art of Almadel of Solomon* from British Library, MS Sloane 2731 and collated with Sloane 3648 and 3825 appears as an appendix to Jan R. Veenstra's article "*The Holy Almandal:* Angels and the Intellectual Aims of Magic," in *The Metamorphosis of Magic from Late Antiquity to the Early Modern Period*, edited by Jan N. Bremmer and Jan R. Veenstra (Leuven: Peeters, 2002).[2]

---

[1] The *Almadel* of the *Lemegeton* should not be confused with *Armadel*—a completely different work, available as *The Grimoire of Armadel*, translated by S. L. MacGregor Mathers (York Beach: Samuel Weiser, 1980 and 1995); nor should these be confused with the *Arbatel of Magick*, a collection of forty-nine magical aphorisms which is the first section of an otherwise lost nine-part tome said to have been employed by John Dee.

See Joseph H. Peterson's translation, *Arbatel: Concerning the Magic of the Ancients* [ORIGINAL SOURCEBOOK OF ANGEL MAGIC] (Lake Worth: Ibis Press, 2009)—also at Peterson's TWILIT GROTTO: www.esotericarchives.com > Classical Grimoires. *Arbatel* also appears in the collection titled *The Fourth Book of Occult Philosophy*, edited... by Stephen Skinner (London: Askin Publishers, 1978; rpt Berwick [ME]: Ibis Press, 2005—see listing below). Also on the Internet, find *Arbatel* at The CHAOS MATRIX: http://www.chaosmatrix.org/library/books/lesserkey/lesserkey4.pdf.

[2] *The Holy Almandal* is a practical manual of ritual magic which "may have roots extending back into Persia and the Far East, but its medieval versions were thoroughly Christianized" [page 192]; however, *Almandal* and *Almadel* are of "diverse traditions." [page 209] (cited from Veenstra's "*Holy Almandel*...").

Some efforts have offered complete, or near-complete, editions of *Lemegeton*. All segments but Notary Art appear in Kevin Wilby's *Lemegetton: A Medieval Manual of Solomonic Magic* [Sloane MS 3648] (Dyfed: Hermetic Research Series NUMBER 5, 1985). In his article, "The *Lemegetton* Revealed," (in *The Hermetic Journal*, Issue 29, ed. Adam McLean, 1985), Wilby says that Notary Art "is fragmentary and nowhere near complete," referring to it as the "corrupted fifth part." Wilby is even harsher in the FOREWORD to his book, *The Lemegetton*, referring to "the fifth and final book" as "the only blemish I found in this masterly work," deeming Notary Art "literary tripe."

A so-so photocopy (with some pages missing) of British Library Sloane MS 2731 (which is in English) and a remarkably poor typescript comprise Nelson and Anne White's *Lemegeton: Clavicula Salomonis, The Complete Lesser Key of Solomon the King* (Fremont: Technology Group, 1979; 2nd edition, once available at www.techgroupbooks.com—an unfortunately now-defunct site which proved that one picture is, indeed, worth a thousand words).

The edition from the International Guild of Occult Sciences (hereafter I.G.O.S.), *King Solomon's The Lemegeton: Lesser Key* (or *The Lemegeton: King Solomon's Lesser Key*) (Palm Springs: I.G.O.S., 1997) contains the Whites' photocopy slightly enlarged with a transcription which is neat and readable. Neither the Whites' nor the I.G.O.S. version includes Notary Art, save for a few "sample pages," stating that Notary Art is "quite obviously not a 'book,' but rather a collection of notes and explanations which should have been presented with the first book, The Goetia" (the Whites' edition, page 57); and "a scattered and undeveloped jotting down … at best supplementary notations" (I.G.O.S. edition, page 65).

Robin E. Cousins[1] observes that Notary Art is, in fact, omitted from Sloane 2731, the MS used by the Whites and I.G.O.S. According to Cousins,[2] Wilby based his edition on a manuscript (Sloane MS

---

[1] In *Elizabethan Magic*, edited by Robert Turner (Longmead: Element Books, 1989), page 140.
[2] *Ibid.*, page 141.

3648) which contains the Notary Art, but—as noted above—he saw fit to exclude it from his "complete" edition.

Another "complete" edition, *Lemegeton: The Complete Lesser Key of Solomon*, edited by Mitch Henson, with revised illustrations by Jeff Wellman (Jacksonville: Metatron Books, 1999), also omits Notary Art. Explaining this omission, Henson says, "Both the content and the context of *Ars Notoria* show no affinity for the listings of spirits that mark the bulk of the material contained in *The Lesser Key of Solomon*."

In his introduction, Henson states, "The text for this edition is a composite derived from Sloane Ms 3825 and 2731 from the British Library. These are the most complete and internally consistent manuscripts available," adding further on, "For this edition, we have reproduced all of the illustrations from Sloane Ms 2731." Henson's *Lemegeton*, now out of print, has become one of the most sought-after—and high-priced—editions.

A text entitled *Ars Notoria: The Notary Art of Solomon*, translated into English in 1657 by Robert Turner of Holshott (not to be confused with Robert Turner, the present-day author/editor, cited in notes 32 and 35) has been published in a collector's edition (Seattle: Trident Press, 1987 and 1997) along with some support material: "An Astrological Catechisme," "Solomon and the *Ars Notoria*" from Lynn Thorndike's *History of Magic and Experimental Science*, and "*Ars Notoria* in Manuscript" by Adam McLean. This is clearly not the *Ars Notoria* referred to by the Whites, I.G.O.S., and Henson.[1]

A low-cost edition of this work, titled variously *Ars Notoria: The Magical Art of Solomon, Showing the Cabalistical Key of Magical Operations* or *The Magical Art of Solomon, being the Ars Notoria: A Grimoire* [KABBALISTIC GRIMOIRE SERIES III], edited by Darcy Kuntz without the sundry additions, was put out by Holmes Publishing

---

[1] Clair Fanger states (in "Plundering the Egyptian Treasure," *Conjuring Spirits*, page 219), "There is no modern edition of the Ars Notoria, and the relation of the seventeenth-century text (found in Agrippa's *Opera [Omnia]* and the Turner translation) to the medieval manuscript tradition remains unexamined."

Group [Edmonds] in 1998 and remains available in a more recent reprint edition.

A handsome reproduction of Frederick Hockley's 1839 transcription of—and occasional additions to—Robert Turner's translation of *Ars Notoria: The Notary Art of Solomon* has been published by Teitan Press (York Beach, 2015). This edition includes an introduction by editor Alan Thorogood and an essay, "'The Philomath': In Search of Robert Turner of Holshot," which is "…a significant 24-page biographical study (with bibliography)" by Robin Cousins.[1]

On the *Ars notoria*, refer to the following:

- *Conjuring Spirits*
    - Camille, Michael. "Visual Art in Two Manuscripts of the Ars Notoria"
    - Fanger, Claire. "Plundering the Egyptian Treasure: John the Monk's *Book of Visions* and its Relation to the *Ars notoria* of Solomon"
    - Klaassen, Frank. § THE ARS NOTORIA within "English Manuscripts of Magic, 1300-1500: A Preliminary Survey"
- Klaassen's section, "The Notary Art" (CHAPTER 4, § 1) in RELIGION, SCIENCE, AND THE TRANSFORMATIONS OF MAGIC: MANUSCRIPTS OF MAGIC 1300-1600, Ph.D. dissertation: Toronto: University of Toronto, 1999 (pages 109-129)
- Klaassen's chapter, "The Ars Notoria and the Sworn Book of Honorius" in *The Transformations of Magic: Illicit Learned Magic in the Later Middle Ages and Renaissance* (University Park: Penn State University Press, 2012).
- Julien Veronèse's "Magic, Theurgy, and Spirituality in the Medieval Ritual of the *Ars notoria*," in *Invoking Angels*.
- Sophie Page's chapter, "The *Ars notoria* and Its Monastic Audience," in *Magic in the Cloister: Pious Motives, Illicit Interests, and Occult Approaches to the Medieval Universe* (University Park: The Pennsylvania State University Press, 2013.

---

[1] An earlier version of Cousins' essay under the title "Robert Turner of 'Holshot' (c. 1620-1665?): The Astrological Botanist and the Books of the Elizabethan Magi," was included in *Elizabethan Magic*, by Robert Turner [and other contributors] (Longmead: Element Books, 1989), pages 128-150.

"The Philomath" as it appears in Teitan's *Ars Notoria* "has been fully revised and updated with recently discovered material" (—Cousins, *Ars Notoria*, page xxvii).

So, what actually *is* the fifth book of the *Lemegeton?* While not really contradicting the White/I.G.O.S. assessment, Benjamin Rowe offers an alternative and more positive take on the *Lemegeton's* fifth book. In the introduction to his *Ars Nova – Book Five of the Lemegeton* (June 1999),[1] Rowe states that in some manuscripts (such as the one from which he transcribed, Sloane MS. 2731 – the same as the Whites' and I.G.O.S.), the fifth book is an addendum containing notes on *Goetia*. This book has been mistakenly called *Ars Notoria* instead of the correct name, *Ars Nova*. Rowe suggests quite convincingly that the last couple of pages of the manuscript are out of order, and, thus, *Ars Nova* consists of two leaves rather than one. These final pages of *Lemegeton* can be seen in the photocopies of the White and I.G.O.S. editions.[2]

In apparent agreement with Rowe, Stephen Skinner notes[3] that whenever *Ars Nova* has been transcribed, it has been read incorrectly as a continuous text rather than as columns. Thus, according to Skinner, the only printed edition of *Ars Nova* which is transcribed in the correct order appears in Skinner & Rankine, *The Goetia of Dr Rudd* (London: Golden Hoard, 2007), APPENDIX 9, pages 414-421; more on *The Goetia of Dr Rudd* below.

The Lesser Key of Solomon, edited by Joseph H. Peterson (York Beach: Red Wheel/Weiser, 2001), includes a complete text – all five books, including *Ars Notoria* – with other pertinent material, including a preface from one of the MS editions of the *Lesser Key*, addenda from two others, and Johann Weyer's *Pseudomonarchia dæmonum*. "I have followed Sloane 3825 for this edition, except for *Ars Notoria*. For the latter, the manuscripts are clearly dependent on Robert Turner's translation. I have therefore used his 1657 printed edition as my primary source." (INTRODUCTION, page *xiii*) However, Peterson adds (at his website, ESOTERIC ARCHIVES

---

[1] Formerly at Rowe's site, *Norton's Imperium: Enochian Magick Papers & Links* > "Classics of Magic," at www.hermetic.com/browe-archive; now, "This topic does not yet exist." Go to The CHAOS MATRIX: http://www.chaosmatrix.org/library/books/lesserkey/lesserkey5.pdf.

[2] The LESSER KEY collection with *Ars Nova*—not *Ars Notoria*—is included in The Embassy of Lucifer's *Clavicula Solomonis*—mentioned above in note 20. The Embassy's *Ars Nova* is identical to Rowe's version, including the footnote numbers in the text—*without the footnotes*.

[3] In an email to me, October 4, 2009.

http://www.esotericarchives.com/notoria/notoria.htm.), "Unfortunately [Turner's version] omit[s] the drawings of the *notae* or mystical drawings which are the centerpiece of this art. Their omission adds greatly to the confusion of the text. Unfortunately, Turner further adds to the confusion by omitting some of the internal references to the missing figures." Intelligently prepared, nicely printed, reasonably priced: Peterson's is by far the best edition available.

Finally, there is *The Goetia of Dr Rudd: The Angels & Demons of Liber Malorum Spirituum seu Goetia Lemegeton Clavicula Salomonis / with study techniques of evocation in the context of the angel magic tradition of the seventeenth century / being a transcription of Dr Rudd's 'Liber Malorum Spiritum seu Goetia' from Harley MS 6483, with other pertinent extracts from manuscripts Harley MS 6482, Sloane MS 3824 and Wellcome MS 3203*, by Stephen Skinner and David Rankine (London – Singapore: Golden Hoard Press, 2007). The question "Why another edition of the *Lemegeton*?" is taken up in the introduction. I have condensed:

1. The manuscript contains much material which no other version does. …
2. We wanted to show how the system of magic in the *Lemegeton* was developed and actually practiced by working magicians in the seventeenth century. …[1]
3. The seals in this manuscript are beautiful and more carefully drawn than in any other manuscript …
4. This version explains the preparation and protection of the magician, specifically what precise angel he should use to compel each individual demon, and the use of the Brass Vessel. These key practical details are not present in any other edition of the Goetia.
5. We wanted to trace where the *Lemegeton* material comes from and to demonstrate that its roots reach back at least to the thirteenth century, and the connections between angel magicians and those evoking in the grimoire tradition, which in the case of this manuscript proves to be identical. …

---

[1] For a critical assessment of Rankine and Skinner's hypothesis of an "alleged secret tradition emanating from Dee," see Egil Asprem's *Arguing with Angels: Enochian Magic & Modern Occulture* (Albany: State University of New York Press, 2012), pages 40-42.

The Goetia of Dr Rudd is Volume III of SOURCEWORKS OF CEREMONIAL MAGIC by Skinner and Rankine (see note 10 on page 4 above). It contains *Goetia, Theurgia Goetia, The Art Pauline,* and *The Art Almadel*—but not *Ars Notoria* because "it is not a workable system as it appears in these manuscripts," *i.e.,* without the crucial *notæ* illustrations.

2. a. <u>Grimorium Verum</u>

Here again we can turn to Waite (pages 96-100, 159-183, 236-240, with numerous other references) and Shah (pages 64-68; 75-112).

An attractive edition was put out by Trident Press (Seattle: 1994 & 1997): *Grimoirium Verum:* CONTAINING THE MOST APPROVED KEYS OF SOLOMON WHEREIN THE MOST HIDDEN SECRETS BOTH NATURAL & SUPERNATURAL ARE IMMEDIATELY EXHIBITED ... translated from the Hebrew by Plangiere, Jesuite Dominicaine, in "library," cloth, and, in this rare case, paperback editions.

The I.G.O.S. version contains the text in both French and English (Palm Springs: 1996).

The most complete edition available is, not surprisingly, that of Joseph H. Peterson (Scotts Valley: CreateSpace Publishing, 2007), which offers not only an English translation but complete French and Italian texts. Peterson's careful work accommodates academics and practitioners alike.

Jake Stratton-Kent has "reconstructed a working text from the corrupted French and Italian versions of this important grimoire" in *The True Grimoire:* ENCYCLOPEDIA GOETICA, VOLUME 1, first published as a limited-edition hardcover (2009) which quickly sold out, subsequently reprinted in a quality paperback, called the "Rouge Edition" ([UK]: Bibliothèque Rouge/Scarlet Imprint, 2010).

There is an inexpensive on-demand paperback edition: *The True Grimoire,* by Solomon, the Hebrew Rabbi, edited by Denise Alvarado [PLANET VOODOO'S CLASSIC HOODOO REFERENCE SERIES] ([West Liberty]: Planet Voodoo/ CreateSpace, 2010). Other Hoodoo and Conjure books in Planet Voodoo's series include *The Gypsy Wisdom Spell Book* (2009), *The Voodoo Doll Spell Book* (2010), and *the Voodoo Hoodoo Spell Book* (2011).

See also *Crossed Keys, Being a Chimeric Binding of Both the Black Dragon and the Enchiridion of Pope Leo III*, translated with commentary by Michael Cecchetelli, with additional notes by Peter Grey, edited by Alkistis Dimech ([UK]: Scarlet Imprint, 2011). The BLACK DRAGON offers an apparent amalgam of *Grimorium Verum*, the GRAND GRIMOIRE (or RED DRAGON), and the GRIMOIRE OF HONORIUS.

2. b. TRUE BLACK MAGIC

There are conflicting descriptions of this text. Butler outlines a MS containing 45 talismans with details of their workings and "all magical characters known unto this day" from a Hebrew original (*Ritual Magic*, page 80). Waite (page 100) refers to it as "simply an adapted version of the KEY... [and] like the *Grimorium Verum*, it is exceedingly confused, and is rendered almost unmeaning by the omission of the practical part." Waite does, however, quote and paraphrase it frequently:

- page 146 on abstinence
- pages 147-148 on baths
- page 149 on inks
- page 154 on instruments
- page 166 on pen and ink

- pages 174-176 on parchment
- pages 177-179 on cleaning
- pages 300-302 for love
- pages 306-307 for invisibility

Joseph Peterson has translated the same text from which Waite drew as *True Black Magic*, i.e., *La Véritable Magie Noire* (Kasson: Twilit Grotto Press, 2017) — author listed as "Iroé Grego," the supposed compiler of the "original" text. This edition shows French and English on facing pages. In his introduction (page i), Peterson refers to it as "one of [the] many variants of The Key of Solomon." This version "preserves some older elements not included in Mathers' edition," e.g., a prayer for exorcising water and a chapter on incenses — along with the more usual planetary pentacles.

2. c. THE GRAND GRIMOIRE

THE GRAND GRIMOIRE, also called the *Red Dragon*, is described and quoted by Waite (pages 100-103 and 241-264). Shah introduces it and from it offers an operation for conjuring Lucifuge (pages 68-74).

There is an artful limited edition (500 copies) from Trident/Ars Obscura (Seattle: 1996) translated by Gretchen Rudy from the 1612 Italian edition; this has been reprinted by Trident in a $100 "library edition" with an optional $25 slipcase (2006). I.G.O.S. has its typically pricey edition titled *The Red Dragon, or the Art Concerning Commanding the Celestial Spirits — The Grand Grimoire*, translated from the 1521 French and Latin text by Robert Blanchard (Palm Springs: I.G.O.S. Research Society, 1995), which gives the text in rather clumsy English adorned with illustrations from a printed French edition.

There is an "economy" version of *The Grand Grimoire* edited by Darcy Kuntz [KABBALISTIC GRIMOIRE SERIES IV] (Edmonds: Holmes Publishing Groups, 2001).

The Authentic Red Dragon (Le Véritable Dragon Rouge) ... followed by The Black Hen (La Poule Noire), published by Teitan Press (York Beach: 2011), reprints an early nineteenth-century French edition (even though dated 1521) with an English translation by Joshua A. Wentworth, along with a highly entertaining introduction by Silens Manus. Manus says of the text, "[I]t is very obviously a variant of the text known as the *Grand Grimoire,* and in common with this and other similar grimoires the *Dragon Rouge* is not a work of 'high culture.' ... It is manifestly also not a work of spirituality or 'high magic,' but instead reflects mundane desires and interests..." (— page xvii).

3. The *Grimoire* & SWORN BOOK of Honorius

Distinction should immediately be made between the SWORN BOOK of Honorius (*Liber iuratis*) and the later, derivative—and diabolical—*Grimoire,* also called the *Constitution of Honorius.* Unfortunately, these titles are often interchanged (as with the I.G.O.S. edition discussed below).

The *Grimoire* is treated in the books we have already cited: Butler, pages 89-97; Waite, pages 103-110; and Shah, pages 253-280.

The Grimoire of Pope Honorius "from a [German] manuscript from the Infernal Library of a Schwabian farmer," translated by Kineta Ch'ien, was published in a limited edition in 1999 by Trident Books (Seattle); both the English and German are included. The text is somewhat different from the one(s) treated by Butler, Waite, and Shah, though introduced by *The Constitution of Pope Honorius* given in French and English, the English of which is identical to Shah (pages 255-6), and quite similar to Waite (pages 107-9). Included in the Trident edition is some welcome support material, such as a "Bibliographic Prolegomenon" by John Davis, an "Examination of the Editions of the Grimoire," and yet another text, *Coniurationes Demonum,* put into English by Matthew Sullivan.

A mere 65 copies of *The Grimoire or Book of Spells of Pope Honorius* were published by the Society for Esoteric Endeavor (2006),[1] which offers a facsimile of a nineteenth-century copy of Honorius scribed by one Frederick George Irwin, a member of Societas Rosicruciana in Anglia. There is also *The Infernal Conjurations of the Notorious*

---

[1] Ref. http://www.caduceusbooks.com/honourius.htm. The final words of the webpage: "Please note all copies of this title have sold."

Grimoire of Honorius, Circa 1670 from Finbarr International (Kent [UK]: 2009).[1] I have not seen either.

The Complete Grimoire of Pope Honorius by David Rankine and Paul Harry Barron (London: Avalonia, 2013) includes "a partial translation of Wellcome MS 4666 [which is in French], with numerous additions translated from the French editions of the Grimoire of Pope Honorius dated 1670 [the so-called "Rome edition"], 1760 [BL[2] shelfmark 8632.a.3] & 1800 [BL shelfmark 8630.aa.21], and a new translation of the German edition of 1845 [from Scheibel's *Das Kloster*]" (—title page [my brackets—DK]). *The Complete Grimoire...* presents "the entire corpus of this grimoire in print for the first time" (—back cover).

A translation of the SWORN BOOK, or *Liber sacer sive liber juratus*—as distinct from the *Grimoire*—was done by Daniel Driscoll: *The Sworn Book of Honourius the Magician, As Composed by Honourius through counsel with the Angel Hocroell* (Berkeley Heights/Gillette: Heptangle Books, 1977 & 1983), using British Museum (now British Library) MSS Sloane 313 and Royal 17A XLII. Printed as a fancy collectable, this work is now difficult and expensive to obtain. With all this, it is incomplete and frequently inaccurate. Further, the entire text is set in a somewhat distracting Old English font.

I.G.O.S. published a hardbound typescript, variously titled *Medieval Grimoire of Honorius, Grimoire of Honorius,* and *Handbook of Honorius the Magus*, translated by Robert Blanchard (Palm Springs: 1993). Even though it is called "*Grimoire,*" this work is actually a version of the "*Liber sacer* or *Liber juratus,*" *i.e.,* SWORN BOOK of Honorius, as described by Lynn Thorndike in *History of Magic and Experimental Science* (New York: Macmillan Company/Columbia University Press, 1923-1958), volume II, chapter XLIX, "Solomon and the Ars Notoria," pages 283-285—the same text as Daniel Driscoll's.

The best edition of this material is *The Sworn Book of Honorius: Liber Iuratus Honorii by Honorius of Thebes*, with text, translation and commentary by Joseph Peterson (Lake Worth: Ibis Press, 2016),

---

[1] Ref. http://www.finbarrinternationalbooks.com/our-books/black-magic/infernal-conjurations-of-the-notorious-51-detail. The final words of the webpage: "This is a Black Magic Book."
[2] BL = British Library

which shows the complete text in Latin and English on facing pages, along with a well-researched introduction.[1]

Refer to *Liber Iuratus Honorii: A Critical Edition of the Latin Version of the Sworn Book of Honorius*, by Gösta Hedegård [ACTA UNIVERSITATIS STOCKHOLMIENSIS: *Studia Latina Stockholmiensa*] (Stockholm: Almquist & Wiksell International, 2002). The text is in Latin; the 46-page introduction, however, is in English.

Section IV of Hedegård's reconstructed Latin text, "de composicione sigilli Dei vivi et veri" (pages 67-71), has been translated into English by Colin D. Campbell as APPENDIX B of *The Magic Seal of Dr. John Dee: The Sigillum Dei Aemeth* (York Beach: Teitan Press, 2009). This *Seal of God*, sometimes called the *Seal of Solomon*, is a prominent feature of the Honorius text.

On the Honorius material, see the following:

- *Conjuring Spirits*:
  - Kieckhefer, Richard. "The Devil's Contemplatives: The *Liber iuratus*, The *Liber visionum* and Christian Appropriation of Jewish Occultism."
  - Klaassen, Frank THE LIBER SACER OR SWORN BOOK OF HONORIUS within "English Manuscripts of Magic, 1300-1500: A Preliminary Survey."
  - Mathiesen, Robert. "A Thirteenth-Century Ritual to Attain the Beatific Vision from the *Sworn Book* of Honorius of Thebes."
- *Invoking Angels*:
  - Fanger, Claire. "Covenant and the Divine Name: Revisiting the *Liber iuratis* and John of Morigny's *Liber florum*."
  - Mesler, Katelyn "The *Liber iuratus Honorii* and the Christian Reception of Angel Magic."
  - Veenstra, Jan R. "Honorius and the Sigil of God: The *Liber iuratus* in Berengario Ganell's *Summa sacre magice*."

---

[1] Online, refer to Joseph H. Peterson's "Liber Juratus Honorii or Sworne Booke of Honorius" based on the English translation of Royal MS 17Axlii (16th century) with variant readings from British Library Sloane MSS 3853, 3854 and 3885, at http://www.esotericarchives.com/juratus/juratus.htm. This version was posted online in 1998. Peterson's introduction to the online Honorius text reads,

Liber Juratus is one of the oldest and most influential texts of Medieval magic. The prologue says the text was compiled to help preserve the core teachings of the sacred magic, in the face of intense persecution by church officials. This may be a reference to the actions of pope John XXII (1316-34). I believe the almost legendary reputation of this work led to the forgery of the so-called *Grimoire of Pope Honorius*, a ridiculous work so despised by Eliphas Levi and A. E. Waite.

- Klaassen, Frank. Religion, Science, and the Transformations of Magic: Manuscripts of Magic 1300-1600. Ph.D. dissertation (Toronto: University of Toronto, 1999), pages 129-135.
- _____. "The Ars Notoria and the Sworn Book of Honorius" in *The Transformations of Magic: Illicit Learned Magic in the Later Middle Ages and Renaissance* (University Park: Penn State University Press, 2012).
- Chardonnens, László Sándor. "Necromancing Theurgic Magic: A Reappraisal of the *Liber iuratus* Extracts and the Consecration Ritual for the *Sigillum Dei* in an Early Modern English Grimoire," in *Magic, Ritual, and Witchcraft*, Volume 10, Number 2 (Philadelphia: University of Pennsylvania Press, Winter 2015), pages 172-198.

4. *Semiphoras & Shemhamphoras Salomonis Regis* (hereafter *S&S*)

S&S is surrounded by a mish-mash of material derived from Agrippa, pseudo-Agrippa, Jewish magic (*Shimmush Tehillim*), folk magic, and fragments from the Faustian school in a collection titled *The Sixth and Seventh Books of Moses* (New York: Wehman Brothers, n.d. [1880]; Carbondale: Egyptian Publishing Company, n.d.; Chicago: The de Laurence Company, 1919).

The texts of *The Sixth Book of Moses* and *The Seventh Book of Moses*, along with seals in Hebrew and magical script, are English translations from Johann Scheibel's *Das Sechste und Siebente buch Mosis* (Stuttgart: 1849), which is volume six of Scheibel's *Bibliothek der zauber geheimnis – und offenbarungs-bucher*. The *S&S* texts also trace their printed origins back to German collections, namely volumes 3 and 4 of J. C. Horst's *Zauberbiliothek* (6 vols., Mainz: 1821-6); and volume 3 of Scheibel's *Das Kloster* (12 vols., Stuttgart and Leipzig: Theodor Thomas, 1846).[1]

---

[1] Other items from *Das Kloster* (vols. 2 and 5, respectively): *Libellus Magicus*, transcribed and edited by Stephen J. Zietz (1999), at http://www.hermetics.org/pdf/grimoire/Libellusjesuitus.pdf, and *Praxis Magica Fausti*, at http://athenaeum.asiya.org/Praxis_Magica_Fausti.pdf [defunct link]. Both are described and quoted by Waite (*Black Magic*, Weiser edition, pages 102-4/323-326; *Ceremonial Magic*, Bell edition, pages 110-112/329-333). *Libellus Magicus*, under the title *Verus Jesuitarum Libellus*, is presented in both Latin and English at Twilit Grotto: http://www.esotericarchives.com/solomon/jesuit.htm.

In 1982, there appeared the profoundly disappointing *New Revised Sixth and Seventh Books of Moses and the Magical Uses of Psalms*, edited by Migene Gonzolez-Wippler (Bronx: Original Publications). The text and especially the introduction are rife with errors.[1]

In 2008, Joseph H. Peterson produced a nicely-printed edition of *The Sixth and Seventh Books of Moses* (Lake Worth: Ibis Press), which offers serious treatment of this hybrid collection of translations: clear, correct texts and diagrams, with an informative foreword, notes, and nine supplemental appendices—surely the best edition.

Interestingly, "The Seven Semiphoras of Adam" and "The Seven Semiphoras of Moses" within *S&S* closely match passages in the seventh book of *Liber Salomonis: Sepher Raziel*, discussed below. For the *Semiphoras* §§ in *S&S*, see Wehman, Egyptian, and de Laurence—pages 116-140; Gonzolez-Wippler—pages 125-164; Peterson, APPENDIX 3, pages 141-168.

5. *Liber Salomonis*, British Library[2] Sloane MS 3826

Until fairly recently (2003), *Liber Salomonis* had not been treated at length in any printed source, though Sloane MS 3826 is described in Waite's *Ceremonial Magic* (pages 20-21) and referred to here and there by Shah and Butler. Thorndike mentions this MS only once in *History of Magic*.[3]

The first section of *Liber Salomonis* refers to itself as "Cephar Raziel," "Sephar Raziel," "booke of Raziel," and "booke of Razeelus," *i.e.*, *Sepher Raziel*. Solomon is indicated as the recipient and redactor—not the author—of the book in the narrative which introduces the text. However, most instructions begin, "Salomon

---

[1] My open letter to Original Publications (cc. Llewellyn Publications) dated March 10, 1986, states, "To my dismay, Migene Gonzolez-Wippler's edition fails to clean up or clarify this book, and, to my shock, the editor has actually further muddled and mystified the text with misleading information and just plain bad writing. It took no great scholarship to arrive at the [twelve] points that shall follow, showing the shoddiness of the editor's work. This note represents only a few hours of rooting around in my *home* library, which is far from extensive."

[2] Manuscripts were designated "British Museum" until 1997, when the designation changed to "British Library."

[3] Volume II, CHAPTER XLIV, "Solomon and the Ars Notoria," page 281, adding an interesting, albeit doubtful, speculation in note 2: "Perhaps the same as 'Sefer ha-Yashar' mentioned by Haya Gaon in the eleventh century: Gaster, *The Sword of Moses*, 1896, p. 16."

said...." Others begin, "Hermes said...," "Adam said...," "Nathaniel said...," "Moyses said...," and "Raziel said...." Narrative passages refer to Raziel as the source of the book and to Adam as the original recipient.

Sepher Raziel contains seven treatises:
1. Clavis..."of astronomy and of the starres" (ff 5ᵛ-11ᵛ)
2. Ala..."the vertues of some stones of herbes and of beasts" (ff 12ʳ-27ʳ)
3. Tractatus Thymiamatus...of suffumigations and of allegations of them and divisions" (ff 27ʳ-34ʳ)
4. The "Treatise of tymes of the year of the day and of the night ... when anything ought to be done by this booke" (ff 34ʳ-46ʳ)
5. The "Treatise of Cleanesse...of Abstinence" (ff 46ʳ-51ʳ)
6. "Samaim" which "nameth all the heavens and her angels and the operations or workings of them" (ff 51ᵛ-53ᵛ)
7. The "booke of Vertues...and miracles...the properties of the ark of magicke and of his figures and of the ordinance of same" (ff 53ᵛ-57ᵛ)

For a full transcription of these treatises, see below pages 72-160. Stephen Skinner provides a modern English version of *Sefer Raziel* below, pages 163-248, and an excellent introduction to the range of "Raziel" traditions (see pages 13-23).[1]

The rest of Sloane MS 3826 consists of
1. *Incipit Canon*: The rule of the book of consecration... (ff 57ʳ-60ʳ)
2. Orisons (ff 60ʳ-65ʳ)
3. Magical directions (ff 65ʳ-83ᵛ)[2]

---

[1] A very similar *Sefer Raziel* appears at ESOTERIC ARCHIVES, "*Sepher Raziel* (Sl. 3846) Book of the Angel Raziel" (edited by Joseph H. Peterson ... © 1999, 2006), at http://www.esotericarchives.com/raziel/raziel.htm.

[2] Robert Mathiesen (in the article listed below, page 29) lists "Sloane 3826...*ff.* 58-83?" [Mathiesen's question mark] among the manuscript versions of the SWORN BOOK at the British Library, though he places it with those which "preserve the original Latin text." Portions of 3826 are in Latin (see above), but the bulk of the text is in English. Gösta Hedegård refutes the identification with the SWORN BOOK (*Liber Iuratus Honorii*, pages 13-14, note 37), quoting Rachel Stockdale that 3826 *ff.* 58—62 contain "The rule of the booke of Consecration or the manner of working, with some orisons." Hedegård then refers to Waite (*Book of Black Magic*..., page 35), stating that the treatises of this part of 3826 "extract matter" from Honorius works; Hedegård allows that this "may possibly be right" (page 14, note 13).

The two paragraphs on *fol.* 68 begin, "Dixit Thebit Pencorat..." and "Thebit said...." The reference is to Thabit ben Korra, or Tabit ibn Korrah, or Qurra (c.836-c.901), member of the pagan sect, the Sabians (mainly of the city Harran, Thabit's birthplace). A prolific and eclectic writer, philosopher, and

4. *Liber Lunæ* (ff 84ʳ-94ʳ)[1]
5. *Raphael*: The Invocation of Oberon Concerning Physick &c (ff 98ʳ-99ʳ)
6. The Call of *Bilgal*, One of the 7 etc. (fol. 99ᵛ)
7. An Experiment for a Fayry (fol. 100ʳ)[2]
8. *Beleemus De imaginibus* (ff 100ᵛ-101ʳ)

Sloane MS 3826 is in English, except for
1. the opening lines of paragraphs in *Liber Salomonis* and *Incipit Canon*
2. the Orisons
3. the invocation, constriction, ligation, and license of *Raphael*
4. *Beleemus De imaginibus* (BELEMUS ON THE IMAGES [of the planets]).

Printed notices of Sloane 3826 and *Sefer Raziel*:

- Åkerman, Susanna. "Queen Christina's Latin *Sefer-ha-Raziel* Manuscript," in *Judaeo-Christian Intellectual Culture in the Seventeenth Century: A Celebration of the Library of Narcissus Marsh (1638-1713)*, [INTERNATIONAL ARCHIVES, 163] edited by Allison P. Coudert, Sarah Hutton, Richard H. Popkin, and Gordon M, Weiner (Dordrecht: Kluwer Academic Publishers, 1999), pp. 20 and 25, note 25.
- Cresswell, Julia. *The Watkins Dictionary of Angels* (London: Watkins Publishing, 2006). Cresswell used Sloane 3826[3] as her "base text" in compiling this grand list of "angels and angelic beings."

---

translator (he rendered the Greek philosophers—*e.g.*, Archimedes, Aristotle, Euclid—into Arabic or Syriac), Thabit was an authority on the occult, particularly on the subject of images. Indeed, he is cited in *Picatrix* and the works of Albertus Magnus and Peter de Abano.

[1] See *Liber Lunæ*..., listed below under "Printed notices...," page 29.

[2] See Donald Tyson, "An Experiment for a Fairy," appended to my transcription of "*Liber Lunæ* and other selections" at http://www.digital-brilliance.com/contributed/Karr/Solomon/LibLun.pdf, pages 35-43. Tyson offers an amended text of Sloane *fol.* 100ʳ with practical commentary.

[3] Cresswell used my original e-transcript version in *Esoterica*, the on-line journal edited by Arthur Verslius (Michigan State University, 2003): *Liber Salomonis: Sepher Raziel* –
  Part 1 at http://www.esoteric.msu.edu/VolumeV/Raziel1.html;
  Part 2 at http://www.esoteric.msu.edu/VolumeV/Raziel2.html.
  Liber Lunæ and other selections also appears, oddly formatted, at *Esoterica*:
    http://www.esoteric.msu.edu/Liber/LiberLunae.html.
  Corrected and revised versions of these texts appear in print as *Sepher Raziel also known as Liber Salomonis*... and *Liber Lunæ*, and on-line at Colin Low's HERMETIC KABBALAH:
    http://www.digital-brilliance.com/contributed/Karr/Solomon/index.php.
  The 2003 transcription of the MS in its entirety was printed in a very limited comb-bound edition (six copies) as *Liber Salomonis, or Cephar Raziel, and Liber Lunæ and other selections from British Library Sloane MS 3826* (Ithaca: KoM, 2003).

- Harrison, Peter. *The Fall of Man and the Foundations of Science* (Cambridge: Cambridge University Press, 2009), page 18.
- Karr, Don; and Nachshon, Calanit. *Liber Lunæ – Book of the Moon from Sloane MS 3826 / Sepher ha-Levanah.* [SOURCEWORKS OF CEREMONIAL MAGIC, volume 7] (Singapore: Golden Hoard Press, 2011; second edition [paperback], 2017). Transcription and contemporary English version of *Sloane MS 3826 fols. 84ʳ-94ʳ*, transcription of *Sloane MS 3826 fols. 54ʳ-83ᵛ*, *Sepher ha-Levanah* in Hebrew and annotated English translation.
- Karr, Don; and Skinner, Stephen. *Sepher Raziel also known as Liber Salomonis, a 1564 English Grimoire from Sloane MS 3826.* [SOURCEWORKS OF CEREMONIAL MAGIC, volume 6] (Singapore: Golden Hoard Press, 2010). Transcript and contemporary English version of *fols. 2ʳ-57ʳ*.
- Klaassen, Frank F. RELIGION, SCIENCE, AND THE TRANSFORMATIONS OF MAGIC: MANUSCRIPTS OF MAGIC 1300-1600 (Ph.D. dissertation: Toronto: University of Toronto, 1999): page 133 (ref. *Liber sacer i.e.*, "Honorius material"), page 207 (as an example of a seventeenth-century collection combining ritual and scholastic image magic), page 259 (listed under "Seventeenth Century [MSS]").
- Láng, Benedek. *Unlocked Book: Manuscripts of Learned Magic in the Medieval Libraries of Central Europe* [MAGIC IN HISTORY SERIES] (University Park: The Pennsylvania State University Press, 2008), page 91, note 21.
- Maddison, Francis, and Turner, Anthony. "The Names and Faces of the Hours," in *Between Demonstration and Imagination: Essays in the History of Science and Philosophy Presented to John D. North*, edited by Lodi Nauta and Arjo Vanderjagt (Leiden: Brill, 1999), pages 143-4: *Tables 18* and *19*.
- Mathiesen, Robert. "A Thirteenth-Century Ritual to Attain the Beatific Vision from the *Sworn Book* of Honorius of Thebes," in *Conjuring Spirits: Texts and Traditions of Medieval Ritual Magic*, edited by Claire Fanger (University Park: Pennsylvania State University Press, 1998): page 145 (Sloane 3826 *ff*. 58-83 is listed as a MS of the *Sworn Book of Honorius*).
- "M. Plessner, article on 'Balinus' in *Encyclopedia of Islam* (new edn. 1959) I, page 995." This entry appears on the British Library reference form which accompanies the microfilm version of MS Sloane 3826, from which my transcriptions have been done.

- Page, Sophie. "Uplifting Souls: The *Liber de essential spirituum* and the *Liber Razielis*," in *Invoking Angels: Theurgic Ideas and Practices, Thirteenth to Sixteenth Centuries*, edited by Claire Fanger (University Park: The Pennsylvania State University Press, 2012).
- Savedow, Steve. "Sepher Raziel Manuscripts" = an appendix to *Sepher Rezial Hemelach: The Book of the Angel Rezial* (York Beach: Samuel Weiser, Inc., 2000).[1]
  Also on-line at the *Alchemy Web Site*, "organised by Adam McLean," at http://www.alchemywebsite.com/raziel.html.
- Shah, Idries. *Oriental Magic* (New York: E. P. Dutton & Co., 1956; rpt 1973): page 191, BIBLIOGRAPHY, Grimoire References, *Chaldea:* "The following 'Black Books' of the sorcerers have traces of Chaldean magical rituals or processes attributed to Chaldean origin: Sefer Raziel (The Book of Raziel). B.M. Sloane 3826."
- Shah, Idries. *The Secret Lore of Magic* (Secaucus: Citadel Press Inc., 1958): pages 288, 289, 290, and 310; ref. abbreviation (SR).
- Thorndike, Lynn. *History of Magic and Experimental Sciences*, volume II: THE FIRST THIRTEEN CENTURIES (New York: Columbia University Press 1923): page 281.
- Waite, Arthur Edward. *Book of Black Magic and of Pacts* (London: Redway, 1898; rpt. New York: Samuel Weiser, Inc., 1972): pages 33-4 of the Weiser edition.
- Waite, Arthur Edward. *The Book of Ceremonial Magic* (London: Rider, 1911; rpt. New York: Bell Publishing Company, 1969): pages 20-21 and 22 of the Bell edition. (*The Book of Ceremonial Magic* is a revised version of *Book of Black Magic and of Pacts*.)

---

[1] Savedow's *Sepher Rezial Hemelach* offers a text from the Jewish folk magic tradition—an entirely different stream from our *Liber Salomonis/Sepher Raziel*.

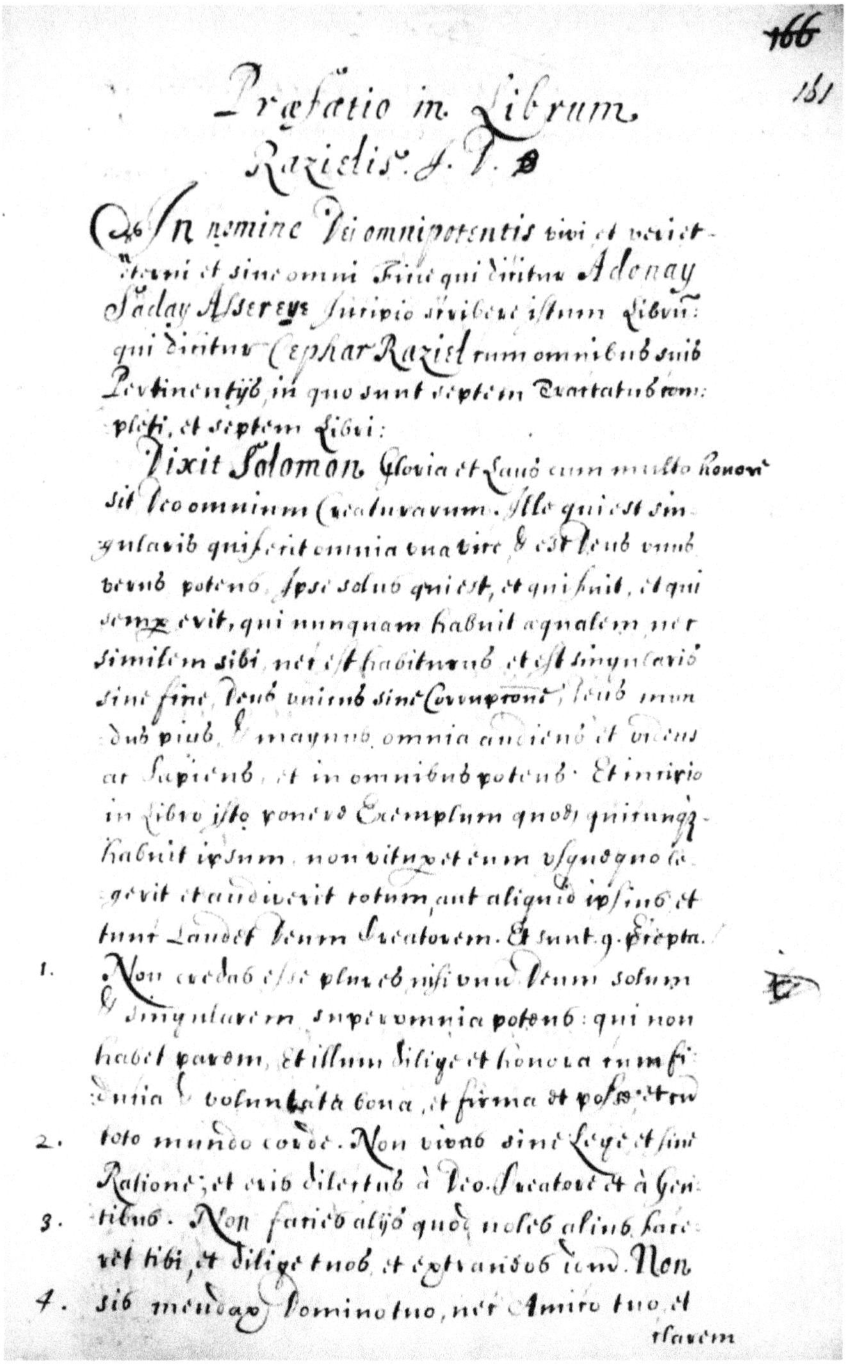

166
181

Præfatio in Librum
Razielis.

In nomine Dei omnipotentis vivi et veri et-
terni et sine omni Fine qui dicitur Adonay
Saday Asserey: Incipio scribere istum Librum:
qui dicitur Cephar Raziel cum omnibus suis
Pertinentijs, in quo sunt septem Tractatus completi, et septem Libri:
Dixit Salomon Gloria et Laus cum multo honore
sit Deo omnium Creaturarum. Ille qui est singularis qui fecit omnia sua virtute & est Deus unus
verus potens, Ipse solus qui est, et qui fuit, et qui
semper erit, qui nunquam habuit æqualem, nec
similem sibi, nec est habiturus et est singularis
sine fine, Deus verus sine Corruptione, Deus mun-
dus pius & magnus, omnia cernens et videns
ac Sapiens, et in omnibus potens. Et incipio
in Libro isto ponere Exemplum quod quicunque
habuit ipsum non utatur eum usquequo le-
gerit et audiverit totum, aut aliquid ipsius et
tunc Laudet Deum Creatorem. Et sunt 9. Præcepta.
1. Non credas esse plures nisi unum Deum solum
& singularem super omnia potens: qui non
habet parem, et illum dilige et honora cum fi-
dentia & voluntate bona, et firma et pura et in
2. toto mundo corde. Non vivas sine Lege et sine
Ratione; et eris dilectus à Deo Creatore et à Gen-
3. tibus. Non facies alijs quod nolles alius face-
ret tibi, et dilige tuos et extraneos tuos. Non
4. sis mendax Domino tuo, nec Amico tuo et
fratrem

Figure 3. First page from the Latin *Librum Razielis* or *Cephar Raziel* Sloane MS 3847 f.161.

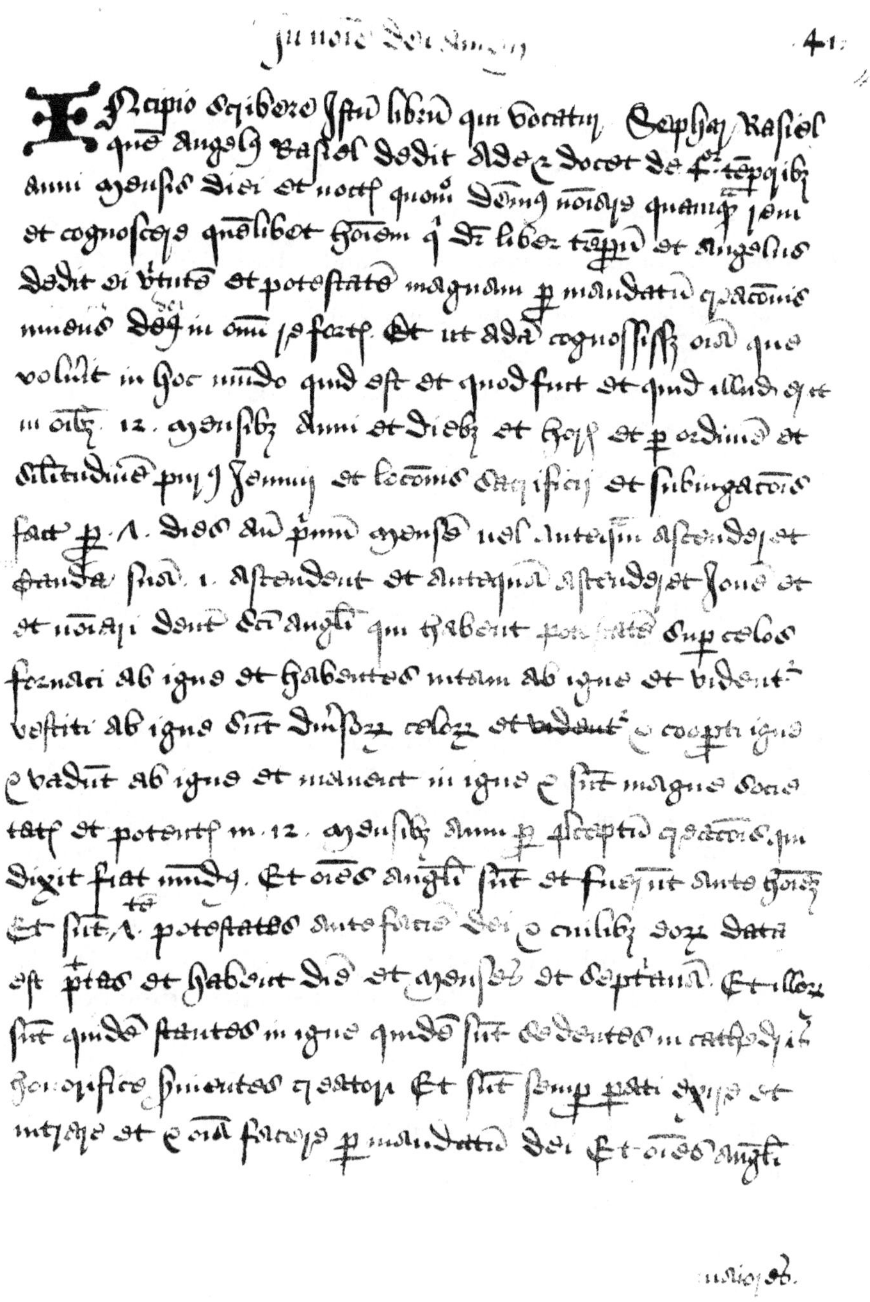

Figure 4: First page of the Latin *Sephar Rasiel* in Sloane MS 3853, f. 46. Early 16th century. Note the ambiguous initial letter of *C/Sephar Rasiel* in the first line.

Introduction to the Manuscript

Liber Salomonis comprises folio pages 2^r-57^r of British Library Sloane MS 3826; it contains seven treatises (as described in its own fol. 3^r):

1. *Clavis* "of astronomy and of the starres" (ff 5^v-11^v)
2. *Ala* "the vertues of some stones of herbes and of beasts" (ff 12^r-27^r)
3. *Tractatus Thymiamatus* of suffumigations and of allegations of them and divisions" (ff 27^r-34^r)
4. The "*Treatise of tymes* of the year of the day and of the night when anything ought to be done by this booke" (ff 34^r-46^r)
5. The "*Treatise of Cleanesse of Abstinence*" (ff 46^r-51^r)
6. "*Samaim*" which "nameth all the heavens and her angels and the operations or workings of them" (ff 51^v-53^v)
7. The "*Booke of Vertues and miracles* — the properties of the ark of magicke and of his figures and of the ordinance of same" (ff 53^v-57^v)

Liber Salomonis refers to itself as "Cephar Raziel" (ff 2^v, 3^r, 4^r, 12^r, 34^r), "Sepher Raziel" (fol. 2^r), "booke of Raziel" (ff 20^r, 46^r, 57^r), and "booke of Razeelus" (fol. 3^v). Solomon is indicated as the recipient and redactor, not the author of the book in the narrative which introduces the text (ff 2^v-3^v), though most instructions begin, "Salomon said." Others begin, "Hermes said" (ff 9^r, 11^r, 18^v, 24^r, 28^v, 30^r, 31^r, 32^r, 33^v), "Adam said" (fol. 16^r), "Nathaniel said" (fol. 47^r), "Moyses said" (ff 4^r, 4^v), and "Raziel said" (ff 6^r, 16^v, 22^r, 26^r, 28^v, 31^v, 34^v, 36^r, 37^r, 38^v). Narrative passages refer to Raziel as the source of the book (e.g., ff 34^r and 36^r).

The rest of Sloane MS 3826 consists of:

1. *Incipit Canon*: The rule of the book of consecration (ff 58^r-60^r)
2. Orisons (ff 60^r-65^r)
3. Magical directions (ff 65^r-83^v)
4. *Liber Lunae* (ff 84^r-97^v)
5. *Raphael*: The Invocation of Oberion Concerning Physick &c. (ff 98^r-99^r)
6. The Call of *Bilgal*, One of the 7 etc. (fol. 99^v)
7. An Experiment for a Fayry (fol. 100^r)
8. *Beleemus De imaginibus* (ff 100^v-101^r)

Liber Salomonis

In various communications, I have expressed my opinion that Sloane MS 3826 was a sixteenth-century Christian product, though one which borrowed from Jewish, Arabic, and Græco-Roman scholastic and folk sources. In a note to me (January 28, 2007), Sophie Page offered an informed and most welcome emendation to my view in the form of an abridged segment of an early draft of her article, 'Uplifting Souls: The *Liber de essentia spirituum* and the *Liber Razielis*,' which eventually appeared in Claire Fanger (ed.), *Invoking Angels: Theurgic Ideas and Practices, Thirteenth to Sixteenth Centuries* (University Park: Pennsylvania State University Press, 2012:

> The most explicit transmission of Jewish magical material into the Christian Latin tradition of magic was the translation of works associated with the name "Raziel," an angel present in Jewish angelology and Arabic astrological texts who was said to have revealed a book of secrets to Adam. Various esoteric and magical treatises attributed to Raziel and based on the practical use of divine and angelic names circulated among late medieval Jews. The earliest known reference in Latin is a citation by the Christian convert Petrus Alfonsus [or Alfonsi] (1062-1110) of a certain *Secretum secretorum*, which claimed to have been revealed to Seth, the son of Adam, by the angel Raziel. By the mid-thirteenth century, these magic texts were circulating more widely in Latin. In 1259, Alfonso [X, (1221-1284)] directed the translation of a work entitled *Liber Razielis* from Latin into Castilian by the cleric Juan d'Aspa. The Castilian version does not survive, but the Latin original put together by Alfonso survives in two complete and several partial copies, as well as various early modern abridged vernacular versions. The Alfonsine *Liber Razielis* is structured in the form of seven books said to have been brought together by Solomon. Nine related texts from the Solomonic and Hermetic magical traditions were added by Alfonso's scribes as appendices. Although the preface cites a single Hebrew original for the seven volumes, it is likely that the structure was partly a creation of Alfonso himself and his translators.
>
> The following post-1500 manuscripts contain abridged vernacular copies of the Alfonsine *Liber Razielis* or the *Liber Sameyn* only (the sixth book). This is not an exhaustive list, and I have only personally examined those in the British Library: MS Yale, Beinecke Rare Books Library Osborn MS fa. 7 (late s. xvi, English); British Library MSS Sloane 3826 (s. xvii,[1] English), ff. 1-57, Sloane 3846 (s. xvi, English), ff 127-55; MS Lyon 970 (s. xvii, xviii, French); MSS Alnwick Castle 596 (s. xviii, Italian, the *Liber Sameyn*), pp. 1-42 and 96 (Italian, Latin, English, the *Liber Sameyn* only); MS Lübeck, Bibliothek der Hansestadt, Math. 4º 10 (s. xvi/xvii, German); MS Dresden N. 36 (s. xviii, German); Prague, National Museum Library MS XVII F25 (1595, Czech, trans. Ioannes Polenarius). MS British Library Add. 16,390 (s. xvii) has a Hebrew extract with

---

[1] Should be xvi century.

a title in Italian. Where no folio references are given, the catalogue entry suggests that the *Liber Razielis* travels alone.

Suggested bibliography: J. Dan, "Raziel, Book of," *Encyclopedia Judaica* 13 (Jerusalem, 1971), 1592-93; A. Garcia Avilés, "Alfonso X y el *Liber Razielis*: imagines de la magia astral judía en el *scriptorius* Alfonsi," in *Bulletin of Hispanic Studies*, Volume 74, Number 1: January 1997, pp. 21-39 (Carfax Publishing/Liverpool University Press); Alfonso d'Agostino, *Astromagia* [MS. Reg. Lat 1283a] (Naples: Liguore, 1992). On the later *fortuna* of the *Liber Razielis* in Spain and elsewhere: F. Secret, "Sur quelques traductions du Sefer Raziel," *Revue des études Juives*, 128 (Paris: 1969), pp. 223-45. On magic at the Alfonsine court, see also N. Weill-Parot, *Les images astrologiques au Moyen Âge et a la Renaissance* (Paris: Honor Champion, 2002), pp. 123-138)."

In her introduction to *The Watkins Dictionary of Angels* (London: Watkins Publishing, 2006), Julia Cresswell writes (page 9) of Sloane MS 3826,

"I would suggest that although the manuscript may be sixteenth century, some of the language is rather old-fashioned for that date, except perhaps for an old person writing in the early sixteenth century. I would guess that the text is a reworking of an earlier one, pushing the origin of the material back into the Middle Ages."

Liber Salomonis is in the present book literally transcribed, line-by-line, with no changes in spelling or wording. Spelling in the MS is quite inconsistent; e.g., within a few lines of each other, we find "wing," "winge," "wyng," and "wynge." Using superscript and other features, I have imitated the look of the text as closely as typographically possible. Note that superscripted <u>letters</u> belong to the text and usually indicate contractions; superscripted <u>numbers</u> refer to footnotes. All Latin headings are in *italics*. Manuscript folio numbers are given in square brackets.

Following that, for ease of reading, Stephen Skinner has edited a modern English version of the same text.

For printed notices of Sloane MS 3826 see the Bibliography.

- Don Karr

Sepher Raziel - Liber Salomonis
British Library Sloane MS 3826, folios 2-57
transcription by Don Karr

Sepher Raziel

[2ʳ]

In noie Dei potentis vibi et veri et aeterni &c
In the name of Almighty God living and very and ever-
lasting and without all and which is said Adonay Saday
Ehye Asereye I begin to write this booke which is said
Sephar Raziel with all his appertenances in which be seven
treatises complete or fulfilled that is vii bookes.

Dixit Salomon Gloria et laus et cu multo honore &c
Salomon said glory and praysing with much honor be to
God of all Creatures, he that is singular which made all
things at one tyme. And he is one God very mighty
he alone that is and that was and which evermore
shall be, and which has never an end or any like him
neither is he like to have. And he is singular without
end, Lord alone without corruption, holy cleane meeke
and great all things seeing and hearing and wise and
in all things mighty. And I begin this booke to put
an ynsample that whosoever that hath it blame it not
till he have red and heard all or somewhat of it, and
then prayse the God maker of all things.

These be the ix precepts *Incipiunt praecepta*
Heere beginneth the precepts

Non credas esse plures nisi unu~ singulare &c
1. Ne trowe thou no to be moe or many but one singular
alone upon all things which hath none like him and him
love with all dread and honor with all trust and with good
will and stable and with might and with all they cleane
2. heart. Ne live thou not without lawe, and thou shall
3. be loved of God thy creator and of folks. Ne do thou
not to another man yf thou wouldest not the same. Ne
4. be thou not a lyer to the Lord neither to thy friend
and say thou such soothes that be to thy profit and not
5. harme. Ne love thou not neither fellowship thou more
with unwise men then with wisemen. And evermore love

[2ᵛ]

thou many wisdoms and good sciences and all thy will
6. and thy lyfe in them. Ne speakest thou not before thou
have thought, and that thou do consider it in thine
7. hart ere thou do it. Neither discover thou not thy privityes
to a woman, neither to a childe, neither to a foole, neither
8. to a dronkᵉ woman. No prove thou not a medicine neither

venym in thy self before thou provest it in an other. Ne
9. blame thou not a booke before thou prophesy neither a wise
man till thou have proved thou. And if thou with holdest
these ix precepts in thee evermore thou shalt profite more
and more. *Postqua sensus et scire et posse vo=*
luntas vera &c After that witt and knowledge and
might and very will overcometh all things with good witt
and good discretion. Therfore I will expound or make open
his booke which is of great power and of great vertue.
I, Salomon put such knowledge and such a distinction
and explanation in this book^e to every man that readeth or
studyeth in it, that he may know^e whereof he was and
from whome he came. Knowe ye that after I Salomon
had xxx yeeres within an half in the vth day of the
month of Hebreys which was the vith ferial day, the
sonne being in the signe of Leonis. In that day was sent
to me from Babilony of some prince that was greater
and more worshipfuller then all men of this tyme some
booke that is said Cephar Raziel which cont vii bookes and
vii treatises.

Nota tempus in quo Salomon fuit p^o adeptus istu libre
et quomodo et a quo venit sibi
Knowe thou the tyme in which Salomon gott the booke and
howe and of whom it came to him.

Iste liber est magnae virtutis et magnae secretiae This
booke is of great vertue and of great privity, the name of the
prince that sent it to me was Sameton and of the two
wise men that brought it to me was said Kamazan and
the other Zazont.

[3^r]
The name of this booke expound^{ed} in Latine is Angelus magnus Secreti Creatoris That is to say the great Angel
of the secret creator And in Hebrew Cephar Raziel it
is the book^e after Adam written in language of Caldey
and afterward translated in Hebrew. And know each man that
read^{e}s it that in it all *Semiforax* that is to say the great
name complete with all his names whole and even. and with
his vertues and his sacraments And I found it in 7 bookes that
is 7 treatises. And know ye that I found the first and the
last full dark^e and the five middle more plain and although
I found them dark^e I opened them as much as I could or
might. And the 7 treatises of this book^e be these..

Sepher Raziel

1. The first is said Clavis for that in it is determined of Astronomy and of the stares for without them we may do nothing.
2. The second is said Ala for that in it is determined of the vertues of some stones of herbes and of beasts
3. The third is said Tractatus Thymiamatu^s for that there is determined in it of suffumigations and of Allegations of them and divisions
4. The ivth is said the Treatise of tymes of the year of the day and of the night for that in it is determined when anything ought to be done by this book^e
5. The vth is said the Treatise of Cleanesse for that there is determined in it of Abstinence
6. The sixt^h is said Samaim for in that treatise it nameth all the heavens and her angels and the operations or workings of them
7. The viith is the book^e of Vertues for that there is determined in it of vertues and miracles for there be told the properties of the ark of magicke and of his figures and of the ordinance of same.

And the I beganne to write all these treatises in a new^e volume for that one treatise without another serves not to the wholeness of the work^e Therfore I made an

[3^v]
whole book^e to be made of the treatises. Therfore Salomon said to his writer Clarifaton that he could write it, which I know well the language of Caldy of Indy of Hebrew and of Syne and their right explanation. Methelis Salomon said that after Clarifaton had corrected it and had dressed it, it should be the better and ordained it in the best maner that he might. And Clarifaton said, which was the writer of Salomon, that this booke is full of great privity and that it was sent of full great honor And that it was sent to Salomon for most price and most love. And everiche treatise of these vii was was written by themselves. But although it be so that Clarifaton said that it ought to be but one booke alone by itself for none of these saith he should suffice without another, wherefore he said it were necessary that they were all together Whereupon Salomon ordained that all the said 7 treatises were but one book^e as they ought to be and as they ought to be read and wrought.

Liber Salomonis

And he ordayned it much better then the ph^{il}o$^{[soph]}$rs orday=
ned, and also he taught how a man ought to do his
work^e by it. And he put every treatise by itself
and every chapter by itself and ordayned all till
the end of the book^e. And he putt into this booke Semiforas
that is the book^e of 17 vertues how it ought to be written
and of which Ink^e, and of which parchment and with what pen
and with what man, and in which time and what day and
in what night and in what hour. After that Salomon
expounded in the book^e of Razeelus and how it ought to
be kept Cleanly and with great honor

Dixit Salomon qui videt et non cognoscit &c
Salomon said who so seeth and knoweth not is as he
that is born^e blind^e and knoweth not colors and who
that heareth and understandeth not is such as if he
were a deaf^e man. And who so considereth and knoweth
not the consideration is such as if it were of a dronkerd

[4^r]
And whom that speaketh and cannot expound the reason is
as a dombe man. And who that readeth playne bookes
and understandeth them not is as it were he dreameth.
These proverbs Salomon said in this booke ffor as Salomon
said in this booke is hit that Cephar Raziel the angel
said to Adam which was the first man in this world and
after it which Moyses said to other prophets in soothes
and we troweth it so.

Dixit angelus Salomoni vt o^{mn}es tuæ operationes &c
The angel said to Salomon that all thy workhings and
petitions and willes be fulfilled, and it shall be made
in all hitt that thou shalt covet that it be in thy might
It behoveth that when thou hast this book^e of this or of
Another example or exemplar that thou write it in
Inst maner in virgin parchemt and that it be not filthy
neither of a dead beast or in vealime (vitulino) or in
parchmyn of sylke, or in samatyne,[1] or in cleane clothe
or in parchmyn of a lamb or of a virgin kidde or of a
virgin ffawne, and this is better than any other.
And the Ink^e with which thou shalt write be it of cleane
galles and let it be made with good white wyne & whole
and with gum^e and vitriol and masticke & thyme and

---

[1] Above "samatyne" is written "sattin."

croco. And the third day when it hath taken residence
and shall be clensed putt [1] thou therein a little of <u>Algoba
and A</u>lmea,[2] and putt therein of good muske or muske more
than of those three. And put thou therein Amber and Bal-
samu^s myrryam and lignus aloes and when the Inke
shall be made, boyled with masticke and with thyme and with
lingo aloes and with somewhat of Thymiamat and Muculazarat and thou clense it well with a clean^e thinne
cloth^e, and the cloth be it threefold. And afterward putt
therein musk^e and Ambram and Almenus & Algana
and Balsami^s and Myrrha^s all well grounden & then

[4^v]
shalt meddle all this with the Inke full well together
And let the inke be so still for the space of 3 days well
covered in a fayre place And know^e thou that with this
ynke thou shalt write all the holy names of God and
of his angels and of his saints, and all things in which
his holy great name is [3] nempned and written. And all
things that thou willest truly to be fulfilled with thy well
pleasing or with thy service. And what ere thou puttest
in this ynke, be it newe and bright and pure and good
[4] And the penne that thou shalt write the holy names
be it of a green^e reed^e gathered early ere the sunne
[5] arise. And he that shall gather it be he clene & washen
& in running water or in a quicke well and also let
him be clothed with cleane clothes, and the moon^e being
waxing with Caput Draconis or with Jove, for that
they be true and very. And when thou shalt gather it, thou
shalt behold of looke toward the East and thou shalt say
thus *Adonai et Saday jubate me ad complendu^s voluntates meas eo^s axundine ista.* That is to say Help
ye me to fulfill my willes with this reed^e. and when this
is said thou shalt cutt one reede or twayne or as many
as thou wilt with one stroke. And as Moyses said the knife
be it well playne sharpe and whole as thoughe we should
cutt of an neck^e with it. And thou take the reed^e with thy

---

[1] Above "putt" is written "& strained."
[2] A marginal note offers an alternative to Almea: Alinza.
[3] Above "is nempned" is written "named."
[4] A marginal note 'pen.'
[5] An indistinct marginal note here reads: "it might be done / in the new of / the ☾ whiles / the ☾ dothe / increase when / she applieth / to caput dra / conis by o / or to the ☌ of or / △ of ♃ for if / they be true / & very good."

Liber Salomonis

cleane hands, and make thou of it a gobbets. And when thou
wilt cutt the penne, cutt it ere the sunne arise or when
it ariseth. With this penne and with this ynke thou shalt
write all the names of God holy and severall. And as
often as thou writest the name of the Creator be thou
clean^e and [1] solleme & serened & in a clean^e place. And
thou shalt first ere thou write by iii dayes be bathed in
clean^e water, but rather thou shalt be clean^e by 9 days
an house or clean^e place made very clean^e with beesoms

[5^r]
and washen watered and suffumed And ordeyne so that when
thou writeth, hold thou thy face toward the East & write thou
from morning till midday till that thou eate. And after that
thou hast eaten and dronken thou shalt not write in it any
thing. And if thou wilt write Semiforax with his strengthes
the number of the mone, be it even. And most in the day of the
mone or of morning or of Jovis or dius. & be thou word of
Saturne and of Sol upon all. And Salomon said If thou
puttest into the ynke of the bloud of vowter or of a furtur or
of a gander (wholly or all white) the ynke shall be much the
better and the more vertue

Also I say that if there were of Sapher powdered Sma=
ragdo, gagnisia & topasia the ynke shall be complete or
fulfilled. And with this Inke and with this penne ought to be
written all the names of Semiforas and know^e thou yt
he that shall write this book^e ought to be clean^e & fasting
bathed and suffumed with precious aromatickes, that is with
spices well smelling. And it shall be great profit to thee
and to him that maketh it or writeth it. And each man yt
hath written this booke or hath holden it in his house, ev'more
hold^e he God in his mynde and his holy Angels & hit
for which he hath made it. & let him put in his mynde in
which tyme of the 4 tymes of the day with his ougth or of
the tymes of an hower And ev'more let him put in
his mynde to his 4 tymes of an hower to which they ought
to be as *invenies in libro prophetar^{um}*

---

[1] Above "and solleme" (and in the margin) is written "solitarie."

Sepher Raziel

Dixit Salomon sicut si esset castru^m etc [Book 1]
Salomon said as though there were a castle full
strong and his highenes ful great and high and en=
hansed and well on each side with walles invironed and
the gates in one place well strong and stable or fyrme
and with keyes closed and locked. Therfore it behoveth it
who that would open the gates of that close castle and
holsomly would enter into it both without travel of gyfte and
without bruising of his body It is necessary to have the same

[5^v]
keyes and none other of this castle and of his gates &
of his closings Thus I say this that it is for to knowe
the starres and their names and their figures and their
natures, and when they should be good and when they should
be evill, And thus I say of the fixe and of the 7 erraticis
neverthelesse Consider how evermore the nature of the
Circle of the xii signes that is thee towards. And therfore
it behoveth each man that hath this booke, that he holde it
clenly and that he keep^e it with great reverence & with
great hono^r. And who that hath it, and can reade it, let
him not reade it, but if he were before full cleane of body
and with great witte.
And I make every man to knowe or weel that he ought
not to worke by this book^e in vayne, neither without wytte
nor without lawe or reason. And this is when every man
doth to the contrary, or when and Reptiles, or wood beasts
should lett thee or do the harme. And knowe thou though^e
thou have might and trust for to worke by this booke &
although thou might have great trust in this, yet thou shalt
not worke, but with great right or lawe or with much reason
And understand thou of all the contrary, and if thou
worchest otherwise by this booke then thou shouldest and
much might let thee that is to say if thou worchest without
reason, or if thou were uncleane or evill in thy self.

o *Clavis istius libri est cognoscere et scire loca*
The key to this booke is to knowe and will the places
of the vii bodyes above and their natures and their
sciences and the domes, and all their vertues after yt
it appeared in the earth to me

o   o *formata debet esse omnis figura cu^s ex vero*
Eache figure ought to be formed with very or true en=

sample therfore I put the figure of the key in this booke
that no man true that without reason and profitt it be
made. And I put in figure and key with the shafte to the

[6ʳ]
similitude or likenes that there is one soleyme Lord one god
which never had neither shall have any even or like to him
In the Quadriture or in that, yt is fower cornered yt
signified that there be 4 elements and no moe. And in
this key is one triangle which signifyeth knowing might
and will for whome these three no man may do any thing
in the worlde neither attayne to any profit. And Salo=
mon said that the shafte of this key is as Raziel said to
Adam unite or one head, and the quadrate is as 4 vertues
that be in herbes and words and beasts, and they be to the
similitude of elemts which openeth and doeth all. And the
7 wards be 7 Angels which have might in the 7 heavens, and in the 7 dayes of the weeke as furthermore
I shall teache you.

And the triangle signifyeth man which is in body and soule
and spirit, and these above said leadeth togither all the
worlde as it was compounded in highnes & lownes.

Pastquã hucusq diximus oportetnos dicere &c
After that we have said hitherto it behoveth us now to
say for this booke that which is said of the key of the 7 bre=
thren. And these 7 brethren have among themselves 12
realmes for to devide or to depart, and in each realme
be 30 cityes, and in every city be 60 castles and in
every eiche castle 60 Caldee yt is to say feeldy or wilde
townes. And this exemplar Salomon found and made
distinction and said there is one father and he hath 7
sonnes and these 7 sonnes be germanyes ffor after that
they be of the same father germayn. And the Elder is
most heavy among all the other. And the middle in the
middle more ordinate then all. And thither lightly be in
the middle in fellowshipping hit evermore, so they twene
of these be not much severed from hit. And the 7 bre=
thren Salomon said be Sabaday Saturnus. Zedel Jupiter

[6ᵛ]
Madyn Mars Hamyna Sol Noga Venus Cocab
Mercury Labana that is to say Luna Knowe thou
the houses of the planetts. And Salomon putt names

Sepher Raziel

to the xii realmes of the of Germanyes and they be called
signes and he beginneth to make distinction. And he
gave to their fighter that is to say to Mars that he should
rest, and that he should not fight in the realme of the
signe of Arietis and of this vertue he is in the realme
of the East, he gave him in the realme of the worlde
the signe of Scorpionis that he should fight strongly
and that he should never rest, and he is in the eight
realme from the first. And afterward he gave to
the fayre Noga that is to say Veneri twey realmes
of which one hath the half seale of Tauri that is
from the highnes of his head with his horns till to the
navell. And their as the viith from the first that is
Libra, and after while Venus is above that is in the
Northe, and otherwhile beneath that is in the South.
And so he hath inherited in twey parts And then he
gave to the painter (which is the writer) that is Mer=
curius twey realmes of which one hath twey men embraced
that is clipping togither himself, that other hath a
fayre virgin winged and nevermore would be divided
or departed from wemen for those Images be such
and he displeaseth evermore to go much from the South
into the Northe. And he gave to the Malix that is to
say Lune for that he goeth evermore one realme
And for that she will note stande much in her house
& her signe is a fish that is said Cancer which hath
many feete, and signifyeth be this that he will go much
for that he is under other brethren, this suffer alone
And he gave to the middle brother, which is the Lord of all

[7^r]
other, and he commandeth to all and is more adorned for fay=
rer arrayed, therfore he gave to him one realme full strong in
heate and his signe is as the Lion, that sheweth him Lord
upon all beasts, so is he stronger and of more Lordshippe
upon all his brethren. And then remayned twey brethren
of the par^{ty} of the South and theld or tooke twey realmes, one
about another for this that he should never overcome
in the signe of the realme well meridionall or south, and
he is one beast with one forme in his front, and the signe of
that other realme is a man that holdeth with many waters
and this brother is said the old Sabaday. And then ta=
keth that other brother for heritage on his right syde
the realme with the signe of half a man and half a horse

Liber Salomonis

and it is said Sagittarius, and on the left syde of Pisces.

Knowe you heere the natures of the Signes
And Salomon said Aries is a sign fiery hot &
dry, choleric, and so is Leo and Sagittarius and they
have might in the East.
Taurus is earthy, cold and dry, melancolious & so
is Virgo and Capricornus and they have might in
the South.
Gemini is airy, hot and moist & sanguine and so is
Libra & Aquarius & they have might in the West.
And Cancer is watery feminine moist and flegmatic
and so is Scorpio and Pisces & they have might in
the North.

Iam diximus de naturis et signis et eor~ complexionib^{us}
Now we have said of natures and sign^{e}s and of the
complexions of them, so we meane to say of natures
and of the complexions of germanyes and what they
signifyeth.
The first higher that is said the old Sabaday is Saturnis the nature of which is cold and dry for that is

[7^v]
much straight and melancholious and signifyeth father
and wroth and discord in lands.
The second is said Zedek and he is temporate for that
he is betweene the old Sabady and the hott Madyn and
Zedek is hott and moyst and sanguine in savor sweete &
it draweth to good ayer, and it signifyeth good and honor
and vertue.
The third is the fighter Madyn and he is hott and dry
evill and lover and bremer, ravisher & a lyer.
The fowrth is Hamyna Sol middle among other hott
and mighty and worshipfull and all thither brethren
shameth or dreadeth him and he is much soothfast and
strong.
The fifth is the fayre Noga colde and moyst, glad
flegmaticke fatt and fleshy and well seeming in all her
members and chere, and he signifyeth good soughts
and he is much glad among wemen.
The sixt is the writer and the forespeaker Cocab, this
holdeth himself with all & serveth to all, and signifyeth
writers and tydings and voyces after that he shall be with
it yt which everich^e he holdeth him self, when he is with it

Sepher Raziel

The viith brother is Labana & it is Malx and it is
colde and moist and it signifyeth brethren and beareth
each moneth and manndem^{en}ts of brethren to brethren
after that it is severed from them.

Deinde loquamur de septem fr̃ibus quare dicuntur
clavis &c And then speake we of the vii brethren
why they be said the keyes of the world (and which this
world may not excuse neither excuseth) and these were
formed as 4 brethren which be said the 4 elements, and
they have after signification witt and discretion & might
complete and honesty and strength, and everiche may
do in his hemisphere that is empire as an Emperor
in his empyer, or as a prince in his Lordship. Also they
have might over the 7 parts which we sayen clymates. And

[8^r]
knowe thou that these be mighty upon all beasts heere
formed.
And Salomon said prophets clippeth these brethren
vii quicke spirits, and holy and wise men said that they
were 7 lampes burning or 7 candlesticks of light & of
life, and all prophets clipeth them 7 heavenly bodyes which
be vii planets and of commonalty they be said 7 starres.
And the 7 brethren be kept of 4 beasts full of eyen before
and behinde which be the partyes of heaven East West north
and South, and they have might in the 4 parts of the
worlde and in 4 tymes and in 4 natures with her com=
plexions and withal her parties and in all her 4 ele=
ments and with these togither is hed and meeved all things
moveable by the Commandements of God that put them
in their places.

Dixit Salomon sicut fuerunt semp status superius
Salomon said As there were evermore states above
without corruption so know^e thou that there is nowe and
shall be evermore. And for this we understand the
bodyes above cleane and good and made without corrup=
tion. And that neather-bodyes uncleane evill treated and
broken, and eache day they fayleth and bend corrupted
And this corruption resteth not neither is made very
of the which we understand that the neatherbodyes might
not excuse the over bodyes. And all things which we seene
beneath have roote and beginneth from things above
ffor things above be with lyfe and without dolor and things

Liber Salomonis

beneath be the contrary, have death and dolor And things
above have during without corruption and things beneath
each day fayleth and be corrupted and minished. All pro=
phets seene that if there lacked any one of the over bodyes
that is of these that be much above ten thousand betwixt
those that we see and those that we not see. Knowe thou
that it were a great precipitation and destruction and
confusion in lande and in sea and in the 4 elements if

[8ᵛ]
any of the bodyes above were broken or were evill trea=
ted And if there fayled one of the 7 brethren the earth
shoulde come agayne to his first state, and all the ele=
ments were confused. And if any of them had corpo=
rally received corruption knowe thou that all things
were destroyed that received soule or lyfe. And knowe
thou that as the 4 elements be turned downeward so
be they not turned without some reason of the 7 above
And this sayeth the Ph[ilosoph]er when the sonne is destroyed
eache lyfe and eache soule is destroyed. And when the
mone is destroyed the ligatures or buildings of the sea
be destroyed. And knowe thou that Saturnus is
earthly and holdeth all the earth in a ballance that is
not moved. And Jupiter holdeth the ayer, and Mars
the fyer, and Sol the day and men, And Venus holdeth
the fayre parts of the worlde, and Mercurius reasons
and Luna holdeth the hearts seas waters and their powers.
And knowᵉ thou that everiche (After that it were or shall
be in this exaltation) ordeyned and bounden with the sonne
ytˢ reasons and words and speeches should be good betwixt
men. And as often as Mercury were joined in Virgo
in the same point with Sol direct and not retrograde, make
we subtill things and reasonable And as ofte as Sol
were in Aries, so many yeeres unlike he giveth us. And
as ofte as Saturnus were in Libra so many mutations
he giveth in landes. And as ofte as Jupiter is ioyned with
Saturne in an earthly signe so many divers mutations or
changings he giveth. And he changeth lawes & seates
and Lordshippes and thus understand thou in other com=
plexions of planetts after the states of them and their
beholdings that is said Aspectus.

[9ʳ]
Et dixit Hermes istam rationem super capita oia &

And Hermes said this reason upon the heads of beasts
Saturnus hath the right eare, Venus the lefte and Sol
the right eye and Luna the lefte. Mercurius the mouth.
These 7 hooles have they in power above upon the head
of a man. And Salomon said that a man is a measure
which is said Palmus made with hande in which bene all
the vertues of the worlde and of the 7 planetts and
that is only the head of a man wherefore everiche man
is likened to his starre and to his elements.
And Salomon said when I founde a spirit above re=
trograde or combust or evill treated thus I say that his
body was evill treated beneath in which it was like or he
signified in it. And who that were so wise that he knowe
his signe and his planet and his starre above and his
signification he might do good and evill to himself &
likewise so to other men. And as the nativityes of beasts
be denyed such wurchings you shall do with helpe
of God.

Postqua diximus de 12 signus et planetis &
After that he said of the 12 figures & planetts
& of radiis of them we say that eche planet that were
in Ascendent and if there be another in the same As=
cendent it is named coniunction, and how much the
latitude or bredth shall be lesse so much the coniunction
is said to be stronger and if there be more latitude
the coniunction is the feebler. And so I say to thee
in the middle of heaven. And if the poynte of the 12
houses which be in the stronger places of all houses I
say the poynte of the first degree of the house, and eche
starre that were lesse and hath upon himself another
the like is said that it hath power and goeth upon another

[9ᵛ]
from starre to starre And thus each starre that diverseth
from another by 60 degrees before and after It is
said aspectus sextilis that is the sixt beholding And
each planet that differeth 90 degrees before and be=
hinde It is said in aspectu quarto that is in the fourth
beholding. And each planet that diverseth or differeth
by 120 degrees before and behinde It is said in aspectu
tertio, that is in the third beholding. And each pla=
net that differeth by 180 degrees is in opposition
in that that it is said in the contrary place. These

be the 7 beholdings and no moe duo tertii, duo
quarti & duo sextile and unus opposites that is to
say twayne in the third, twey in the fourth, and twey
in the sixt and one contrary against another. The
coniunction is complete then they be in one degree
Double coniunction if twey good or temporate sheweth
double good, as twey evill by the contrary sheweth
much evill The sextilis beholding the ascendent
avayleth one good if trino and twey trino avayleth
in the beholding ascendent one good fortunate in the
ascendent. And twey quarties in the beholding the
ascendent avayleth one greevous or heavy (if there
were evill starres) and twey opposita avayleth one
infortunate in the ascendent or in the opposite. And
twey quarti avayleth as much as a starre falling
or combust or retrograde this is letted in the Ascen=
dent one fortunate or twey in the Ascendent and
another of sextile and another of trine beholding
the ascendent sheweth much good hasty or highing
Twey evill in the ascendent or one with another in
opposito that is in the contrary or falling sheweth

[10ʳ]
greevous or long impediment. And if they be falling and
letted it shall be worse. One fortunate in the Ascendent
beholding of twey trinis it sheweth much good and how
much there were no witnesses upon the figure of
which thou enquireth and searcheth or fo which thou worchest
so much it shall be the better And if three planets be=
holden the Ascendent with good beholding and twey evill
the good shall overcome the evill and so of the other
One infortunate in the Ascendent beholding twey quar=
tis sheweth much greefe. Caput draconis is much
better than Cauda Eache planet in his head of the same
degree it more Lordship in the figure for that it is twey
in latitude to the way of the sonne and it profiteth in
going toward the party of the north. Eache planeth in
the tayle of the dragon is minishing of his worke yt
goeth towards the south.
Luna coniunct or Joyned with Saturne and Mars in
the Ascendent it constrayneth and threatneth divels
Satunus maketh divels strength & great power
Luna coniunct or Joyned with Jove and Venus in the
ascendent it sheweth great dilection and great love

in every good thing.
Luna joyned with Mars & Saturne in the ascendent it
sheweth impediment except the planet were of good
receiving.
Luna joyned with Sol in the one poynt sheweth great
grace and if that they were good
Luna ioyned in falling and to mercury in the
Ascendent it sheweth the contrary
Luna in the ascendent by her self signifyeth after the
planet to the which she is Joyned
Luna with Caput draconis in the ascendent sheweth good
Luna with Cadua draconis or combust or ioyned with

[10ᵛ]
a starre letted or in evill sitting it sheweth much
evill when caput draconis and Luna were with
capite Saturni or that Luna or Saturnis were there
and that their werke of celson made it signifyeth upon
buildings of devills fowle and evill.
Each planet that is with dracon of another & both be
ioyned togither it sheweth a very soothe or try worke
and more in the ascendent. And if caput draconis
were of Jovis or Luna and these twey coniunct or
Joyned in the ascendent it sheweth much good and in=
ceasing of good and honor And if it were in Cauda
not only when there were twey Cauda draconis that
is of Luna and of other they be full evill when Luna
were with them. When Caput draconis Luna were
with Caput draconis Martis and Luna and Mars
in the like poynt it sheweth strength and might. And
if Cauda with Cauda and Luna with Mars togither
it is full greevous and evill after everiche is
evill so is the place or beholding of one another.
Caput draconis and Luna in capite. Aries (Luna
& Sol in Zamin) sheweth great might and great honor
and by the contrary in Libra beneath with Cauda dra=
conis. Caput draconis with capite veneris sheweth
much love and cauda draconis the contrary
Caput draconis that is to say mercury with caput
draconis and Luna sheweth werke of reason and of
voice and many sounds, and in Cauda Luna with
Mercury & Saturne it sheweth us the beholding of
many experiences.
Luna in capite sui draconis sheweth and if there

Liber Salomonis

Were Jupiter or Venus it shall do the werke of Jovis
or of Venus and it shall profit in all good worke as these
be good. Luna if it be in Cauda draconis and Mars

[11^r]
and Saturne with it or that they beholdeth it with evill be=
holding it sheweth as evill as we have said of Saturne
and Martis.
And we have said that Saturnis nourisheth devills and
Mars draweth and thresheth and figureth them. And
Saturnus gathereth togither many divels Venus and
Saturnus gathereth togither devills and wyndes from
beneath. A good starre in the ascendent and Luna
Joyned with a good starre sheweth much good. And the
beginning in all hit in which were d^{e}us quartae that is
the Lord of the 4th house and if the 4th house is well
beholden of good, all the one of the thing shall be good
And when the Lord of the 4th house were evill and evill
intreated it sheweth noy and evill. The signe of the
Ascendent sheweth the body o The Lord of the Ascen=
dent of the planet that is in the Ascendent or which behol=
deth it sheweth his spirit and the Lord of the hower
signifyeth his soule and his will, and this understand
thou in other domes The body and soule and the
spirit for these three knowe thou that they maketh the
body of a man safe and whole.

Dixit Hermes Saturnus exaltatur in Libra &c
Hermes said Saturnus is enhanced in Libra, and
Jupiter in Cancer, and Mars in Capricorne and
Sol in Aries. And Venus in Pisces and Mercurius
in Virgo and Luna in Tauro.
And knowe thou that Saturnus gladdeth or Joyeth in
The xii house, and Mars in the vith and Sol in the
ixth and Venus in the vth and Mercurius in the Ascen=
dent that is the first house and Luna in the 3^d house
And the Ascendent hath 12 vertues, and each planet
that is in it upon eache place of the circle. The xth

[11^v]
house hath xi vertues. The xith house hath 10
vertues. The viith nine, the 4th eight vertues
the vth house hath 7 vertues, the ixth house hath 6.
The third 5. The second 4. The 8 three, the xiith two

and the vi house hath one vertue. And evermore
consider thou in all things, that thou shalt do upon the
planets how it be in the xii houses & thou shalt
profitt if thou choosest well. And Salomon said to
eache man that worketh by this booke, It behoveth that
he knowe all these things, that is reasons which heere I
will not expound to thee, that is thou knowe in which
tyme of the yeere thou were borne of the 4 tymes
of the yeere. And in which moneth of the moneth of Luna
And begin thou from the Lunation of the moneth of
Mercury (where ever Luna prima were) And all
Secrets and privity be it asked in Saturne with all
deepenes, and honor and substance be it asked upon
Jove. And all strifes and battaile and hasting be it
asked upon Mars. And all cleannes & Lordship of
sol. And all fayrenes and dilections or loves and
fatnes be it asked of Venus. And all reasons & witts
& subtiltyes of Mercury. And of these 7 thou shalt aske
evermore counsel where thou findest them in their
houses and signes And they shall shewe to thee
so deeme thou upon them in all good and evill.
Now we have fulfilled heere with the helpe of God
The treatisy that is said *Liber Clavis* That is the
booke of the Key.

    Heere endeth the first booke and heere
    beginneth the second

Liber Salomonis

[12ʳ] [Book 2]

Dixit Salomon sicut alae avium sunt membra &c
Salomon said as the wings of the fowles or byrds
be members that leadeth the fowles to the place where
they desire to be, so by the vertue of stones & of herbes
and of beasts, that liveth in flying, in swimming in going
and in creeping thou might attayne to that thou wilt
if thou chooseth the nature of them.
The propertyes and vertues. And therfore we clipeth
this booke Ala that is wings for without wings neither
fowles neither fishes mought move themselves, and so as
winges beareth bodyes to highnes upwards and to fun=
daments downwards and to Longitude and latitude
that is to length and bredth, so by the vertue of
stones and of herbes with grace and with much might
of Semiforas Knowe thou that thou might attayne
that thou coveteth to do as to heale and to make sicke
or to stande or to goe.

Dixit Salomon sicut lapides sunt mundiores &c
Salomon said as stones be cleaner cleerer and
fayrer then golde and in vii vertues of this worlde as
be in stones herbes wordes and beasts, so I say that in
the beginning of this booke Cephar Raziel that was
crowned with vii stones of great power he put them
in this booke The first was Rubinus – i – Carbunclo
the second Smaragdus, the third Saphirus the
fourth Berillus, the fifth Topasius, the sixt fagun=
cia, the viith Adamas and the vertues of these
stones Raziel hath spoken. And he said that they
were crowned of 7 angells which have might over the
7 heavens and of the 7 dayes of the weeke. And Raziel
said knowe eache man that hath this booke that in this
booke be the more vertues of this worlde And the first
vertues of this booke that is said of 4 wings be the

[12ᵛ]
vertues of stones whereof knowe thou that by stones
alone thou might do wonderfull things if thou hast well
knowen as thou shouldest doe with all other Images and
that thou keepe them clenely and reverently.

Sepher Raziel

De prima ala
Et dixit Salomon scias quod in prima ala sunt &c
And Salomon said knowe thou that in the first ala
or winge be 24 precious stones great and of great
power to the similitude and signification that there
be 24 howers in the day and night. And Salomon
began & said I put and sett the first stone car=
1 bunculu Rubinus for that it is brighter and cleerer
and fayrer and of more price above all other stones
And I will say of his color and his power and his
vertue, and of his seale and of his figure that might
to be in it. And thus I shall say in all other
stones, eache stone signifyeth durability or lastingnes
without end. The color of Rubinus is as the color of fyre
sparkling and his power is that he shineth by night
as a starre or as a flame of fyre sparkling. And the
vertue of it is that it maketh good color of men that
beareth it reverently, and it encreaseth his goods
of this worlde among other men, and the Image which
thou oughtest to putt in it ought to be a draco that is
a Dragon well fayre with dread.
2 The second stone is Topazins of which the color is citrine
as of golde. His power is that if it be put in a caldron
with fervent hott or boyling water it withholdeth the
water that it may not boyle, which is for great power
for making colde, and the vertue of it is that it ma=
keth a man chaste that beareth it with him and it giveth
benevolence or well willing of great Lords and his
figure is a falcon.

[13^r]
3 The third stone is Smaragdni and this stone is greene
and fayre upon all greenenes, and it is not heavy as others
are and his power is to keepe the light and it healeth
the face and it doth many wonderfull things. And his
vertue is to increase riches, and who that beareth it in
golde prophesyeth things to come. And the signe of it
is Scarabeus that is a maner of flye.
4 And the iiii[th] stone is Faguncia the color of which is redde
as the graynes of an apple. Of these sothely there be
well coloured some and some a little and some in the
middle maner. His power is that beareth it is not
infect with alien infirmity, his vertue is that is that he giveth

Liber Salomonis

health and hono^r and keepeth the man that beareth it
whole in wayes or in Journeys, and his figure is a Lyon
well figured.
5 The vth stone is a crysopazine of which the colo^r is greene
and when it hath similitude as though it had golden
drops, and his power is to defend a man from the
Podagrie, and his vertue is that it maketh to prophesy
things to come (if it were in the hand cleane and
chast) and his figure is the image of an asse.
6 The sixt stone is Saphirus the color of which is full
leady and fayre (as the color of the pure cleane heaven)
His power is that he healeth all infirmityes that axeth
in men of Inflamation and greevance of the eye. And it
clenseth them much. And if in this stone be graven
the head of a man with the beard it delivereth a man from
prison and from all pressure and oppression and this
stone accordeth to the great power of Lords & of kings
If this stone be kept clenely reverently & chastly, &
that it be good oriental with it a man might attayne
great honor and the profitt of it that he searcheth and
coveteth And some man putteth therein the signe of a ram. Aries

[13^v]
7 The vii^th stone is Berillus the color of which is of the
eye or of sea water, and some of them be round and
some of five corners. The stone ought to be cleere
within and cleane. And his power is to chaffe the hand
closed of him that beareth it. And if it be sett in golde
it giveth great frindshippe betwixt twey men, if thou
touchest them with it. And his figure is Rana that is
a ffrogge & it is of great power to make concord and
love.
8 The viii^th stone is Onyx this stone is full blacke
and his power is to give him that beareth it many
dreadfull dreames and dreads, and he that beholdeth
himself in it hath power upon all divels in constray=
ning them and in clipping and gathering them to=
gither in speculo tabilio conjuring as it behoveth
and his figure is the head of a camell or twey
heads betwixt two eares that be said Mirti
9 The ix^th stone is said sardius the color of which is
red and fayre, and his power is to make other stones
fayrer his vertue is to give good color to him that
beareth it. And it is putt in golde, and if there be

graven in it Aquila that is an Eagle it giveth great
hono^r
10 The xth stone is Crysolitus that is of golden color
and sparkling as fier. His power is to gather togither
divels and windes and his vertue is to defend the
place where it is from evill spirits and from dead
men that they do not there any evill and that divels
obey there. And his figure is Vultur that is a wontor
11 The xi^th stone is said Eliotopia. And it is a stone
of great power of which the color is greene and fayre
shining and cleere with drops like bloud well redde
within this stone is said the stone of wisemen of prophets

[14^r]
and of philosophers. And this is honoured for twey things
for the color is like Smaragdo in greenenes and in
rednes to rubine. The price of this stone overcometh the
price of other and of his vertues and propertyes. The
power of this stone is that if it be put in any broad vessell
full of water to the sonne it resolveth the water into vapor
And it maketh it to be raysed upward till that into the forme
of rayne it be converted downeward. His vertue is that who
that beareth it in his mouth or in his hand closed he may
not be seene of any man, with this stone a man may have
power upon all divels, and make eache Incantation or In=
chantment that he will. And in this stone ought to be graven
Vespertino thus he sayth. But I trowe it be Vespertilio
that is a Backe or a rermouse.
12 The xii^th stone is Cristallus of which the color is of water
congealed with colde. his power is that he putteth abstray
of fyer from him. and his vertue is that he increaseth to
nourishe much mylke and good. and thou may take in it
what vertue thou wilt, after as the hower shall be in
which thou shalt work^e. and after as the Image shall be
which thou hast made (although they be many) and yet be
seene easily. Knowe thou that it hath many vertues. and
his figure is a gryffon that is a fowle and a beast that
he hath 4 feete & 2 wings and he is a great beast.
13 The xiii^th stone is Cornelia and it is likened to water
in which is bloud as the loture or washing of bloud. And his
power is to staunche bloud of the nostrells. And if there
be graven in it a man well clothed holding a yard or a
rodde in his hande, it giveth honor to him yt beareth it
14 The xiiii^th stone is Jaspis and it is thicke darke greene

and redde. and there be some greene and cleere and they
be better then the other. and there be some redde thicke and
dropped. And his power is that who that beareth it is not
[14ᵛ]
letted with venyme neither with serpent, neither with
Attercope neither with scorpion. And it defendeth a
man from fever if in it be graven Leo Aries or
Sagittarius
15 The xvth stone is Iris and it is likened to cristall
or to gelly, and it hath corners and if any man put
it in a house to the beames of the sonne so that the
beames passé through it or by it the color appeareth
of the raynebowe. And for this cause it is said Iris
that is the raynebowe. And this is the might for it
hath vi corners, and the vertue of it is to keepe the
place which it is with health & honesty, and there ought
to be graven in it a man armed that beareth a bowe
and an arrowe.
16 The xvith stone is Corallus and it groweth in rocks
of the sea as Arbor inuersa that is as a tree over=
turned, and it hath branches as a tree, more till two
and three palames or palmes and no more. And when
it is drawen up it is greene and tender, and then it
is dryed in the ayer and it is made redde & harde as
another. And otherwhise it is founden white. And
know thou that the redde be better. And where this
stone were it keepeth the house and the vineyarde
or the place from tempest pestilence and torment
And it keepeth the place with health and it defendeth
a man from malefets i maleficis and from evill
inchantments. And his Image is a man like to him
that holdeth a sword in his hande.
17 The xviith stone is presius or prassius and it is of
greene color thicke and fayre. and it helpeth malefets
an giveth to them grace to his ministry And Taurus

[15ʳ]
ought to be graven in it, that is a Bull.
18 The xviiith stone is said Catel and it is of great power
both in deedes and in vertues. the color of which is like to
Berill, but for it is darker then it, although it have
within full cleere and cleane beames and strakes And
there be founde some of vi corners and other some
of v. And his power is to inclepe devills and to speake

with them. And his vertue is, if thou maketh in thee blanke
of water and bringeth the roote of Apii and the stone
hanged to the necke in the skynne of an Asse suffumed
with masticke thure and croco and that thou inclepeth what
dead man thou wilte that is knowen to thee and other
knowe thou that anone he shall appeere to thee. And
he shall be with thee in the same tyme And grave thou
in it Lapwing and before Dragancia^{m} which is a middle
herbe and it is said Colubrina.
19 The xixth stone is Celonites And it is greene as
an herbe and his power is that it waxeth & decrea=
seth as the moone, and his power is also to make peace
and concorde betwixt twey if in it were graven the
signe of a swallowe.
20 The xxth stone is Calcedonius and it is white
as betwixt cristall and berill or as gyfus thicke
bright, his power is to overcome plees. His vertue
is to holde a man whole in an alien land and his
Image is a man that holdeth his right hand straight
forth to heaven.
21 The xxith stone is Ceramius This stone is of di=
vers colors after divers elements and divers londs
otherwhiles white, and otherwhiles browne greene &
redde And elsewhere it is likened to Iron and somewhere
to copper and sulphur and it hath as it were rundlets

[15^{v}]
paynted and little droppes and his power is to defend
a place from thunders and lightnings, and his vertue
is to defend from all enemyes. And write thou in it or
one p^{rte} or syde Raphael Michael & Gabriel
and on the other side panuteseron micrason Saidalson
and if thou beareth it with thee and hast it in thy power
thou shalt overcome all thine enemyes and thine
adversaryes.
22 The xxiith stone is Metestus[1] and it hath the color
of wyne upon it. a white cloth or of a rose or violet
and this hath might to chase away feends and his
vertue is to defend from dronkennes and his figure
is Ursus that is a Beare.
23 The xxiii stone is Magentis or magnes and it is

---

[1] Above "Metestus" is written "amatyst."

Liber Salomonis

of great weight and like to ferro brumeto. His
power is that he draweth dead Iron as nayles knives
and swords and his vertue is that with it thou moght
be in what house thou wolte, and do what thou wolt
with men and with things of the house suffuming the
house of it, and with this men made inchantments
and grave thou in it a man armed when Luna were in
Aries or Scorpio joyned with Mars, and sol beholding
them with a trine aspect. And knowe thou that what
maner of Images thou gravest in this stone such in=
chantments thou might attayne, and beare it with thee
and thou shalt profitt.
24 The xxiiii[th] stone is Adamas as it is middle color
and the better hath somewhat of greenenes And his
power is that with it other stones be graven. And ther=
fore we have putt it out more strange & more openly
and his power or vertue is to keepe the members of
a man safe and whole And this stone is more, and is

[16[r]]
better set at price in inchantments & invocations of
wyndes spirits and devills And with this thou maiest
send whatever fantasy thou wilt, and his figure is of
5 corners and know[e] each man who that will beare
within a precious stone be he pure and cleane when
he will do anything with them And eschewe he or keepe
himself from uncleanenes and keepe he them reve=
rently in a quiche or in a cleane place And Raziel
said In the hower in the which thou wilt do of Semiforas
beare the ii stones abovesaid and thou shalt profitt.

Dixit Salomon sicut avis corpus volare non potest &c
Salomon said As the body of a fowle ne may not fly
without wynge neither go where he cometh, so by sci=
ence of one thing above we might not fulfill that we
desire And for this we putteth the second keye in this
book[e], and we sayne it the second for that it maketh the
second opening, for as the world is closed with 4
elements so this book[e] is closed with 4 sciences and
4 vertues. and now we have said of stones now say
we of herbes. Knowe thou that in herbes are
vertue of the most that may be. And some of naturals
of this worlde beth that liveth of them as ther that have
reason and some that flyeth, and some which swimeth and
which goeth and which creepeth. And knowe thou that of

Sepher Raziel

trees and herbs some liveth much and some liveth midly
and some liveth litle, and yt is the similitude of beasts
And knowe thou also that among herbes there be some
with which thou may do good or evill, as to heale & to make
sicke, and so understand thou in these that shall be said
furthermore hereafter And Adam said By a tree
come wretchedness into the worlde, that is by the tree

[16ᵛ]
I synned in it. And Raziel said an herbe shall be thy
Lyfe. And Salomon said A tree shall be & shall waxe
Or growe of which the leaves shall not fall and it shall
Be medecine of men.

    The second wynge is to the similitude
      of 24 howers and of 24 herbes

1 *Prima herba est Acil vel almabum &c*
The first herbe is Acil almalie and it is said corona
regia and in Latin Rosmarinus This herbe hath
a middle tree and good odor and litle leaves and his
power is to chafe and comforte the brayne. And if
an house be suffumed with it it chaseth away devills
the same doth Peonia
2 The second herbe is Artemisia and this is mother
and first if other, but for that other is said Corona
regis that is to say the crowne of a kynge we had
putt it first of this they sayden all that in all things
thou doest thou shalt putt of it And the leafe is middle
greene over thone side and white on thother side
And it waxeth or groweth midly. And with this thou
shalt steepe windes [1] and all spirits that thou wilt
and thou shalt profitt.
3 The iii herbe is Cannabis [2] and it is long in shafte
and clothes be made of it, the vertue of ye Joyce
of it is anoynt thee with it and with the Joyce of
artemisia and ordayne thee before a mirror of steele
clepe thou spirits, and thou shalt see them, and thou
shalt have might of bynding and losing devills and
other things
4 The iiii herbe is said feniculus and it hath small

---

[1] Above "windes and" is written "stop or stacke."
[2] Above "Cannabis and is written "hempa."

Liber Salomonis

leaves and a long staffe and it is an holy herbe and
worshipfull, and it is medecyne of the eyen, and it

[17ʳ]
giveth good light and it chaseth away spirits and evill
eyne in the place [1] where it is, the roote of it chaseth
away evill things and helpeth in sight.
5 The vth herbe is Cardamomm^{us} and it is hott and of
good complexion and it is of middle highnes and it
giveth gladnes to him that useth it and gathereth togither
spirits. Eate thou of this when thou steepest or maketh
invocation and if thou wilt make fume of it.
6 The vith herbe is Anisu^{s} and it is of chastity Joyne it
to camphire, and thou shalt see that spirits shall dread
thee, and it is a cleane herbe, and it maketh one to see
secret things and privy, and the fume of this ascendeth
much.
7 The viith herbe is Coriandru^{s}, and this withholdeth the
spirit of a man much with tother, and it maketh a man also
full of sleepe and this gathereth much togither ye spirits
wherefore evermore they standeth with it, so that it is
said that if with this and apis and insquiano thou make
fumigacions compounded with much lazaias cicuta
anon it gathereth togither spirits, and therfore it is
said herba spiritum.
8 The viiith herbe is said Petroselim^{um} which hath great
might for to chase away the spirits of roches, and his
vertue is to breake the stone in the bladder of him that
useth it.
9 The ixth herbe is ypericon or hipericon and it is a
middle herbe thirled the Joyce of it seemeth bloud, this
is of great power for with the joyce of it, and with croco
Arthemisia and with fume of radicis valerianae if it be
written upon what frindshippe thou wilte of a prince
of spirits of the ayer and devills. Knowe thou that anon
it shall be that thou covestest And so upon spirits and wyndes
10 The xth herbe is Apium. this is of great power upon

[17ᵛ]
wyndes and devills and fantasyes and it is shawdded
and towhiched to shade with the cloud Alcisse for in it
be wyndes and devills, and this alone maketh Albafortu͂

---

[1] Above "in the place' is written "that is withouten." The final word, "withouten," is not clear and could be read differently.

Vazebelil i Mortagon and they be much contrary, for
one is kepte with heavenly angels, and another is kepte
with devills i.Apin^(u~) And this beareth the stone of the
reynes and a woman with childe use ~~shee~~ it ~~not for~~ it
noyeth ~~to~~ the childe, and it gathereth togither divells
when suffumigacions is made with insqrmo and arthe=
misia Apinm suffumed by 7 nights with fagax al=
meit and gathered clenly and the roote of it putt
and dryed and then tempered with aqua lapides suffume
thou thee by environ when thou wilt and thou shalt
see fantasyes and devills of divers maners.
11 The xith is Coriandru^s of the second kynde which maketh
one muche to sleepe. And if thou maketh suffumigacions
of it and croco and insqrmo & apio papavere nigro
grounden togither evenly and tempered with succo ci=
cutae and with msk, and then suffume thou the place
where thou wilt hide treasure in when Luna is Joyned
with Sol in angulo terra that is to say in the corner
of the earth. And know thou that the like treasure
shall never be found. And who that would take it
away shall be made fooles. And if in the hower of de=
position of the golde or silver or of the stones or
Images thou suffumeth them with thure musk suco=
lingo aloes cost evermore devils keepeth that
place and evill wyndes. And knowe thou that it might
never be dissolved or foredome agayne without sever or
and Image made thereto by the poynt of starres.
12 The xiith herbe is Satureja and this is of great
vertue and good odor and who that beareth it with him

[18^r]
with auricula muris in the day of veneris it giveth him
grace of goods and it taketh away from ther place wyndes
and evill fantasyes.
13 The xiiith herbe is said sca [1] And this is middle
in length and hath litle leaves This ought to be hol
den worshipfully in holy places and in churches, for it
defendeth the places from evill things And with this
prophets made dead men speake that were dead
by many dayes or fewe. In place where as any evill
he hath no might if he that beareth it stepeth them not

---

[1] Some speculation on this has led us to the reading "scammony," namely, the bindweed *Convolvulus scammonia*.

And it giveth them might upon which things he woulde
and this herbe put upon the place where devills be
closed, and it constrayneth them and byndeth them
least that they might have power to move them selves
And Salomon said I founde in the booke of hermits
that who that taketh water in the 4th hower of the
night upon the tombe of a dead man with what spi=
rits he would have speech withall caste he water
upon the tombe with this herbe ysope And the
water be it suffumed with costo succo musco and say
surgo surgo surgo That is to say rise rise rise
and come and speak to me, and do this by 3 nights
and in the third night he shall come to thee and he
shall speake with thee of what thing thou wilte.
14 The xiiii[th] herbe is psyllium which is of great vertue
for it sheweth or maketh open in the ayer the other
mought not to do it maketh to see spirits in the cloudes
of the heavens and this with scicorda & garmone and
the tree which swimeth which is said arbor Cancri and
malie with rore madii and with the tree that sheweth
by night, and it is said herba lucens that is herbe

[18ᵛ]
shining if thou makest with these an ointment with
the eyne of a whelpe and with the fatnes of a harte
thou mightest go suerly whether thou wolt in on hower
15 The xv[th] herbe Majorana, this keepeth an house
by itself and defendeth from evill infirmityes and
Hermes said that gentiana and valerina and
maiorana avayleth much upon great princes and
upon great men.
16 The xvi[th] herbe is Draguntia. This is of great
power, and the highnes of the roote of it Joyned with
the tong of Colubrj which is lett quicke, and the herbe
be gathered when sol is in the first degree of Cancri
and Luna beholdeth mercury or Joyned with him
knowe thou that who that toucheth clansures or locke
they shall be opened to him anone And Hermes said
that it gathereth togither wyndes & spirits If man
dragora were with it and Capillus dezoara.
17 The xvii[th] herbe is Nepita and if this with maio=
rana and athanasia & trifolio and salvia hermita
edera and artemisia with ysope being ioyned & ga=
thered togither cresente luna die Jovis That is

to say in the wenyng of the mone in the day of
Jovis in the morowe when the sonne waxeth from
the first degree of Aries till into the first of Cancer
and when thou shalt gather him be thou clene and
washen worshipfull and stand thou towards the east
knowe thou that the house and place is amended
where these nyne herbes were wyned togither And
put them upon the gate of thy house and thou shalt
profitt evermore And the 9 herbes ioyned be
like to rubyne.

[19ʳ]
18 The xviiiᵗʰ herbe is Linum suffumigacions of the
Seed of this with semine psylly – i – azartachona & radix
Violae and apii maketh to see in the ayer things to come
and to say many prophesies
19 The xixᵗʰ herbe is Salvia this is of great vertue
and the long leife of it is as ligna agni and sharpe
this breaketh or defendeth evill shades & evill spirits
from the place where it is, and it is good for an hole
man to beare with his for it holdeth a man whole, but
a sicke man holdeth it not with him.
20 The xxᵗʰ herbe is Sauina, and some men say that it
is a tree ^ of love [1] and dilection who that can chese it
And if this with somewhat of croco and lingua co=
lubri be borne with him a ring of gold and somewhat
of provinca surely goe thou before the king or before
whomsoever thou wolt And most if thou put with it
the stone that is said Topazius or if thou wilt beril=
lum And if this ring were made when Luna is ioyned
to Jove in trino from sol it were much the better
And it is said annulus solis that the ring of the
sonne, and it is of health against infirmityes, and it is
of grace of vertue and of honoʳ.
21 The xxiᵗʰ Nasturciũ This holdeth the
members whole, and if there were with it origan and
pulegin͂ and arzolla and be borne togither with thee
and thou eatest of them thou shalt be whole within
and without And so if thou annoyntest thee with them
and were suffumed with marrubio albo or reubarbaro
and herba thuris it shall defend thee from many
infirmityes

---

[1] At the caret mark ^ above the words "of love" is written, "This is a tree."

22 The xxii[th] is an herbe that is said Canna ferula

[19ᵛ]
This is full dreadfull and greevous and strong in
worke. And if thou takest the Joyce of it and the Joice
of cicuta and Jusquiami and sapsi barbate and san=
dalu~ rubr~ papaver nigr~ with confection made fume
thou what thou wolt and thou shalt see devills and
things and strannge figures And if Apin were with
this Knowe thou that from eache place suffumed
devills should flye, and if thou wolt thou might de=
stroy evill spirits. This suffumigacions is full
evill and dreadful for the fume of it and the
worke overcometh in malice and worcheth most evill
and most strongly if Luna were with Saturne or
in opposition with marte that is in opposition with
Mars.
23 The xxiii[th] herbe is Calamintum and it is like=
ned to mynte and it is of great vertue in good
suffumigacions, and if there is with it menta and
palma xpi i. pioma theis beholden taketh away
evill spirits from a place And evermore it is
against fantasyes.
24 The xxiiii[th] herbe is Cicoria. This is full good
in all ^ exercisannce [1] if it be ioyned with erigo &
pentaphyllon and ypericon and vrtica & verbena
and all be togither and be borne at the necke and
under the feete and be there the herbe of vii knots
and of vii leaves. l. Martagon and liliu~ domesticu[s]
and sylvestre that is tame and wylde and herba
angelica who ever hath these under his feete or
sytteth above and putteth the other herbes to the
necke and hath vii rings of vii metals in the fi=
gures Knowe ye that he shall have might in

[20ʳ]
bynding and in losing and in enchanting and for to
do good and evill in eache place that thou wolt making
suffumigacions of these 9 things thure albo thymiama=
te mastiche musco ligno aloes cassia cinamono and
of them suffume thee with the things above said in envy=
ron and say these names Raphael Gabriel Michael

---

[1] Above "exercisannce" is written "exonization."

Sepher Raziel

Cherubin Seraphin arrielim pantaseron micraton san=
daton complete mea͠ petitione͠ et mea͠ voluntate͠. That
is to say fulfill ye my peticion or asking and my will
and they shall fulfill it to thee. These be the more names
of the more 9 angels abovesaid And knowe thou them
and keepe them, and some men said that they be the 9
orders of Angels.

Heere endeth the 24 reasons upon the vertues of
herbes of the second wynge and these experiments
were new writen on party in Raziel although Sa=
lomon put two of these three of the sawes of hermes
And the herbes be put in the booke of Raziel for
that with them we may be excused and worke with herbs
as with Semiforas with fasting and with words in good
and in evill And let no man Joyne himself to Se=
miforas till he knowe himself the first and
in the second And thus we shall say all thing that
shall be to us necessary with the helpe of God.

De tertia ala
Dixit Salomon super ala tertia sicut corpus solis &c

Salomon said upon the third wyng as the body of the
sonne is more appeering and mighty upon all other
bodyes and brighter and fayrer and cleener So the
vertues of sensible beasts which flyeth and sendeth out

[20ᵛ]
voices and sayeth And so beasts of the third wyng
have power upon the twey first wyngs of stones and
of herbes And he put therefore in the Raziel 24
beasts with their names and vertues and states. And
the figures be 24 distincte or departed a twey. And
I would putt upon eache Element 6 beasts everiche
distinct from other and everiche of his kynde. And
as the fyer is the high Lord and distinct from the
4 elements so the lese of them all is purer and Cle=
ner among them. Therfore I beginne to say upon
the beasts of fyer ffor as everiche of the 4 ele=
ments hath his beast beneath so the fyer hath his
above pure and cleane without corruption And this
fyer that is above is not expounded of wax trees neither
of oyle neither of other composition but it is simple
And the things that liveth in it beth angels cleane
and cleere and bright like to the beames of the

sonne or of a starre, and like to the flame of fyer
or of a sparke of fyer or to the color of quickesilver
or of pure golde. And this similitude is naturall in
the beasts of the fyer And the figures of them bene
seeme such as the lightening in similitude and in
deed for as an Eomoest is a messenger to the
creator so they be ready anon to good and evill and
they seme like things & prophets that upon the
4 elements be heavens with their beasts of which we
should say furthermore.
The second spirit is much cleane but darker then
The overer and it is likened to the wynde & his figure
Is after that he would take after some of the 4

[21r]
Elements to which he is Joyned. And he formeth himself
in this maner either by water or by cloude or by moist=
nes or by thicknes of some darkenes or he receiveth
some body as fume of some kynde by falling on it either
by voce or by shape of a beast elemented by these he
taketh forme after that the nature above disposeth
3 The third beast of which wise men sayne is that evermore he fellowshippe a spirit And most the corpulent
and thicke of the spirit And therfore his figure is found
by night in places of dread and it is heard and seene and
that ofte tyme and the color of it is like to tpari 1 after
the nature of hower ere it is made, otherwise to the
similitude of the body of which it went out of, wherfore
some men seith otherwhiles the soules of bodyes in church
hayes And of these soules said the wise Hermes and
the prophet that the soule that goeth out & hath might
is not neither was but a man or a woman And upon
such maner of soules speaketh wisemen and clepeth
them spirituall for goodness heavenly fro~ symplenes.
4 The iiiith beast is the wynde eache day we heare that
we seyne not although we other & hearen not. And
the worke of the wynde be seene of the eyne after
the part from which they cometh And he hath such
nature that if he be orientall or meridionall that
is East or south he is hott And if he is occidentall
or septentrionall that is west or north he is colde
This we seene to have great power for it beareth
cloudes and waters and tempests and gayles and it
stirreth and troubleth the seas and breaketh tree, and

this is said quicke ayer as the fyer above is said
quicke fyer and simple. And therfore the elementes
above said double or twey folde That is to say fixe &

[21ᵛ]
moveable, moveable it is because it dwelleth in
the corners of the earth although it descendeth from
above ffor the 7 above byndeth and loseth it for
of them it descendeth and of them it was formed &
this is a great figure in sea in Ayre and in land
as it cometh temperate.
5 The vᵗʰ beast or vision is a fantasy that is a shade
to the similitude of divers colors or maners come
pounded of divers togither And this forme is made
in desert place or in a corrupte ayre or otherwhile
it descendeth from hills to the similitude or lightnes
of knights, and they be said exercitus antiquus, that
is an olde house And otherwise upon matters to
similitude of fayre women and well clothed
or in medes, and some say that they be faceˢ. And
otherwhiles this befalleth in a man, for corruption
or malice of complexions and of humoʳˢ that be
in a man And they be said Demoniaci for that it
ascendeth the head and falleth upon the eyne and
such corruption maketh to see many fantasyes
6 The sixt beast is said Demon this descendeth
in highnes to lownes ad he was formed of pure
matter without corruption wherfore he fayleth not
but shall evermore dure although he hath taken
thicknes in darknes of the lownes of the earth. And
he is pure in matter and strong in body And of this
sayth the wise man that he knoweth all things that
is, And by him Philosophers have answers
and wise men all things of which they would knowe
the soothenes and he dwelleth evermore in darknes
and in obscurity and he is never severed from them

[22ʳ]
And of this sayth the prophet that he hath power of ta=
king away forme and shapes of which he would in the
earth after the will of the creatoʳ And he said a bright
angell mighty and fayre as the forme of the sonne
and of the mone and of the starres or of an angell or
of a cloude or of a fowle or of a fyshe or of a man or

of a beast or of a reptile that is a creeping beast or
any other forme which he woulde And all these abovesaid
without them knowe thou that they be impalpable or unhappy to be felt. That is that they neither may be taken
with hand nor towhiched with foote for they be spirits or
wyndes And knowe thou that everiche of the abovesaid
when it befalleth in the elements he taketh a body of them
although the lyfe of them be of fyer And the dwelling of
them in the fyre and their deads fury for they be fury.
And Raziel said upon these vi that invocation of them
and opening and constrayneth and bynding and losing
and also to do good and evill by them All is made with
cleanes and therefore who that would clepe them or
have the service of them & with orison and fasting and
fumigation and with praysing of God must do as Heere=
after thou shalt heare furthermore.

Animalia aeris tertiae alae vocantur aves &c
Beasts of the ayer of the third winge be cleped
fowles for that they flyeth and they be of 4 mevings
one is said running another flying and swiming and
going and creeping
Now say we of flyeing and beginne we first of
1 Aquila that is an Egle for that is a fowle flying
much in highnes and he hath Lordship upon all other
fowles, and he is very and true in his deeds and in
Lordship and in hono^r among all other fowles. The

[22^v]
Eagle hath such a nature that he taketh his sonnes
or byrds when they be litle and ascendeth them into
a place when the sonne is highe, and then he dresseth
the face of them to the sonne. And if they beholdeth
strongly the sonne he deemeth them to be his children
and good and if they beholdeth not the sonne he deem=
eth them not to be his children but thinketh them
evill and letteth them fall and dye And one feather
of him fretteth another fether, and he seith farre
by one league or rule a litle beast, a great beast
soothly he seith by 9 leagues or by a dayes Journey
The eyne of him with the hart have great vertue and
Grace to a kynge or to a lord of a lorde for that

Sepher Raziel

Giveth to him grace in ^[1] realme.
2 The second fowle is Vultur that is a vouter this
hath great vertue in all his members, the head of
him helpeth against all dreames and against crafte
of magicke and his feete helpeth against malefette
And if an house be suffumed with 9 fethers of him
it putteth out from it evill spirits The gall of it
helpeth the eyne better then anything of y^e worlde
The eyne of him putt in the skynne of a serpent, and
The tong of him putt in a cloth of red sylke wrapped
with them helpeth in clauses in which thou covetest to over=
come and for to wynne the love of another Lord. The
wings of him putt upon a bed defendeth a man sleeping
from all evill wyndes greevances and evill spiritts
neither may they lett in all the house, neither any other
fantasyes have power or other things.
3 The third fowle is falco that is falcon of whome the
Vertue is that of great Lords he is sett at much price

[23^r]
they bene of the highnes of his right wyng overcometh
plees both ravishing and in taking away alien things
and the highnes of his lefte wyng taketh away evill
fevers But we ought not to sley venative fowles
neither hounds although they have many vertues in them
selves. And knowe thou that how many members be
in every beast fowle fishe or reptile so many vertues
distincte hath every member by himself.
4 The iiiith fowle is a Turtur simple and good never=
thelesse if thou takest the male and the female together
and burnest them togither in a new pott with croco and
vervinca and cichoria gathered togithere by them which thou
wilt ioyne togither if thou castest the powder of these
upon them knowe thou that anon they shall be ioyned to=
gither, and it giveth great love to them that beareth the
powder with them
5 The vth fowle is said Upupa that is a Lapwing
having a crest of fethers in the head as a cocke &
he hath many vertues this hath one bone in his wings
and it gathereth togither divels and spirits of the ayer
the property of him is that whoever taketh the hart of
him and wrappeth it in hony, and the assoone as he may

---

[1] Above ^ is written "his."

Liber Salomonis

swallowe it and drinke the mylke of a white cow of a
red or of a blacke. Know thou that it maketh a man to
say things to come. And he hath another vertue for
who that cutteth the necke where the cocke croweth
not neither may be hard neither the voice of an hound
neither where wheate is sowen and when he cutteth
if his necke inclepe he devils, and then bear[e] he with
him the half deale of the bloud and of that other half
deale anoynt he himself and evermore shall go with

[23^v]
him one of the devills that is to witt he whome he
can inclepe which shall say to him many things
6 The vi[th] is said Ciconia that is an haysoucke who
that fleyeth him in the day of Luna and taketh the
bloud of the hart of him and anoynt himself with it
And eateth the flesh with somine faeminli and with
cardamoms and garyophillo And eare he eate it
suffume he himself with good odors and with thure
masticke and cinamom and other such. And know
thou that he shall have grace of enchanting
which he woll and of coniuring and constraining
the spirits of the ayer and other spirits that goeth
upon rivers and wells These vi fowles abovesaid
bene exemplar upon all other And when thou wilt
knowe the vertue of any fowle do thou after the
precept of this booke.
Raziel upon the booke of visions of Angells upon
the beginning of tymes in the 12 months as heere
after thou shalt see furthermore

Dicamus de viscubus mavis et alys &c
Say we of fishes of the sea and others upon vi of
Them that is to witt of the more and the middle that
I should shew the vertues of them.
1 The first fishe is Balena the fatnes of which made
liquid and kepte by the space of vii yeeres & more
for how much it is thelder so much it is the better
it healeth a man from eache gowte and evill mynde
if he anoynt himself with it. And if he annoynteth his
head with the bloud of him it helpeth him much and
yeeldeth him strong and more whole and it maketh

[24^r]

Sepher Raziel

him to see true visions. The sperma of him is said Ambra
If they suffumeth tombs with this it gathereth togither
The spirits above downwords and each peticion & axing
It maketh to give answere. And Hermes said There is not
suffumigacions for to inclepe spirits as Ambra & lignum
aloes, costus, muscus' crucus and bloud of lapwing with
thymyamati for these be meat and drinke & gladnes
of spirits of the ayre, and these things gathers them togither strongly and full soone. And wise men sayne that
the sperme and bloud and hart of a Balene be princi=
palls for to command the wyndes & spirits
2 The second fish is said Dolphin And he is the king of
the sea ffor as the eagle hath might among fowles
and the Lion among beasts so in this maner hath the
dolphin in the sea. And who that annoynteth with the bloud
of the clothes of twey friends it maketh them enemyes
or casteth the dry bloud upon them. And who that bea=
reth the hart of him maketh him hardy
3 The third fishe is Cancer this hath vi feete take
and brenne him in panno livido and with the powder
frote thy teeth softly it healeth them and maketh them
fayer, and cureth the canker in the mouth, if thou
casteth it upon the fyer with somewhat of Stercoris
humani combusti it gathereth togither spirits.
4 The fourth is bright as an horne betwixt palemes
and whitenes that is to say piscis candis or sepia
This fish hath many propertyes and that knoweth well
enchantments and prophets which made with this their
enchantments and transfiguracions so that when
they would that a house should seem full of water
or that a river should enter by the gate They tooke

[24ᵛ]
this fish and with thymyamati and ligno aloes and
roses they fumed an house and they cast therein of
the water of the sea, and then it seemed that the house
were filled with water And if they cast bloud therein
then it seemed all bloud, and so if they cast snowe there=
in it seemeth snowe. And when they would that the
earth shoulde seeme to quake then they cast therein
the earth of a plowe, and so the made there divers
similitudes in all things according or after the thing
which they put in the fumigacion. And knowe thou that
it dweth so much and so long as the suffumigacions

Liber Salomonis

is or lasteth in the house. And with the gall of him
also they made many enchantments, ffor that this
beast is much unlike to other.
5 The vth fishe is Murena and he is lentiguus
the vertue of it is that enchanters beareth the
powder of him with them to make enchantments with.
6 The vi[th] fishe is Rana viridis And if thou take
it or touché it upon what woman thou wilte and
nempnest the names of the Angells of the moneth
in which thou werte borne as I thinke which be furthermore within in libro visionn[is] thou might do both
good and evill of what woman thou wilte, and know
thou that of these fishes and of all other thou maist
knowe the vertues of moneths and understand
thou by like things in all other things.

Primie~ animal est leo ista bestia est valde fortis
The first beast is a Lyon This beast is full strong in
The brest and in the cheeks And he is of strong beholding

[25[r]]
and looking so that when other beasts seeth him they be
moved togither with dread and the skynne of him is of full
vertue that if it be putt with other skynnes it destroyeth
them and maketh them bare. And who that taketh the biting
toothe of him that is cleped dens caninus and putteth
it in golde it is good to take away and to take alyen things
and the same doth wolfes toothe. And if thou maketh a
purse of the harte of a Lyon full of bloud musco & almea
et ligno aloes thymyamati and it were gathered & put
upon whome thou wylt and thou maketh it hott. Know thou
that in that hower he shall love the much and shall doe
thy bidding. And if thou inclepest with the bloud of a goate
the prince of Divels he shall be ready anone to do thy
commandement and so more kynge or he for whome thou
doest, and the same I say for great women.
2 The second beast is Elephant that is an Oliphant and
He is ful great, and when he is risen of hard he lyeth &
when he falleth of hard re riseth, for that thereto he hath
no knees disposed well, and the bone of the teeth of him
is said Ebur that is Ivory. And if it be put in electna=
ryes it comforteth the feebleness of the hart as much as
margarita and more. And the bloud of him with the liver
comforteth much fasting.

Sepher Raziel

3 The third beast is Cerbus that is an hart which liveth
long for that he remayneth as the moone or as an egle
who that maketh fumigacions of the hornes it chaseth
away serpents, by it self it chaseth away devills.
4 The ivth beast is Catus that is a catte and he seith
better by the night then by the day, and who that ta=
keth of him and of an Irchen and of a rearemouse and
maketh of Alcofol & Alcofolizeth or noynteth his eyne
he seith well by night and by day. And if thou putteth

[25^v]
therein the eyne of an asse thou mightest see whe=
ther the spirits and devills of the ayer goen
5 The vth beast is Mustela that is a wesell, this
bringeth forth her Issue at her moneth after the
sayeng of the poets but not of philosophers, this
helpeth much when he is brent, and the skynne of
him is written for to cause love betwixt tweyne
6 The vith beast is Talpa that is a molewarpe and
dwelleth under the earth and is likened to a mouse
with this beast thou mayest make to come tempests
pestilence, hailes and lightnings & cornflations
and many evill things if thou putteth him bare or
naked upon the earth dead and overturned, and with
this beast thou mayest make discorde and concord with
whome thou wilte, for he is a cursed beast, he healeth
a man of the festure when he is burnt or powder
and Cast in it.
And when thou wilt knowe the vertue of other beasts
do as it is said in libro visionn^{is} upon which aske
thou this of the Lord of the vision that is that it
appears to thee that thou askest and covetest to
knowe of beasts which thou wylte.
This beast seith not neyther hath eyne. And know
thou that the vision of moneths is upon all things
that thou askest or would knowe. And God shall
be with thee if of right thou aske. And knowe thou
that heere is fulfilled the third wyng And now begin
we the fourth wing which is complete or fulfilled
upon all the elements.

Liber Salomonis

[De Quartus Ala]
Dixit Salomon sicut corpus vivũ &c
Salomon said as a quicke body mylde or great is

[26ʳ]
not moved with their feete neither any fowle lesse then
with two wings, neither the world is governed with lesse
then with fowre elements may not neither might not
be lesse then with 4 wyngs which be said to be 4 vertues
wherefore Raziel said that who that shall be filled
with this booke shall be as one of the prophets, he shall
understand all vertues of things and powers of them
and if he withholdeth and worcheth he shall be as an an=
gell. And therfore he putt in this booke 22 elements
of great vertue that is 22 letters or figures which the
sonnes of Adam might not excuse.
1 The first is Aleph א That is A his letter is three
cornered and it signifyeth the lyfe power and highnes
and the principall or beginning in all things These
putteth all things in their figures and in their prin=ciples.
2 The second is said Beth ב That is B and it is
full good in things which we desire in Battaile and in
playe & evermore sheweth goodness and profitt
3 The third is said Gimel ג that is G and it sheweth
evill and grief and Impediment in things
4 The fourth is said Daleth ד that is D this sheweth
turbation and death of some man & harme to him
5 The fifth is said He ה that is H and it sheweth
price, honor and gladnes & it is full good in all things
6 The sixt is said Vau ו that is V and it sheweth
death payne and travaile
7 The vii[th] is said Zain ז that is Z at it sheweth
pennyes and riches
8 The viii[th] is said Heth ח and it signifyeth
Long lyfe and helthe.

[26ᵛ]
9 The ix[th] is said Teth ט that is T and it signifyeth
wrath woodnes and grief
10 The tenth is Iod י that is I and it signifyeth faith
good lyfe and gladnes and all good beginning
11 The xi[th] is said Caph כ hit sheweth very gladnesse
and travaile without profitt

Sepher Raziel

12 The xii[th] is said Lamed ל and it sheweth glad=
nes and honor and profitt
13 The xiii[th] is said Mem מ That is M and it
sheweth greef and otherwise dolor
14 The xiiii[th] is said Nun נ that is N. It signifyeth
restoring of a friend, and a visitation of him & profitt
15 The xv[th] is said Samech ס
16 The xvi[th] is said Ain ע It sheweth occasion
or evill of a woman
17 The xvii[th] is said Pe פ it sheweth health.
18 The xviii[th] is said Phe פ [1] That is ff and it sheweth
bloud is shed of good men and highe
19 The xix[th] is Zade צ It sheweth health
20 The xx[th] is said Coph ק It sheweth hid lyfe
21 The xxi[th] is said Res ר That is R✤ And it shew=
eth a man that is fallen and is risen
22 The xxii[th] is said Thau ת That is T. It sheweth
Greefe and diminution.
Now we have said upon the fowre wyngs upon the
22 letters that be upon the lawes of the table written
And know thou that there be no moe but onlye 22 letters
Which be the roote of Semiforas for with them it is formed
And is caused and is made and without them I may not be

[27[r]]
And some men said that Ca~malie found them. But it is
not sooth ffor the angell Raziel gave them written to
Adam in this booke that is said liber ignis, and with them
all the booke of Semiforas written. And knowe eache
man that readeth this booke that the Creator said to Raziel
to be the names of Semiforas wherfore if thou canst
transpose these 22 letters or figures as it beseemeth
thou shalt attayne the great name of thy Creator
and with it thou might do what thou wilt evermore
with Cleanesse and with the helpe of the Creator.
Now we have fulfilled this booke of the wing like
to the angels that is Pantaseron Mucraton
Sandalon for everich of these hath 4 wings by
commandement of the benigne angell which the Creator
sent to me that this booke were better compounded
and well ordeyned.

---

[1] Two forms of *peh* פ (*peh* and *peh dagesh*) are given, but no *shin* שׁ.

Liber Salomonis

Heere endeth the second booke & beginneth
the third book of Thymiamatibus

Dixit angelus Adae fac Thymiamata &c [Book 3]
The Angell said to Adam make thymiamata
Thymiamata be confections of good odors with which thou
shalt suffume (and thou shalt please to Creacion)
and thou shalt attayne what thou wylt by this
And they of which they be made be peticion things
which thou shalt fynde and of good odor and of good
nature, and of cleane things. And when thou
wilt do it be thou cleane of without all fylthe
and then the angell rested in that hower And Adam
remayned and did what he might And this Salomon
expounded and said I marvaile why this is the booke

[27^v]
of Moyses also ffor the Creato^r said to Moyses
make thou Thymiamata and suffume thou in the
hill when thou wilt speake with me wherfore Salomon
said suffumigacions sacrifice & unction maketh
to be opened the gates of the aire and of the fyre
and of all other heavens. And by suffumigacions a
man may see heavenly things and privatyes of the
Creato^r And each man knowe that they thirleth
The earth water and lownesse And Salomon said
As there be 7 heavens, 7 starres & 7 dayes in
the weeke of which everiche is distinct and is not likened
to his even. So knowe each man that there be 7
suffumigacions which withholdeth with them the vertue
of the 7 starres, and maketh glad the spirits of the
ayre and the angels of heaven and Divels of angels
of the worlde. And therfore for a man yeeldeth to
them hit, that is theirs. Therfore they be pleased
and well apaid for the words which thou sayest of
sayest the names of them or of the Creato^r. And for
this that thou doest when thou washest thee and
for the gift that thou givest to them when thou
suffumest, and these things yeeldeth them earthly
and appearing to thee. And that spirituall & invisible
that is, that neither evill men neither beasts
mongst see thee if thou doest it strongly about thee
and about whome thou doest it.
Thymiamata is made of many things, and these be

Sepher Raziel

Principally upon the vii dayes of the weeke And first
say we of thymiamata of the Saturday for the starre
of him is higher & the angell of him is mighty in ye earth

[28^r]
1 The first Thymiamata is of the Saturday ought
to be of good things and well smelling rootes as is
costus and herba thuris. And that is thymiamata
for good, and so I shall shewe all other as it beseemeth
to good and Thymiamata to another I
shall say in another place
2 Thymiamata of the Sonday is thus Mastick muscus
and other such and all other good gumes and
of good odor in all good and by the Contrary in
all evill
3 Thymiamata of the Monday is foliu^s myrti and
lauri and leaves of good odor and so understand
thou in his contrary.
4 Thymiamata of the Tuesday is Sandalus rubeus
niger and albus and all such trees and eche tree
of Aloes & cypresse and so understand thou of each
tree.
5 Thymiamata of Wednesday is made of all rindes
as cinamon cassia lignea & cortices lauri & muris
and so understand thou in the other
6 Thymiamata of Thursday is nux muscata gari=
ophylli and citruli and the rinde of Aurangiar~
siccar~ & pulverizatar~ that is the rynde of Oranges
dry and powdered & all other fruits of good odor
7 Thymiamata of the Friday is moas rosa viola
& crocus and all other flowers of good odor and in
the contrary to the contrary put yow all Thymiamata stinking
And knowe thou that each Thymiamata of good odor
Gathereth togither his spirits after that his nature
& his color he & his strength is Thus I sayd for good
good, for better better.

[28^v]
And Hermes said of Thymiatibus that
Thymiamata of Luna is cinamonis & ligno
aloes et mastix et crocus et costus, et macis
et myrtus we putteth this that each of the pla=
nets have a parte in it, and all this may be Luna
good and well fortunate by good spices & sharpe

although Salomon made distinction upon the daies
and planette of the spices with the which a man ought
to make thymiamata And he said that of Saturne
is each good roote in good and evill in evill
And of Jovis all fruite, and of martis eche tree
And of solis eche gume and of veneris eche
flower, and of mercury each rinde, and of Luna
eache leafe, and thus understand thou of all other
and eche odoriferous herbe is of veneris. And
Raziel said to Adam that he should make good
Thymiamata. And therfore said Hermes, understand
That eache Thymiamata is made of all good things
as of roote tree rinde leafe flower fruite & gumes
and yet seeds be put in it as Baccae & Cardamomu͠
and waxe, and put thou in it all good thing and
precious, and sithen he said Thymiamata completu͠
And there is some Thymiamata gracu͠ or of greeke
by which heather men were wont to suffume Idols
with. And yet to this day Churches and Altars be
suffumed with it, and it is said Thymaimata Jovis.
And in soothenes who that useth this Thymiamatibus
must be cleane and chaste and of all good lyfe and
will to the Creato^r and he shall profitt.

[29^r]
Dixit Salomon super suffumigata Hermetis q [1] *dur &c*
Salomon said upon the suffumigacions of Hermes which
be said beneath and they be seven maners with which be
1 made sacrifices some be (and the first) which fastesth and
giveth tei things to the Creato^r, and therfore they
trust that they attayne to that that they desire And
it is soothe
2 The second is that they washen & clenseth them
selves and dwelleth cleane and therfore they trow
to attayne their petition & axing & it is soothe
3 The iii^d is that they do almes of God and for the
holy angels of him
4 The iiiith is that they sleyeth and casteth the bloud
in the fyer.
5 The fifth is that they sleyeth and burneth all
6 The sixt is that they prayeth much in howers ordeyned
7 tymes in the day, and 3 in the night

---
[1] The *q* has *ae* written above it.

Sepher Raziel

7 The viith is to make suffumigacion with good things
and well smelling and everiche of these did this
that he might attayne the sothenes of it that he asked
and so he attayned hit by the Commandement of the
Creato^r.

And know thou that suffumigacion overcometh in all
Sothely who that suffumeth best to the eye it proveth
and with this the wisemen excuseth all other. And wit
thou that who can well knowe the natures of suffumigacions
he might easily nigh thilk spirits which
he would enclepe according to the nature of suffumigacion
And evermore consider thou the nature of
the spirit and of the suffumigacion, and the spirits be
constrained by the contrary and be comforted by

[29^v]
like things And it is to wytt that as a wise leache
in giving a medecine to a sicke man removeth
the sickenes and inleadeth health. So suffumigacion
if it be good remeveth the contrary from the place
And with evill suffumigacion be remeved good spirits,
evill and ill spirits also dreadeth for eache
thing more loveth health then sickenesse. And therfore
it is said that Sulphur remeveth both good
spirits and evill, and this is approbation or profitt
way And there is another way for lignu͠ aloes
and none other, and Sulphur chaseth them
away and this is very reason And then I say
that Sulphur gathereth togither his proper spirits
and none other And they be full strong & penetra
tive and thicke and be not severed or departed so
soone from a place But although a place were
suffumed with Sulphur, and then were washen
with water and suffumed with lignu͠ aloes yet it
draweth away the spirits of Sulphur or endureth
or leadeth in his owne. And knowe thou also that
the spirit of Azet that is quicksilver and the
spirit of Thuris be contrary Although spirits
both yet therwith all devills entereth and thirleth
rather or sooner then the spirit of Thuris, wherfore
everich hath full great might, yet and if
thou wilte withdrawe the spirits suffume thou with
thure and they shall go out And so understand thou
of all other spirits good and evill.

Liber Salomonis

And Salomon said that as a physicion putteth
a man pure good oyntmente and cleane and

[30ʳ]
they thirleth the body of a man and healeth so suffumigacions
thirleth the 4 elemts and maketh to see and knowe
heavenly things which were evermore heavenly and which
descendeth from heavens as be angells & spirits of the
ayre and the soules of dead men and divels and windes
of spelunke and of deepenes and fantasies of desert place
And wherfore knowe thou that all spiritualls with right
fumigacon shall obey to thee, and shall come to thee
and they shall do thy co~mandement And Hermes said
that all things that was or is present or shall be that the
overnature Joyned with the neather by ordinance or tyme
and hower maketh one body and understanding that he
can understand and knowe thilke things whereof creatures
have to live and themselves to governe. Therfore
know thou that there be fumes that Chaseth away
spirits and other some that steyeth them and constreyneth
them to come, and other that quickeneth them
and strengthneth them, and giveth them might, and so
by the contrary there be some that destroyeth them
and taketh away their might, and this is the probacion
of this for the fume of an hare chaseth them away
and this he said upon serpents and that chaseth them
away which is fumus amnecae that is the fume of feces
of oyle and that steyeth them is the spittle of a
fasting man. And therfore he said suffumigacion
sufficeth to us in all things beneath. And Raziel
said knowe thou that as water washeth all uncleanesse
and fire maketh liquid or melteth all mettalls & maketh
cleane and fyneth. And as the aire is the lyfe of a man

[30ᵛ]
living, and the earth sustaineth or beareth eche body
and nourisheth each plant, to understand thou that
good thymiamata – i – suffumigacions is fulfilling in
the worke to the Invocations of spirits and of other
things and well proporcioned with the which Thymiamata
is confect or medled, and were in eache hower convenient
of according.

Sepher Raziel

Dixit Salomon propter hoc pono horaˢ et tempus &c
Salomon sayeth ffor this I put the hower and the
tyme in this worke for in all howers in which a man
will speake to a kinge or to a prince he may not speake
to them neither in eache hower which a sonne asketh
of the father any thing he giveth to him. Therfore
it is darke to thee to choose the tyme and the hower
upon these that thou askest. This is therfore tempus
quoddam that is some tyme of Jovis be it done in the
day of Jovis and of Veneris in the day of Veneris
and Martis. And of Saturne in the day of Saturne.
And so of other that be done in Invocations of spirits
and in all praysings of Angells. And the fumigacion
of which is pure and cleane. Knowe thou that it is a
spirituall thing and living and fellowshipping to heavenly
things. And now said Veallia Knowe thou
that no man ought to make suffumigacion of precious
things but if it were before cleane, and with cleane
waters well washen and annoynted with precious oyntments
which he made cleanly and with precious things
as cera alba, balsamo croco and musco abitatmeca
algalia, almea Thure myrrha. Oleo olivary. And this
oyntment be it well kept and well warded in a cleane

[31ʳ]
place of him after that also the clothings be cleane
white newe and good, not broken neither blacke. And
the suffume he himself worshipfully, and the
maner of suffuming himself ought to be made in
vii maners towards the East the North the West
and the south, and towards the heaven above, and
towards the earth beneath, and the viith tyme all
about. And as offe as thou doest this evermore
dresse thy mynde unto God evermore, and pray that
he fulfill thy will. And knowe thou that I founde in
some olde booke that these were the more suffumigacions.
Thus thymiamata gracu˜ masticke, sandulus
galbanuˢ Muschalazerat myrrha and Ambra and these
be collectors of spirits and placators of them. And
Salomon said when thou wilt gather togither the
spirits of the ayre do thou in this maner. Clense
thou thy self in the better maner that thou canst
and go to a pitt where thou wilt knowen to thee
and suffume it and encleape him by his owne

proper name and lathe him or pray him and that
by three nights, and if he answereth not to thee
neither appeareth send thou him to a certaine place
or to an house or to a quadrive that is a place where
4 wayes meeteth or to a yard or gardeine And suffume
thou the pitt towards the vii parts and in the place
where thou bathest also, as I have said And then
knowe thou that he shall come, and he shall appeere
to thee that thou shalt do this.
Et dixit Hermes quod spiritus qui apparent &c
And Hermes said that the spirits which appeareth

[31ᵛ]
in this worlde be these. Some sothely be heavenly
and the prophet clepeth them Angels, and
they be bright and cleere as flame or a starre
as we have said. Other be aire and of the aire
and of many colors greene bright and other such
& of many figures. And other be fiery and they be
bright and red. And other be watery and they be
white and as bright as tinne or Iron burnished
or quickesilver Other be that neigheth to men &
be like to a white cloude or to a white clothe
And other be darke and dime and of divers formes
which be said Divels which be said with the wynde, and
they be in the deepenesse of the sea and of lownesse
Spirits that bring with hailes & lightnings
And wisemen clepeth these huge spirits & strong
Now we have said of the nature of spirits and
putt to thy mynde and thou shalt attayne with the
helpe of God.

Dixit Raziel sicut in aere puro claro &c
Raziell said as in the pure cleere and bright &
cleane and peciable aire all things gladdeth
a wyeth of it. So knowe thou that from fasting
and cleannes and washing of water & prayers
[1] and orison of the Creator. And for naturall and
cleane suffumigacion and very faith or trust thou
might please them which we have said above. And
Raziel said to Adam knowe thou that in all maner
te life of Angells be holy & cleane And the

---

[1] The word "luck" appears here in the margin.

Sepher Raziel

suffuming or suffumigacion is bread of which spirits

[32ʳ]
liveth And fasting and Cleannesse and Clarity sacrifice
with orison be the house of holy altar soules
and trust in the author of good. Wherfore each man
that hath these abovesaid in himself he shall attaine
or neigh and he shall have profitt.
And Salomon said these be that befalleth in suffumigacions,
anon shall come to us fume and then odor
and of the fume a cloude ^ [1] of the cloud an high cloude
and wynde, and of the wynde ascendeth the cloude higher
and of the Cloude an high winde ascendeth higher and
is made a soule And of this the spirit is made higher
and of the spirit and angell of heaven, and of angells
light. And these be caused by cleane suffumigacion. And
know thou that suffumigacions be of vii maners. Some
sothely sharpe, and other penetrative or percing. Other
sweete smelling other stinking, other simple, other meke
other of greefe other sothely of peace, or everich of these
or of these manners is after his odor savor nature and
complexion. Wherfore Hermes said that as coldenes
congealeth water which is colde, and as water of the
sea is congealed with great, and as Azertacona congealeth
the water of wells, and everiche of these congealeth
the water one with coldenes another with hotnes
another by arte another by nature, and the matter is
made one body and one gobbet. And knowe thou that
good suffumigacion gathereth togither and constrayneth
and maketh spirits to appeare in the aire, and secret
or privy things And it maketh them to take a body with
out eyne seeth.
And Salomon said that as the Adamant draweth

[32ᵛ]
Iron to himself, so knowe thou that suffumigacion
gathereth together and draweth the spirits of the
ayre, and maketh them to come to the place where
thou doest it and will gather them togither. And the
wiseman said suffumigacion is like to the roote of
Arzolle ffor as it Joyneth togither gobbette of flesh
into one. So suffumigacions gathereth togither

---

[1] Above the caret mark ^ appears '&.'

spirits of heaven or heavenly which the 4 elements
and they make that they taketh a body, and spirits taketh
fulfilleth that be axed of them and that to
likenes of a mirror to which if there be sett before what
figure thou wylte a like appeareth within the fumigacion
made Cleanly and invocation in the hower
after the spirits proporcionall. The spirits appeareth
to us, and new operations and worchings with
fulfilling upon the thing that thou asketh, and be
thou never deceived in the knowledge of suffumigacions,
and putt thou thy mynde in them lest
they be transposed, and thou shalt fulfill as that
were and after that thou doest as he said.
And Salomon said I will touché somewhat to thee
of the nature of suffumigacions, who that useth it
much it maketh to see in sleepe or in sothenes grene
things and yellowe and divers colors melancholious
fumigacion sheweth leady things Sanguine fumigacion
sheweth red things, and otherwise it is shewing
of purpure color fflegmaticke fumigacion sheweth
white things and fayre. And so understand thou after
that the nature were and the appearing of spirits

[33^r]
and of their colo^r and visions and the worke of them
shall be after the sharpenes of it and the goodnes and
the direction of fumigii that is fulfilling of the thing
after that the Image were formed and the Orison of
the thing nempned and the trust for all is in the
intention of the man and in the hower in which it is done.
Now we have said how every of the planetts hath his
fumigacions Now say we the fumigacions of the xii
signes and of the xxxvi faces of them. Aries holdeth
by himself Mirta^s. Taurus costum. Gemini
masticem. Cancer Musthalazeratis. Leo thus. Virgo
classen. Libra galbanu^s. Scorpio opopanace^s. Sagittarius
lignu^s aloes. Capricornus assa^s fatidu^s. Aquarius Euphorbiu^s.
Pisces Thymiama. The first face of Aries
holdeth Mirta. The second Stamonea the third Piper
nigru~. The first of Tauri Costum. The second Cardamomu~.
The third Cassia. The first of Geminoru~
masticem. The second Cinamomus. The third Cipressu~
The first of Cancer mastu~. The second succu~. The
third anisu~. The first of Leonis thus. The second

lignu~ balsami. The third Nuce~ muscata. The first of
Virginis Sandalos. The second Crocu~. The third mastice~
The first of Librae galbanu~ the second Bofor. The third
mirtum. The first of Sagittarii lignu~ aloes. The
second folia lauri. The third gariofilum. The first of
Capricorni assa. The second Colofoniam, the third piper
longum. The first of Aquarii Euphorbiu~ the second
Reubarbar~ the third Stamonea The first of Piscium.
Thymiama. The second Crocum. The third Sandalum
album.

[33ᵛ]
Nota scdm Hermetem de fumigiis
And Hermes said Aries Leo and Sagittarius
withholdeth eche chollericke spice & bitter
Taurus Virgo and Capricornus melancholious
and stipticke
Gemini Libra & Aquarius sanguine & sweet
Cancer Scorpio & Pisces flegmaticke and of salt savor
And this Salomon holdeth for the naturall
for such spice we give & with them we suffume
And which give to the dayes and to the howers. And the
sunday the first hower is of Solis, and all of the day
altogether we should give this masticke & muscum
as we have said of planets in the beginning if this
booke of Thymiamatu, and to understand thou of all
other knowe thou the suffumigacions of tymes

In primo tempore lignu~ aloes thus et crocu~ &c
In the first tyme lignu~ aloes, thus & crocu~ In
the second tyme Thymiama. Costum mastice. In the
third tyme Sandalus Cassia and mirtu~. In the fourth
tyme muscu~ succu~ and lignu~ balsami. And as he
gave to eche of the 4 tymes their spices or kyndes
so he giveth to eche moneth one spice by order.
Dicamus nunc suffumigia 4 partiu~ mundi &c
Say we now suffumigacions of the 4 partes of the
worlde and of the 4 elements. For all things
that be in this worlde either be compounded of
4 elements or symples Suffumigacions of the 4
partyes of this world be these upon the partyes of the

[34ʳ]
East and the fier serveth Ambra muscus & alba cera yt

Liber Salomonis

is white waxe. Upon the party of the south and the earth
Algalia, almea and teriaca. Upon the party of the west &
the ayre Balsamus, Camphora & olen olivraru˜. Upon the
North & the water Lignu˜ aloes, mix muscata & Maris.
And Salomon said each man that would do any thing
by this booke putt he his mynde to the chapter of thymiamatu˜.
That he knowe the kindes or things & justly
Can meddle them. And so knowe thou that thou might
easily worke by it and without travayle thou might fulfilall
thing that thou desyrest to see. Now we have fulfilled
one Chapiter of fumigiis or fumigacions, and we
will say furthermore yet upon which was or intencion with
the help of God.

Sepher Raziel

Heere beginneth the fourth booke that
speaketh upon tymes of ye yeare

In Dei noie py incipio scribere libris istu &c [Book 4]
In the name of the meeke God I beginne to write
this booke that is said or called Cephar Raziel which
the Angell Raziel gave to Adam. And it shall speake
upon the 4 tymes of the yeere & moneths & dayes with
his night how we should nempe each thing and knowe
each man. That this is said the booke of tymes, and the
Angell gave it that is said might and great b [1] by the
manndement of the Creator quicke God & in all things
mighty. And for that Adam should knowe all things
by which he would knowe in this worlde what it is
what it was and what it should be in all things in the
12 moneths of the yeere and dayes & howers and that
by order and similitude of Cleane fastings and of washings
of sacrifice of suffumigacions made by 7 dayes or the

[34^v]
first mone were, and ere the sonne should assende
his taile the ascendent, and ere the sonne should
ascend upon his starre Zedek Jovis and they should
be nempned in this booke by monthe of holy angells
that have might upon the 7 heavens formed of fyer
and the beholding of them is of fyer and the life of
him is fyer. And they seemed clothed with fyer And they
be covered with fyer. And from the fyer the went out
and in the fyer they dwelleth and they be of great fellowships
mighty upon the xii moneths of the yeere by the
precept of the Creato^r of it which said the world be it and
all angels be, and were before it, and there be vii
powers before the face of it, and to eache of them is
given might and hath a day of the moneth and of the
weeke. And of them some be standing in environ and
some be sitting in chaires with great honor serving
to the Creato^r, and they be evermore ready and
bound to go out and to enter, to come and to go and
to do all good and evill whatsoever is made and to
enchant and to put downe and to cover prily things
and to discover or make revelacion. And all this that
we have said by the manndmt of God, and all the

---

[1] This "b" is smudged out.

Liber Salomonis

more angells and lesse, and the princes of them
with their powers with their odors or with their fellowships
they clipeth themselves everiche with their names
and which be selly . i . heigh or sovereigne evermore
they praise God the Creato^r which formed them. And also
all the powers of all heavens in the moneth and
in the day in which he formed them and they all
speaking to himself togither as men. And Raziel said
that these angells wrote these names and this booke.

[35^r]
And he said that there be 7 angells mighty
upon vii starres and these bene potestates or
powers mighty upon vvi dayes of the weeke And they
be keepers of them and of the xxiiii howers of the day
and of the vii heavens and of the xii signes and of all
other things that governeth the worlde. And Raziel
said to Adam beholde knowe and withhold these vii
powers or potestates which have power in the vii heavens
and the vii starres. The names of which be these Sabaday
that is Saturnus. Zedek that is Jupiter. Madim that
is Mars. Hanina that is Sol. Noga that is Venus
Cocab . i . Mercurius. Labana . i . Luna. The names of
the vii heavens in which they be borne be these Samin
raquia Siagum Mahum. Macon. Zebul. Arabeck
upon Samyn goeth Luna. Upon Raquia goeth Mercurius
and upon Arabeck Saturnus and so understand
thou of other
The names of Angells that have power upon the
vii starres and goeth upon the vii heavens and other
while in their chaires be these Capziel. Satquel
Samael. Raphael. Amael. Michael. Gabriel.
And the power of these is that Capziel is the power
of Sabaday. Satquel of Zedek. And Mamael of Madyn
and Raphael of Hanina. Amael of Noga. Michael
of Cocab. Gabriel of Lubona. And everiche of these
sytteth in his heaven. And the meynees of them all about
and there be divers colors as white blacke red
yellow greene leady pardi viati medled overgilt and
of the color of a pecocke fether and of many other colors
These be the Angels that have power upon the 12
moneths of the yeere. The names of the moneths

Sepher Raziel

[35ᵛ]
be these Nisan yar zinantamus abelul Tisirin
Marquesuam quislep tobez or thebeth Sabat adar
pladar postm♃ The names of potestates be these
And they be 12 capitalls, that is one upon everiche
moneth of Luna and the rather that is the other is
Oriel Sasuyel Amariel. Noriel. Biraquel magnia
saciel. And everiche of these hath so many potestates
helpers more or greater as there be sayes in the
moneth or many other servants of them. And the aforesaid
Angells a man may knowe all things that is
to come in everiche yeere, and in everiche tyme and
in everiche moneth and everiche day and everiche
hower with the proper signes of them who that knoweth
them well if he will knowe of many reynes or fewe
or when they shallbe or if they shall be or no. and
the day and hower when they shall fall. And a man
may knowe by them which is his signe and his starre
and he may knowe of his lyfe if it shall be of long
tyme or of shorte in the worlde sand other things
either for a sicke man or an whole, either for a man
either from a woman. Or he may knowe a subtill understanding
or sharpe he may knowe what is to
come and do with it what he will. And the dayes of
the yeere or of Solis alone (in which may be done the
worching of this booke) 365 and the 4th parte of one
day in the week of dayes. the yeere of Luna be otherwise
360 dayes or four howers and 46 minutes
after the yeere of Luna. And the fulfilling of tyme
in this. In one tyme be 3 monethes, and when the tymes

[36ʳ]
befower sothely till to 12. And knowe thou that Nisan
that is the first moneth entereth in the first day of the
first mone whereat were Luna prima of the moneth
of Martii and so of other. and the first very tyme is
from the first poynt into the which the sonne entereth into
Arietem, till it enter the first poynt of Cancer. And
The 2 from Cancer in Libran, And the third from
Libra to Capricornũ. And the 4th from Capricorno
into Ariente^s. And this is the better distinction of tymes
And in the hower which Raziel gave the booke to Adam
of tymes of moneths and names of things then was Adam

comforted onely wherin thilk day fillen lightnings meved
and thunders and Coruscations appeariden, and there
was in that day great tempest in all the worlde both in the
lande and in the ayre, and in the sea. And in the hower
in which the Angell Raziel opened this booke and gave it
to Adam. Then he gave to him might and strength & surety
in all the words of this booke and myracles that be in it.
And when this booke fell before the face of Adam, then
Adam dread full muche and quoke of great dread And
fell downe unto the earth as though he had bene dead
Then the Angell Raziel said to Adam Rise and
be thou comforted for knowe thou that a very soothfast
spirit hath descended in thee from the hight heavens
which hath lightned thee and hath putt in this hower
in thee knwing and might, and that thou sahlt attaine
that that thou shalt aske. And I say to thee that thou
consider in this booke and beholde in it and by it thou
shalt knowe and understand whatere was and that is

[36ᵛ]
and that shall be after thee And in that hower in
which this booke was given to Adam fier fell upon the
brinke of the floud of paradice And the Angell
ascended by the flame of the fier to the heavens And
an Angell descended in similitude of a white cloude
and spake with him plainely and came to him as a
man well bright and cleere like to the cleerenes
of a starre in his body and full of many other all about
And in ascending when he was severed evermore
Adam was like to a lambe which formed well bright
as the flame of fyre and cleere then the fyre of a
fornace in which golde is purged And then Adam sawe
this and found and knewe that of the Lord of all
worlds which is a great king and mighty things.
This booke was sent for him. And then he considered
and looked in it with holynes and Cleannesse. And
then he beheld in it all things that he would know
in this worlde. And this was the first word that
Adam had with the Angell Raziell And therfore he
considered in it and governed himself by it.
Salomon said upon the foresaid reason above
after that the Angell Raziell said unto Adam that
it behoveth to knowe the tymes and one hower before
another and one tyme before another ffor who that

soweth wheat in Ver it may mot be gathered on
the same Ver. And this is after the temperament
of the party of the northe. And therfore it is necessary
or needful to divide the yeere into 4 parts and a
moneth into 4 partes and an hower into fowre partes

[37^r]
And if thou keepest these divisions and understandest
thou shalt profitt in all that thou wilt, for this is sothe
and all naturall things is made in the tyme and in the
day and in the hower according as the higher or sovereigne
Creato^r hath ordeyned. Raziel said of thou
wilt knowe any thing of this worlde that is of other
that be in the heaven or heavens which be fellowshipped
with the first heavens. Or if thou wilt do any thing yt
be fulfilled to thy will clense thou thy body by 7 daies
that is washe thee and eat thou not a thing of cheste
neither of raven, neither of evill party neither a thing
uncleane neither that is fallen to death, neither a beast
of 4 feete neither other. And eschewe thou thee from
malice and falsenes, and thou shalt not drinke wyne
neither shalt thou eat fishes or any thing which bloud
goeth out. And ioyne thou thee not to a woman pollute
neither menstruate neither enter thou into an house
where is a dead man neither go thou beside the pitt
of a dead man. neither by him that suffereth gonorrhea
and eschewe thou and be thou ware of night lest thou
fall into pollution and keepe thee from lechery and
evill pride. And do thou that thou be evermore cleane
and be thou in Orison or prayer, and keepe thy tong
from saying evill and leasing and fast thou clenely
And keepe thou thy body from doing evill and sinne
And lighten thou the house with orison and prayse the
angells and do thou almes to needy men and charity
and be not thou ioyned to evill men neither to uncleane
and clothe thou thee with cleane clothes the larger that
thou mightest and evermore trust thou unto God and

[37^v]
rise thou early and pray to the Creato^r that he
dresse thee and washe thee and fulfill thy peticion
and thou shalt attayne to that thou askest with God

Liber Salomonis

Nota hanc partem bene
Note well this parte

Primu^m opus istius libri q est necessaiu^m &c
The first worke of this booke that is necessary or
needful in all things that man will do. And when
thou wilt knowe when it is good to do all thing
which thou wilt do. Or thou wilt know when it is good
to do what thing thou wilt of this worlde and thou
canst not any thing thereof understand thou that thou
account by 7 dayes before the first day of the moneth
that is of the moneth of Luna. And in these 7 dayes
ne be thou not pollute, neither eat thou a beast having
bloud, neither drinke thou wyne, neither touch thou
uncleane things, neither ly thou not with a woman
and washe thou thee with cleane water running all
the vii dayes ere the sonne Ascend And hold the
abstinence which we have said and suffume thou
thee when thou were bathed with this ligno aloes
and ambra croco costo camphora and masticke
And then take thou twey quicke turturs and whole without
languor in themselves, or if thou wilt twey white
culvers if thou might have none other. And cut of
the necke fasting with a brazen red knife overgilt
on everiche side cutting. And cut of the necke of that
one turtur on that one side, and that other on that
other, after that drawe out the intrailes but withholde
the bloud in a newe glasen cup & cast it into the fyer.

[38^r]
And wash thou th'entrailes with cleane water. And then
take iii weighte of musk and iii croco and thuris
albi lucidi cinamoni and 10 keyes of gariophylli and
lignu˜ aloes as much And then take 12 grana piperis
nigri and olde white wyne and sandalos and muscu
and camphora and somewhat hony and wyne all these
with wyne, and put all medled in the entrailes of the turturs
and fill them or divide them into 7 parts or 7 members, and
cast on member upon the coles of the fyer in the morrow
ere the sunne arise and that is to understand the 11 hower
of the night. And when thou burnest the members be
thou covered with white cloth and standing thy feete
discalciated that is unhosed and unshowed afterward
the names of angells which be written that is serving

Sepher Raziel

to the moneth in which be written that is serving
to the moneth in which thou doest for they be prayers
and doers there, and knowe thou that each day thou hast
to say the names of angells of that moneth 7 tymes.
And in the 7 dayes thou shalt gather togither the ashen
which thou hast made in thilk 7 dayes of the foresaid 7
members. And the house and the place in which thou shalt
burne be it cleane. And when all this is done thou
shalt dispose or ordeyne a solemne house cleane
severed to thee. And thou shalt spring the aforesaid
ashen upon the earth in the middle of the house and
thou shalt sleep there so that thou shalt do this. And
then when thou entereth the bed thou shalt nempne the
names of the angells strong dreadfull mighty & high
and then sleepe thou. And speake thou with man And then
knowe thou that thou be well certaine and not dreadfull
that there shall come to thee some man and he shall
shew himself to thee in the vision of the night and the

[38ᵛ]
similitude or likenesse of him shall be of a worshipfull man. Then be thou strong and dread thou not
and he shall not leave himself to thee that it be
a vision or a dreame but in very or sooth maner
And aske thou what thou wylte and without doubt
he shall give to thee.

Dixit angelus Raziel volo tibi dicere hoc com=
plemento &c The angell Raziel said I will
say to thee this fulfilling the worching that thou
worke by power and vertue and strength of this
booke in which be written the powers of the moneths
and of dayes ~~and~~ of the yeere and they have power
in everiche moneth and in eache day for evermore
And knowe thou eache man who that governeth himself
with them with cleannesse that they helpeth him
in all his deeds and in all his things. And they
maketh him to knowe all his willes, and they helpeth
him to fulfill at that ever he asketh with great
power and strength and wisedome
The names of the Angells of the first moneth. These   nisan
be the names of the Angells which be mighty and more
mighty in the first moneth which is said Nysan
Oriel malaquiran acia yaziel paltifus

Liber Salomonis

yesmactria yariel araton robica sephatia. Anaya
quesupale semquiel sereriel Malgas Ancason
pacyta abedel ram asdon Casiel nastiafori
sugni aszre sornadaf adniel necamia
caisaat benit quor adziriel
The names of Angels of the second moneth   yar

[39ʳ]
These be the mightier Angells of the second moneth
which is yar in language of Hebrewᵉ Safuel
Saton Cartemat aryel palthia bargar galms nocpis
Aaron manit aadon qwenael quemon abragin yehoc
adnibia parciot marinoc galus gabmion resegar affry
absamon sarsaf alxim Carbiol regnia achlas nadib
absafyabitan pliset. And thou sahlt name the names
of the foresaid Angells of this moneth yar in each thing
which thou shalt name in it and they should helpe thee
and they shall make thee to knowe all thy will.
The names of the Angells of the third moneth. These   Zivitam
be the names of the Angells which be keepers of the
third moneth that is said Zyvan of which the first is
amariel tatgiel casmuch nuscifa almux naamab
mamiazicaraˢ Samysarach naasien. Andas paltamus
abris borhai Salor hac yayac dalia Azigor Mabsuf
abnisor zenam dersam Cefania Maccafor naboon
Adiel maasiel szarhyr cartalion adi ysar. And thou
shalt name these names that be said in all things that
thou doest and thou shalt profitt.
The names of the Angells of the fowrth moneth. These be   Thamuth
the names of the Angells of the fowrth moneth that   Ab elul
is said Thamuth moriel safida Asaf Mazica sarsac
adnyam nagrow galuf galgall danroc saracus remafidda
luliaraf nediter / delgna maadon saamyel amrael
lezaidi Elisafan paschania maday And thou shalt
nempe these names above said in all hit that thou
wilt do and thou shalt profitt.
The names of the Angells of the 5 moneth. These [1]
be the names of the Angells of the 5 moneth that is said

[39ᵛ]
manhi or amariahaya byny madrat amantuliel
cassurafarttis nactif necyf pdgnar tablic mamirot

---
[1] The marginal note here is illegible.

Sepher Raziel

amacia qnatiel reycat qnynzi paliel gadaf
nesquiraf abrac amyter camb nachal cabach
loch macria safe essaf And thou shalt name
these before said in all his that thou wilt do and
thou shalt profitt.

The names of the Angells of the 6 moneth   Ab
These be the names of the angells of the 6 moneth   Elul
that is said Elul. Magnyny arabyel hanyel   marqueslica
nacery yassar rassy boel mattriel naccamarif
zacdon nafac rapion sapsi salttri raseroph malgel
samtiel yoas qualabye danpi yamla golid rasziel
satpach nassa myssa macracif dadiel carciel
effignax. And thou shalt name these names
aforesaid in eache thing which thou wilt do and
thou shalt profitt therein.

The names of Angells of the 7 moneth. These be   Tysirin
Quislip the names of keepers of the vii moneth that is
said Tisirin. Suriel sarican gnabriza szucariel
sababiel ytrut cullia dadiel marhum abecaisdon
sacdon pagulan arsabon aspiramo aquyel safcy
racynas altim Masulaef vtisaryaya abri And
thou shalt name these names abovesaid in each
thing that thou wilt do and thou shalt profitt.

The names of Angells of the 8 moneth. These be   Tobtz
the names of Angells of the eight moneth that   marque=
is said marquesaan karbiel tiszodiel raamyel   sean
nebubael alisaf baliel arzaf rasliel alson

[40ʳ]
naspiel becar paliel elisuaig nap naxas sansani aesal
maarim sasci yalsenac iabynx magdiel sarmas
maaliel arsaferal Manistiorar veaboluf nadibael
suciel nabuel sariel sodiel marcuel palitam. And
thou shalt name these names above said in everich thing
that thou wilt and thou shalt profitt.

The names of the Angells of the 9 moneth. These be the   Quinslip
names of the Angells of the 9 moneth that is said Qwinslep   Scibat
adoniel radiel naduch racyno hyzy mariel azday
mandiel gamiel seriel kery sahaman osmyn sachiel
pazehemy calchihay hehudael nerad minael arac
arariqniel galnel gimon satuel elynzy baqwylaguel
And thou shalt name these names above said in all hit
that thou doest and thou shalt profitt.

The names of the Angells of the 10th moneth. These   Adar

Liber Salomonis

be the names of angells that have might in the 10th
moneth that is said Thebeth Anael aniyel aryor
naflia rapinis raaciel pacuel hahon guanrinasuch
aslaqwy naspaya negri somahi hasasisgafon gasca szif
alzamy maint xatinas sargnamuf oliab sariel Canyel
rahyeziel pansa insquen sarman malisan asirac
marmoc. And thou shalt name these names in it that
thou wilt do and thou shalt profitt.

The names of the angells of the xith moneth. These be the   pladar
names of Angells that keepe the xith moneth that is said
Cynanth and which have might in it Gabriel Israel natriel
gazril nassam abrisaf zefael zamiel mamiel tabiel
miriel sahumiel guriel samhiel dariel banorsasti
satyn nasyel ranfiel talgnaf libral luel daliel guadriel
sahuhaf myschiel And thou shalt name these names before
said in all thing that thou doest in the moneth & thou shalt fulfill

[40^v]
[1] The names of Angells of the 12 moneth These
be the names of the 12 moneth that is said Adar
romiel patiel guriel laabiel addriel cardiel aguel
malquiel samiel sariel azriel paamiel carcyelel
amaluch parhaya ytael beryel cael tenebiel pantan
panteron fanyel falafon masiel pantaron labiel
ragael cetabiel nyahpatuel. And thou shalt name
these names in all things that thou doest and thou
shalt profitt.

The names of Angels if the 13 moneth. These be
the names of angells of the xiii moneth Bisertilis
which is said Adar the laste in marche lantiel ardiel
nasmyel celidoal amyel magel gabgel sasuagos
barilagni yabtasyper magossangos dragos yayel
yoel yasmyel stelmel garasyn ceyabos sacadiel
guracap gabanael tamtiel. These names abovesaid
thou shalt name in all things that thou wylte, and
they shall ful fill all thy will with fasting & washing
and suffumigacion and cleanenesse. And thus
understand thou of every worke. And knowe thou
that the moneths of the Hebrewes and the moneths
of Romans be evened upon the moneth of marche
and knowe thou well this number and thou shalt
proffitt.

---

[1] There is no marginal note here, or marking of the 12th or 13th months.

Sepher Raziel

Scias quod postquaˢ diximus de mensibus &c
Knowe that after that we have said of moneths nowe
we will say the names of the dayes of the weeke with
his angells full strong and mighty upon everiche day
and everiche in his day

[41ʳ]
The names of yᵉ angels yᵗ serveth in yᵉ day of Solis
And these be the names of haie~ and his angell be these
Daniel Elieyl Saffeyeyl dargoyeyl yelbrayeyl comaguele
gebarbayea faceyeyl caran neyeyl talgylnenyl bethaz
rancyl falha hyeyl armaqnieyeyl roncayl gibryl
zamayl mycahe zarfaieil ameyl torayeil ronmeyeyl
remcatheyel barhil marhil barhil mehil zarafil
azrageyl anebynnyl denmerzym yeocyn necyl hadzbeyeyl
Zarseyeyl Zarael anqnihim Ceytatynyn Ezuiah
Vehichdunedzineylyn yedmeyeyl esmaadyn albedagryn
yamaanyl yecaleme detriel arieil armayel veremedyn
unaraxxydin These be the mighty angels on the day
of Solis, and name thou them worthily & thou shalte
proffitt.
The names of the angels in the day of Luna
These be the names of angels that serveth in the
day of Luna. Semhahylyn. stemehilyn Jasyozyn
Agrasinden Aymeylyn Cathneylyn Abrasachysyn
Abrasasyn Layzaiosyn langhasin Anayenyn nangareryn
aczonyn montagin labelas mafatyn feylarachin
candanagyn Laccudonyn Casfrubyn bacharachyn
bathaylyn anmanineylyn hacoylyn balganarichyn
aryelyn badeilyn abranocyn tarmanydyn amdalycyn
sahgragynyn adiamenyn sacstoyeyn latebayfanysyn
caybemynyn nabyalni cyzamanyn abramacyn lariagathyn
byfealyqnyn baiedalin gasoryn asaphin dariculin
marneyelin gemraorin madarilyn yebiryn arylin farielin
nepenielin branielin asrieylin ceradadyn These holy angells
in the day of Luna thou shalt name worthily and
thou shalt profitt.
The names of angels of the day of Martis
These be the names that serveth in the day of martis

[41ᵛ]
And they have power upon red mettall and in his
worches. Samayelyn Tartalyn dexxeyl racyeylyn
farabyn cabyn asymeylyn mabareylyn tralyelyn

rulbelyn marmanyn tarfanyelyn fuheylyn ruffaraneylyn
rabfilyn eralyn enplyn pirtophin brofilyn
cacitilyn naffrynyn impuryn raffeylyn nyrysin
memolyn nybirin celabel tubeylyn haayn reyn
paafiryn cethenoylyn letityelyn rorafeyl cannyel
bastelyn costiryn monteylyn albeylyn parachbeylyn
alyel uaceyl zalcycyl amadyeyl usaryeyel emco=
deneyl dasfripyel unleylyn carszeneyl gromeyl
gabrynyn narbell

  The names of the angels y^t serveth in y^e day of Mercury
These be the names that serveth in the day of
Mercury. Michael Zamirel beerel dufuel
Aribiriel boel bariel meriol amiol aol semeol
Aaon berion farionon kemerion feyn ameinyn
zemeinyn cananyn aal merigal pegal gabal leal
amneal farnnial gebyn caribifin ancarilyn
metorilin nabiafilyn fisfilin barsfilin camfilin
Aaniturla feniturla geniniturla elmia calnamia
rabmia rasfia miaga tiogra bee ylaraorynil benenil
The names of angels in the day of Jovis
These be the names of Angells that serveth in the
day of Jovis Sachquiel pachayel tutiel osflyel
labiel raliel beniel tarael snynyel ahiel yebel
ancuyel Jauiel Juniel amyel faniel ramnel
sanfael sacciniel galbiet lafiel maziel gunfiel
ymrael memieil pariel panhiniel toripiel abinel
omiel orfiel ael bearel ymel syymelyel traacyel

[42^r]
mefeniel antquiel quisiel cunnyryel rofiniel rubycyel
Jebrayel peciel carbiel tymel affarfytyriel rartudel
Cabrifiel beel briel cherudiel
The names of angels in the day of Veneris
These be the names of the angells that serveth in the
day of Veneris Hasneyeyl barnayeyl uardayheil
alzeyeil szeyyeil uachayel zesfaieil morayeil borayeyl
apheieyl arobolyn canesylyn anrylin zarialin marilin
batoraielyn kelfeielyn azraieylin ambayerin ayayeylin
cadneirin alserin afneirin abneyrin nonanrin eazerin
orinyn gedulin hareryn nanylin halilin himeilin resfilin
noraraabilin hatheylin laudulin et effilin thesfealin
patnilin keialin lebraieil ablaieil talrailanrain
barcalin bahoraelin

Sepher Raziel

The names of angels of the day of Saturne
These be the names of angels that serveth in the
day of Saturne or Sabat. Micraton pacryton
pepilon capeiel themiton alsfiton chenyon Sandalson
panion almyon expion papon calipon horrion melifon
aurion temelion refacbilion ononiteon boxoraylon
paxilon lelalion onoxion quilon quiron vixalimon
relion cassilon titomon Murion dedion dapsion
leuainon foylylon monichion gabion paxonion xysuylion
lepiron belon memitilon Saron salion pion Macgron
acciriron felyypon ymnybron raconeal zalibron
These holy angells and blessed be they names in all thy
very workes and keepe thee with them cleane and thou
shalt profitt.
The names of howers of ye night

Ista sunt propria noia horar˜ noctis prima hora &c
These be proper names of howers of the night. The

[42^v]
first hower of the night is said zedrin. The second
biroel the third caym the fourth hacir the
fifth zaron the syxt zzya the seventh Nachlas
the eight Thasras the nynth Saphar The tenth
Halaga The eleventh galcana the xiith Salla
And these be proper names which the xii powers of
the night have. And thou shalt nempne in these
that thou doest and thou shalt proffitt.

 These be the names planets and of their
 angels by the Elements these be the proper
 names

Ista sunt noia ptar˜ 7 et angelor˜ super 4 eta &c
These be the names of the 7 planets and of the
angels upon the 4 elemts as is fyer aire earth
and water for without these and without the 7 above
we may not do anything. The first is the highest
Sabaday and Sabaday is said in the fyer campton
In the aire Srynongoa. In the water Synyn and
In the earth onion. And the names of angels of
Sabaday upon the fyer be these 3 Libiel nybiel
phynitiel. And upon the aire be these 3 Arfigyel
gael nephyel. And upon the water be these Almemel
hoquiel fulitiel. And upon the earth be these Lariel
tepyel esyel. Zedet is nempned upon the fier

Liber Salomonis

Pheon upon the ayre fidon And upon the water
Calidon and upon the earth Mydon. And the names
of the angels of Zedek upon the fyer be these three
Tinsyel Necanynael fonyel. And upon the water
be these 3 Meon ykiel yryniel. and upon the earth

[43ʳ]
Palriel tufiel quyel. These be the names of
the third which is Madyn upon the fyer it is said
Roqnyel upon the aire pyryel upon the water
Tasfien upon the earth Ignofon And the angels
of Madim upon the fyer be these three Kasiel
Cabryel raloyl. And upon the aire be these three
pyroyinel flatoniel carbiel and upon the water
be these three Cazabriel pasaliel zebaliel
These be the names of haie~ upon the fire it is said
yeye upon the aire Don. And upon the water Agla
And upon the earth On. And the angells of haie~ upon
the fyer be these 3 dandaniel Saddaniel ellalyel
And upon the aire be these 3 Karason berriel
oliel. And upon the water be these three Muracafel
pecyrael Michael. And upon the earth be these
homycabel lucifel locariel. Noga is the 5 and
is nempned upon the fyer Dusuyon and on the aire
Clarifon and in the water Narubni and in the
earth Cabras. These be the three angells of Noga
upon the fyer Capciel debitael deparael. And upon
the aire Camirael Cakaziel neraziel and upon
the water Saloniel emyel expaoniel. And upon the
earth paziael amurael salainel These be the
names of Cocab upon the fyer it is said Piztal
and in the aire Cabran and in the water facayl
and in the earth tarzon. And the names of angells
of Cocab upon the fier be these paradiel darifiel
dameyel. And upon the ayer be these ramatiel
loriqniel bengariel. And upon the water be these

[43ᵛ]
Rinafonel Mellyfiel Alatiel And upon the
earth these Alapion beriel rabiel These be
the names of Labona upon the fyer it is said
Claron. And upon the ayre becyla and upon the
water tasfit and upon the earth pantours. And
the names of the angells of Labona upon the fire

Sepher Raziel

be these Gabriel paticael daliel and upon the
aire be these barasiel ztaziel. and upon the
water be these Caziel memyiel pazicaton and
upon the earth be these: Simyllyel Lafaqnael toniel
And name thou these abovesaid in all hit that
thou doest and evermore Consider thou the planet
with which thou wilt worche and thou shalt
proffitt.

  The names of the hais in 4 tymes

Ista sunt noia caelor~ in quatuor temporibus &c
These be the names of the heavens in the 4 tymes
In the first tyme first it is nempned Hacibor
In the second rumcaqnia. In the third Mesfisnogna.
In the fourth Saaemaho. These be the
names of the heavens in the 4 tymes. And when
thou wilt worche and worke, name thou the
names of the heavens in the tyme in which thou worchest.

  These be the names of ye fire in the 4 tymes
In the first tyme the first is named quoyzil in
the second Enlubra. In the third Mezayn In the
fourth aybedyn. And these angels have might upon
the fyer and in the flame Michael rafael rasoiel
acdiel roqniel myriel Indam malqniel gazriel

[44^r]
amynyel cariel yafrael And these thou shalt name
evermore when thou doest any thing in the fyer.
These be the names of the aire in the 4 tymes
in the first tyme it is said ystana in the second furayl
in the third Oadion in the fourth gulynon And the
names of the Angels that have might upon the aire be these
rafael quabriel micha^el[1] cherubyn ceraphin
orychyn pantaceren micraton. Sandalfon barachiel
ragehyel tobiel And name thou them in all thinges
that thou shalt do in the aire and thou shalt proffitt
well with the helpe of God.

Ista sunt noia aquar~ et maris in quottuor temporibus &c
These be the names of the waters of the sea in the 4
tymes. In the first tyme it is nempned Angustiz
In the second Theon. in the third Maddrylk. In the

---

[1] Above ^ is the letter *r*.

Liber Salomonis

fourth Sebillgradon. And the names of angells of the
waters of the sea be these Urpeniel . Armariel
yyamnel abrastos Sapiel uiotan oriel bachmyel
[1] porackmiel acceriel galliel zsmayel. And name thou
them upon waters and upon the sea and thou shalt p^{ro}fitt.

These be the names of the earth in the 4 tymes
In the first tyme it is said ingnedon. in the second
yabassa, in the third Coliel. In the fourth Aradon
And the Angells of the earth be these Samael
yatayel baraniel oriel arfaniel latgriel daniel
affariel partriel bael byeniel. And thou shalte
name these names of Angells upon the earth in these
that thou hast done in it
These be the names of lownesse in the 4 tymes
In the first tyme it is said Hahan in the second
Cipaon. And his angell is Jacyel in the third

[44^v]
meresac and his Angell is Ababaot. In the fourth
aycyhambabo and his angell is Caaniel
These be the names of the 4 parties of the world
in the 4 tymes
In the first tyme the East is said Acbedan
in the second Cardrenac. in the third Abryel
in the fourth Acritael.
These be the names of the north party in the foure
tymes In the first tyme it is said Henniyna
In the second tyme Abodich in the third galdidur
in the fourth Rabbifor
These be the names of the west party
In the first tyme Mahanahym. In the second
Sugor. in the third Zarzir in the fourth Rabiur
These be the names of the south party
In the first tyme Naufor. in the second Alparon
in the third Machniel. in the fourth Thaumy
These be the names in the 4 partyes of the world
In the party of the east these have might or
power guabriel raphael uriel
In the party of the north these Adriel yamiel Zabdiel
In the party of the west these Adtriel Samael Joel
And in the party of the south these Corabiel Sariel Michael
And name thou them upon all things that thou

---

[1] Marginal note "o."

Sepher Raziel

doest in the 4 partyes of the worlde and thou shalt proffitt.

The proper names of ye planets in the 4 tymes
Ista sunt noia stellar~ qui sunt et vadunt &c
These be the names of the seaven starres that be

[45^r]
and goeth in the 7 heavens everiche by himself Sabaday Zedek Madyn Hanina noga Cocab Labana And ewiche of these hath his owne proper name upon the fowre tymes of the yeere as we shall shewe in this chapter beneath. And Salomon said in explanation of this place. Wherfore everiche planet and eche thing beforesaid changeth his name in each tyme for his thing ffor heere standeth some tree and from thilk tree cometh to us fowre things. And of these fower things the first is when it burgeoneth the second is the flower. The third is the fruite the fourth is the seed when it is in it. Therfore the sonne is said in the first tyme hott and moist. In the second hott and dry In the third Colde & dry in the fourth Colde and moyst. These be the worchings of the sonne, and the propertyes of it upon all things for another reason the names of things abovesaid be changed in fower parts of the yeere, for ewiche tyme hath his nature and his Complexion by himself as we have said of water which is in the first tyme temperate and in the second heat and in the third rotton and in the fourth Congealed And so other things of the worlde ewiche by himself. The exam= ple whie Raziel put his name to eache thing. In everiche thing be the 4 lords that have might in eche thing and everiche in his tyme. And it is said that there be 4 elements whereof one is fyer that hath might in the first tyme and so other. Wherefore knowe thou that everiche thing changeth his name

[45^v]
As first we say a man a childe and then a yongling and then a middle man in the fourth tyme an old man. And so things changeth their names who will cleape them a leader and this is in a man And so understand thou of Mettaile and in all things

Liber Salomonis

that waxeth and liveth. And Salomon said and
all other that it was more inst that eache thing
should have 7 names then 4 for that all they
might descend of 4 bodyes, and to them is given
all the might Sothely they put 4 names to
everiche thing that it were more easy to worche
these 4 names be assigned upon the city of David
my fathers and myne which had many names. Sothly
the wiseman Isaac the wiseman said that the
first name was Remusale, and then Jebusale
Jeroboam Jerusalem. And these names this
City received for 4 Lords that were in yt And
everiche putt to his proper name And for this
like things of this worlde receiveth 4 names
in themselves or 7 or more after that God hath
ordeyned. And therfore no man marvaile of these
names of things in 4 tymes. In the higher heaven
that is the first from the ou/ [1] party and it is the 7
from the neather in it serveth Sabaday and his
angell Capciel. In the first tyme Sabaday is
said Cuerues. In the second Palicos. In the third
Quirtipos in the fourth Panpotes. In the sixth serveth
Zedek and his angel is Satquiel and the
name Jovis In the first tyme it is amonor. In

[46ʳ]
second Sahibor. In the third Sayin. In the fourth
Eanynyel. In the 5 heaven serveth Madim and for
his angell Balquiel. And the name of Martis in the
first tyme is said Aaryn. In the second Daron. In the
third Bearon. In the fourth Pantefos. In the fourth
heaven serveth Hamina and his angell Dandaniel
In the first tyme the name of Solis is said halyom
in the second Adocham in the third Cantopos. In the
fourth Pantasus. In the third heaven serveth Noga
and his angell Adzdiel. In the first tyme the name
of Veneris is said Aporodicy In the second Calizo
in the third niniptz. In the fourth Pontos. In the
second heave serveth Cocab and his angell Satquiel
In the first tyme Mercurius is said Armis In the
second Angocus. In the third Tholos. In the fourth
Ancholos. In the first heaven serveth Labana and

---

[1] This is probably "outer."

Sepher Raziel

his angell Anael. In the first Luna is said Salmi
in the second Sarico. In the third Naspilij. In the
fourth Afriqnym. And knowe thou that thou shalt
nempne the names in their fowre tymes and thou shalt
profitt when thou shalt knowe any thing of them.

Liber Salomonis

Heere beginneth the fifth booke
that treateth of Cleannesse

Dixit Salomon revelatũ fuit nitri de isto   [Book 5]
libro &c Salomon said It was shewed to me of
this booke of Raziell and many angells after that
I had the booke and of these which nourished powers

[46^v]
and vertues and matter and strength of the
potestates above, and that by the manndement and
obedience of the Creato^r or maker of the worlde
And they said thus Salomon thou hast asked witt
and wisdome and fairenes and might in will com=
pleate and named full great for evermore upon
earthes.
And knowe that all kings and lesse men shall
come after thee and which should heere speake of
thee should love thee and worshippe thee and should
set price of thee and should prayse thee and
keepe thou this booke, and worche thou with it with
reverence and cleannesse. And Salomon said
to the benigne angell Natanael which hath might
in thaire and this evermore ~~was~~ was fellowshipped
to Salomon which be thilke 7 bodyes which we seene
above bright fayre cleane and cleere w^h ceaseth
never to go neither the wayes of them be void
and they fayleth never but evermore dureth going
their wayes. And it that farryeth more in going
his way fulfilleth it in 30 yeeres. And then they
appeareth such as they were before and which went
before thus they sawe. And thus it us said that
they should be how long God would. And thus
I say of an hundreth yeeres and a 1000 that they
never be changed neither in meving but we have
found them as the Prophets and other olde men
founden. And the angell Natanael said to Salomon.
The 7 bright bodyes which thou seest above

[47^r]
above be put beneath And they in going upwards
holdeth in balance or in rule the 4 elemts beneath
And therfore the meving of them ceaseth not for such
might the Creato^r gave to them. And knoweth thou

that the matter of them is simple and pure without cor=
ruption and evermore durable. And the state of them
is likenes to the Lord that formed although they obey
to him in all things. And Natanael said further=
more to Salomon knowe thou that in the heavens of
the 7 bright bodyes be angels without number mighty
in all thing, and everiche of them hath his proper
mighte and his strength and vertue. And they be
unlike among themselves as men togither or other
beasts And everiche serveth of his office to the creato^r
that formed them or made them. And Salomon
said to Nathaniel which is the lyfe or the might or the
service that these angells doth. And Nathaniel said
the lyfe of them is of cleannesse of Orison and of
trustines and the might of them is of suffumigii
holocausti et sacrificii. And the service of the is when
the Creato^r woll they go from place to place when
any cleane man hath prayed to the Creato^r as it
beseemeth And then they do good or evill as the creato^r
will for in them is power science & will complete
And Salomon said which be these 7 bright bodies
and how be they named and of what thing serveth
everiche And Nathaniel said that same that Raziel
said to Adam, the higher of these that goeth slower
is said Sabaday and all the realmes of his heaven be

[47^v]
full of Ice snowe and haile and wrothe ranco^r
and Coldenes And all the angells that bene there
bene clothed with darkenes full darke. And the great=
nes of them be full high and full long and small
and upon the earthes and upon divels and upon dark=
nesse and coldeness and drinesse. And this hath
power upon wyndes of this nature And they have
power of doing good and evill And the angell of it
is Beel crowned upon all other. In the second heaven
[1] standeth Zedek and all the realmes of him.

   Dixit Salomon rex filius regis David &c
Salomon the king said the sonne of David that
was king of Jerusalem of Jury and Damaske
of Egypt Lord of Babilony prince of science

---

[1] Margin note "for like."

Liber Salomonis

covetouse of cleannesse ensearcher of privityes
keeper of good true men, avoider of leasing of
poore men, of vertues desire upon l^{c}re vertues and
speedfulnes of words busily thinking and most
subtilly in mynde insearching. I have enquired and
knowe that in wordes of power vertue and effecte
and of all humo^{rs} whole and health and there may
be sufficient fulfilling. And he said I see that
the most fame is of wise men and prophetts by
words and books which they have left into testimony
of them And I see that the sonnes of Adam and
of Hermes and of Noe and their sonnes & many
other prophets have left books by their death by
which they should clarify their fame and anents men

[48^r]
glory should remayne. And I see that my father
king David compowned or made some booke in which be
conteyned all orisons which he might knowe and fynde
which sothely latin men that is Romanes clipeth the
psalter which sothe it is if prayers alone and of holt
names of the creato^r it is names the head of Orisons.
In the same booke king David wrote all things that
ever he might knowe of patriarke and of old wise men
to the praising of the creato^r And I king Salomon
sothely long studyeng in holy words with vertues and
miracles I founde to be while there is fulfilled in eche
thing worching trust and will sawe in the books in which
while I studies long found and knowe that Adam and
Hermes and Noe and Moyses and many other most wise
men had great privityes & vertues in their bookes.

Cu~ ergo veteres et antiquos Sapientes &c
When therfore I understand old wise men to have
made bookes how or with what wytt or with what arte
I might knowe the sciences of all the aforesaid
I enquired and there answered unto mean old man of
good mynde and understanding which was cleped zebraymayl
And I said Adam had a maker and a m^r that is to say
o^r Lord his maker and gabriell to m^r ffurthermore
Hermes the discreet and most wise man and Moyses
had a master and a friend that is to witt Cretu^s Also
Aaron sothely had a friend of which therfore is made
resistance that a wise man may not be without a m^r

how arresteth it thou in thee that two may be wise without
one m^r But that thou be wise these I knowe to be

[48^v]
necessary to thee. A wise m^r and discreete long
and continuall study many olde bookes of great wise
men made oft and ofter over red profitt & amended
glad and continuall health of thy body long lyfe
without cares and travailes quiet. The Salomon
said to the wise man Is not this possible to be done
by a shorter way then that thou hast said above
Zebraymayl answered king by a lighter & shorter
way then this ne unknowe thou not to may be done
To whom Salomon said How therfore to whome
the wise man answered agayne saying Open thou
privily and fully the arke of the Testant no man
knowing or understanding in which all secrets or
privityes and olde wisdomes and words of great
power and of vertue thou shalt fynde By which
not only thou shalt knowe things passed but
these also that be present and likewise these that
be to come. The Salomon answered agayne
saying for this that thou hast answered to me I
give thanks to that high and blessed creato^r which
reigneth after that it pleased to him all things with word
alone he formed or made. And there is not any
more noble or mightier then he without whome no
vertue or power is which giveth wisedome to wise
men, he is that is of all things the fyrste sithe
he is without beginning and of all things the last
sith there is no end of him. This is of all thinges

[49^r]
maker and none ymade of whome the raigne or
raigning is and shall be and of whome all worke be
good and of whome he will over all is free sith there
is none that may againe say to him. Whereupon Salo=
mon trowing or trusting to Zebraymayl made the
arke of the testament to be brought before him. And
he sought all the bookes of Moyses and of Aaron of
Adam and of Noe and of their sonnes and of Hermes
and of other prophetts, and of others which he might finde
of the miracle of words and the vertues of them And

Liber Salomonis

he sought all the old Idolls of heathen men & Images
of divers tongs having writings and all things graven
which might be founde by all the parts of the worlds
And he made them to be gathered togithers into his
pallace, and he brought forth M^{rs} of everiche one
of the 72 which should expound to him privy l^{c}res or
hid Y. C. M. Hebrew Caldy Syriacke greeke
writing and that they should expound to him that
which were hidde. And when the l^{c}res were expounded
he sawe the more party to accord with hit in vertues of
words.

*Rex ergo Salomon fecit arca nocte quadam ape=
riri &c* therfore King Salomon made the arke
some might privily to be opened that in the arke with
reasons afterward he should be learned. And
Salomon said After that the sovreigne and Almighty
Creato^r had infused that grace of his spirit in me
I opened the arke of the testament in which I found all

[49^v]
things which long and studiously before I had sought
Among which I found the booke which is cleped Raziel
which the creato^r sent to Ada^m by the angell Raziel when
upon the brinke of the floud of paradice weeping
thilke creato^r he prayed and of him forgivenes of
his sinnes he besought. And I found the booke which
the creator gave to Moyses in the hill when he
made him partner of his privityes In which three
bookes that is three Orisons I found.
The first the prophets clepeth Semiforas which
the creato^r gave to Adam in Paradice
The second booke is which the creato^r gave to Adam
in paradice in the hower of necessity or need
The third is which the creato^r gave to Moyses
in the hill of Sinay after that he had ful=
filled the fasting.
And Salomon said I found in the arke a pott
full of manna, and the yard of Moyses which was
changed into a serpent and efte from a serpent
into a yard And the tables of the lawe and peeces
of the first l^{c}res which Moyses for the sinnes of the
people in his wrothe he broke in the ground sothely
of the arke I found some golden tables quadtrate

Sepher Raziel

or fowre cornered In which were 15 precious stones
twelve tribes or lynages of Israell by similitude
likened And in everiche stone were written the
holy highe names of the creator of the booke
Semiforas out drawen And I found a boxe of
marble having greene color as Jaspis coloured

[50r]
And in this boxe were 7 figures, and in each figure
7 great and virtuous names of the Creator to Moyses
tolde and other 7 which the creator taught Adam in paradice.
And this is a secret or privity which much leaned
and covered ought worshipfully to be kept. I found also
about thextremityes of arke 24 vertuous rings with
names and figures of the creator writt in Semiforas
with divers colors written or figured And I myself
Salomon had one of thilk rings having mynde to the same
In which I knowe to have founden such vertue that when
I said make it to rayne and it rayned And when I said
eft as thou hast made it to rayne so make thilk rayne
to cease agayne and it ceased. And beside Jerusalem
the same realme aswell of tempests as of raines it did
or made And Salomon said I found Semiforas with which
Moyses made the plagues in Egypt, and with which he dryed the
red sea, and with which also he drewe out water out of the
stone, and with which also he knewe all the cleannesse of his
people, and with which also overcame princes and kings and
mighty men, and with which whatever he would do he did
and that which he would destroy he destroyed And with which
fulfilled it at his owne will

Capitulum explanationis hujus nois Semiforas &c
The chapter of explanation of this name semiforam
And it is that that all divells and wynds and men as
well quicke as dead, and all spirits and all bodyes
dreadeth. Wherefore sothely Semiforas is said or
nempned the first secret or privity and of great old
and much yleaned and hidde and of great vertue and
power to gett what ever he would. Semiforas is a word

[50v]
which ought not to be shewed to all men, neither by
hit (but with great necessity or anguish) ought any
man to worche. And then with dread of the creator

he ought cleanely and meekely and devoutly to nempne
it. Also Semiforas is roote and beginning and
foundament of oryson, exemplar of good lyfe trust of
mans body the oryson or prayer of a Just man thilk
creator dreading. And Salomon said about Semiforas
These be necessary with mekeness fasting, with oryson
trust with clarity cleannesse, with patience meekenes
and constancy of a man without which yow might worche
nothing. And with the which whatever thou wilt thou
shalt gett. When all vertues in worching by Semi=
foras ought to be nethelesse these 7 that is meke=
ness trueth patience abstinence trust clarity
mercy ought in him principally to be had or to
abound.

*Si ergo per Semiforas operari volumes oportet
quod simus &c* If therfore we will worche
by Semiforas it behoveth that we be bright or
cleane of body and in trust stedfast and from
falsenesse and leasing fully departed. It behoveth
also to dread the creator and the creatures of
him among which we ought to dread most the sonne
which giveth to us light and darkenes colde and hott
which is cause of changing of tymes and of temperment
of the aire and of herbes. We ought also to knowe
the beholdings of the moone and the moneths which
by hit 12 and s~, 13 by accounted as the said nyssan
yar tina &c And we ought to knowe the waxing

[51ʳ]
and decreasing of the mone when by it all creatures
as the sea flouds and welles and all the neather bodyes
waxing and decreasing taken bloud in the veynes and
marrowe in the head and the bones. After that
the mone taketh waxing & decreasing they be nourished
in thilk Also the enfusiall or melting of
metalls ne doubt thou not the vertue of the mone
to worche. We ought also to knowe Sabaday .i. Sa=
turne by whome hunger and dearth and all anguish
in londs befalleth. We ought also to knowe & dread
Zedek .i. Jove by whome honor and health and righte=
ousnes and all good is had. We should also knowe and
dread Madim .i. Martem of whome chollers & strifes
and hate and battailes and leasing and all evills cometh.

Sepher Raziel

We ought also to knowe and dread Hanina .i. solem by whome we have light and darkenes & cleerenes and by whome tymes as evill unto good into evill be transmuted or changed. We ought also to dreade and know Nogam .i. Venerem by whom^e we have meate and drinke and all necessaries or things that be needful by whome peace and love and dilection among men is made fast and stable. We ought also to dread Cocab .i. Mercury for he is nigher to us then all except the mone by whome merchandise and venditions or sellings and all seculer things be exercised. Therfore behold y^{ow} those that be said and most the spirits abovesaid and thus thou shalt profitt And whatever thou shalt axe of the creator rightfully thou shalt have it.

Liber Salomonis

[51ᵛ]

    Heere beginneth the Sixth book that
    treateth of the names of heavens

Dixit Salomon oẽs coiter horas et malas &c   [Book 6]
Salomon said All men commonly good howers and
evill, and good dayes and evill, good signes and evil
to be they affirmeth And this with many reasons
they Confirmeth And I my self Salomon have
proved the dayes and howers of madim & Sabaday
which I found full greevous for to worche. I have
proved also the howers of zedek and Noga And I
sawe what ever I would worche of them lightly
I wrought. The howers of Cocab and Labana
otherwhile greevous otherwhile good I have proved
to be And I sawe that in the day and in the hower
coᶜia nothing of my will I might fulfill. And know
thou that the spirits abovesaid anentis divers
men diversty be nempned ffor the first in Hebrew
is Sabaday in Arabicke zoal, in greeke orgrue
fenes in Latin Saturnus it is cleped or nempned
And I say therfore that the first hower of the
day of Sabaday is said Sabaday the second zedek
the third Madyn the fourth Hanina the fifth
Noga. the sixth Cocab the 7ᵗʰ Labana And
the howers of the might ought to be nempned to
them. And knowe thou that by the starres above
said and dayes and howers whatever thou wilte
thou shalt understande And thou shalt knowe the
hidde and privy willes of men.

Cumq per Semiforas operari voluerat &c

[52ʳ]
When he would worche by Semiforas first or ever
he beganne any thing it behoveth him to name the 7
names of Angells, for some angells be upon the seven
heavens, and upon the 7 planets and upon the 7 dayes
of the weeke and upon the 7 mettalls and upon the
7 coloʳˢ and upon the 7 words having power, the names
of the which be these Raphael. gabriel. Samael. Michael.
Saquiel. anael. capciel. And these be ordeyned after
that we ought to name and to enclepe them in the 7
dayes early in this maner.

151

Sepher Raziel

Nota oratione~ o angeli supradicti sitis meae quoins
quam volo quaerere auditors et nutri in oibus adintores &c
That is to say Oh the angells abovesaid be ye the
hearers of my question or axing which I will enquire
or axe and to me in all things helpers. Thilke
sothely which we ought to name upon the 7 heavens
and upon the 7 planetts be these Capciel Saquiel
Samael. raphael anael Michael gabriel. And in all
Things in cleping these angels thou shalt profitt.
When therfore there be 7 heavens that is to witt
Samaym Raaqu Saaquin Maon Mahon Zebul
Araboch And these be 4 partyes of the worlde
that is East West north and south which Angels
in everiche heaven, and in what party serveth we say

  These be the angels of the first heaven

In primo caelo q vocat' Samaym in quatuor ptibus &c
In the first heaven that is cleped Samaym in the
fowre partyes of heaven serveth these
ffrom the party of the north Alael hiaeyel urallim
veallu~ baliel basy unascaiel ffrom the party of the

[52ᵛ]
south these be Duraniel darbiel darquiel hanin
anael nahymel alscini. soquiel. zamel. hubayel bactanael
Carpa;iel. ffrom the party of the East be these
Gabriel Gabrael Odrael Modiel Raamyel Janael
ffrom the party of the west be these Abson soquiel

  Angels of the Second heaven

In secundo caelo quod vocat' Roaquya a parte septen=
rionis &c In the second heaven that is cleped Roaquya
from the party of the north serveth these angells Tyel
Jarael yanael Nenael. Nenel quian. uetamuel ffrom
The party of the south be these Mylba nelia
balyer Calloyel cyoly batriel. ffrom the party
of the East be these Maachin another lᶜre hath
Carmiel Carcoyel betabaat. ffrom the party of the
west is Anulus yesararye in which is written the
names of macareton & in many maners expounded

  Angels of the third heaven

In tertio caelo q vocat' Saaquin a parte Septen=
Trionis &c In the third heaven that is cleped

Liber Salomonis

Saaquin ffrom the party of the north serveth these
Poniel penael penat Raphael carmiel. Doranel.
ffrom the party of the south be these parna sadiel
lyenyel vastamel sanael samyel ffrom the party
of the east be these Satquiel quadissa taramel
taryestorat amael hufrbria another l^{c}re hath heere
last hifaliel

Angels of the fourth heaven

In quarto cael q dicit^r Maon serviunt isti a parte
Septentrionis &c In the 4th heaven that is said
Maon these serveth from the part of the north

[53^r]
Rahumiel haynynael bacyel serapiel matiel serael
In the party of the south be these saoriel mahamel
gadiel hosael vaanyel verascyer. In the party of the east
be these Capiel braliel braaliel raguel gael
Daemael calcas atragon In the party of the west
be these Lacana astagna nobquin sonatas yael yas
yael lael yyel.

Angels of the fifth heaven

In quinto caelo isti sunt q dicitur Mahon. In the
Party of the north serveth these hayel hanyel veal
quiel margabiel saeprel mamyel. In the party of
the east be these Lanyfiel anther l^{c}re hath barquiel
zaquiel sanficiel zoaziel aciel farbiel uranacha
In the party of the west be these Anhael pabliel
uslael Bortaz suncacer zupa faly paly.

Angels of the Sixth heaven

In sexto caelo q vocat^r cebul dices a parte septen=
trionali &c In the sixt heaven that is cleped Cebul
thou shalt say from the north parte est Deus fortis
et potens sine fine that is to say God is mighty
and strong without end ffrom the party of the south
thou shalt say Deus sanctus patiens et misericors
that is to say God holy patient and mercifull ffrom
the parte of the east thou shalt say Deus magne
excelse et honorate per saecula. that is to say great
god highe and worshipped by worlds ffrom the
party of the west thou shalt say Deus sapiens clare

et juste Deus tua clementia et sititate exoro q
quaestione mea et opus meu et labore meu hodie

[53ᵛ]
complete et integer verficere digneris qui vivis
et regnas deus per o. s. s. amen that is to say
God wise cleere and righteous. God thy mekenes
and thy holynes I beseech, that question and
my worke and my travaile do daily fulfill and
hallow thou vouchsafe to ful fill that liveth and
reigneth God by all worlds of worlds so mote it
be Amen.

    Angels of the seaventh heaven

*In septimo cael est Semiforas scriptu in libro
vitae &c* In the seaventh heaven Semiforas is
written in the booke of lyfe. In the name of the meke
and mercifull god of Israel and of paradice
and of heaven and of earth and of the seas and
of hills and of Creatures.

Liber Salomonis

Heere beginneth the seaventh booke
that treateth of names and of the
vertues of them
Incipiunt srae et verba et noia Semiforas &c [Book 7]
Heere beginneth the l͡re and words and names
of Semiforas which god the Creato͡r gave to Adam
in paradice. In which be fowre letters which to the
4 parties of the worlde and to the 4 elements
and to the 4 complexions and to the 4 natures
of the beasts they be likened such they be יהוה הוהי [1]
And these be letters piteously and devoutly and
meekely name thou that peticion in all things
be fulfilled. Salomon said ther be to be said that
there are 7 semiforas. And the first is the

[54ʳ]
Semiforas of Adam in which be conteyned 4 chapters
The first is when Adam spake with the creator in paradice.
The second is when he spake with the angells
The third is when he spake with the divels. The 4th
is when he spake with men and with fowles & fishes and
beasts and reptiles and wilde beasts. The fifth
when he spake with seeds and herbes and trees and
all growing things. The 6 when he spake with wyndes
and with the 4 elemts. The 7th when he spake with the
sunne and the moone and the starres And by the 7 vertues
of Semiforas whatever he would do he did, and
what ever he would destroy he destroyed. And this
Semiforu Adam had when the Creato͡r enspired grace
into him.
          The first Semiforas

Primũ Semiforas est quando creator Adam formavit &c
The first Semiforas is when the creator formed Adam
and putting him in paradice nempned or named

גגגג [2] יהוה הוהי [1] that is to say

---

[1] At this place are eight poorly formed Hebrew letters. Since no transliteration is given, it is impossible to determine with any certainty which letters are intended, given the similarities among the Hebrew letters ה *heh* (H), ח *chet* (Ch), and ת *tav* (T or Th), and, if badly written, between ו *vav* (V) and י *yud* (Y). My best guess is that the letters are supposed to show the *tetragrammaton* forward and backward: יהוה הוהי YHVH HVHY.

[2] Eight letters resembling those discussed in a previous note are written here, but crossed out.

yana. the natures and vertues of which above we
have declared. If in great necessity or need thou
namest this name meekely and devoutly before the
creato^r grace and helpe ne doubt thou not to finde.

The Second Semiforas

Secundũ Semiforas est quando Adã locutus fuit &c
The second Semiforas is when Adam spake with the
Angell which brought to him these letters written the
example of which is such אשר אהיה [2] That is
yeseraye. And the name thou shalt name when thou
wilt speake with angells. And then thy question and thy

[54^v]
worke without doubt shall fulfill

The third Semiforas

Tertiu Semiforas est qu locutus est cu daemonibus &c
The third Semiforas is when he spake
with devils and with dead men and of them counsel
he enquired, and they sufficiently to him answered
And all this he did with these l^cres of which this is
the explanation Adona Sabaoth Adonay Cados
Addona Annora And these l^cres thou shalt name
when thou wilt gather togither wyndes or divels
or serpents

The fourth Semiforas

Quartũ Semiforas est qu aialia et sps &c
The fourth Semiforas is when he bound and
loosed beasts and spirits and that with these 7 names
Lagume Lamizirm Lanagzlayn Lagri Lanagala
Lanatozin Layfyalasyn And when thou wilt bynde
or loose beasts thou shalt name the names abovesaid

The fifth Semiforas

Quintu Semiforas est qu arbores et sementa &c
The fifth semiforas is when he said or names the
7 natures with which he bound seeds and trees And
these they be Lihaham Lialgana Liafar Vialurab

---

[1] Four letters are shown which look like variations of *gimel*, but nothing close to *yana* in Hebrew.

[2] Again, here are eight letters with little or no likeness to the word they represent. Some do not even resemble Hebrew letters.

Liber Salomonis

Lelara Lebaron Laasasilas. And when thou wilt bynde seeds or trees thou shalt name the names abovesaid And thou shalt bynde

The Sixt Semiforas

Sextu Semiforas est magnae virtutis &c The sixt Semiforas is of great vertue and power of which These be the names ~~La~~ Letamynyn Letaglogen Letafiryn Babaganaritin Letarimitin Letagelogin

[55ʳ]
Letafalazin these names thou shalt name when thou wilt that the elemts and wyndes fulfill thy will in all things

The Seventh Semiforas

Septinu Semiforas est magnu et virtuosu &c
The seventh Semiforas is great and vertuous for they be names of the Creatoʳ which thou oughtest to name in eache thing and in all thy workes inclepe. And they be these Eliaon yaena Adonay cados ebreel Eloy Ela Egiel ayom sath adon sulela Eloym deliom yacy Elim delis yacy Zazael pabiel man myel enola dylatan saday alina papym another lᶜre saena alym catinal uza yarast calpi calsas safna nycam Saday aglataon sya emanuel Joth lalaph om via than piel patriceion chepheron baryon yael And these thou shalt name in eache tyme that thou workest upon the 4 elements and whatever thou wilte do by them it shall be destroyed and fordone.

Heere beginneth the Semiforas that Moyses had

Incipit Semiforas q dᵉus dedit Moisi &c Heere beginnethe semiforas that oʳ Lord gave to Moyses and it is divided into 7 Chapters of which the first is when Moyses ascended the hill and spake with the flambé that environed the bush and the bush seemed to burne and nevertheles it burned not. The second when he spake with the Creatoʳ in the hill. The third was when he divided the red sea and passed through it.

[55ᵛ]
The iiiiᵗʰ when the yard was changed into a

157

serpent and the serpent devoured other. The vth is
in which the name that was written in the forehead
of Aaron. The vith is when he made the brazen
adder and the Calf in brasse with the plagues of the
Egyptians he smote. The viith is when he rayned
Manna in desert, and drewe out water of the stone
and let out the Children of Israel from Captivity.

    Cap primu~

Haec sunt noia quae dixit Moises qu est &c These
be the names that Moyses when he ascended the
hill and spake with the flambe Maya afi zye
yaremye une bace sare binoe maa yasame roy
lyly leoy yle yre cyloy zalye lee or see loace
cadeloy ule meha ramechi ry hy fossa tu mimi
sehie nice yelo habe uele. hele ede quego ramaye
habe. And when thou namest these names devoutly
knowe thou thy worke without doubt to be fulfilled

    Capitulu~ secundu~

Haec sunt noia quae dixit creator &c These be
the names which the Creato^r said to Moyses when he
ascended the hill and spake with him Abgincam
loaraceram naodicras pecaccecas acaptena yeger
podayg saccosicum These be the names with which
the temple of Bozale was founded. These be the
names of the prophets when with the Angels with
which the 4 partyes of the worlde were sealed with which
thou mightest do many miracles And beware least thou
name them but chaste and cleane and three dayes

[56^r]
fasting, and what ever thou wilt do by them thou shalt
do trustelye

    Capitulu~ tertiu~

Haec sunt noia quae Moses dixit &c These be the
names that Moses sayd when he divided the red sea
ena elaye sayec helame maace ~~lehaha~~ lehahu. lehahu
alielie q°re azaye boene hyeha ysale mabeha arayha
arameloena qleye lieneno feyane ye ye malice
habona nechee hikers And when thou wilt have
grace of any man, these names thou shalt name devoutly
and meekely and thou shalt have

Liber Salomonis

Capitulu~ Quartu~

Haec sunt noia quae dixit Moses &c These be the names that Moses said when the ^[1] yard was changed into a serpents of the enchanters and the prophets micraton piston yeymor higaron ygniron tenigaron mycon mycondasnos castas laceas astas yecon cuia tablinst tabla nac yacuf And these foresaid names thou shalt name when thou wilt ful fill thy question or axing

Capitulu~ quintu~

Haec sunt noia quae scripta evant in pple Aron &c These be the names that were written in the people of Aron when he spake with the Creato^r Saday haleyos loez elacy citonij hazyhaya yeynimeysey accidasbaruc huadonenu eya hyebu ueu uaha oyaha eye ha hia zalia haliha eyey yaia el ebehel ua ua ua Keepe well these names abovesaid for they be holy and vertuous, and these thou shalt name that thou mayst get what thou askest of the Creato^r.

[56^v]

Capitulu~ Sextu~

Haec sunt noia quae scripta errant in virga Moysi &c These be the names that were written in the yard of Moyses when he made the brazen serpent and destroyed the golden calf when all that dronke in the well had a beard. yana yane sia abibhu uanoia accenol tiogas yena eloym ya uehu yane hayya uehu ahiacmed. And these names Conteyned in themselves in any vertues for with them thou shalt destroy evill and all enchantm^ts And presume thou not to name them in the 7 works

Capitulu~ septimu^s

Haec sunt noia quae Moyses dixit qu pluit &c These be the names that Moyses said when Manna rayned in desort and drew out water of the worke and ledde out from Captivity the Children of Israel Saday samora ebon pheneton eloy eneiobceel messias Jahe yana or eolyen

---

[1] Above the caret mark ^ is written "rod."

Sepher Raziel

When thou wilt do any marvelles, or if thou were
in any anguish these names thou shalt name. And
in all things thou shalt feele the helpe of them
and the vertue. And when thou hast done this
rehearse thou these words by which the names afore
said be expounded Deus vive verax magne fortis
poleus pie sancte munde oi bonifate plene benedicte
due benedictu˜ nomen tuu tu completer nostra compleas
questione tu factor fac nos ad fine uri operis
provenire tu largitor nobis integru complementu
uri operis elagire to sancta et misericors nobis
miserere nomen tuu yeseraye sit per secula benedictu˜
Amen. That is to say God quicke very great

[57ʳ]
strong mighty meeke holy cleane full of all goodnes
blessed Lord be thy name thou fulfiller
fulfill our question thou maker make us to come
to thend of our worke Thou holy and mercifull
have mercy of us Thy name yeseraye be it
blessed by worlds Amen. In the name of souereigne
almighty Creatoʳ I beginne the explanacion of
his name yeseraye that is to say God without
beginning and without end Angilae is the name of
a prophet and properly written in a golden plate of
living men And whoever beareth it upon himself
and how long he hath it with him he shall no
dread sodeyne death.

Heere endeth the booke of Raziel
of the seaven treatises

Liber Salomonis

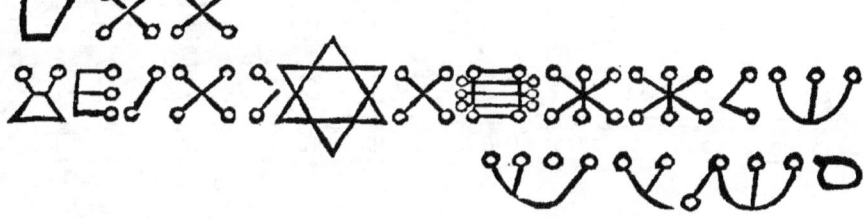

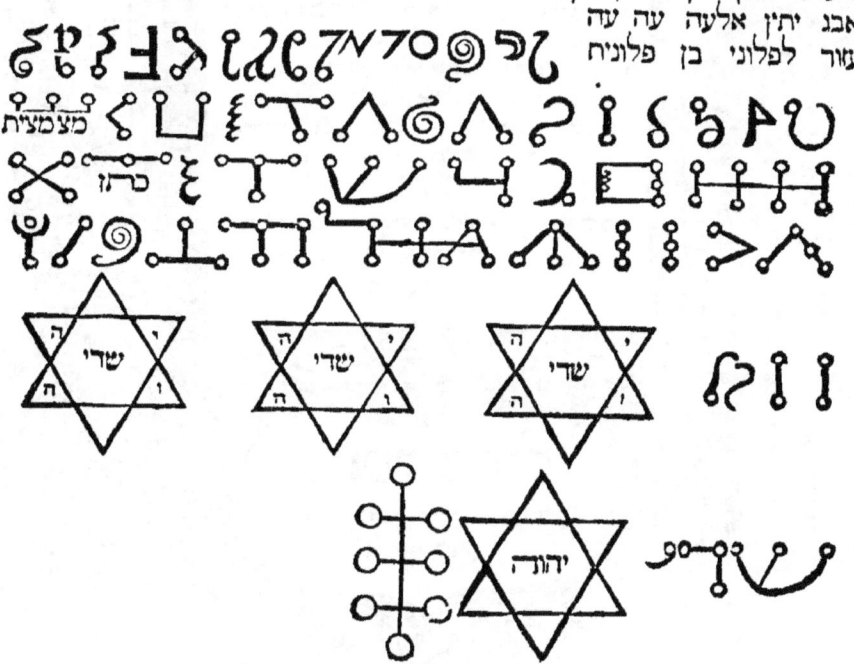

Figure 5: Page from the Hebrew edition of *Sepher Raziel ha-Melakh*, 1701 showing illustrations of amulets which do not occur in the present *Sepher Raziel* text helping to support the fact that it is from a different Raziel tradition.

Figure 6: Title page from the Hebrew edition of *Sepher Raziel ha-Melakh*, 1701.

Sepher Raziel - Liber Salomonis

British Library Sloane MS 3826, folios 2-57

rendered into modern English, with modernised spelling, punctuation, paragraph breaks, word order, and with its contractions expanded

modern English text
edited by Stephen Skinner

Sepher Raziel

Modern English Text

In the course of rendering the text into modern English, the spelling has been modernization, and the punctuation clarified. Paragraph breaks, and occasionally sentence breaks, have been silently introduced to clarify the meaning, and to help make the divisions of the manuscript more clear. In a number of cases the word order has been changed to match modern understanding, without loss of meaning. Contractions both in the Latin and the English have been expanded. The Latin has not been translated, because the scribe, in each case, has provided a translation or summary immediately after each Latin passage. Excess personal pronouns such as 'he' and 'you' used in Middle English[1] have been silently removed. For example 'know you' has been rendered simply as 'know' or eliminated altogether where its repetition becomes tedious. The verb 'to be' has also been adjusted to reflect modern usage. Redundant words have been silently dropped, so for example in a phrase like 'destroyed and fordone', the second word has been dropped as 'fordone' means 'destroyed.'

Where significant words have been inserted to clarify the meaning they are enclosed in square brackets. Simple connective words (like 'and', 'or', 'because', 'then', 'there', 'that'), definite/indefinite articles ('the', 'a'), or prepositions ('on', 'by', 'in', 'over', above'), have been added or deleted silently where necessary to improve the meaning. If there is any uncertainly as to the meaning, then the reader can simply refer to the original text transcription printed earlier in the present book.

Some words will appear to have been arbitrarily changed. This is because a number of words in English have completely changed in their underlying meaning since the time this manuscript was composed. You should not, for example, be surprised to find 'said' in the original changed to 'called' in the modern English version, or 'proved' changed to 'tested', or 'very' changed to 'true' or 'truth', or 'quick' changed to 'living', or 'clean' changed to 'pure', or 'cleanness' changed to 'purity', or 'price' changed to 'high esteem', or 'point' changed to 'degree', or 'star' changed to 'planet' where needed, or 'will' sometimes (as the context demands) changed to 'wish' and 'full' sometimes changed to 'very.' These changes reflect the original meaning and intention of the author, and can be confirmed by consulting any Middle English dictionary.

The original names of stones and herbs have been retained with the modern word, plus alternate Latin word, following in square brackets.

---

[1] Middle English as defined by W. W. Skeat in his dictionary of Middle English, is the period 1150-1580, which certainly covers the presumed date of the present manuscript, 1564.

Liber Salomonis

[*Praefatio* - Preface]

[2ʳ] *In nomine Dei [omni]potentis vibi et veri et aeterni &c.*

In the name of Almighty God living, true and everlasting and outside of all [creation] and which is called[1] Adonay, Saday, Ehye Asereye,[2] I begin to write this book which is called *Sepher Raziel*[3] with all his appurtenances, in which there are seven Treatises complete or fulfilled, that is in 7 books.

Dixit Solomon gloria et laus et cum multo honore &c.

Solomon spoke glory and praise, and with much honour, to the God of all Creatures, he that is singular [unique], which made all things at one time. And he is the one true God and mighty, he alone is, and was, and always shall be, who has no end, nor is there any [other] like him, neither is he like [any other]. And he is unique without end, Lord alone without corruption, holy, pure, meek and great, seeing and hearing all things, wise, and in all things mighty. And I begin this book to make an exemplar, [so] that whosoever has it, blame it not till he has read and heard it all, or somewhat of it, and then praise God, maker of all things.

These are Nine Precepts [to be observed in this practice].

Incipiunt praecepta. Here begins the precepts:

Non credas esse plures nisi unum [Deum solum &] singularum &c.[4]

1. Do not believe [God] to be many, but one unique, alone among all things, which has none like him, and love him with all awe and honour, with all trust and with good will, and a stable [intent], and with might, and with a pure heart.

2. Do not live without law, and you shall be loved by God your Creator, and by folks [your family].

3. Nor do to another man, if you would not [have] the same [done to you].

4. Do not be a liar to the Lord, nor to your friend, but say such truth that is to your profit, and not to do harm.

---

[1] 'Said' is used in the original manuscript in many places where the sense is obviously 'called', and so it has been uniformly replaced with 'called' in these places.
[2] A more familiar transliteration of these Hebrew godnames would read: 'Adonai Shaddai Eheieh Asher Eheieh.'
[3] It later refers to itself as *Cephar Raziel*.
[4] The Latin catchlines have sometimes been supplemented from the Latin of Sloane MS 3847.

Sepher Raziel

5. Do not love associating more with unwise men than with wise men. And always love [2ᵛ] much wisdom and good sciences, and [put] all your will and your life into them.

6. Do not speak before you have thought, and consider it in your heart before you do it.

7. Do not show your private parts to a woman, nor to a child, nor to a fool, nor to a drunken woman.

8. Do not test a medicine, nor its venom, on yourself, before you test it on another.[1]

9. Do not blame a book before you prophesy,[2] nor [confirm] a man to be wise till you have tested [him].

And if you hold these Nine Precepts to you always, you shall profit more and more.

Postquam sensus et scire et posse voluntas vera [vestra] &c.

After that, understanding, knowledge, might and truth will overcome all things with good understanding and discretion. Therefore I will expound, or make open, his book which is of great power and of great virtue. I, Solomon, supply such knowledge, and such distinction and explanation, in this book [so] that every man that reads or studies it, may know whereof he was, and from whom he came.

[*Introductio Libri* – Introduction of the Book]

Know that after I, Solomon, had 30 years [of reign] plus a half [year], [till] the fifth day of the month of Hebrews, which was the sixth day of the Sun being in the sign of Leo. In that day there was sent to me from Babylon by some Prince, that was greater and more reverenced then all men of that time, a book called *Cephar Raziel* [3] which contained 7 books and 7 Treatises.

Nota tempus in quo Solomon fuit quo adeptus istum libre et quomodo et a quo venit sibi

Know the time in which Solomon received the book, and how and by whom it came to him.

Iste liber est magnae virtutis et magnae secretiae

---

[1] This appears to be the wrong way around ethically.
[2] Prophesy here means have the magical powers of a prophet of old, not just being able to foretell the future.
[3] *Cephar Raziel* is an alternate spelling for *Sepher Raziel*, the *Book of Raziel*. In Hebrew it is כפר רזיאל. In the Latin of Sloane MS 3847 it is called '*Sephar Raziel*.'

Liber Salomonis

This book is of great virtue and [has] great secrets. The name of the prince that sent it to me was Sameton, and the two wise men that brought it to me were called Kamazan,[1] and the other Zazont.[2] [3r] The name of this book as expounded in Latin is *Angelus Magnus Secreti Creatoris*, that is to say the 'Great Angel of the Secret Creator,'[3] and in Hebrew *Cephar Raziel*. It is the book of Adam written in the language of Caldey [Chaldaean] and afterwards translated into Hebrew. And each man that reads it knows that in it are all the *Semiforas*,[4] that is to say the great name [of god] complete with all his names, whole and even, and with his virtues and his sacraments.

[The Seven Treatises]

And I found it in 7 books, that is in 7 Treatises. And know that I found the first and the last very dark,[5] and the five middle [Treatises] more plain, and although I found them dark I opened [understood] them as much as I could or might.

And the 7 Treatises of this book are these:

1. The first [treatise] is called *Clavis* [Key] for in it is explained Astronomy and the stars [planets], for without them we may do nothing [magically].

2. The second is called *Ala* [Wing] for in it is explained the virtues of some stones, of herbs, and of beasts.[6]

3. The third is called *Tractatus Thymiamatum* [Treatise of Perfumes] in it is explained [the virtues] of suffumigations,[7] their choice,[8] and their divisions.[9]

4. The fourth is called the *Treatise of Times of the Year*, [*Temporum Anni*], of the day, and of the night, in it is explained when anything ought to be done by this book.

---

[1] 'Karmazail' in Sloane MS 3846. 'Karmazayl' in the Latin of Sloane MS 3847.

[2] 'Zozont' in the Latin of Sloane MS 3847.

[3] Here we have yet another title for this manuscript: *Great Angel of the Secret Creator*.

[4] It is not just the 72 letter name Shem ha-Mephorash. It is written Semhamforash/Semphorax in the Latin of Sloane MS 3847. The Semiforas are the formulae or lists of names given in the last Treatise this book. In two places in the present manuscript, it is also written 'Semiforax.' 'Semiphoras' is also the name of related Solomonic manuscripts mentioned in the Introduction.

[5] Difficult to understand.

[6] In the present text, the supposed explanation of why the second book is divided into four 'wings' is very stretched, artificial and unconvincing, as if the scribe was seeking to justify something he himself found inexplicable.

[7] We have refrained from modernising 'suffumigation' throughout as it is not easily replaceable by a single word like 'perfume' or 'cense', and 'fumigate' definitely doesn't give the right meaning. It means to use perfumed smoke or incense, with the objective of ritually cleansing a thing or place, or to attract or dispel sprits therefrom.

[8] 'Allegationibus' in the Latin of Sloane MS 3847.

[9] The Greek word for incense is *Thymiama*, and becomes *Thymiamata* in the plural (incenses). *Thymiamatōn* (from *Revelations*) is the genitive case of the plural.

5. The fifth is called the *Treatise of Purity* [*Tractatus Munditia*] for in it is explained Abstinence.

6. The sixth is called *Samaim* ¹ [Heavens] for in that Treatise it names all the heavens and their angels, and their operations or workings.

7. The seventh is [called] the *Book of Virtues* [*Liber Virtutum*], for there is explained virtues and miracles, and there are told the properties of the Ark of Magic, and of its figures, and of its provisions.

And then I began to write all these Treatises in a new volume for [just] one Treatise without another serves not to [explain] the wholeness of the work. Therefore I made [3ᵛ] a whole book up of the Treatises. Therefore Salomon said to his writer Clarifaton,² that he could write it, which I know well the languages of Chaldaean, of Indy [Indian], of Hebrew and of Syrian,³ and their right explanation. Solomon secondly said that after Clarifaton had corrected it and had arranged it,⁴ it should be better, and he arranged it in the best manner that he might. And Clarifaton, who was Solomon's writer, said that this book is full of great secrets, and that it is worthy of very great honour. And that it was given to Solomon with high esteem and much love. And every Treatise of these 7 [treatises] was written by themselves. Clarifaton said that it ought to be but one book alone by itself, for none of these [Treatises], said he, would suffice without the others, therefore he said it is necessary that they are all [kept] together.

Whereupon Solomon ordained that all the said 7 Treatises were but one book, as they ought to be, and so they ought to be read and wrought. And he ordained it much better than the philosophers ordained, and he also taught how a man ought to do his work from it. And he put every Treatise by itself and every chapter by itself and arranged all till the end of the book. And he put into this book the Semiforas, that is the book of 17 virtues, how it ought to be written, and with what ink, and on what parchment, and with what pen, and with what man, and in which season, and on what day, and in what night, and in what hour. After that Solomon expounded how the *Book of Razeelus* [Raziel] ought to be kept, purely and with great honour.

Dixit Solomon qui videt et non cognosit &c.

Solomon said, "who sees and knows not, is like he that is born blind and knows not colours, and whoever hears and understands not, is such as if he

---

¹ Hebrew for 'heaven.'
² The Latin version of Sloane MS 3847 has 'Clarephaton' and 'Clarefatoni.'
³ '*Siriacum*' in the Latin of Sloane MS 3847.
⁴ 'Drossed' meaning 'dressed up', hence 'edited.' '*Diregibat*' is the Latin of Sloane MS 3847, from 'dirigo' meaning 'to arrange in order.'

were a deaf man. And who considers and knows not the consideration is, such [a person] is as if he were a drunkard. [4r] And whoever speaks and cannot expound the reason, is as a dumb man. And whoever reads plain books and understands them not, is as if he were a dreamer."

[Qua charta debet Scribi…Quo Encausto…Quo Calamo]

[The Parchment, the Pen and the Ink]

These proverbs Solomon wrote in this book, for Solomon wrote in this book *Cephar Raziel* [1] what the angel said to Adam, who was the first man in this world, and after that, what Moses said to other prophets, in truth, and we believe it to be so.

Dixit Angelus Salomoni ut omnibus tua operationes &c.

The angel said to Solomon that all your workings and petitions shall be fulfilled, and all that you covet shall be made [available], and be in [your] power. It is your duty that when you have this book, or another copy of it, that you write it [out] the first time on virgin parchment, and [see] that it [the parchment] is not filthy, neither [just on the skin] of a dead beast, [but] on vealime (*vitulino*),[2] or on parchment of silk, or on satin,[3] or on clean cloth, or on parchment of a lamb, or on a virgin kid,[4] or on a virgin faun, and this [latter] is better than any other.

And the ink with which you write [should] be [made] of clean [oak] galls, and let it be made with good whole white wine, and with gum,[5] and vitriol, and mastic & thyme and crocus.[6] And the third day when it has taken residence [7] and is cleansed, and strained, add therein a little of *algoba* and

---

[1] The English scribe wrote 'Cepher' or 'Cephar' for 'Sepher', the Hebrew for 'book.' The Latin of Sloane MS 3847 however clearly shows '*Libro Razielis.*'
[2] Vellum, or prepared sheep skin. The reference is to the use of lime to clean the flesh off the skin in order to make it into parchment.
[3] In Sloane MS 3826 this is 'Samatyne' (with 'sattin' written above it), but in Sloane MS 3846 it is just written as 'satin.' This suggests, but it is not in any way conclusive, that Sloane MS 3826 is possibly the older of the two versions.
[4] Young virgin goat.
[5] Usually gum tragacanth.
[6] The wine is the main liquid part of the ink. The oak galls and (small quantity of) vitriol help to remove any oiliness from the parchment at the point where the pen is writing. The gum tragacanth helps glue the ink to the parchment. The mastic, thyme and crocus are part of the magical tradition that the ink should be perfumed. The other necessary, but omitted, ingredient is soot which provides the black of the ink.
[7] Settled.

Sepher Raziel

almea,¹ and add therein good musk, more than the three [other perfume ingredients]. And add therein ambergris and balsamic myrrh, and *lignum aloes*.

And when the ink is made, boil it with mastic, thyme and *lignum aloes*, and with somewhat of Thymiamata ² and Muculazarat ³ and cleanse [filter] it well with a clean thin cloth, and [let] the cloth be [folded] threefold. And afterward put therein musk, *ambram* [ambergris], *almenus & algana*, balsam and myrrh, all well ground & then [4ᵛ] mix all this very well with the ink. And let the ink be still for the space of 3 days well covered, in a fair place. And know that with this ink you shall write all the holy names of God, his angels, and of his saints, and all things in which his holy great name is named and written. And all things that you want will truly be fulfilled, pleasing to your wishes, and serviceable to you. And whatever you put in this ink, [make sure] it is new and bright and pure, and [written with] a good pen.

[*De modo faciendi Calamum* – of the Method of making the Reed]

And the pen that you shall write the holy names, [should] be a green reed, gathered early before the Sun ⁴ arises. And he that shall gather it, [must] be clean & washed in running water, or in a living/flowing well, and also let him be clothed with clean clothes, and [let] the Moon be waxing, with Caput Draconis or with Jupiter, for that they be true [usable]. And when you shall gather [the reed pen], you shall look toward the East, and you shall say thus *"Adonay et Saday juvate me ad complendum voluntatem meam [ac voluntates meas cum] arundine ista."* That is to say "[Adonai and Saday] help me to fulfill my wishes with this reed." And when this is said you shall cut one reed, or two, or as many as you wish, with one stroke. And as Moses said that the knife must be plain, sharp and whole, as though we should [need to] cut a neck with it. And you take the reed with your clean hands, and make of it a gobbet [small piece]. And when you cut the pen, cut it before the Sun arises, or as it arises. With this pen and with this ink you shall write all the names of God holy and several. And as often as you write the name of the Creator, be pure and solemn, alone, serene & in a pure place. ⁵

---

¹ A marginal note offers an alternative to Almea: Alinza.
² Incense, from the Greek θυμιαματον, *thymiamaton*. See *Revelations* 5:8 "bowls of gold full of incenses." See Appendix 1 for modern the equivalents of the other incense ingredients.
³ Not in the OED. 'Mukul' is a type of myrrh produced in Zufar. 'Muql' is a type of bdellium.
⁴ An (indistinct) marginal note: "it must be done in the new of the ☾ [Moon] while the ☾ [Moon] increases, when she applies [moves towards] Caput Draconis, or towards the ☌ [conjunction] with, or △ [trine] with ♃ [Jupiter], for if so the [time] will be very good."
⁵ 'Cleanliness' or purity is mentioned frequently in this manuscript, even to the extent of

Liber Salomonis

And you shall first, before you write, for 3 days be bathed in clean water, but rather you shall be pure for nine days [in] a house or clean place, made very clean with beesoms [brooms], [5ʳ] and washed, watered and censed. And arrange it so that when you write, you hold your face toward the East & write from morning till midday, after that you [may] eat. And after you have eaten and drunk you shall not write anything. And if you wish to write Semiforas, [taking advantage of] its powers, then the number of the [days of the] Moon, should be even.[1] And mostly do it on the day of the Moon [Monday], or in the morning, or of Jupiter [Thursday] or Venus [Friday], & [begin writing in the hour] of Saturn, and of the Sun over all.[2]

And Solomon said, "If you add into the ink the blood of a vowter [vulture], or of a turtur [turtle dove], or of a gander (wholly or all white), the ink shall be much the better, and [have] more virtue. Also I say that if there were *sapher* [sapphire][3] powdered, *smaragdo* [emerald],[4] *gaynisia* & *topasia* [topaz][5] in it, [then] the ink shall be complete or fulfilled."

And with this ink, and with this pen, ought to be written all the names of Semiforas, and know that he that shall write this book ought to be pure & fasting, bathed and censed with precious aromatics, that is with good smelling spices. And so it shall be of great profit to you, and to him that makes it or writes it. And each man that has written this book, or has held it in his house,[6] always [shall he] hold God in his mind, and his holy Angels & [the purposes] for which he has made it. And let him keep in his mind in which time (of the 4 times of the day), he ought to [work], or at what time of the hour. And always let him keep in his mind to his 4 times, in an [appropriate] hour to which they ought to be as *Juvenies* in *Libro Prophetarum*.

---

having one of the seven Treatises wholly devoted to it. Although washing and wearing clean clothes forms part of the requirements, it is really meant in the sense of 'moral purity.' Contrary to the popular impression that magic involves depravity, the emphasis of all serious works on magic, and all serious practitioners, is on the purification and the purity of the operator, so that they are in a sufficiently morally strong position to deal with any 'spiritual creatures', be they angels, spirits or demons.

[1] In other words, only on the 2nd, 4th, 6th, 8th, 10th, 12th and 14th day after New Moon.
[2] The last phrase is not clear, but might suggest 'during daylight hours.'
[3] Symbolic of the Virgin Mary.
[4] Symbolic of Hermes Trismegistus.
[5] Sometimes 'topas' was also used to indicate a chrysolite, peridot or yellow sapphire.
[6] Mediaeval Jews considered the *Sepher Raziel* so potent that the mere possession of the book in the house was believed to help prevent fires, a serious concern in the ghettos of Mediaeval Europe. However, at present we have no certainty that the Mediaeval Hebraic *Sepher Raziel* is connected in any direct way with the present text.

[Liber Primus - The First Book]

[Liber Clavis, the Book of the Key of Astronomy and of the Stars][1]

Dixit Solomon sicut si esset Castrum &c.

Solomon said that [this method is] as though there is a strong castle great, high, enhanced and well [fortified] on each side and with walls surrounded, and the gates in this place are strong and stable, or firm, and with keys closed and locked. Therefore it obliges [anyone] who would open the gates of that closed castle, and wholesomely enter into it, without work or gift [bribe], and without bruising his body [in battle], to have the same [5ᵛ] keys, and none other, of this castle and of its gates and of its closings.

Thus I say that it is [necessary] for [you] to know the stars and their names and their figures and their natures, and when they should be good and when they should be evil. And this I say of [both] the fixed [stars] and of the 7 erratics [the planets]. Consider [also] how the nature of the Circle of the 12 [Zodiacal] Signs [effects it].

And therefore it is the duty of each man that has this book, to hold [understand] it purely, and keep it with great reverence & with great honour. And he who has it, and can read it, let him not read it before he [has a] very pure body, and [then read it] with great understanding. And I make every man know that he ought not to work with this book in vain [disrespectfully], neither without understanding, nor without law or reason. And when any man does to the contrary, [it] as [if] reptiles, or wild beasts do him harm.

And know though you have power, and trust to work by this book, & although you might have great belief in this, you should not work, except with great right or law [on your side], or with much [good] reason. And understand, if on the contrary, you work otherwise by this book than you should, [it] might greatly hinder you: that is to say if you work without [good] reason, or if you are unclean or evil in yourself.

---

[1] The beginning of the first book, the *Clavis,* is not marked in the English manuscript, but as this section begins the discussion of astrological matters, and first mentions keys, it is likely that this was the beginning of the first of the seven Treatises or books, which is called *Liber Clavis* on its last page. The Latin of Sloane MS 3847 marks the beginning of this chapter on the next page where [*Clavis Libri*] is marked. But 12 lines later it re-headines the page with '*De Astronomia Liber Primus*', so its divisions are not quite as logical as they initially seem.

Liber Salomonis

[Clavis Libri]

Clavis istius libri est cognoscere et scire loca

The key to this book is to know and examine the places of the 7 bodies above [the planets], and their natures and their sciences, and their Houses, and all their virtues, after it appeared in the earth to me.

Formata debet esse omnis figura cum exemplo vero

Each figure ought to be formed with a true example, therefore I put the figure of the key in this book,[1] [in order] that no true man, without [good] reason, shall profit by it. And I put in the figure a key with a shaft, to [6r] [symbolize] that there is one solemn Lord, one god, which never had, nor shall have, any even or like to him. In the quadrature [quarter part of the figure], there are four corners that signify that there are 4 Elements, and no more. And in this key is [also] one triangle, which signifies knowledge, might [power] and will, for [without] these three [things] no man may do anything in the world, nor attain to any profit.

[Et dixit Salomon quod hastilo huinum Clavis]

And Solomon said that the shaft of this key is as Raziel said to Adam, with unity or one head; and the quadrate is as the 4 [types of] virtues that are in [stones], herbs, words, and beasts, and they be in the likeness of [the 4] Elements which open and do everything. And in the 7 wards [zones] be 7 Angels which are mighty in the 7 Heavens, and in the 7 days of the week, as furthermore I shall teach you. And the triangle signifies man which is [divided] into body, soul and spirit: and these things abovesaid, lead to all the world, as it was compounded [generated] in highness & lowness.

Pastquam hucusque diximus oportet nos dicere &c.

After what we have said hitherto, it is the duty of us now to say, in this book, that which is said of the key of the 7 brethren [planets]. And these 7 brethren have to divide among themselves 12 realms [Signs], and in each realm are 30 cities [degrees], and in every city are 60 castles and in every castle there are 60 *Caldee*,[2] that is to say *feeldy* [fields?], or wild *forones* [towns?].[3]

And this example Solomon found, and made distinctions, and said, "there is

---

[1] There is no figure or key present in the manuscript. However Guillaume Postel (1510 – 1581), a French Kabbalist, designed a similar key which might have been modelled on this description.

[2] 'Villa campostris' in the Latin of Sloane MS 3847. The meaning is probably rooms.

[3] A metaphor for the 7 planets wandering in the 12 Zodiacal Signs, each one of which has 30 degrees, divided into 60 minutes, in turn divided into 60 seconds of arc.

a father and he has 7 sons [the planets], and these 7 sons are siblings, for they are [born] of the same father. And the eldest [Saturn] is the most heavy among all the others. And the middle [the Sun] is in the middle, and regulates then all. And there it is lightly in the middle in relationship with them, so [no planet] is separated from it [by more than] two [places]."[1]

And the 7 brethren [planets] Solomon said are Sabaday or Saturn; Zedek or Jupiter; [6ᵛ] Madym or Mars; Hamyna[2] or the Sun; Nogah or Venus; Cocab or Mercury; and Labana, that is to say the Moon.[3] Know also the [favourable] Houses of these planets. And Solomon put names to the 12 realms, which are called Signs, of the siblings [the planets], and he begins to make distinctions [between them].

[Attribution of the 7 Planets to the 12 Zodiacal Signs]

And he [Solomon] gave to the fighter, that is to say to Mars, that he should rest, and that he should not fight in the realm of the Sign of Aries, and of this virtue he is in the realm of the East, he also gave him in the realm of the world the sign of Scorpio, that [there] he should fight strongly and that he should never rest, and he is in the eighth realm from the first [i.e. Scorpio].

And afterward he gave to the fair Nogah, that is to say Venus, two realms [Signs], of which one has the half figure of Taurus, which is from the highness of his head with his horns till the navel. And [counting] as the seventh from the first, that is Libra, and after Venus is above in the North, and otherwise beneath that in the South.

And so she has inherited in two parts. And then he gave to the painter (which is the writer) that is Mercury, two realms, of which one has two men embracing [Gemini] that is clinging together, and that other has a fair virgin winged [Virgo], and nevermore would he be divided or departed from women, for those images be such, and he dislikes always to go far from the South into the North.[4]

And he gave to the Malix,[5] that is to say the Moon, for she is always moving, [just] one realm. And for that she will not stand [still] much in her house & her Sign is a fish that is called Cancer, which has many feet, which signifies

---

[1] Using the Earth-centric model, with the planets being in order Moon, Mercury, Venus, Sun, Mars, Jupiter, Saturn, no planet is more than two positions away from the Sun.
[2] Hamyna or Hamina is used in Honorius' *Liber Juratus* to indicate the Sun. Hamina is used in the Latin version of *Sepher Raziel* Sloane MS 3847.
[3] These names are simply the Hebrew names of the days of the week.
[4] The path of the planet Mercury remains close to the ecliptic.
[5] Malix = Matrix? Astrologers thought of the Moon as the womb or 'matrix' of life.

that she will travel much, for she alone is under the other brethren.[1]

And he gave to the middle brother, which is the Lord of all [7r] others [the Sun], and who commands all, and is more adorned and far fairer arrayed, therefore he gave to him one realm very strong in heat, and his Sign is as the Lion [Leo], that signifies him as Lord over all beasts, so is he stronger and more Lordship [aristocratic] than all his brethren.

And there remained two brethren [planets] in the part of the South which [each] take two realms, one about another that he should never overcome in the Sign of the southerly realm. He is a beast with one form in his front [and one in the back, Capricorn], and the sign of that other realm is a man that holds many waters [Aquarius], and his brother [planet] is called the old Saturn.

And then take that other brother [Jupiter]. For heritage, on his right side the realm with the Sign of half a man and half a horse called Sagittarius, and on the left side [the Sign] of Pisces.

[The Nature of the 12 Zodiacal Signs]

Know the nature of the Signs. Solomon said that Aries is a sign fiery hot & dry, choleric, and so is Leo and Sagittarius and they have strength in the East. Taurus is earthy, cold and dry, melancholic & so are Virgo and Capricorn, and they have strength in the South. Gemini is airy, hot and moist & sanguine and so is Libra & Aquarius, and they have strength in the West. And Cancer is watery, feminine, moist and phlegmatic and so is Scorpio and Pisces, and they have strength in the North.

Iam diximus de naturis et signis et eorum complexionibus

Now we have explained about natures and Signs, and of their complexions, so we now mean to explain about their natures, and of the complexions of the siblings [the planets] and what they signify.

[The Nature of the 7 Planets]

The first and highest [planet] is called the old Sabaday or Saturn, the nature of which is cold and dry, for that is [7v] very straight and melancholic, and it signifies father, wrath, and discord in lands.

The second is called Zedek [Jupiter] and he is temperate for he is between the old Saturn and the hot Mars, and Jupiter is hot and moist and sanguine, in savor sweet, and it draws to good air, and it signifies good, honour and virtue.

---

[1] Below all the other planets in the Earth-centric model of the universe.

The third is the fighter Mars, and he is hot and dry, evil and a lover, and fierce, a ravisher & a liar.

The fourth is Hamina or the Sun, middle among the others, hot and mighty and [worthy of] reverence, and all the other brethren are ashamed and regard him with awe, for he is very true and strong.

The fifth is the fair Nogah [Venus], cold and moist, glad, phlegmatic, [appearing] fat and fleshy, and well seeming in all her limbs and countenance, and she signifies good events, and she is very happy among women.

The sixth is the writer and forespeaker [1] Cocab [Mercury], that holds himself with all & serves all, and he signifies writers, news, and voices, after which he shall be with that which everyone holds close.

The seventh brother is Labana [the Moon] & it is Malix, and she is cold and moist, and she signifies brethren and [marks out] each [lunar] month, and [conveys] the commandments of brethren to brethren, after she is parted from them.

Deinde loquamur de septem fribus quare dicuntur clavis &c.

And then we speak of the 7 brethren, why they are called the keys of the world (and this world may not be neglected), and these were formed from the 4 brethren which are called the 4 Elements, and they afterward have signification, understanding and discretion, complete power, honesty and strength, and every [one] may do in his hemisphere that [which is his] empire, as an Emperor in his empire, or as a prince [may do] in his Lordship. Also they have rulership over the 7 parts, which we call the climates. And [8r] know that from these rule all beasts here formed.

And Solomon said that prophets call these brethren the 7 living spirits, and holy and wise men said that they were 7 lamps burning, or 7 candlesticks of light & of life,[2] and all the prophets call them the 7 heavenly bodies which are the 7 planets, and commonly they are called the 7 planets. And the 7 brethren are kept of 4 beasts, full of eyes before and behind, which are the [four] parts of heaven: East, West, North and South. And they have rulership in the 4 parts of the world, and in 4 times, and in 4 natures, with its complexions and with all its parts, and in all its 4 Elements. And with these together is led, and moved, all things moveable by the Commandments of God, that put them in their places.

---

[1] Bewitcher or prophet. Prophet also meant having the magical powers of a prophet. Forespeaker can also mean advocate or barrister. These are both typically mercurial professions.
[2] Suggestive of the Jewish *menorah* or 7 branched candlestick, which used to be a symbol of Judaism, in the same way the Star of David is now.

Liber Salomonis

Dixit Solomon sicut fuerunt sempus status superius.

Solomon said, "as there were always states above, without corruption, so there is now and shall be for ever more." And from this we understand that the bodies above are pure, good, and made without corruption. And that the lower bodies are unclean, evil, treated and broken, and each day they fail and are bound and corrupted. And this corruption rests not, neither is it made true of that which we understand, so that the lower bodies might not neglect the upper bodies. And all things which we see beneath have roots and begin from the things above: for things above are with life and without dolor, and things beneath be the contrary, and have death and dolor.

And things above are without corruption, and things beneath each day fail, are corrupted and diminished. All prophets have seen that if we lacked any one of the upper bodies (there be more than ten thousand [stars], between those that we see and those that we see not), there would be a great precipitation, destruction and confusion in land, and in sea, and in the 4 Elements [below], if [8ᵛ] any of the bodies above were broken or were evilly treated. And if any one of the 7 brethren failed, then the earth should come again to its first state, where all the Elements were confused. And if any of them [the upper bodies] had corporally received corruption, all things would be destroyed that receive a soul or life.

And know that as the 4 Elements are turned downward, so they are not turned without some reason [or motion] of the 7 [bodies] above. And thus say the philosophers, that when the Sun is destroyed so each life and each soul is destroyed. And when the Moon is destroyed the ligatures or bindings of the sea are destroyed. And know that Saturn is earthy and holds all the earth in a balance that is not moved. And Jupiter holds air [in balance], and Mars [holds] fire, and the Sun [holds] the day, and men. And Venus holds the fair parts of the world, and Mercury [holds] reason, and the Moon holds the hearts, seas, waters and their powers. And know that everyone (after it were, or shall be, in this exaltation) is regulated and bound to the Sun, [so] its reasons, words and speeches should be good between men.

And when Mercury is in conjunction in Virgo (in the same degree) with the Sun, [moving] direct and not retrograde, this makes things subtle and reasonable. And as often as the Sun is in Aries, so many years [of life] unlike he gives us.[1] And as often as Saturn is in Libra so many mutations

---

[1] This is rather stating the obvious, for the Sun passes through Aries once a year, for every year of one's life.

he gives us in lands. And as often as Jupiter is in conjunction with Saturn in an earthly Sign, so he gives us many mutations or changes. And he changes laws & seats and Lordships (of the planets) and thus, in other complexions of the planets (after their state) their relationships are called Aspects. [9r]

Et dixit Hermes istam rationem supra capita [animalium] &c.[1]

And Hermes said this reason: on the heads of beasts Saturn [corresponds with] the right ear, Venus the left [ear], the Sun the right eye, and the Moon the left [eye]. Mercury [has] the mouth. These 7 apertures have power over the head of man. And Solomon said that man is the measure, which is [exemplified in his] palm, [part of his] hand, in which is [reflected] all the virtues of the world and of the 7 planets, and that is only the head of a man, wherefore every man is likened to his star and to his Elements.

And Solomon said, "when I found a spirit [planet] retrograde [2] or combust [3] or evilly treated, thus I say that his body will be evilly treated beneath, in whichever [part] it was like, or [the part of his body] signified [by the afflicted planet]. And he who is so wise that he knows [his natal chart], his Sign, and his planet, and his star above, and his signification, he is [able to] do good and evil to himself & likewise to other men. And as the nativities of beasts be denied such workings, you shall do so with the help of God."

Postquam diximus de 12 Signis et Planetis &c.

And after that he said of the 12 figures & planets & of their *radiis* [rays],[4] we say that each planet that is in Ascendant, and if there be another [planet] in the same Ascendant, this is named 'conjunction', and by how much the latitude (or breadth) shall be less, by so much the conjunction is said to be

---

[1] The text now begins to quote Hermes, as well as Solomon. The following paragraph appears as a marginal note in Sloane MS 3846: "But Hermes saith, That there are seven holes in the head of an Animall, distributed to the seven Planets, viz. the right ear to Saturne, the left to Jupiter, the right nostrell [nostril] to Mars, the left to Venus, the right eye to the Sun, the left to the Moon, and the mouth to Mercury. The severall Signes also of the Zodiack take care of their members. So Aries governs the head, and face, Taurus the neck, Gemini the armes..."
The two do not agree on all the attributions, but it is not clear which manuscript is the oldest.

[2] Retrograde is normally applied to a planet, not a spirit. It is said of a planet that appears to move backwards when viewed from the Earth.

[3] Literally 'catches fire', said of a planet which comes too close to the Sun in the sky, thereby losing much of its virtue. This is usually defined as within 3 degrees of the Sun, but this term is sometimes extended as far as 8.5 degrees from the Sun. The only exception is the planet Mars which gains in strength by its proximity to the Sun.

[4] In the sense that *radiis* is used by al-Kindi to remark on the effect of the rays of the planets.

stronger, and if there be more latitude [between the two planets] so the conjunction is the feebler. And so I say to you in the middle of heaven. And if the degree of the 12 Houses which are in the stronger places of all the Houses, [that is] the first degree of the House, and each star that were less and has over himself another the like, is said that it has power and goes over another [9ᵛ] from star to star.

[De Aspectibus]

[The Aspects]

And thus each planet that diverges from another by 60 degrees, before or after, is in *aspectus sextilis* [Sextile aspect] that is the 'sixth aspect.' And each planet that differs 90 degrees, before or behind, is called in *aspectu quarto* [Square aspect], that is in the 'fourth aspect.' And each planet that diverges or differs by 120 degrees, before or behind, is called in *aspectu tertio* [Trine aspect], that is in the 'third aspect.' And each planet that differs by 180 degrees is in Opposition, in that it is in the contrary [opposite] place. These are the 7 aspects and no more *duo tertii, duo quarti & duo sextile* and *unus opposites*, that is to say two in the third, two in the fourth, and two in the sixth and one contrary against another.

The conjunction is 'complete' when [the planets] are within one degree [of each other]. Double conjunction if two [planets are] good or temperate, [and this] signifies double good, but if two [planets are] evil, to the contrary, it signifies much evil. The *sextilis* [aspect] to the Ascendant, avails one good, if in *trino* [Trine aspect] and [if] two *trino* avail in the aspect the Ascendant, one good, fortunate in the Ascendant. And two *quartiles* [Square aspects] in the aspect to the Ascendant, avails one grievously or heavily (if they are evil planets) and two opposite avails one unfortunate [aspect] in the Ascendant or in the opposite [Opposition aspect].

And two *quarti* [Square aspects] avails as much as a star falling or [one that is] combust or retrograde, and this is hindered in the Ascendant [by] one fortunate [aspect], or two in the Ascendant and another of Sextile and another of Trine aspecting the Ascendant, signifies much good, and speedy travelling. Two evil [planets] in the Ascendant, or one with another in Opposition, that is in the contrary, or falling, signifies [10ʳ] a grievous [heavy] or long impediment. And if the [planets] are [in their] fall and hindered, it shall be worse. One fortunate in the Ascendant aspect of two *trinis* [Trine aspects] signifies much good, and how much there were no witnesses over the figure of which you enquire and search, or for which you work so much, it shall be the better. And if three planets aspect the Ascendant with good aspects, and two with evil [aspects], the good shall overcome the evil, and so [it is true] of the other [configurations]. One unfortunate [planet] in the Ascendant aspecting two *quartis* [Square aspects] signifies much grief.

Caput Draconis is much better than Cauda [Draconis].[1] Each planet in its head [Caput] of the same degree has more Lordship [influence] in [reading] the [astrological] figure, for if it is [within] two [degrees] in latitude away from the [path] of the Sun, it profits in going toward the part of the North. Each planet in the tail of the dragon [Cauda Draconis] is diminishing in its work if it goes towards the South. The Moon in Conjunction or joined with Saturn, and Mars in the Ascendant, constrains and threatens devils.[2] Saturn makes devils of strength & great power.

The Moon in Conjunction, or joined with Jupiter and Venus in the Ascendant, signifies great delectation and great love of every good thing. The Moon joined with Mars & Saturn in the Ascendant signifies impediment, except where the planets were receiving good [influences]. The Moon joined with the Sun in the same degree signifies great grace, and that they are good. The Moon joined in its Fall to Mercury in the Ascendant signifies the contrary. The Moon in the Ascendant by herself signifies [the nature of] the planet to which she is joined. The Moon with Caput Draconis in the Ascendant signifies good. The Moon with Cauda Draconis, or combust, or joined with [10ᵛ] a hindered [badly aspected] planet, or in an evil sitting, signifies much evil when Caput Draconis and the Moon are with Capite Saturn,[3] or the Moon or Saturn were there, and their work of *celson* signifies the building of devils foul and evil.

Each planet that is with the Dracon [Caput or Cauda] of another [planet] & with both in Conjunction, or joined together, signifies a truth or true work, and more so in the Ascendant. And if Caput Draconis were with Jupiter or the Moon, and these two conjunct, or joined in the Ascendant, it signifies much good and an increase of good and honour. And if it were in Cauda [Draconis] not only when there were two Cauda Draconis (that is of the Moon and of another [planet]) and they will be very evil when the Moon is [conjunct] with them. When Caput Draconis and the Moon are with Caput Draconis and Mars and the Moon, and Mars is in the same degree, it signifies strength and might. And if Cauda with Cauda, and the Moon with Mars,

---

[1] Caput and Cauda Draconis are the Head and Tail of the Moon, poetic terms for the Moon's turning points as it wanders North and South of the Equator. The Indian equivalents are Rahu and Ketu.
[2] Possibly a useful astrological configuration for the timing of evocations.
[3] Head of Saturn, an astrological Part.

Liber Salomonis

together it is very grievous [heavy] and evil, after everyone is evil, so is the place or aspecting of one to another.

Caput Draconis and the Moon in Capite Aries (the Moon & the Sun in Zamin) signifies great might and great honour, and to the contrary, if it is in Libra beneath with Cauda Draconis. Caput Draconis with Capite Venus signifies much love, and Cauda Draconis [signifies] the contrary. Caput Draconis, that is to say Mercury with Caput Draconis and the Moon, signifies a work of reason, and of voice, and many sounds, and in Cauda the Moon with Mercury & Saturn, it signifies the observing of many experiences. The Moon in Capite *sui* Draconis signifies [good], and if there were Jupiter or Venus [in conjunction], it shall do the work of Jupiter or of Venus, and it shall profit in all good work as these be good [aspects]. The Moon, if it is in Cauda Draconis, and Mars [11r] and Saturn with it, or that they are aspected to it with an evil aspecting, it signifies evil, as we have said of Saturn and Mars. And we have said that Saturn nourishes devils, and Mars draws and threshes and figures them.[1] And Saturn gathers together many devils. Venus and Saturn together gather devils and winds from beneath.[2]

A good planet in the Ascendant, and the Moon joined [in Conjunction] with a good planet, signifies much good. And the beginning in all in which were *deus quartae*, that is with the Lord of the fourth House; and if the fourth House is well aspected and good, every one of the things shall be good. And when the Lord of the fourth House is evil, and evil entreated, it signifies annoyance and evil. The Sign of the Ascendant signifies the body of the Lord of the Ascendant of the planet that is in the Ascendant, or that which aspects it signifies his spirit, and the Lord of the hour signifies his soul and his will, and this you must understand in other *domes* [Houses]. The body, soul and the spirit, for these three make up the body of a man, safe and whole.

[The Houses]

Dixit [Salomon et] Hermes, Saturnus exaltatur in Libra &c.

Hermes said, "Saturn is enhanced in Libra, and Jupiter in Cancer, and Mars in Capricorn, and the Sun in Aries. And Venus [is enhanced] in Pisces, and Mercury in Virgo, and the Moon in Taurus. And Saturn gladdens or is happy in the twelfth House, and Mars in the sixth, and the Sun in the ninth, and Venus in the fifth, and Mercury in the Ascendant (the first House), and the Moon in the third House."

---

[1] Maybe, Mars either punishes them, or it shapes their manifested form.
[2] There is an interesting association of demons with evil winds from the Underworld, possibly derived from the word '*spiritus*', which is the Latin for air or breath.

The Ascendant has 12 virtues, and each planet that is in it rules each place of the circle [horoscope]. The tenth [11ᵛ] House has 11 virtues. The 11th House has 10 virtues. The seventh [House] has nine [virtues], the fourth [House has] eight virtues, the fifth House has 7 virtues, the ninth House has 6 [virtues]. The third [House] has 5 [virtues]. The second [House] has 4 [virtues]. The eighth [House] has three [virtues], the 12th [House] has two [virtues], and the sixth House has one virtue.

And for always consider in all things, what you should do with the planets, how they are in the 12 Houses, and you shall profit if you choose [the best astrological configuration of planets in Houses]. And Solomon said, "to each man that works by this book, it is well that he know all these things, for reasons which here I will not expound to you, that is you [should] know in which time of the year you were born, [which] of the 4 times [seasons][1] of the year. And [born] in which month of the Moon."[2]

And begin [counting the months] from the Lunation of the month of Mercury (wherever the Moon *prima* is). And [about] all Secrets and private matters ask Saturn with all seriousness; and [about] honour and substance ask Jupiter. And for all [matters] of strife and battle and speed, ask Mars. And for all [matters] of purity & Lordship ask the Sun. And for all [matters] of fairness and delectation, or loves and fatness, ask Venus. And for all reasons, understandings & subtleties [ask] Mercury. And of these 7 [planets] you shall always ask counsel from [the positions] where you find them in their Houses and Signs. And they shall show you, so consider them in all good and evil [configurations]. Now we have finished here, with the help of God, the Treatise that is called *Liber Clavis,* which is the 'Book of the Key.'

Here ends the First Book and here begins the Second [Book].

---

[1] Throughout the manuscript, 'times' has been changed to 'seasons', where that is its actual meaning.
[2] This is the lunar month of the year (as in the Jewish calendar) beginning circa March, rather than the standard Western solar calendar month, beginning in January.

[*Liber Secundus* - The Second Book]

[*Ala*, the Virtues of some Stones, Herbs, Beasts and Words]

[12ʳ] *Dixit Solomon sicut alae avium sunt membra &c.*

Solomon said, "as the wings of the fowls or birds are the limbs that lead the birds to the place where they desire to be, so by the virtues of stones & of herbs and of beasts, that live in flying, in swimming, in going [upon the face of the earth], and in creeping, you might attain to that which you desire if you choose their [correct] nature."

The properties and virtues. And therefore we call this book *Ala*, that is 'wings', for without wings neither birds nor fishes might move themselves, and so as wings bear bodies to highness upwards and to the foundations downwards, and to longitude and latitude, that is to length and breadth, so by the virtue of stones and of herbs, with grace, and with much power of Semiforas [they will carry us].[1] Know that [through them] you might attain that which you covet, such as to heal and to make sick, or to stand, or to go.

Dixit Solomon sicut Lapides sunt mundiores &c.

Solomon said, "stones are purer, clearer and fairer than gold, and in the 7 virtues of this world which are in stones, herbs, words and beasts, so I say in the beginning of this book *Cephar Raziel*, that is crowned with 7 stones of great power, he put them in this book."

The first [stone] is Rubinus Carbunclo [red carbuncle], the second Smaragdus [emerald], the third Saphirus [sapphire], the fourth Berillus [beryl], the fifth Topasius [topaz], the sixth Faguncia [hyacinth], the seventh Adamas [diamond], and [about] the virtues of [all] these stones Raziel has spoken. And he said that they are crowned by 7 angels, which have power over the 7 heavens, and over the 7 days of the week. And Raziel said, "each man that has this book, has in this book all the virtues of this world." And the first virtue of this book, called the *Four Wings*, is the [12ᵛ] virtue of stones, wherefore know that by stones alone you may do wonderful things, if you know well (as you should do) all the other [magical] Images [for engraving them], and you keep [store] them purely and reverently.

---

[1] This is a rather strained and overly long rationalisation as to why this treatise is called the four 'Wings.'

Sepher Raziel

De Prima Ala – the First Wing

[Stones]

Et dixit Solomon scias quod in prima Ala sunt &c.

And Solomon said that in the first *Ala*, or 'wing', there are 24 precious stones of great power, corresponding to and signifying the 24 hours of the day and night.

[1.] And Solomon began & said, "I chose for the first stone Carbunculu[m] Rubinus [red carbuncle] because it is brighter, and clearer, and fairer, and [held in] more high esteem above all other stones. And I will describe its [1] colour, and its power and its virtue, and of its seal, and of its figure that might be [engraved] in it. And thus I shall explain for all other stones, each stone signifying durability, or [long] lastingness without end." The colour of Rubinus is as the colour of a sparkling fire, and its power is that it shines by night, as a star or as a flame of sparkling fire. And the virtue of it is that it makes good colour of men that bear [wear] it reverently, and it increases his goods of this world among other men, and the Image which you ought to put in it ought to be a *draco*, which is a Dragon well [formed] with reverence.

2. The second stone is Topazins [*Topazius/Thopasius* – ancient topaz],[2] of which the colour is citrine, as of gold. Its power is that if it is put in a cauldron with fervent, hot, or boiling water, it holds the water so that it may not boil,[3] which is [because of its] great power for making cold, and the virtue of it is that it makes a man chaste that carries it with him, and it gives benevolence (or willingness) of great Lords, and its figure is a falcon. [13r]

3. The third stone is Smaragdu[m] [*Smaragdum* - emerald] and this stone is green and fair over all greenness, and it is not heavy as the others are, and its power is to keep the light, and it heals the face, and it does many wonderful things. And its virtue is to increase riches, and whoever wears it [mounted] in gold prophesies things to come. And the sign of it is a Scarabeus [beetle] that is a manner of filth.[4]

4. And the fourth stone is Faguncia [*Hiacynthum* – hyacinth], the colour of which is red, as the grains [pips?] of an apple. Of these [stones] there are [some] well coloured ones, and some of a lesser [colour], and some in the

---

[1] The text refers, in each case, to the stone as 'he' or 'his.' We have changed this to 'it' and 'its.'

[2] For clarification, the Latin term in each case is taken from the (sometimes faulty) Latin of Sloane MS 3847 without correction.

[3] The stone that causes water not to boil is *hephaestites*, which is what Albertus Magnus called topasion. This is not the modern topaz, nor the stone mentioned by Pliny.

[4] The scarabeus, or dung beetle, was the insect associated with the ancient Egyptian god Kephra.

Liber Salomonis

middle. Its power is that bearers of it will not be infected with an alien illness, its virtue is that it gives health and honour, and keeps the man that wears it whole in ways and in journeys, and its figure is a Lion well figured.

5. The fifth stone is a Crysopazine [*Chrisopazium* – chrysoprase], of which the colour is green, and it is as though it had golden drops [in it], and its power is to protect a man from the podagrie,[1] and its virtue is that it makes [its wearer] prophesy things to come (if it is [held] in a hand that is pure and chaste), and its figure is the Image of an ass.

6. The sixth stone is Saphirus [*Saphyrus* - sapphire], the colour of which is [ranges between] very leady [grey] and fair (as the colour of a pure heaven). Its power is that it heals all infirmities that affect men [especially] inflammation and illness of the eye. And it cleans them much. And if in this stone be engraved the head of a man with a beard, it will deliver a man from prison, and from all pressure and oppression, and this stone accords with the great power of Lords and of kings. If this stone be kept purely, reverently & chastely, & if it be a good [quality] oriental [sapphire], a man might [with it] attain to great honour and to the profit that he searches [for] and covets. And some men put therein the sign of a ram, Aries. [13ᵛ]

7. The seventh stone is Berillus [*Berillus/Beryllus* - beryl], the colour of which is of a [blue] eye, or of sea water, and some of them are round, and some have five corners. The stone ought to be clear within, and pure. And its power is to warm the closed hand of him that bears it. And if it be set in gold it gives great friendship between two men, if you touch them with it. And its figure is Rana, that is a [genus of] frog, and it has great power to make concord and love.

8. The eighth stone is Onyx [*Onix/Onyx*], this stone is very black and its power is to give him that bears it many dreadful dreams and dread, and he that sees himself in it has power over all devils, in constraining them and in calling [them], and gathering them together in *speculo tabilio*,[2] conjuring as it requires, and its figure is the head of a camel, or two heads between two ears, that are called Mirti.

9. The ninth stone is called sardius [*Sardus/Sardius* – carnelian], the colour of which is red and fair, and its power is to make other stones fairer, its virtue is to give good colour to him that bears it. And if it is set in gold, and if there is engraved in it Aquila, the Eagle, it gives great honour.

10. The tenth stone is Crysolitus [*Chrisolitium* – chrysolite, 'Greek topaz'], that

---

[1] Gout, inflamation of the joints, especially in the toes.
[2] Used in evocation, so that the spirits evoked can be seen in a skrying speculum or crystal.

is of golden colour and sparkling as fire. Its power is to gather together devils and winds, and its virtue is to protect the place where it is [kept] from evil spirits, and from dead men, so they do not do there any evil, and [to ensure] that devils obey [the wearer]. And its figure is a vulture, which is a vowter.

11. The 11th stone is called Eliotopia [*Elitropia* - heliotrope]. And it is a stone of great power, of which the colour is green and fair shining and clear with drops like blood, red within. This stone is called the stone of wise men, of prophets, [14r] and of philosophers. And this is honored for two things: for the colour is like Smaragdo in greenness, and in redness [like] to ruby. The high esteem of this stone's virtues and properties overcomes the esteem of other [stones]. The power of this stone is that if it be put in any broad vessel full of water, [open] to the Sun, it dissolves that water into vapor. And it makes [the vapour] to be raised upward, till in the form of rain it is converted [to cloud and falls] downwards. Its virtue [works] for him who bears it in his mouth, or in his closed hand, so that it may not be seen by any man. With this stone a man may have power over all devils; and make any incantation or enchantment that he wishes. And in this stone ought to be engraved a Vespertino, thus he says. But I believe [the image should instead] be a Vespertilio, that is a bat or a dormouse.[1]

12. The 12th stone is Crystal [*Christallus* - crystal], of which the colour is of water congealed with cold [i.e. ice]. Its power is that it withdraws fire from [the body]. And its virtue is that it increases or nourishes [with] much good milk. And you may create in it whatever virtue you wish, [according to] the hour in which you shall work. And afterwards the Image shall be what you have made (although they are many) and that are seen easily.[2] Know that it has many virtues, and its figure is a griffin, which is [both] a fowl and a beast, with 4 feet and 2 wings, and it is a great beast.

13. The 13th stone is Cornelia [*Cornelina* - carnelian], and it is likened to water in which is blood, as the lotion,[3] or washing of blood. And its power is to staunch the blood of the nostrils. And if there is engraved in it a man well clothed, holding a staff or a rod in his hand, it will give honour to him that bears it.

14. The 14th stone is Jaspis [*Jaspis* - jasper], is thick dark green and red. And there are some green and clear [varieties], and they are better than the others, and there are some [varieties which are] red, thick and dropped [marked

---

[1] Vespertilio is Latin for 'bat.'
[2] Its magical action is determined by the Image engraved in it.
[3] The old meaning of 'lotion' was the water in which something has been washed, rather than a cream.

with spots]. And its power is that whoever bears it is not [14ᵛ] hurt by venom, neither from a serpent, nor a spider,[1] nor a scorpion. And it protects a man from fever, if it is engraved [with the Sign of] Leo, Aries or Sagittarius.

15. The 15th stone is Iris [*Yris/Iris*], and its [appearance] is likened to crystal or to jelly, and it has corners; and if any man put it in a house [open] to the beams of the Sun, so the beams pass through it, and by it the colour appears of the rainbow. And for this reason it is called Iris, which is the [goddess of the] rainbow. And this is its strength, for it has 6 corners, and the virtue of it is to keep the place where it is [kept], with health & honesty, and there ought to be engraved in it a man armed, that bears a bow and an arrow.

16. The 16th stone is Coral [*Corallus*], and it grows on rocks of the sea, as *arbor inverse*, that is as a tree overturned, and it has branches as a tree does, [some] more than two or three palms [in width] and no more. And when it is drawn up [from the sea] it is green and tender, and after it is dried in the air, it is made red & hard as another [stone]. And otherwise it is found white. And know that the red is the better [variety]. And where this stone is, it preserves the house and the vineyard, or the place, from tempest, pestilence and torment. And it keeps the place healthy, and it protects a man from evil doers and evil deeds, and from evil enchantments. And its Image is a man holding a sword in his hand.

17. The 17th stone is Presius or Prassius [*Prasius*], and it is a green colour, thick and fair, and it helps [against] evil deeds, and gives them grace to their ministry. And Taurus [15ʳ] ought to be engraved in it, that is [the image of] a Bull.

18. The 18th stone is called Catel [*Catel*],[2] and it is of great power both in deeds and in virtues, the colour of which is like Beryl, but it is darker than that, although it has within it very clear and pure beams and streaks. And some [varieties] are found with 6 corners and others with 5. And its power is to call in devils, and to speak with them. And its virtue is, if you make in your water and bring the root of *apii*,[3] and the stone is hung on the neck with the skin of an ass, censed with mastic, *thure* [frankincense] and crocus, and you call [invoke] whatever dead man you wish ([one] that is known to you), he shall soon appear to you. And he shall be with you at the same time [immediately]. And engrave in it [the image of] a Lapwing and [add] Dragantium, which is a middle herb, that is called Columbrina.[4]

---

[1] Sloane MS 3846 has the obsolete word 'Attercoppe' for 'spider.'
[2] 'Catel' is Middle English for chattel, property or wealth.
[3] *Apium* or celeriac.
[4] Columbrina gum. Or maybe Adderwort, the fern *Ophioglossum vulgatum*.

Sepher Raziel

19. The 19th stone is Celonites [*Colonites*]. And it is green as a herb, and its power is that it waxes & decreases as the Moon does, and its power is also to make peace and concord between two, if in it is engraved the sign of a swallow.

20. The 20th stone is Calcedonius [*Calcidonium* - chalcedony], and it is white as between crystal and beryl, or as *gifus* thick and bright, its power is to overcome pleas.[1] Its virtue is to preserve a man whole [healthy] in an alien land, and its Image is a man that holds his right hand straight out to heaven.

21. The 21st stone is Ceramius [*Ceramius*]. This stone is of many colours after many elements and many lands, otherwise it is white, or brown, green & red. And elsewhere it is likened to iron, and somewhere to copper and sulphur, and it has, as it were, discs [15ᵛ] painted and little drops, and its power is to protect a place from thunder and lightning, and its virtue is to protect [the wearer] from all enemies. And write in it, or one part or side, 'Raphael Michael & Gabriel', and on the other side 'Panuteseron, Micrason, Saidalson', and if you bear it with you, and have it in your power, you shall overcome all your enemies and adversaries.

22. The 22nd stone is Metestus [*Amestitum* - amethyst], and it has the colour of wine, a white cloth, or of a rose or violet, and this has strength to chase away fiends, and its virtue is to protect [you] from drunkenness; and its figure is Ursus, which is a bear.

23. The 23rd stone is Magentis or magnes [*Magnes* - magnetite], and it is of great weight and like to *ferro brumeto* [magnetic iron?]. Its power is that it draws [out] dead iron, [such] as nails, knives and swords, and its virtue is that with it you may be in whatever house you wish, and do whatever you wish with men, and with the things of the house, censing the house with it, and with these men make enchantments. Engrave on it a man armed, when the Moon is in Aries, or Scorpio is conjunct with Mars, and the Sun aspected to them with a trine aspect. Whatever manner of Images you engrave on this stone, such enchantments you may attain to, carry it with you, and you shall profit.

24. The 24th stone is Adamas [*Adamas* - diamond], as it is of middling colour, and the better [varieties] have somewhat of greenness. And its power is that, with it, other stones can be engraved. And therefore we have put it out [explained it] more strangely & more openly, and its power or virtue is to keep the limbs of a man safe and whole. And this stone is more [beneficial], and is [16ʳ] more highly esteemed for enchantments & invocations of winds,

---

[1] Depositions or pleas made in court. In other words, to help win a court case, by overturning your opponent's depositions.

spirits and devils. And with this you may send whatever fantasy you wish [to another person], and its figure has 5 corners, and each man who bears it within a precious stone, [must] be pure when he does anything with it. And avoid or keep yourself from uncleanness, and keep them [the stones] reverently in a *quiche*, or in a pure place. And Raziel said, "in the hour in which you [invoke] Semiforas carry the two stones abovesaid, and you shall profit."

Sepher Raziel

[De Secundus Ala – the Second Wing]

[De Herbis - Herbs]

Dixit Solomon sicut avis corpus volare non potest &c.

Solomon said, "as the body of a fowl will not fly without wings, nor go where it comes, so [without] the science of the one thing [outlined] above we might not fulfill that which we desire. And for this [to work] we supply the second key in this book, and we say the second book makes the second opening, for the world is closed [sealed] with 4 Elements, so this book is closed with 4 sciences and 4 virtues."

As we have explained stones, now we will explain herbs. Know that in herbs are the most virtues. And some of the natural [things] of this world are those that live and have reason, and some that fly, and some which swim, and [some] which go [upon the earth], and [some] which creep.

And know that of trees and herbs some live much [flourish], and some live mildly, and some live little, and that is the same as for the beasts. And know also that among herbs there are some with which you may do good or evil, so as to heal & to make sick, and so understand what shall be said furthermore hereafter. And Adam said, "that by a tree [1] came wretchedness into the world, that is, by the tree [16ᵛ] I sinned." And Raziel said, "a herb shall be your Life." And Solomon said, "[there is] a tree that shall wax (or grow) of which the leaves shall not fall, and it shall be a medicine for [all] men." The second 'wing' [section] is about the correspondence of the 24 hours and the 24 herbs.

1. *Prima herba est Acil almalie &c.* The first herb is *Acil* or *Almabum* and it is called *Corona Regia*, and in Latin Rosmarinus [*Rosmarina* - rosemary]. This herb has a middle [sized] trunk and good odour and little leaves, and its power is to warm and comfort the brain. And if a house is censed with it, it chases away devils, the same as does Peony.

2. The second herb is Artemisia [*Arthemesia*], and this is mother and first [among all] other [herbs], but for it is called *Corona Regis*, that is to say the crown of a king. We [would] have put it first [in this list], because in all things you do, you should use it. And the leaf is mid-green over one side, and white on the other side. And it grows mildly [slowly]. And with this you shall stop winds, and [invoke] all spirits that you wish, and you shall profit.

---

[1] The Tree of the Knowledge of Good and Evil.

3. The third herb is Cannabis [*Cannabis* [sic] - hemp] and it is long in the stem, and clothes are made of it. The virtue of the juice of it, is to anoint yourself with it (and with the juice of artemisia) and set yourself before a mirror of steel and call spirits, and you shall see them, and you shall have the ability to bind and loose [set free] devils, and other things.[1]

4. The fourth herb is called Feniculus [*Feniculus* - fennel], and it has small leaves and a long staff, and it is a holy herb and reverential, and it is medicine for the eyes, and it [17r] gives good light, and it chases away spirits and the evil eye from the place where it is, and the root of it chases away evil things and helps in sight.

5. The fifth herb is Cardamommus [*Cardomonium* - cardamom], and it is hot and of good complexion, and it is of middle highness, and it gives happiness to him that uses it, and it gathers together spirits. Eat this when you call [spirits] or make an invocation, and if you wish, make smoke of it.[2]

6. The sixth herb is Anisus [*Anisum* - aniseed], and it has [the qualities] of chastity. Join it to camphor, and you shall see that spirits shall dread you, and it is a pure herb, and it makes one to see secret and private things, and the smoke of it ascends much.

7. The seventh herb is Coriandrus [*Coriandrum* - coriander], and this holds the spirit of a man much with the other, and it makes a man also full asleep, and this gathers together many spirits, wherefore always they stand with it. So it is said that, if with this and *apis* [honey?] and *jusquiami*,[3] you make fumigations, compounded with much *lazaias cicuta*,[4] soon it gathers together spirits, and therefore it is called *'herba spirituum'* [herb of spirits].

8. The eighth herb is called Petroselinum [*Perroselinum* - parsley] which has a great power to chase away the spirits of roches [roaches?], and its virtue is to break [up] the stone in the bladder of any that use it.[5]

9. The ninth herb is Ipericon or Hipericon [*Hipericon* - hypericon], and it is a middle [height] herb, [which when] pierced the juice of it seems [like] blood. This [herb] is of great power, for with the juice of it (and with crocus and artemisia, and with the smoke of *radicis valerianae* [root of valerian]), it [can be used] to write upon [a talisman] what friendship you wish of a Prince of

---

[1] This is a standard magical experiment to anoint yourself with these juices, and using a steel skrying mirror, to see the spirits that you invoke.
[2] Burn it on hot coals.
[3] *Hyoscamus niger*.
[4] *Cicuta* = water hemlock.
[5] To break up calculus or stones in the kidneys or urinary tract.

the spirits of air, and [other] devils, and soon it shall be that [you will get that which] you covet. And so [likewise] over [other] spirits and winds.

10. The tenth herb is Apium [*Apium* – celeriac, parsley]. This has great power over [17ᵛ] winds and devils and fantasies [phantoms], and it is [both] the shadow and the exhalation¹ of the cloud Alcisse. For in it are winds and devils, and this alone [calls the spirits] Albafortum, Vazebelil and Mortagon, and they [these spirits] are very contrary, for one is kept [lives] with the heavenly angels, and another is kept [lives] with the devils in Apium.

And this [herb] cures the kidney-stone, but a woman [pregnant] with child [should not] use it as it annoys [irritates] the child, and it gathers together devils when suffumigations are made [of it, together] with *insqrmo* [*jusquiami*],² and artemisia. Apium is censed for 7 nights with *fagax almeit* gathered purely, and the root of it kept and dried, and then tempered with *aqua lapides* [water stones?]: cense [your surroundings] when you wish, and you shall see fantasies and devils of many types.

11. The 11th is Coriandrus [*Coriandrum* - coriander] of the second kind, which makes one sleep. And if you make suffumigations of it, with crocus and *insqrmo* [*jusquiami*],² *apia* and *papavere nigro* [black poppy], ground together evenly, and tempered with *succo, cicutae* ³ and with musk, and then cense the place where you hide treasure, when the Moon is in conjunction with the Sun in *angulo terra* [earth angle], that is to say in the corners of the earth. And know that such a [hidden] treasure shall never be found [by other people]. And anyone who would take it away shall be made fools [of]. And if in the hour of depositing the gold or silver, or of the [precious] stones, or images you suffume [them] with *thure* [frankincense], musk,⁴ *succo* [succory], *lignum aloes*, and *costus*,⁵ and always devils [shall] keep that place [safe from robbers] and evil winds. It [the protection] will never be dissolved or destroyed again, without separation, or [without using] an image made thereto at the [precise] degree of the planets.⁶

12. The 12th herb is Satureia [savory], and this is of great virtue and good odour, and whoever bears it with him, [18ʳ] with *auricula muris* [mouse-ear

---

¹ '*Umbro et nebula*' in the Latin of Sloane MS 3847 meaning 'shade and fog.'
² *Hyoscamus niger* or black henbane.
³ '*Cicuta*' is water hemlock or cowbane. *Succo* is succory. This is a very psychotropic mixture.
⁴ The sexual secretion of the preputial gland of the male musk deer, highly prized in perfumery.
⁵ The root of *Costus Arabicus* or the fragrant root of *Saussurea lappa*, from Kashmir.
⁶ This is a procedure for thwarting other magicians who might wish to use magic to find and free treasures from their spirit guardians. For more detail about these techniques see David Rankine [ed.] *The Book of Treasure Spirits: a grimoire of magical conjurations to reveal treasure... by invoking spirits, fallen angels, demons and fairies*, Avalonia, Hay, 2009.

hawkweed], in the day of Venus [Friday], will get grace of goods, and it takes away from that place [all evil] winds and evil fantasies.

13. The 13th herb is called *sca* [*Centaurea*].[1] And this is middle in length and has little leaves. This ought to be held reverently in holy places and in churches, for it protects these places from evil things. And with this [herb] prophets made dead men speak, that had been dead by many days or few.

In places where there is any evil, it has no power if he that bears [this herb] calls them not. And it gives him rule over whatever things they wish, and [if you] put this herb upon the place where devils are confined, it constrains them and binds them, least that they might have power to move themselves.

And Solomon said, "I found in the *Book of Hermitis* [2] that whoever takes water in the fourth hour of the night [and puts it] upon the tomb of a dead man, of whatever spirits he wishes to speak, he should cast the water upon the tomb with this herb hyssop." And the water is censed with *costo, succo, musco* [costus, succum, musk], and [he should] say "surgo, surgo, surgo." That is to say "rise, rise, rise and come and speak to me", and do this for three nights, and in the third night he [the spirit] shall come to you, and he shall speak with you of whatever things you wish [to know].

14. The 14th herb is psyllium [*Serpillum* – fleabane/wild thyme], which is of great virtue for it signifies or makes open in the air what the other powers do not. It makes [you] see spirits in the clouds of the heavens, and [put] this with *scicorda* [3] & *garmone* and the 'tree which swims' (which is called *arbor cancri* and *malie*) with *rore madii,* and with the tree that signifies by night, and it is called *herba lucens,* that is a shining herb. [18ᵛ] If you make with these an ointment with the eye of a whelp and with the fat of a hart [deer], you may go surely wherever you wish in an hour.

15. The 15th herb Majorana [*Majorana* - marjoram], keeps a house and protects [it] from evil infirmities, and Hermes said that *gentiana* [gentian], *valerina* [valerian] and *maiorana* [marjoram] have power over great princes, and over great men.

16. The 16th herb is Dragantia [*Dragantia*].[4] This is of great power, and the highness of the root of it, joined with the tongue of a *colubri* [snake] which is

---

[1] The Latin version clearly shows *Centaurea*.
[2] For *Liber Hermetis* see the 17th century Sloane MS 3847, fol. 84-100: Hermes Trismegistus, *Liber Magicus* or *Liber Hermetis tractans de 15 stellis 15 lapidibus 15 herba et 15 harum rerum figuris*.
[3] In Sloane MS 3846 it is '*cicorea*' or chicory. The rest of the ingredients in this sentence are difficult to identify.
[4] Columbrina. Or maybe Adderwort, the fern *Ophioglossum vulgatum*.

left alive. And [if] the herbs are gathered when the Sun is in the first degree of Cancer, and the Moon aspects Mercury, or is in Conjunction with him [Mercury], whosoever touches [it to] closures or locks, they shall be soon opened for him.

And Hermes said that it gathers together winds & spirits, if mandragora is [mixed] with it and *capillus* [hair of] *dezoara*.

17. The 17th herb is Nepita [*Nepta*], and if this [is put] with maiorana [marjoram] and *athanasia* & *trifolio* and *salvia* [sage], *peruca, edera* and artemisia with *ysope* [hyssop],[1] being joined & gathered together, [during] the crescent Moon, on the day of Jupiter [Thursday], that is to say in the waning of the Moon, in the day of Jupiter, and in the following day, when the Sun waxes from the first degree of Aries till the first [degree] of Cancer, [then it is most effective]. And when you shall gather it be pure and washed, reverential, and stand [facing] towards the East, know that the house and place is improved where these nine herbs were twined together. And put them upon the gate of your house, and you shall profit always. And the nine herbs joined are like to rubies. [19r]

18. The 18th herb is Linum [*Lumen*], suffumigations of the seed of this with *semine psylly* and *azartachona* & *radix violae* and *apii* [celeriac] makes [you] see in the air things to come, and to make many prophesies.

19. The 19th herb is Salvia [*Salvia* – sage].[2] This is of great virtue and the long leaf of it is as *ligna agni* and sharp. This breaks or protects evil shades & evil spirits from the place where it is [kept], and it is good for a man to bear it with him, for it keeps a man whole, but a sick man [should] not hold it.

20. The 20th herb is Sauina [*Samna*], and some men say that it is a tree of love and affection, whoever can choose it. And if this with somewhat of crocus and *lingua colubri* [snake tongue], are set in a ring of gold, with somewhat of territory [you may] surely go before a king, or before whomsoever you wish. And [it is] most [potent] if you put with it the stone that is called Topazius [topaz], or if you wish beryllium [beryl]. And if this ring is made when the Moon is in Conjunction with Jupiter in a trine [aspect] to the Sun, it would be much better. And [this herb] is called *annulus solis*, which is the 'ring of the Sun', and it is [good] for health against infirmities, and it is [good] for grace, virtue, and for honour.

---

[1] In Sloane MS 3846: "*maiorana & Athanasia & trifolio & Saluia, peruca, edera & arthemesia* with *ysopo.*" So we have replaced '*hermita*' with '*peruca.*'
[2] *Salvia divinorum* has many interesting psychotropic properties.

21. The 21st [herb is] Nasturcium [*Nasturtium* – nasturtium]. This keeps the limbs whole, and if there are with it *origan*,[1] *pulegium*,[2] and *arzolla*,[3] which are carried together by you, and you eat them, you shall be whole within and without. And so if you anoint yourself with them and are censed with *marrubio albo* [white horehound] or *reubarbaro* [rhubarb] and *herba thuris* [boswellia], it shall protect you from many infirmities.

22. The 22nd is an herb that is called Cannaferula [*Cana ferula*].[4] [19v] This is a very dreadful, grievous [heavy] and strong [herb] in work. And if you take the juice of it, and the juice of *cicuta* [water hemlock], *jusquiami* [*hyoscamus niger*], *sapss barbati*, *sandalum rubrum* [red sandalwood], *papavero nigrum* [black poppy], and with this confection make smoke, [you may obtain] whatever you wish, and you shall see devils and things, and strange figures. And if Apinum is [mixed] with this, know that from each place so censed devils should flee, and if you wish you may destroy evil spirits [with it]. This suffumigation is very evil and dreadful, for the smoke of it overcomes in malice, and [it] works most evilly and most strongly if the Moon is [in Conjunction] with Saturn, or in Opposition with Mars.

23. The 23rd herb is Calamintum [*Calonietum* – calamint], and it is likened to mint, and it is of great virtue in good suffumigations, and if there is [mixed] with it *menta* [mint], *palma ppi*[?] and *pioma*[?], observe that it takes away evil spirits from a place. And always it is [useful] against fantasies [phantoms].

24. The 24th herb is Cicoria [*Cichorea* – chicory]. This is very good in all exorcisms [5] [especially] if it is joined with *eringo* [eryngium] & *pentaphylon* [Cinquefoil, snake grass, *potentilla reptans*], hypericon, *urtica* [stinging nettle] & verbena, and all together, worn around the neck, and under the feet, and [they] are then [called] the herb of 7 knots and of 7 leaves.

Martagon and *lilium domesticus* [domestic lily] and sylvestre (both tame and wild), and the herb angelica: whoever has these under his feet or sits above [them] and puts the other herbs on his neck, and has 7 rings of 7 metals on his fingers, knows that he shall have power in [20r] binding and in losing [spirits], and in enchanting, and to do good and evil in each place that he wishes, [by] making suffumigations of these 9 things: *thure albo* [white frankincense], *thymiamata*, *mastiche* [mastic], *musco* [musk], *lignum aloes*, cassia,

---

[1] Any plant of the genus *Origanum*, especially majoram or oregano.
[2] The herb pennyroyal, *Menta pulegium*.
[3] Lady's thistle or *Silybum marianum*.
[4] This might possibly be asafoetida, as in *Ferula asafoetida*.
[5] 'Exocism' can mean the evocation of spirits as well as their banishment.

cinnamon, and with them suffume with the things abovesaid in the surrounding area, and say these names: "Raphael, Gabriel, Michael, Cherubim, Seraphim, Arelim, Pantaseron, Micraton, Sandaton, *complete meaum petitionem et meam voluntatem.*" That is to say, "fulfill my petition and my wish," and they shall fulfill it for you. These are the names of the nine angels abovesaid. And know them and keep them, and some men say that they are the 9 orders of Angels.[1]

Here ends the 24 reasons concerning the virtues of herbs of the second 'wing' [section] and these experiments were newly written in [*Sepher*] *Raziel*, although Solomon put in two of these, [and] three of [them were] the sayings of Hermes.

And the herbs are put in the *Book of Raziel* so that with them we may be absolved, and work with herbs, as with Semiforas, with fasting and with words for good and for evil [purposes]. And let no man join himself to Semiforas till he knows himself first, and second. And thus we shall explain all things that shall be necessary, with the help of God.

---

[1] In fact Raphael, Gabriel, and Michael are archangels, but Cherubim, Seraphim, and Arelim are orders of angels. Pantaseron has been found as far afield as a Norwegian runic Christian lead tablet from the thirteenth or fourteenth century, but is probably from a Greek Christian source. Micraton is an angel of Saturn. 'Sandaton' is likely to be Sandalphon. See also "Panthaseron, Mucraton, and Sandalon" at folio 27r.

Liber Salomonis

De Tertia Ala – [the Third Wing]

[Beasts, Birds and Fish]

Dixit Solomon super alam tertiam sicut corpus solis &c.

Solomon said about the third 'wing' [section]: "as the body of the Sun is more visible and rules all other [heavenly] bodies, and is brighter, fairer and purer, so the virtues of sensible beasts which fly and send out [20ᵛ] voices [are above other beasts]." And so beasts of the third 'wing' have power over the [other] two 'wings' [sections] of stones and of herbs. And he [Solomon] therefore put in the [*Sepher*] *Raziel*, 24 beasts with [details of] their names, virtues and states. And the figures are 24 distinct or departed [divided] in two. And I put over each Element 6 beasts, everyone distinct from the other, and everyone of its [own] kind. And as fire is the high Lord, and distinct from the [other] 4 Elements, so the least of them all is purest among them.

[Spirit 'Beasts' of the Elements]

[1.] Therefore I begin to speak [first] of the beasts [i.e. spirits] of fire, for as every one of the 4 Elements has its beast beneath [on Earth], so fire has its [beast] above, pure and without corruption. And the fire that is above, is without corruption. And this fire is not expounded [made] of wax, trees, nor of oil, nor of [any] other composition, but it is simple. And the things that live in it are the angels, pure, clear and bright, like to the beams of the Sun or of a star, and like to the flame of fire, or a spark of fire, or the colour of quicksilver, or of pure gold. And this likeness is natural in the beasts of fire. And their figures seem like the lightening in likeness and in deed, for as an Evrizon [1] is a messenger of the Creator, so they are ready to do [both] good and evil, and they seem like things & prophets that [rule] over the 4 Elements, are heavens with their beasts, of which we shall say furthermore.

[2.] The second spirit is pure, but darker than the other, and it is likened to the wind, & its figure takes after some of the 4 [21ʳ] Elements to which it is joined. And it forms itself in this manner either by water, or by cloud, or by moistness, or by thickness, or by some darkness, or it receives some body as smoke of some kind, by falling in it either by *voce* [call?] in the shape of an 'elemented' beast, and from these it takes form, after the nature above stated.

3. The third beast of which wise men tell is [one] that always associates with a spirit, and mostly the corpulent and thick [part] of that spirit. And therefore its figure is found by night in places of dread, and it is heard and seen, and

---

[1] 'Orison' in Sloane MS 3846.

that often time, and the colour of it is like to a spirit [?], after the nature of the hour before [when] it was made, otherwise [it is] in the likeness [shape] of the body from which it went out of, therefore some men see the souls of bodies in churchyards. And of these souls, said the wise Hermes, and the prophet, the soul that goes out and has power is not, nor was, but a man or a woman. And over such manner of souls speak wise men, and [they] call them 'spiritual' for [their] goodness, [and] 'heavenly' from [their] simpleness.

4. The fourth beast is the wind: each day we hear but we see not, although we and others hear it not. And the work of the wind is seen by the eye, after the direction from which it comes. And it has such nature that if it is oriental [East] or meridional [South] it is hot. And if he is occidental [West] or septentrional [North] it is cold. This [wind] we see has great power, for it bears clouds and waters, and tempests and gales, and it stirs and troubles the seas and breaks trees, and this is called 'living air', as the fire above is called living fire, and simple. And therefore the Elements above are of double or twofold [nature], that is to say fixed and [21ᵛ] moveable: moveable it is because it dwells in the corners of the earth, although it descends from above, for the 7 [planets] above bind and lose it, for from them it descends, and from them it was formed, & this is a great figure in the sea, in air, and in land, it comes temperately.

5. The fifth beast, or vision, is a fantasy [phantom], which is a shade like many colours or manners, it comes compounded of many [colours] together. And this form is made in desert places, or in a corrupt air, or otherwise it descends from hills, in the likeness of knights, and they are called *exercitus antiquus,* which is an 'old army.' And otherwise [they come] in the likeness of fair women and well clothed, or in *meᶜdes*[?], and some say that they are [just] faces. And otherwise this befalls a man, for corruption, or malice of complexions, and of the humors that are in a man. And they are called *Demoniaci* for they ascend to the head and fall upon the eye, and by such corruption [of our senses] make [us] to see many fantasies [phantoms].

6. The sixth beast is called a Demon, and it descends from highness to lowness, and it was formed of pure matter without corruption wherefore it fails [dies] not, but shall always endure, although it has taken thickness in the darkness of the lowness of the earth. And it is pure in matter and strong in body. And of this [beast] says the wise man, it knows all things that are, and by him Philosophers have [been given] answers, and wise men [also have answers to] all things [about] which they wish to know the truth, and it dwells always in darkness and in obscurity, and it is never separated from them. [22ʳ] And of this says the prophet, that it has the power of taking [any]

form and shape, of which it would in the earth, after the will of the Creator.

And he tells of a bright angel, mighty and fair as the form of the Sun, and of the Moon, and of the stars [planets], or of an angel, or of a cloud, or of a fowl, or of a fish, or of a man, or of a beast, or of a reptile that is a creeping beast, or [he may take] any other form which he wishes. And all these abovesaid [beasts] are impalpable and unhappy to be touched. That is that they neither may be taken with hand nor touched with the foot, for they are spirits or winds. And know that everyone of the abovesaid, when it falls into the elements, it takes a body from them, although their life is of fire. And their dwelling is in fire, and their deeds fury, for they are fury.

And Raziel explained about these 6 [beasts], their invocation, opening, constraining, binding and losing [them] to do good and evil with them. All is made with pureness, and therefore whoever would call them, or have their service, [must] with orison and fasting, and censing, and with the praising of God, must do as hereafter you shall hear furthermore.

[Birds]

Animalia aeris tertiae alae vocantur aves &c.

Beasts of the air of the third 'wing' are called birds for they fly, and they have four movements: one is called running, another flying, and swimming, and going [upon the earth], and creeping. Now we will tell of flying [animals] and begin with the first [bird].

1. Aquila that is an Eagle [*Aquila*], for that is a fowl flying high, and he has rulership over all other birds, and it is true in its deeds, and in rulership and in honour among all other birds. The [22ᵛ] Eagle has such a nature that he takes his sons, birds, when they are little and ascends into a place when the Sun is high, and then he arranges their faces to the Sun. And if they observe strongly the Sun, he deems them to be his children and good, and if they do not observe the Sun, he deems them not his children but thinks them evil, and lets them fall and die. And one of his feathers interlaces another feather; and he can see far: at one league (or rule) [he can see even] a little beast, but a great beast truly he can see at 9 leagues, or at a day's journey [distant]. His eye with his heart has great virtue, and [gives] grace [fit] for a king, or a lord, as that [his heart] gives to him grace in his [own] realm.

2. The second fowl is a Vulture [*Vultur*], which is a *vouter*, this has great virtue in all his limbs, his head helps against all dreams and against magic craft, and his feet help against evil deeds. And if a house is censed with 9 of his feathers it drives out from it evil spirits. His gall helps the eye better then

anything in the world. His eye put in the skin of a serpent, and his tongue wrapped in a cloth of red silk, with them helps in clauses, which you wish to overcome, and to win the love of another Lord.[1] His wings put upon a bed protects a sleeping man from all evil winds, grievances, and evil spirits, nor may they enter into the house, nor may any other fantasies have power [there].

3. The third fowl is *falco*, which is a falcon, of whom the virtue is that of great lords, he is set with much high esteem. [23ʳ] They [the virtues] are of the highness of his right wing [which] overcomes [legal] pleas, both ravishing and in taking away alien things, and the highness of his left wing takes away evil fevers. But we ought not to slay game birds, nor hounds, as they have many virtues in themselves. And know how many limbs are in every beast, fowl, fish or reptile, as so many distinct virtues has every limb.

4. The fourth fowl is a Turtur [turtledove] simple and good. Nevertheless if you take the male and the female together and burn them in a new pot with crocus, *vervinca* [vervain?], *cichoria* [chicory] gathered together or joined together: if you cast the powder of these upon them [the lovers?] soon they shall be joined together, and it attracts great love to them that bear the powder with them.

5. The fifth fowl is called Upupa, that is a Lapwing, having a crest of feathers on its head like a cock, and it has many virtues. This [bird] has one bone in its wings, and [the bone] gathers together devils and spirits of air. The property of it is that whoever takes its heart and wraps it in honey, and as soon as he swallows it and drinks the milk of a white cow, of a red, or of a black [cow], it makes a man to [prophesy] things to come. And it has another virtue, [for anyone] who cuts its neck when the cock crows [at sunrise], neither may be heard, nor the voice of a hound, nor where wheat is sown. And when he cuts its neck he [can] call in devils, and then he [should] carry with him half the blood, and of that other half anoint himself, and [so] always shall go with [23ᵛ] him one of the devils that he called, and it shall tell to him many things.

6. The sixth [bird] is called Ciconia [stork], that is a haysoucke [a hedge-sparrow][2] that flees on the day of the Moon [Monday] and takes the blood of the hart [deer] and anoints himself with it. And [you should] eat the flesh with *somine faeminli* and with cardamoms and *garyophillo* [cloves], and when [you] eat it [you should] suffume yourself with good odours, and with *thure* [frankincense], mastic, cinnamon, and other such. [If you do this then you] shall have the grace of enchanting whatever [you] wish, and of conjuring and

---

[1] Possibly refers to the clauses of an indenture that bound someone to their current Lord.
[2] It is hard to see how this bird can be both a stork and a hedge-sparrow.

Liber Salomonis

constraining the spirits of air, and other spirits that go over rivers and wells.

These 6 birds abovesaid are exemplary over all others. And when you wish to know the virtue of any fowl, [find them] after the precepts of this book *Raziel* from the *Book of Visions of Angels*, from the beginning of times, in the 12 months, as hereafter you shall see furthermore.

[Fish]

Dicamus de piscibus maris et alys &c.

The explanation of fish of the sea and others, more than 6 of them, [some] that are more [potent], and [some that are in] the middle, so I will show you their virtues.

1. The first fish is Balena [whale] the fat of which [if it is] made [into] a liquid and kept for the space of 7 years & more (for how much it is aged, so [by this] much it is better) heals a man from gout, and [from an] evil mind, if he anoint himself with it. And if he anoints his head with its blood, it helps him greatly and makes him strong and more whole, and it makes [24r] him to see true visions. Its sperm is called *ambra* [ambergris]. If they cense tombs with this, it gathers together [the spirits]. The spirits above [are moved] downwards, and for each petition & asking, it makes them give an answer.

And Hermes said, "there is no [better] suffumigation to call in spirits than *ambra* [ambergris] & *lignum aloes, costus, muscus* [musk], crocus, and the blood of a lapwing with thymiamata, for these are meat and drink & happiness for the spirits of air, and these things gather them together strongly and rapidly." And wise men say that the sperm, blood and heart of a Balene [whale] are excellent for commanding the winds & spirits.

2. The second fish is called a Dolphin. And he is the king of the sea, for as the eagle has might among birds, and the Lion among beasts, so in this manner has the dolphin in the sea. And whoever anoints with their blood, the clothes of two friends, [so] it makes them enemies, or [if he] casts the dry blood upon them. And whoever bears its heart makes himself hardy.

3. The third fish is Cancer [the crab] which has 6 feet. Take and burn [cook] him in a *panno livido* [bruising pan?], and with the powder rub [polish] your teeth softly so that it heals them, and makes them fair [whitens them], and cures the canker in the mouth. And if you cast it upon the fire with somewhat of *stercoris humani combusti* [human dung], it gathers together spirits.

4. The fourth [fish] is a bright horn [*cornu lucidi*] between paleness and whiteness [in colour], that is to say *piscis candis* or sepia. This fish has many properties and well knows enchantments; and prophets made with this [fish]

their enchantments and transfigurations. So that when they wanted that a house should seem to be full of water, or that a river should [seem to] enter by the gate, they took [24ᵛ] this fish, and with thymiamata and *lignum aloes*, and roses, they censed the house, and [then] they cast therein sea water, and then it seemed that the house was filled with water. And if they cast blood therein [instead of sea water] then it seemed all [filled with] blood; and so if they cast snow therein it seemed [full] of snow. And when they wished that the earth should seem to quake, then they cast therein the earth from a plough, and so they made there many likenesses of all things, according to the thing which they put in the incense. And know that [this effect] dwells as much and as long as the suffumigations last in the house. And with the gall of this fish they also made many enchantments, for this beast is unlike any other.

5. The fifth fish is a Murena [eel] and he is lentiguus [spotted]. The virtue of it is that enchanters bear the powder of the fish with them to make enchantments.

6. The sixth fish is *Rana viridis* [green frog]. And if you take it or touch it upon whatever woman you wish, and name the names of the Angels of the month in which you were born, which are furthermore [listed] within *Libro Visionnis*,[1] you may do both good and evil with any woman you wish. And know that of these fish, and of all others, you must know the virtues of the months, and understand similarly in all other things.

[Beasts]

Primieum Animal est Leo ista bestia est valde fortis

[1.] The first beast is a Lion. This beast is very strong in the breast and in the cheeks [buttocks]. And he is of strong countenance, [25ʳ] and looking so that when other beasts see him they are all moved with dread, and his skin is of great virtue, [such] that if they be put with other skins, they destroys them and make them bare. And whoever takes [the lion's] biting tooth that is called *dens caninus* [canine tooth] and mounts it in gold, it is good to take away and to take alien things, and the same goes for the wolf's tooth. And if you make a purse of the heart of a Lion, full of blood, *musco* [musk] *& almea* and *lignum aloes*, thymiamata, and it is gathered & put upon whom you wish, and you make it hot, know that in that hour he shall much love you, and shall do your bidding.

And if you call [spirits] with the blood of a goat, the prince of devils shall be ready soon to do your commandment, and so [even] more the king [of devils], or he from whom you do, and the same I say for great women.

---

[1] John Morigny's *Liber Visionem*.

Liber Salomonis

2. The second beast is the Elephant, that is an Oliphant, and he is very great, and when he has risen hard he lays, & when he falls hard he rises, because he has no well disposed knees, and the bone of his teeth is called Ebur, that is Ivory. And if it [ivory] is put in electuaries, it comforts the feebleness of the heart as much as margarita and more.[1] And his blood with his liver comforts much fasting.

3. The third beast is Cerbus [*Cervus* – stag], that is a hart, which lives long, for he remains as the Moon, or as an eagle, [and he] who makes fumigations of the horns, chases away serpents, and by itself it chases away devils.

4. The fourth beast is Catus, that is a cat, and he sees better by the night than by the day, and whoever takes from him, and from a hedgehog, and from a dormouse, and makes an Alcosol & Alcosolizat,[2] or anoints his eye, so he sees well by night and by day. And if you put [25ᵛ] therein the eye of an ass, you may see where the spirits and devils of the air go.

5. The fifth beast is Mustela, that is a weasel, which brings forth her issue at her month, after the sayings of the poets, but not of the philosophers, this helps much when he is brent [burnt], and his skin is said to cause love between the two.

6. The sixth beast is the Talpa, that is a mole, and it dwells under the earth and is likened to a mouse. With this beast you may make to come tempests, pestilence, hail and lightning & cornflations [conflagrations?], and [he will cause] many evil things if you put him bare or naked upon the earth, dead and overturned, and with this beast you may make discord and concord between whoever you wish, for he is a cursed beast, he heals a man of the fisture [3] when it is burnt, or powdered, and cast in it.

And when you wish to know the virtues of other beasts, do as it is instructed in *Libro Visionnis*,[4] and ask this [question] of the Lord of the vision that appears to you,[5] what you ask and want to know, for [the qualities of] beasts which you wish [to know]. This beast [the mole] sees not, nor has an eye. And know that the vision of *moneths* [?] is over all things that you ask or wish to know. And God shall be with you, if [it is] for a right [cause] you ask.

And know that here is fulfilled the third 'wing.' And now we begin the fourth 'wing' which is complete or fulfilled about all the Elements.

---

[1] An electuary is a herb, or other medicinal substance, mixed with honey, to make it more palatable.
[2] Methods of preparing herbs with alcohol. Alcosol is a colloidal solution in alcohol.
[3] A non-healing tubular boil.
[4] John of Morigny, *Liber Visionem* used as a technique for obtaining knowledge.
[5] The angel or spirit guide that will appear to you in your vision.

Sepher Raziel

[De Quartus Ala – the Fourth Wing]

[De Verbis – Words]

Dixit Solomon sicut corpus vivum &c.

Solomon said, "as a living body moderate or great is [26ʳ] not moved with[out] its feet, neither is any fowl [moved with] less than with two wings, nor is the world governed with less then four elements, [so this book] may not have less than 4 'wings,' which are said to be 4 virtues." Wherefore Raziel said that whoever shall be filled with this book shall be as one of the prophets, he shall understand all the virtues of things and their powers, and if he possess it and work on it, he shall be as an angel. And therefore he [Raziel] put in this book 22 elements of great virtue, that is the 22 [Hebrew] letters (or figures), which the sons of Adam may not neglect.

1. The first [letter] is Aleph א that is A. His letter is three cornered and it signifies life, power and highness, and the principal or beginning of all things. This puts all things in their figures and in their principles.

2. The second is called Beth ב that is B, and it is very good in things which we desire in battle, and in play, & it always signifies goodness and profit.

3. The third is called Gimel ג that is G, and it signifies evil and grief and impediment in things.

4. The fourth is called Daleth ד that is D. This signifies the perturbation and death of some man & harm to him.

5. The fifth is called He ה that is H, and it signifies high esteem, honour and gladness & it is very good in all things.

6. The sixth is called Vau ו that is V, and it signifies death, pain and work.

7. The seventh is called Zain ז that is Z, and it signifies money and riches.

8. The eighth is called Heth ח [that is Ch], and it signifies long life and health.

[26ᵛ] 9. The ninth is called Teth ט that is T, and it signifies wrath, anger and grief.

10. The tenth is Iod י that is I, and it signifies faith, good life, and gladness, and all good beginnings.

11. The 11th is called Caph כ [that is K], and it signifies true gladness, and work without profit.

12. The 12th is called Lamed ל [that is L], and it signifies gladness, honour and profit.

13. The 13th is called Mem מ that is M, and it signifies grief, and otherwise dolor.

14. The 14th is called Nun נ that is N. It signifies the restoration of a friend, and a visitation by him, & profit.

15. The 15th is called Samech ס [that is S].

16. The 16th is called Ain ע [that is O]. It signifies the [menstrual?] occasion, or the evil of a woman.

17. The 17th is called Pe פ [1] [that is P]. It signifies health.

18. The 18th [17th] is called Phe פ [2] that is ff, and it signifies that blood is shed of good men and high [men].

19. The 19th [18th] is [called] Zade צ [that is Tz]. It signifies health.

20. The 20th [19th] is called Coph ק [that is Q]. It signifies hidden life.

21. The 21st [20th] is called Res[h] ר that is R+. And it signifies a man that has fallen and is risen.

[The 21st is called Shin ש that is Sh.]

22. The 22nd is called Thau ת that is T. It signifies grief and diminution.

[Iam diximus de quatuor Alia super]

Now we have explained about the four 'wings', and about the 22 letters that the laws of the table were written.[3] And know that there are no more [Hebrew letters], but only the 22 letters, which are the root of Semiforas, for with them it is formed. And [it] is caused and is made [with them], but without them it may not be.

[27r] And some men said that Cammalie found them. But it is not true, for the angel Raziel gave them, written, to Adam in this book that is called *Liber Ignis*,[4] and with them all the book of Semiforas was written. And each man that reads this book, knows that the Creator said to Raziel [that these letters are] to be [used in] the names of Semiforas, wherefore if you transpose these 22 letters (or figures) as it seems [best], you shall attain the great name of your Creator, and with it you might do what you wish,

---

[1] The hard *peh*, or *peh dagesh*, with a dot in the middle of the letter.
[2] Two forms of *peh* are given, but no *shin*.
[3] The assumption is that Moses' Tablets of the Law were written in Hebrew on Mt Sinai.
[4] *Book of Fire*.

always with pureness and with the help of the Creator.[1]

Now we have fulfilled this book of the 'wing' like to the angels that are Panthaseron, Mucraton, and Sandalon,[2] for every one of these has 4 wings by commandment of the benign angel which the Creator sent to me, [in order] that this book is better arranged and well arranged.

Here ends the Second Book & [here] begins the Third Book of Thymiamata.

---

[1] A description that neatly sums up the aim and rationale behind the Kabbalah.
[2] See "Pantaseron, Micraton, Sandaton" at folio 20r.

[*Liber Tertius* – The Third Book]

[*Tractatus Thymiamatus* of Suffumigations]

Dixit angelus Adae fac Thymiamata &c.

The angel said to Adam make thymiamata.[1] Thymiamata are confections of good odours with which you shall suffume (and you shall please the Creator) and you shall attain what you wish by this [action]. And those [things] of which they are made are petition things,[2] which you shall find and [are] of good odour and of good nature, and of pure things. And when you do it, be clean of all outward filth, and then the angel rested in that hour. And Adam remained and did what he might. And this Solomon expounded and said, "I marvel why this is the book [27ᵛ] of Moses also, for the Creator said to Moses 'make Thymiamata, and suffume it in the hill when you wish to speak with me.'"[3] Wherefore Solomon said "suffumigations, sacrifice & unction make to open the gates of air, and of fire, and of all the other heavens."

And by suffumigations a man may see heavenly things and the privities [secrets] of the Creator. And each man [must] know that they pierce the earth, water, and lowness. And Solomon said that as there are 7 heavens, 7 planets, and 7 days in the week, of which everyone is distinct, so know that there are 7 suffumigations which hold within them the virtue of the 7 planets, and makes glad the spirits of air, and the angels of heaven, and devils, or angels of the world. And therefore if a man yields it to them, that is theirs.

Therefore they [the angels and devils] are pleased and glad of the words when you say their names, or that of the Creator. And for this, which you do when you wash, and for the gift that you give to them when you suffume: these things yield them earthly and [make them able to] appear to you. And spiritual & invisible that is, [so] that neither evil men, nor the beasts amongst [you], see you if you do it strongly about you, and about whom you do it. Thymiamata is made of many things, and these are principally [based] upon the 7 days of the week. And the first thymiamata is of Saturday, for his planet [Saturn] is the highest & his angel is mighty on the earth. [28ʳ][4]

---

[1] As defined in the next sentence, mixtures of perfumes or incenses to be burned on hot coals to produce smoke to purify things. These perfumes are also designed to attract spirits. It literally means 'incense', from the Greek θυμιαματον, *thymiamaton*. See Appendix 1 for incense nomenclature.

[2] Things that will help your petition or prayer.

[3] A reference to Mt. Sinai, or simply to the 'high places' of worship.

[4] Saturday is the first day of the week for Jews.

Sepher Raziel

[Perfumes of the Days]

1. The first thymiamata of Saturday [Saturn] ought to be [made] of good things and well smelling roots, as is costus and the herb *thuris*. And that is thymiamata for good, and so I shall show all others as it seems for good; and then thymiamata for another [bad purpose] I shall explain in another place.

2. Thymiamata of Sunday is [*thur*], mastic, *muscus* [musk], and other such, and all other good gums, of good odour [are useful] in all good [operations], but to the contrary [bad odours are useful] in all evil [objectives].

3. Thymiamata of Monday is *folius myrti* [myrtle] and *lauri* [laurel] and [other] leaves of good odour, and so understand [the opposite is true] for its contrary.

4. Thymiamata of Tuesday is *sandalus, rubeus, niger* and *albus*,[1] and all such trees, and each tree [wood] of aloes & cypress, and so understand [the benefit] of each tree.

5. Thymiamata of Wednesday is made of rinds, as cinnamon, *cassia lignea* [cassia wood] & *cortices, lauri* [laurel] & *muris* [hawkweed?], and so understand for the other [purposes].

6. Thymiamata of Thursday is *nux muscata* [nutmeg], *gariophylli* [cloves] and *citruli* [citrus] and the rind of *aurangiarum* [oranges], *siccarum & pulverizatarum*, which is [in other words], the rind of oranges dry and powdered, & all other fruits of good odour.

7. Thymiamata of Friday is the flowers of rose, viola & crocus and all other flowers of good odour; and for the contrary [purposes], to the contrary, use all stinking thymiamata.

And know that each thymiamata of good odour gathers together spirits after its [good] nature, its colour & its strength. Thus I said for good [use] good, for better [use] better. [28ᵛ]

And Hermes said of thymiamata that:

Thymiamata of the Moon is cinnamon & *lignum aloes*, mastic, crocus, *costus, macis* [mace], *myrtus* [myrtle], and we make this such that each of the planets has a share in it, and all this may be the Moon good and fortunate, by good spices & sharp, although Salomon made distinction between the days and planets of the spices, with which a man ought to make thymiamata. And he [Hermes] said that of Saturn, each good root [is used] in good, and evil [root is used] in evil [magic]. And of Jupiter all fruit, and of Mars each tree. And of

---

[1] The three varieties of sandalwood: red, black and white.

the Sun each gum, and of Venus each flower, and of Mercury each rind, and of the Moon each leaf, and thus understand of all the others, and each odoriferous herb is of Venus.

And Raziel said to Adam that he should make good thymiamata. And therefore said Hermes, understand that each thymiamata is made of all good things, as of root, tree, rind, leaf, flower, fruit & gums, and that seeds are [also] put in it, as are *baccae* [berries] & cardamom, and wax, and put in all good things and precious, and afterwards he called this '*Thymiamata Completum.*'

And there is some 'Greek Thymiamata' by which heathen men were used to suffume Idols. To this day Churches and Altars are [still] censed with it, and it is called 'Thymiamata of Jupiter.' And in truth, he who uses this thymiamata must be pure and chaste, and of a good life, and [with good] will towards the Creator, and so he shall profit. [29r]

Method of Using the Thymiamata

Dixit Solomon super suffumigata Hermetis quae dure &c.

Solomon said about the suffumigations of Hermes below, that there are seven manners [of using them] which are:

1. [The first is to] make sacrifices (of the first [born]), with fasts, and give things to the Creator, and therefore they [who do this] believe that they attain to that which they desire. And it is true.

2. The second is that they wash & purify themselves and dwell pure, and therefore they think to attain their petitions & asking, & it is true.

3. The third is that they do alms for God, and for his holy angels.

4. The fourth is that they slew [sacrifices] and cast the blood in the fire.

5. The fifth is that they slew [sacrifices] and burn all [of the sacrifice].[1]

6. The sixth is that they pray much in specific hours, 7 times in the day, and 3 [times] in the night.

7. The seventh is to make suffumigation with good things, and good smelling [incenses], and every one of those that did this might attain the truth of whatever he asked, and so he attained it by the Commandment of the Creator.

---

[1] Typically a Jewish practice, prior to the destruction of the Temple in Jerusalem in 70 C.E.

And know that suffumigation overcomes all [other methods].[1] Truly, whoever suffumeth best, to the eye it proves, with this the wise men dismiss all other [methods]. And understanding that he who can know the nature of suffumigations, might easily [come] near such spirits, which he wishes to call, according to the nature of the suffumigation. And always consider the nature of the spirit and [the nature] of the suffumigation, as the spirits are constrained by the contrary [thing] and are comforted by [29v] similar things. And this is like a wise doctor in giving a medicine to a sick man, removes the sickness and leads to health.

So suffumigation, if it is good, removes the contrary [evil spirits] from the place. And with evil suffumigation are removed good spirits, evil and ill spirits also dread that, for each thing loves health more than sickness. And therefore it is said that sulphur removes both good spirits and evil, and this is proven in a profitable way. And there is another way for *lignum aloes* and none other, and sulphur chases them away and this is the true reason. And then I say that sulphur gathers together its [own] proper spirits, and none other. And they are very strong & penetrative and thick, and are not departed soon [easily] from a place. But although a place is censed with sulphur, and then is washed with water, and [then] censed with *lignum aloes*, it draws away the spirits of sulphur, or endures or leads in its own [spirits].

The spirit of Azet [Azoth], that is quicksilver [mercury], and the spirit of *thuris*, are contrary [to each other], although spirits, yet all devils enter and pierce [quicksilver?] rather or sooner than the spirit of *thuris*, wherefore every one has very great strength. But if you wish to withdraw the spirits, suffume with *thure* [frankincense], and they shall go out. And so understand of all other spirits, [both] good and evil.

And Solomon said, that as a physician applies to a man pure good ointment and pure, and [30r] it pierces the body of a man and heals [it], so suffumigations pierce the 4 Elements, and makes [one] to see and know heavenly things which were always heavenly, and which descend from heaven, as do angels & spirits of air, and the souls of dead men, and devils, and the winds of spelunke [caves], and of the deepness and fantasies [phantoms] of desert places. And all spiritual [creatures], with the right fumigation, shall obey you, and shall come to you, and they shall do your commandment. And Hermes said that all things that were, or are present, or shall be, that the above nature [is] joined with the lower by ordinance, for time and hour makes one body, and understanding that he can understand

---

[1] This suggests that suffumigation is a replacement for the animal sacrifice of the old Temple.

Liber Salomonis

and know such things, how creatures have to live and govern themselves.

Therefore know that there are fumes that chase away spirits, and other sorts that strengthen them, and constrain them to come, and other that enliven them and strengthen them, and give them might, and so to the contrary there are some [fumes] that destroy them and take away their might, and this is the proof of it: for the smoke of a hare chases them away, and this he said about serpents, and *fumus amnecae* chases them away, that is the smoke of dregs of oil, and what constrains them is the spittle of a fasting man.[1]

And therefore he said suffumigation suffice for us in all things beneath [on Earth]. And Raziel said that water washes [away] all uncleanness, and [likewise] fire makes liquid, or melts, all metals & makes them pure and fine. And as the air is the life of a living man, [30ᵛ] and the earth sustains or bears each body and nourishes each plant, understand that good thymiamata or suffumigation is fulfilling in the work of the invocation of spirits; and of other things [ensure that] the thymiamata is well proportioned [when it] is confected or melded, in each hour convenient [to its manufacture] according [to its planetary qualities, etc.]

Dixit Solomon propter hoc pono horas et tempus &c.

Solomon said, "I [should] put [fix] the hour and the time for this work, for in all [auspicious] hours in which a man wishes to speak to a king, or to a prince, he may not [be able to] speak to them; nor in every hour in which a son asks of the father for any thing, does he give [it] to him." Therefore it is dark [unclear] to you to choose the [correct] time and the hour for these [things] that you ask.

This is therefore the *tempus quondam* [relevant measure of time], is some time of Jupiter, be it done in the day of Jupiter, and of Venus in the day of Venus, and Mars. And of [the hour of] Saturn in the day of Saturn: and so for other [planets] that [must] be done in the invocation of spirits, and in all praising of [praying to] angels. And the fumigation [must be] pure. Know that it is a spiritual thing, living and being associated with heavenly things, and now called *Veallia*. Know that no man ought to make suffumigation of precious things unless he is pure, and with pure waters well washed, and anointed with precious ointments, which he made purely and with precious things [such] as *cera alba* [white wax], *balsamo* [balsam], *croco* [crocus] and *musco* [musk], *abitatmeca*, *algalia* [civet],[2] *almea*, *thure* [frankincense], myrrh, and *oleo*

---

[1] An interestingly concrete reason for fasting before taking part in evocations.
[2] The obsolete Spanish word 'algaliar' means to perfume with civet.

olivary [olive oil].

And this ointment [must] be well kept and well protected in a pure [31r] place, after that also [see] that your clothing is pure, white, new and good, not broken nor black [stained]. And cense yourself reverently, and the manner of suffuming yourself ought to be made in the 7 directions: towards the East, the North, the West and the South, and towards the heaven above, and towards the earth beneath, and the seventh time all about. And as often as you do this, address your mind unto God, and pray that he fulfills your desires.

I found in some old book that these were the best suffumigations. Thus *Thymiamata Graecum*, mastic, *sandulus* [sandalwood], galbanum, Muschalazerat,[1] myrrh, and *ambra* [ambergris], and these are collectors of spirits and their placators. And Solomon said that when you wish to gather together the spirits of air do it in this manner. Cleanse yourself in the best manner that you can, and go to a pitt [2] known to you and suffume it, and call him [the angel or spirit] by his own proper name and call him or pray [to] him, and that [repeat] on three nights, and if he answers not, nor appears, take him to a certain place, or to a house, or to a quadrive [crossroads] that is a place where 4 ways meet, or to a yard, or garden. And suffume the pitt [enclosure?] towards the 7 directions, and in the place where you bathe also, as I have said. And then know that he shall come, and he shall appear to you if you do this.

Et dixit Hermes quod spiritus qui apparent &c.

And Hermes said that the spirits which appear [31v] in this world are these. Some truly are heavenly and the prophet calls them angels, and they are bright and clear as flame or a star as we have said. Others are of air and of many colours green, bright, and other such and of many figures. And others are fiery and they are bright and red. And others are watery, and they are white and as bright as tin or burnished iron, or quicksilver. Others that are neighed [denied] to men are like to a white cloud, or to white clothes. And others are dark and dim and of many forms, which are called Devils, which are called with the wind, and there are [others] in the deepness of the sea and of lowness, spirits that bring with [them] hail & lightning. And wise men call these huge spirits & strong. Now we have explained the nature of spirits, and [so] put your mind to it, and you shall attain with the help of God.

---

[1] In the Latin of Sloane MS 3847 it is 'Muschullaroth.' However this could be Malabathron or Malabatrum (Indian Bay leaves) which was the Classical Graeco-Egyptian incense of Jupiter.

[2] This could refer to an enclosure or arena, a pond, an underground chamber, or even a grave.

Liber Salomonis

Dixit Raziel sicut in aere puro claro &c.

Raziel said, as in the pure, clear, bright, pure and peaceable air, all things gladden a joy [?] of it. So know that [success comes from] from fasting, purity, washing of water, prayers, and orisons to the Creator. And from natural and pure suffumigation, and true faith, or belief, which may please them [the angels] which we have mentioned above. And Raziel said to Adam, know that in all manners the life of angels is holy & pure. And the suffuming or suffumigation is bread on which these spirits [32ʳ] live. And fasting and pureness and chastity, sacrifice with orisons, are the house of holy altar souls, and trust in the author of [all] good. Wherefore each man that has these abovesaid [qualities], he shall attain, and he shall have profit.

And Solomon said, "this is what happens in suffumigations: soon shall come to us smoke, and then odour, and of the smoke a cloud, and of the cloud a high cloud and wind, and on the wind the cloud ascends higher, and of the cloud a high wind ascends higher, and is made a soul. And of this the spirit is made higher, and of the spirit an angel of heaven, and of this angels [of] light." And these [things] are caused by pure suffumigation. And know that suffumigations [incenses] are of 7 manners. Some truly sharp, and others penetrative or piercing. Others sweet smelling, others stinking, others simple, others meek, others of grief, others truly of peace, every one of these, or of these manners, is after [the nature of] his odour, savor, nature and complexion.

Wherefore Hermes said that as coldness congeals water [into ice] which is cold, and as the water of the sea is congealed with great [cold], and as Azertacona congeals the water of wells, and everyone of these congeals the water; one with coldness, another with hotness, another by art, another by nature, and the matter is made [into] one body and one gobbet [piece]. And know that good suffumigation gathers together and constrains and makes spirits to appear in the air, and [reveal] secret or privy things. And it makes them to take a body, without eye seen.

And Solomon said that as the Adamant draws [32ᵛ] iron to itself, so suffumigation gathers together and draws the spirits of air, and makes them to come to the place where you do [the experiment], and [it] will gather them together. And the wise man said suffumigation is like the root of *arzolle* [Lady's thistle], as it joins together gobbets of flesh into one. So suffumigations gather together the spirits of heaven, which [then] the 4 Elements make them take a body, and spirits take [and] fulfill what is asked of them, and that [spirit may be drawn] into a likeness in a mirror, which if [you] there are sat in front of it, whatever figure you wish appears within the fumigation, made purely, an invocation in the hour after the spirits proportional.[1] The spirits appear to us, and new operations and workings with fulfillment of the thing that you ask, and don't be deceived in the knowledge of suffumigations, and apply your mind to them lest they be transposed [confused], and you shall fulfill [your wishes], after you do it as he [Solomon] said.

And Solomon said, "I will touch somewhat on the nature of suffumigations, whoever uses it much makes to see [visions] in sleep, or in reality, green things, and yellow, and many colours. Melancholic fumigation signifies grey things; sanguine fumigation signifies red things, and otherwise it is shown of a purple colour; phlegmatic fumigation signifies white things and fair. And so [you can] understand what their nature is [from] the appearance of the spirits, [33r] and of their colour and visible [appearance]." And their work shall be the sharpness of it, and the goodness, and the direction of *fumigii* [censing] that is fulfilling the thing, after the Image was formed, and the orison of the thing [spirit] named, and the trust for all is in the intention of the man, and in the hour in which it is done. Now we have said how every one of the planets has his fumigations.

Now we will state the fumigations of the 12 Signs and of their 36 Faces.[2]

[The Perfumes of the Zodiac]

Aries holds by himself mirtal [myrtle].

Taurus	costum [costus].
Gemini	masticem [mastic].
Cancer	musthalazeratis.
Leo	thus [olibanum].
Virgo	classen [oil of sandalwood].
Libra	galbanum.
Scorpio	opopanaces [oppoponax].
Sagittarius	lignum aloes [oud].
Capricorn	assafoetida.
Aquarius	euphorbium.
Pisces	thymiama [thyme].[3]

---

[1] The reference is probably to the proportional planetary hour, which is one twelfth of the time between sunrise and sunset, rather than to an evenly divided clock hour of 60 minutes.
[2] The 12 Zodiacal Signs are divided into 36 Faces, like the 36 Decans. The first list above lists the suffumigation of the first Face as if it was the suffumigation of the whole Sign.
[3] Note that although 'thymiamata' refers to blended incense, 'thymiama' means the herb tyme.

Liber Salomonis

The first Face of Aries holds mirtal.[1] The second stamonea. The third piper nigrum.

The first of Taurus [holds] costum. The second cardamom. The third cassia.

The first of Gemini masticem. The second cinamomus. The third cipressum.

The first of Cancer mastum [camphor]. The second succum. The third anisum.

The first of Leo thus. The second lignum balsami. The third nucem muscata.

The first of Virgo sandalos [sandal]. The second crocum. The third masticem.

The first of Libra galbanum. The second bofor. The third mirtum [mortum].

[The first of Scorpio oppoponax.] [2]

The first of Sagittarius lignum aloes. The second folia lauri. The third gariofilum.

The first of Capricorn assa[foetida]. The second colofoniam, the third piper longum.

The first of Aquarius euphorbium, the second reubarbarum, the third stamonea.[3]

The first of Pisces thymiama. The second crocum. The third sandalum album.[4]

[33ᵛ] *Nota sedum Hermetem de fumigiis.*

And Hermes said, "Aries, Leo and Sagittarius hold each choleric [suffumigations, and are] spicy & bitter; Taurus, Virgo and Capricorn [have] melancholic [suffumigations] and are styptic [astringent]; Gemini, Libra & Aquarius [have] sanguine and are sweet; Cancer, Scorpio & Pisces [have] phlegmatic and are of a salty savor."

And this Solomon holds for the nature of such spices we give, & with them we suffume. And which [suffumigations are] given to the days, and to the hours? For Sunday, the first hour is of the Sun, and all of the day all together: we should give this [day] mastic & *muscum* [musk] as we have said of planets in the beginning of this 'Book of Thymiamata', and to understand of all others, know the season of suffumigations.

In primo tempore lignum aloes thus et crocum &c.

In the first season [5] [use] *lignum aloes, thus* [frankincense] *& crocum* [crocus].

---

[1] The first third of the Sign Aries. See Appendix 1 for translation of names of the incenses.
[2] The second and third Face are not given.
[3] The last two rhubarb and stamonea are often reversed.
[4] For details of the suffumigations of the 36 Faces see Table N12-N14; for details of the Faces/Decans other attributes see Tables H54-71 in Stephen Skinner, *Complete Magician's Tables*, Golden Hoard, Singapore, and Llewellyn, St. Paul, 2006.
[5] Spring.

In the second season *thymiama, costum, mastice*.

In the third season *sandalus, cassia,* and *mirtum* [myrtle].

In the fourth season, *muscum, succum* and *lignum balsami*.

And as he gave to each of the 4 seasons their spices, or kinds, so he gave to each month one spice [each] in order.

Dicamus nunc suffumigia 4 partium mundi &c.

We now tell of the suffumigations of the 4 parts of the world and of the 4 Elements. For all things that are in this world are either compounded of the 4 Elements, or simples.

Suffumigations of the 4 parts of this world [and of the 4 Elements] are these:

About the parts of the [34ʳ] East, and fire, serve *ambra* [ambergris], *muscus* [musk] & *alba cera* (that is white wax).

About the parts of the South, and earth, *algalia* [civet], *almea* and *teriaca*.

About the parts of the West, and air, *balsamus*, camphor & *oleo olivrarum*.

About the [parts of the] North, and water, *lignum aloes, nux muscata* [nutmeg] & *maris* [the sea?].

And Solomon said, "each man that wishes to do any [magical] things [using] this book [should] study the chapter on thymiamata, [so] that he knows the kinds of things & can justly mix them." And so you might easily work by it, for without work you might [not] fulfill all things that you desire to see. Now we have fulfilled our Chapter of *fumigiis,* or fumigations, and we will say furthermore about that which was our intention, with the help of God.

[Here ends the Third Book & here begins the Fourth Book][1]

---

[1] For a more complete listing of the various incenses, their Latin names and modern equivalents, plus their botanical names, see Appendix 1.

[The Fourth Book]

[*Treatise of Times* of the Day and of the Night][1]

Here begins the Fourth Book that speaks about the times of the year

In Dei nomine pii incipio scribere libris istu &c.

In the name of the meek God I begin to write this book that is said or called [2] *Cephar Raziel* which the Angel Raziel gave to Adam. And it shall speak about the 4 seasons of the year, & months & days, [each] with his night, [and] how we should name each thing, and know each man. This is called the *Book of Times*, and the Angel that gave it is called mighty and great by the commandment of the Creator, the living God, [who is] in all things mighty.

And [this Book was given in order] that Adam should know all things in this world, what it is, what it was, and what it should be, in all things in the 12 months of the year, and [all the names of the] days & hours, and that by order and likeness, by pure fasting, and by washings, by sacrifice, by suffumigations made on the 7 days [of the week], [especially] on the [34ᵛ] first [day of the] Moon, and before the Sun should ascend his tail, the Ascendant, and before the Sun should ascend over the planet Zedek, or Jupiter, they should be named in this book by the mouth of the holy angels, that have rulership over the 7 heavens formed of fire, and their observing is of fire, and their life is fire.

And they seemed clothed with fire. And they are covered with fire. And from fire they went out, and in fire they dwell, and they are of great friendship [help], ruling the 12 months of the year by the precepts of the Creator who called the world into being, and all the angels [into being], and existed before it, and there are 7 powers before the face of it, and to each of them is given a rulership, and [each] has a day of the month, and of the week [given to him]. And of them, some are standing around, and some are sitting in chairs with great honour serving the Creator, and they are always ready and bound to go out, and to enter, to come and to go, and to do all good and evil whatsoever, and to enchant and to put down and to [un]cover secret things and to find [out] or make revelation.[3]

And all this that we have said, by the commandment of God, and [by the

---

[1] This Chapter is entitled *Temporum Anni* in the Latin version of the text.
[2] Here 'said' is used in the same sense as 'called.' Where appropriate 'said' is changed to 'called' where it is used elsewhere in the manuscript in this sense.
[3] It is interesting that the angels should be said to be equally able to do good as well as evil things.

Sepher Raziel

commandment of] all the greater angels and lesser, and their princes with their powers, with their odours, or with their associations, they call themselves, every one, by their names which are selly [marvelous], [blessed], high and sovereign always, and they praise God the Creator which formed them. And also all the powers, of all the heavens, in the month, and in the day in which he formed them, and they are all speaking together as men. And Raziel said that these angels wrote those names and this book. [35ʳ] And he said that there are 7 angels ruling over the 7 planets, and these be *potestates* or powers,[1] ruling over the 7 days of the week. And they are the keepers [of the days of the week], and of the 24 hours of the day, and of the 7 heavens, and of the 12 Signs [of the Zodiac], and of all other things that govern the world.

[The Planets in the 7 Heavens]

And Raziel said to Adam, "behold, know and hold [understand] these 7 powers or *potestates*, which have power in the 7 heavens, and [over] the 7 planets."

The names of [the planets] are these: Sabaday that is Saturn, Zedek that is Jupiter, Madim that is Mars, Hanina that is the Sun,[2] Nogah that is Venus, Cocab [Kokab] that is Mercury, and Labana [Levanah] that is the Moon.

The names of the 7 Heavens in which they are born are these: Samin, Raquia, Siagum, Mahum, Macon, Zebul, Arabeck.[3] Over Samyn goes the Moon. Over Raquia goes Mercury and over Arabeck [goes] Saturn, and so understand the others. The names of Angels that have power over the 7 planets, and rule over the 7 heavens, and others while in their chairs are these: Capziel, Satquel, Samael, Raphael, Amael, Michael, Gabriel. And the power of these is that Capziel is the power of Sabaday; Satquel of Zedek; Mamael of Madim; Raphael of Hanina; Amael of Nogah; Michael of Cocab; Gabriel of Labana. And every one of these sits in his [own] heaven. And their meynees [retainers/descendants?] all about, and they are of many colours as white, black, red, yellow, green, leady [grey], *pardi viati,* mixed, gilt [golden], and of the colour of a peacock's feather, and of many other colours.

[The 12 Hebrew Months]

These are the Angels that have power over the 12 months of the year. The names of the months [35ᵛ] are these: Nisan, Yar, Zivan, Tamus, Ab, Elul,

---

[1] *Potestates*: category of angels.
[2] The name for the Sun is sometimes spelled Hamina and sometimes Hanina in the manuscript.
[3] A more modern transliteration of the Hebrew heavens is Shamayim [Moon], Raqia [Mercury], Shechaqim [Venus], Zebul [the Sun], Ma'on [Mars], Makon [Jupiter], and Araboth [Saturn].

Liber Salomonis

Tisirin, Marquesuam, Quislep, Tobez or Thebeth, Sabat, Adar, *postadar postmodo*.[1] The names of the *potestates* [Powers] are these. And they are the 12 capitals, that is, one over every [lunar] month of the Moon, rather that is the [first 7 months only:] Oriel, Sasuyel, Amariel, Noriel, Biraquel, Magnia, Saciel. And every one of these has so many *potestates*, helpers, more or greater as there are days in the month, or many other servants.

And [using] the aforesaid angels, a man may know all things that are to come in every year, and in every season, and in every month, and every day, and every hour, with the proper signs. Whoever knows them well, he will know of [the destiny of kings and queens, their] many reigns or few, or when they shall be, or if they shall be or not, and the day and hour when they shall fall [from grace].

And a man may know by them which is his Sign and his planet, and he may know of his life, if it shall be long or short in the world, and other things, either for a sick man or a whole [man], either for a man or for a woman. Or he may know a subtle understanding, or sharp [understanding], he may know what is to come, and do with it [that knowledge] what he wish. And the days of the year, or of the Sun, alone [are] 365 and the quarter part of one day (in the week of days). The year of the Moon is otherwise 360 days and four hours and 46 minutes, [calculated] after the year of the Moon.[2] And the fulfilling of seasons in this: if one season is 3 months, and then the [four] seasons [36r] truly [add] to 12 [months].

And know that Nisan, which is the first month, begins on the first day of the first Moon (the Moon *prima*) of the [calendar] month of March, and so [it is] for the other [Hebrew months]. The first season is truly [calculated] from the first degree in which the Sun enters into Aries, till it enters the first degree of Cancer. And the second [season is] from Cancer to Libra. And the third [season] from Libra to Capricorn. And the fourth [season] from Capricorn unto Aries. And this is a better distinction of seasons [than the Western civil calendar]. And in the hour which Raziel gave the Book to Adam, [with details] of seasons, of months and the names of things, then was Adam comforted [because] in the same day lightning struck, and thunders and coruscations appeared, and there was in that day a great tempest in all the world, both in the land, and in the air, and in the sea. And [this happened] in

---

[1] This is a slightly garbled rendering of the 12 Jewish lunar months beginning in March-April: Nisan, Iyar, Sivan, Tammuz, Ab, Elul, Tishri, Marchesvan, Kislev, Tebet, Shebat, Adar, followed by an occasional thirteenth month. This is another indication that the original of this grimoire (or at least this section) was Hebrew.
[2] This presumes a year of 12 lunar months calculated as 30.02 days each month.

Sepher Raziel

the hour in which the Angel Raziel opened this book and gave it to Adam.

Then he [Raziel] gave to him [Adam] might, strength & surety in all the words of this book, and the miracles that are in it. And when this book fell [open] before the face of Adam, Adam regarded it with very much awe, and quaked in great dread. And [he] fell down onto the earth as though he had been dead. Then the Angel Raziel said to Adam, "rise and be comforted for know that a steadfast spirit has descended in you from the high heavens which has lightened you, and has been put in this hour in you, the knowledge and power that you shall attain [anything] that you shall ask."

And I say to you, that you [should] consider this book and observe it, and by it you shall know and understand whatever was, and is, [36ᵛ] and that shall be after you. And in that hour in which this book was given to Adam, fire fell upon the banks of the rivers of paradise. And the Angel ascended by the flame of fire to the heavens. And an Angel descended in likeness of a white cloud and spoke with him plainly, and came to him as a man, very bright and clear, like to the clearness of a star in his body, and full of many other [stars] all about. And in ascending when he was separated, always Adam was like a lamb which grew very bright, as the flame of fire, and clear as the fire of a furnace in which gold is purged.

And then Adam saw this, and found [this], and knew the Lord of all worlds who is a great king, and mighty [in all] things. This book was sent for him. And then he considered and looked in it with holiness and purity. And then he beheld in it all things that he would [want to] know in this world. And this was the first word that Adam had with the Angel Raziel. And therefore he considered it, and governed himself by it.

Solomon said, "for the aforesaid reason that the Angel Raziel said unto Adam that it is well to know the seasons, of [the difference of] one hour to another, and of one season to another", for whoever sows wheat in Spring [knows that] it may not be gathered in the same Spring, [but only in the appropriate season, Autumn]. And these [seasons] are after the temperament of the parts of the North[ern hemisphere]. And therefore it is necessary or needful to divide the year into 4 parts [seasons] and the month into 4 parts [weeks] and an hour into four parts. [37ʳ] And if you keep these divisions and understand them you shall profit in all that you wish, for this is true, and all natural things are made in the season, and in the day, and in the hour, according to how the high sovereign Creator has ordered [it]."

Raziel said [using this Book], "you will know anything of this world, that is of the other [worlds], or that is in the heavens which are associated with the first heavens. Or if you [wish to] do any thing that fulfills your wish, cleanse your body for 7 days, that is, wash, and eat not a thing of the chest [coffin], nor of the raven, nor of evil parts, nor a thing unclean, nor that [which] has fallen to its death, nor a beast with 4 [cloven] feet, nor other. And avoid malice and falseness, and you shall not drink wine, nor shall you eat fish, or any thing from which blood goes out. And do not join [sexually] to a polluted woman, nor a menstruating [woman], nor enter into a house where there is a dead man, nor go beside the grave of a dead man, nor go near him that suffered gonorrhea, and avoid and be aware of night lest you fall into pollution, and keep from lechery and evil pride. And see that you are always pure, and are in Orison or prayer, and keep your tongue from saying evil [things] and lying, and fast purely."

And keep your body from doing evil and sin. And lighten the house with orisons, and praise the angels, and do alms to needy men, and do charity, and do not join with evil men, nor with unclean [men], and clothe yourself with clean clothes, a larger [size] than you might [normally use], and always believe in God, and [37ᵛ] rise early, and pray to the Creator that he dress you and wash you, and fulfill your petition [prayers], and [so] you shall attain to that which you ask of God.

[The First Work and Sacrifice]

Nota hanc partem bene. Note well this part.

Primum opus istius libri que est necessarium &c.

The first work of this book is necessary, or needful, in all things that man does. And then you want to know when it is good to do all the things which you do. Or you will know when it is good to do whatever thing you wish of this world, and you cannot do anything thereof [unless you] understand that you [must] count by 7 days, before [beginning with] the first day of the month that is of the Moon. And in these 7 days you [must not] be polluted, nor eat a beast having blood, nor drink wine, nor touch unclean things, nor lay with a woman, and wash yourself with clean running water each of the 7 days, before the Sun ascends. And hold [understand] the abstinence which we have said, and cense yourself, when you are bathed, with this: *lignum aloes* and *ambra* [ambergris], crocus, *costo* [costus], camphor and mastic.

And then take two living turtledoves, whole without languor in themselves, or if you wish two white doves, if you might have none other.[1] And cut off

---

[1] Turtledoves were common ancient Hebrew sacrifices. They appear in Solomon's *Song of Songs* 2:12 in a sensual context. They were considered emblems of devoted love.

Sepher Raziel

the neck, fasting, with a brazen red knife over gilt [with] on both sides a cutting [edge]. And cut the neck of one turtledove on one side, and the other [turtledove] on the other [side], after that draw out the entrails, but save the blood in a new glass cup & cast it into the fire. [38r].[1]

And wash the entrails with clean water. And then take 3 weight of musk, and 3 crocus, *thuris albi lucidi* [bright white frankincense], cinnamon and 10 *keys* of *gariophylli* [cloves] and *lignum aloes* the same [amount]. And then take 12 *grana piperis nigri* [grains of black pepper], and old white wine, and *sandalos* [sandalwood], and *muscu* [musk], and camphor, and somewhat [of] honey and [mix] all these with wine, and put it all melded in the entrails of the turtledoves and fill them or divide them into 7 parts or 7 'limbs', and cast one 'limb' upon the coals of fire in the morrow [the following day] before the Sun arise, and that is the 11th hour of the night.[2]

And when you burn the 'limbs' be covered with white cloth and standing [with] your feet bare, that is unhosed [without stockings] and without shoes, and afterward [write] the names of angels which are written that serve the month, that is serving the month in which you do it, for there are prayers and doers there, and know that each day you have to say the names of the angels of that month 7 times. And in the 7 days you shall gather together the ashes which you have made in the same 7 days of the aforesaid 7 'limbs.' And the house and the place in which you shall burn it [should] be clean. And when all this is done, you shall arrange a solemn house, clean [pure] and separated [from other houses] for you. And you shall sprinkle the aforesaid ashes upon the earth, in the middle of the house, and you shall sleep there, so that you shall do this.

And then when you enter the bed, you shall name the names of the angels strong, dreadful, mighty & high, and then sleep. And speak with the man. And then you may be very certain, and not dreading, that there shall come to you some man, and he shall show himself to you in a vision of the night, and [38v] his likeness shall be of a holy man. Then be strong and dread [him] not, and he shall not leave you, [know] that it is [not] a vision or a dream, but in a true manner. And ask what you wish, and without doubt he shall give it to you.

Dixit angelus Raziel volo tibi dicere hoc complemento &c.

The angel Raziel said, "I will say to you that this fulfilling of the working, is by the power, virtue and strength of this book in which are written the

---

[1] This, and the following paragraph, appear in a slightly different form in 'The Prayer of Adam' in the first part of the *Sepher ha-Malbush*. See Savedow (2000), Book One, page 7.
[2] In other words the hour before sunrise.

Liber Salomonis

powers of the months, of days, and of the year, and they have power in every month, and in each day, for always. For each man who governs himself by them, with purity, they have helped him in all his deeds, and in all his things. And they make him to know all his wiles, and they helped him to fulfill all that he ever asked, with great power, strength and wisdom."

[The Angels of the 12 Hebrew Months]

The names of the Angels of the first month.[1] These are the names of the Angels which are mighty, and more mighty in the first month, which is called **Nysan [Nisan]**:[2] Oriel, Malaquiran, Acia, Yaziel, Paltifus, Yesmactria, Yariel, Araton, Robica, Sephatia. Anaya, Quesupale, Semquiel, Sereriel, Malgas, Ancason, Pacyta, Abedel, Ram, Asdon, Casiel, Nastiafori, Sugni, Aszre, Sornadaf, Adniel, Necamia, Caisaat, Benit, Quor, Adziriel.

The names of Angels of the second month.[3] [39r] These are the mightier Angels of the second month which is **Yar [Iyar]** in [the] language of Hebrew: Safuel, Saton, Cartemat, Aryel, Palthia, Bargar, Galms, Nocpis, Aaron, Manit, Aadon, Qwenael, Quemon, Abragin, Yehoc, Adnibia, Parciot, Marinoc, Galus, Gabmion, Resegar, Affry, Absamon, Sarsaf, Alxim, Carbiol, Regnia, Achlas, Nadib, Absafyabitan, Pliset. And you shall name the names of the aforesaid Angels of this month Yar in each thing which you shall name it in, and they should help you, and they shall make you to know all your wishes.

The names of the Angels of the third month.[4] These are the names of the Angels which are the keepers of the third month that is called **Zyvan [Sivan]** of which the first is Amariel, Tatgiel, Casmuch, Nuscifa, Almux, Naamab, Mamiazicaras, Samysarach, Naasien, Andas, Paltamus, Abris, Borhai, Salor, Hac, Yayac, Dalia, Azigor, Mabsuf, Abnisor, Zenam, Dersam, Cefania, Maccafor, Naboon, Adiel, Maasiel, Szarhyr, Cartalion, Adi, Ysar. And you shall name these names that are called, in all things that you do, and you shall profit.

The names of the Angels of the fourth month. These are [5] the names of the Angels of the fourth month that is called **Thamuth [Tammuz]**: Moriel, Safida, Asaf, Mazica, Sarsac, Adnyam, Nagrow, Galuf, Galgall, Danroc, Saracus, Remafidda, Luliaraf, Nediter / Delgna, Maadon, Saamyel, Amrael,

---

[1] Margin note "nisan." The margin notes over the next few pages are often indistinct, and not very helpful, being mostly a repetition of the Hebrew month name.
[2] The modern transliteration of the names of each Hebrew lunar month is printed in bold in square brackets.
[3] Margin note "yar"
[4] Margin note "zinatam."
[5] Margin note "enamus Ab elul."

Sepher Raziel

Lezaidi, Elisafan, Paschania, Maday. And you shall name these names abovesaid in all that you do, and you shall profit.

The names of the Angels of the fifth month.[1] These are the names of the Angels of the fifth month that is called [39ᵛ] Manhi or Amariahaya **[Ab]**: Byny, Madrat, Amantuliel, Cassurafarttis, Nactif, Necif, Pdgnar, Tablic, Mamirot, Amacia, Qnatiel, Reycat, Qnynzi, Paliel, Gadaf, Nesquiraf, Abrac, Amyter, Camb, Nachal, Cabach, Loch, Macria, Safe, Essaf. And you shall name these beforesaid in all that you do, and you shall profit.

The names of the Angels of the sixth month.[2] These are the names of the Angels of the sixth month that is called **Elul**: Magnyny, Arabyel, Hanyel, Nacery, Yassar, Rassy, Boel, Mattriel, Naccamarif, Zacdon, Nafac, Rapion, Sapsi, Salttri, Raseroph, Malgel, Samtiel, Yoas, Qualabye, Danpi, Yamla, Golid, Rasziel, Satpach, Nassa, Myssa, Macracif, Dadiel, Carciel, Effignax. And you shall name these names aforesaid in each thing which you do, and you shall profit therein.

The names of Angels of the seventh month.[3] These are the names of the keepers of the 7ᵗʰ month that is called **Tisirin [Tishri]**: Suriel, Sarican, Gnabriza, Szucariel, Sababiel, Ytrut, Cullia, Dadiel, Marhum, Abecaisdon, Sacdon, Pagulan, Arsabon, Aspiramo, Aquyel, Safcy, Racynas, Altim, Masulaef, Vtisaryaya, Abri. And you shall name these names abovesaid in each thing that you do, and you shall profit.

The names of Angels of the eighth month.[4] These are the names of Angels of the eight month that is called **Marquesaan [Marchesvan]**: Karbiel, Tiszodiel, Raamyel, Nebubael, Alisaf, Baliel, Arzaf, Rasliel, Alson, [40ʳ] Naspiel, Becar, Paliel, Elisuaig, Nap, Naxas, Sansani, Aesal, Maarim, Sasci, Yalsenac, Iabynx, Magdiel, Sarmas, Maaliel, Arsaferal, Manistiorar, Veaboluf, Nadibael, Suciel, Nabuel, Sariel, Sodiel, Marcuel, Palitam. And you shall name these names abovesaid in every thing that you wish, and you shall profit.

The names of the Angels of the ninth month.[5] These are the names of the Angels of the ninth month that is called **Qwinslep [Kislev]**: Adoniel, Radiel, Naduch, Racyno, Hyzy, Mariel, Azday, Mandiel, Gamiel, Seriel, Kery, Sahaman, Osmyn, Sachiel, Pazehemy, Calchihay, Hehudael, Nerad, Minael, Arac, Arariqniel, Galnel, Gimon, Satuel, Elynzy, Baqwylaguel. And you shall

---

[1] The margin note here is illegible.
[2] Margin note "Ab Elul Marqueslica."
[3] Margin note "sirmi Quinslip."
[4] Margin note "Tobtz Marquesaan."
[5] Margin note "Quinslip Scribat."

Liber Salomonis

name these names abovesaid in all that you do, and you shall profit.

The names of the Angels of the tenth month.[1] These are the names of Angels that have might in the tenth month that is called **Thebeth [Tebet]**: Anael, Aniyel, Aryor, Naflia, Rapinis, Raaciel, Pacuel, Hahon, Guanrinasuch, Aslaqwy, Naspaya, Negri, Somahi, Hasasisgafon, Gasca, Szif, Alzamy, Maint, Xatinas, Sargnamuf, Oliab, Sariel, Canyel, Rahyeziel, Pansa, Insquen, Sarman, Malisan, Asirac, Marmoc. And you shall name these names in all that you do, and you shall profit.

The names of the Angels of the eleventh month. These are the names of Angels that keep the 11th month that is called **Cynanth [Shebat]** and which have might in it: Gabriel, Israel, Natriel, Gazril, Nassam, Abrisaf, Zefael, Zamiel, Mamiel, Tabiel, Miriel, Sahumiel, Guriel, Samhiel, Dariel, Banorsasti, Satyn, Nasyel, Ranfiel, Talgnaf, Libral, Luel, Daliel, Guadriel, Sahuhaf, Myschiel. And you shall name these names beforesaid in all things that you do in the month & you shall fulfill [your aims]. [40v]

The names of Angels of the twelfth month. These are the names of the 12th month that is called **Adar**: Romiel, Patiel, Guriel, Laabiel, Addriel, Cardiel, Aguel, Malquiel, Samiel, Sariel, Azriel, Paamiel, Carcyelel, Amaluch, Parhaya, Ytael, Beryel, Cael, Tenebiel, Pantan, Panteron, Fanyel, Falafon, Masiel, Pantaron, Labiel, Ragael, Cetabiel, Nyahpatuel. And you shall name these names in all things that you do, and you shall profit.

The names of Angels if there [is a] thirteenth month.[2] These are the names of Angels of the 13th month Bisertilis which is [also] called **Adar,** the last in March: Lantiel, Ardiel, Nasmyel, Celidoal, Amyel, Magel, Gabgel, Sasuagos, Barilagni, Yabtasyper, Magossangos, Dragos, Yayel, Yoel, Yasmyel, Stelmel, Garasyn, Ceyabos, Sacadiel, Guracap, Gabanael, Tamtiel. These names abovesaid you shall name in all things that you wish, and they shall fulfill all your wishes, with fasting & washing, and suffumigation and purity.

And thus understand of every work. And know that the months of the Hebrews and the months of the Romans are evened [coincide at] the month of March, and know well this number, and you shall profit.[3]

---

[1] Incorrect margin note "Adar."
[2] Because the 12 lunar months do not quite fill a solar year, at irregular intervals a thirteenth month (with the same name) is introduced, so that the first lunar month does not slip backwards in time.
[3] March was considered the beginning of the year by Hebrews, Romans (until the introduction of January and February) and Europeans (until Elizabethan times). Other cultures also saw

Sepher Raziel

[The Angels of the 7 Days of the Week]

Scias quod postquam diximus de mensibus &c.

Know that we have told of the months, now we will tell of the names of the days of the week, with their angels, very strong and ruling over every day, and each in his [own] day. [41r]

The names of the angels that serve in the day of the Sun [Sunday].

And these names of the **Sun** and his Angels are these: Daniel, Elieyl, Saffeyeyl, Dargoyeyl, Yelbrayeyl, Comaguele, Gebarbayea, Faceyeyl, Caran, Neyeyl, Talgylnenyl, Bethaz, Rancyl, Falha, Hyeyl, Armaqnieyeyl, Roncayl, Gibryl, Zamayl, Mycahe, Zarfaieil, Ameyl, Torayeil, Ronmeyeyl, Remcatheyel, Barhil, Marhil, Barhil, Mehil, Zarafil, Azrageyl, Anebynnyl, Denmerzym, Yeocyn, Necyl, Hadzbeyeyl, Zarseyeyl, Zarael, Anqnihim, Ceytatynyn, Ezuiah, Vehichdunedzineylyn, Yedmeyeyl, Esmaadyn, Albedagryn, Yamaanyl, Yecaleme, Detriel, Arieil, Armayel, Veremedyn, Unaraxxydin. These are the mighty angels on the day of the Sun, and name them worthily & you shall profit.

The names of the angels in the day of the Moon [Monday].

These are the names of Angels that serve in the day of the **Moon**: Semhahylyn, Stemehilyn, Jasyozyn, Agrasinden, Aymeylyn, Cathneylyn, Abrasachysyn, Abrasasyn, Layzaiosyn, Langhasin, Anayenyn, Nangareryn, Aczonyn, Montagin, Labelas, Mafatyn, Feylarachin, Candanagyn, Laccudonyn, Casfrubyn, Bacharachyn, Bathaylyn, Anmanineylyn, Hacoylyn, Balganarichyn, Aryelyn, Badeilyn, Abranocyn, Tarmanydyn, Amdalycyn, Sahgragynyn, Adiamenyn, Sacstoyeyn, Latebaifanysyn, Caybemynyn, Nabyalni, Cyzamanyn, Abramacyn, Lariagathyn, Bifealyqnyn, Baiedalin, Gasoryn, Asaphin, Dariculin, Marneyelin, Gemraorin, Madarilyn, Yebiryn, Arylin, Farielin, Nepenielin, Branielin, Asrieylin, Ceradadyn. These holy angels in the day of the Moon you shall name worthily and you shall profit.

The names of angels of the day of Mars [Tuesday].

These are the names [of the Angels] that serve in the day of **Mars**. [41v] And they have power over red metal and in his [Mars] works: Samayelyn, Tartalyn, Dexxeyl, Racyeylyn, Farabyn, Cabyn, Asymeylyn, Mabareylyn, Tralyelyn, Rulbelyn, Marmanyn, Tarfanyelyn, Fuheylyn, Ruffaraneylyn, Rabfilyn, Eralyn, Enplyn, Pirtophin, Brofilyn, Cacitilyn, Naffrynyn, Impuryn,

---

the beginning of Spring as the beginning of the year, and the Chinese still take February 4th/5th as the beginning of the solar year (with March being the middle of Spring).

Raffeylyn, Nyrysin, Memolyn, Nybirin, Celabel, Tubeylyn, Haayn, Reyn, Paafiryn, Cethenoylyn, Letityelyn, Rorafeyl, Cannyel, Bastelyn, Costiryn, Monteylyn, Albeylyn, Parachbeylyn, Alyel, Uaceyl, Zalcycyl, Amadyeyl, Usaryeyel, Emcodeneyl, Dasfripyel, Unleylyn, Carszeneyl, Gromeyl, Gabrynyn, Narbell.

The names of the angels that serve in the day of Mercury [Wednesday].

These are the names [of the Angels] that serve in the day of **Mercury**: Michael, Zamirel, Beerel, Dufuel, Aribiriel, Boel, Bariel, Meriol, Amiol, Aol, Semeol, Aaon, Berion, Farionon, Kemerion, Feyn, Ameinyn, Zemeinyn, Cananyn, Aal, Merigal, Pegal, Gabal, Leal, Amneal, Farnnial, Gebyn, Caribifin, Ancarilyn, Metorilin, Nabiafilyn, Fisfilin, Barsfilin, Camfilin, Aaniturla, Feniturla, Geniniturla, Elmia, Calnamia, Rabmia, Rasfia, Miaga, Tiogra, Bee, Ylaraorynil, Benenil.

The names of angels in the day of Jupiter [Thursday].

These are the names of Angels that serve in the day of **Jupiter**: Sachquiel, Pachayel, Tutiel, Osfleel, Labiel, Raliel, Beniel, Tarael, Snynyel, Ahiel, Yebel, Ancuyel, Jauiel, Juniel, Amyel, Faniel, Ramnel, Sanfael, Sacciniel, Galbiet, Lafiel, Maziel, Gunfiel, Ymrael, Memieil, Pariel, Panhiniel, Toripiel, Abinel, Omiel, Orfiel, Ael, Bearel, Ymel, Syymelyel, Traacyel, [42r] Mefeniel, Antquiel, Quisiel, Cunnyryel, Rofiniel, Rubycyel, Jebrayel, Peciel, Carbiel, Tymel, Affarfytyriel, Rartudel, Cabrifiel, Beel, Briel, Cherudiel.

The names of angels in the day of Venus [Friday].

These are the names of the Angels that serve in the day of **Venus**: Hasneyeyl, Barnayeyl, Uardayheil, Alzeyeil, Szeyyeil, Uachayel, Zesfaieil, Morayeil, Borayeyl, Apheieyl, Arobolyn, Canesylyn, Anrylin, Zarialin, Marilin, Batoraielyn, Kelfeielyn, Azraieylin, Ambayerin, Ayayeylin, Cadneirin, Alserin, Afneirin, Abneyrin, Nonanrin, Eazerin, Orinyn, Gedulin, Hareryn, Nanylin, Halilin, Himeilin, Resfilin, Noraraabilin, Hayeylin, Laudulin, Et, Effilin, Thesfealin, Patnilin, Keialin, Lebraieil, Ablaieil, Talrailanrain, Barcalin, Bahoraelin.

The names of angels of the day of Saturn [Saturday].

These are the names of Angels that serve in the day of **Saturn** or Sabat: Micraton, Pacryton, Pepilon, Capeiel, Themiton, Alsfiton, Chenyon, Sandalson, Panion, Almyon, Expion, Papon, Calipon, Horrion, Melifon, Aurion, Temelion, Refacbilion, Ononiteon, Boxoraylon, Paxilon, Lelalion, Onoxion, Quilon, Quiron, Vixalimon, Relion, Cassilon, Titomon, Murion, Dedion, Dapsion, Leuainon, Foylylon, Monichion, Gabion, Paxonion, Xysuylion, Lepiron, Belon, Memitilon, Saron, Salion, Pion, Macgron, Acciriron, Felyypon, Ymnybron, Raconeal, Zalibron. These holy angels, blessed are they names, [use them] in all your true works and keep them pure, and you shall profit.

The Names of the Hours of the Night

Ista sunt propria nomina horaram noctis. Prima hora &c.

These are the proper names of hours of the night. The [42ᵛ] first hour of the night is called Zedrin. The second [is called] Biroel; the third Caym; the fourth Hacir; the fifth Zaron; the sixth Zzya; the seventh Nachlas; the eighth Thasras; the ninth Saphar; the tenth Halaga; the eleventh Galcana; and the twelfth Salla. And these are the proper names which the 12 powers of the night have. And you shall name in these [in all] that you do, and you shall profit.

These are the names of the planets and their angels by the Elements, these are their proper names.

Ista sunt nomina planetarum 7 et angelorum super 4 elementa &c.

These are the names of the 7 planets and of the angels over the 4 Elements fire, air, earth, and water, for without these, and without the 7 planets above, we may not do anything [magical].

The first is the highest [planet] Sabaday, and Sabaday [**Saturn**] is called in fire Campton. In air [it is called] Srynongoa. In water Synyn, and in earth Onion. And the names of angels of Sabaday over fire are these three: Libiel, Nybiel, Phynitiel. And over air are these three: Arfigyel, Gael, Nephyel. And over water are these: Almemel, Hoquiel, Fulitiel. And over earth are these: Lariel, Tepyel, Esyel.

Zedek is named over fire Pheon; over air Fidon. And over water Calidon; and over earth Mydon. And the names of the angels of Zedek [**Jupiter**, the second planet] over fire are these three: Tinsyel, Necanynael, Fonyel. [Angels over air are missing] And over water are these three: Meon, Ykiel, Yryniel; and over earth: [43ʳ] Palriel, Tufiel, Quyel.

These are the names of the third [planet] which is Madyn [**Mars**]: over fire it is called Roqnyel; over air Pyryel; over water Tasfien; over earth Ignofon. And the angels of Madim [Mars] over fire are these three: Kaliel, Cabryel, Raloyl. And over air are these three: Pyroyinel, Flatoniel, Carbiel, and over water are these three: Cazabriel, Pasaliel, Zebaliel. [Angels over earth missing].

These are the names of Hamina [the **Sun**, the fourth planet] over fire it is called Yeye, over air Don. And over water Agla. And over earth On. And the angels of Hamina [the Sun] over fire are these three: Dandaniel, Saddaniel, Ellalyel. And over air are these three: Karason, Berriel, Oliel. And over water are these three: Muracafel, Pecyrael, Michael. And over earth are these:

Liber Salomonis

Homycabel, Lucifel, Locariel.

Nogah [**Venus**] is the fifth [planet] and is named over fire Dusuyon, and on air Clarifon, and in water Narubni, and in earth Cabras. These are the three angels of Nogah over fire: Capciel, Debitael, Deparael. And over air: Camirael, Cakaziel, Neraziel, and over water: Saloniel, Emyel, Expaoniel. And over earth: Paziael, Amurael, Salainel.

These are the names of [the sixth planet] Cocab [**Mercury**]. Over fire it is called Piztal, and in air Cabran, and in water Facayl and in earth Tarzon. And the names of the angels of Cocab over fire are these: Paradiel, Darifiel, Dameyel. And over air are these: Ramatiel, Loriqniel, Bengariel. And over water are these: [43ᵛ] Rinafonel, Mellifiel, Alatiel. And over earth these: Alapion, Beriel, Rabiel.

These are the names of Labona [Levanah, the **Moon**] over fire it is called Claron. And over air Becyla, over water Tasfit, and over earth Pantours. And the names of the angels of Labona over fire are these: Gabriel, Paticael, Daliel and over air are these: Barasiel, Ztaziel. And over water are these: Caziel, Memyiel, Pazicaton and over earth are these: Simyllyel, Lafaqnael, Toniel. And name these abovesaid in all that you do, always. Consider the planet with which you will work, and you shall profit.

The Names of the Heavens in the 4 Seasons.[1]

Ista sunt nomina caelorum in quatuor temporibus &c.

These are the names of the Heavens in the 4 seasons. In the first season it is named Hacibor. In the second [season it is called] Rumcaqnia. In the third Mesfisnogna. In the fourth Saaemaho. These are the names of the Heavens in the 4 seasons.

And when you will work, name the names of the Heaven, in the season in which you work. These are the names of fire in the 4 seasons. In the first season [Spring] the first is named Quoyzil; in the second [season, Summer] Enlubra. In the third [season, Autumn] Mezayn. In the fourth [season, Winter] Aybedyn.

[Names of the Angels of the 4 Elements]

And these angels rule over **fire** and in the flame:
Michael, Rafael, Rasoiel, Acdiel, Roqniel, Myriel, Indam, Malqniel, Gazriel,

---

[1] The following sections on the different names of the elements, sun and moon, etc in different seasons, appear in a quite different form in 'The Prayer of Adam' in the first part of the *Sepher ha-Malbush*. See Savedow (2000), Book One, page 11-28. The structure is similar, but the names attributed are very different.

[44ʳ] Amynyel, Cariel, Yafrael. And these you shall name these always when you do anything in fire.

These are the names of **air** in the 4 Seasons:
In the first season it is called Ystana, in the second Furayl, in the third Oadion, in the fourth Gulynon. And the names of the Angels that rule over air are these: Rafael, Quabriel, Michael, Cherubyn, Ceraphin, Orychyn, Pantaceren, Micraton, Sandalfon, Barachiel, Ragehyel, Tobiel. And name them in all things that you shall do in air, and you shall profit well, with the help of God.

Ista sunt nomina aquarum et maris in quatuor temporibus &c.

These are the names of the **waters** of the sea in the 4 seasons:
In the first season it is named Angustiz. In the second Theon. In the third Maddrylk. In the fourth Sebillgradon. And the names of angels of the waters of the sea are these: Urpeniel, Armariel, Yyamnel, Abrastos, Sapiel, Uiotan, Oriel, Bachmyel, Porackmiel, Acceriel, Galliel, Zsmayel. And name them over waters and over the sea and you shall profit.

These are the names of **earth** in the 4 seasons:
In the first season it is called Ingnedon, in the second Yabassa, in the third Coliel. In the fourth Aradon. And the Angels of earth are these: Samael, Yatayel, Baraniel, Oriel, Arfaniel, Latgriel, Daniel, Affariel, Partriel, Bael, Byeniel. And you shall name these names of Angels ruling over earth.

These are the names of **lowness** [underworld?] in the 4 seasons. In the first season it is called Hahan in the second Cipaon. And his angel [name] is Jacyel. In the third [season] [44ᵛ] Meresac and his Angel is Ababaot. In the fourth Aycyhambabo, and his angel is Caaniel.

These are the names of the 4 parts of the world in the 4 seasons. In the first season the East is called Acbedan, in the second Cardrenac. In the third Abrthel, in the fourth Acritael. These are the names of the North parts in the four seasons. In the first season it is called Henniyna. In the second season Abodich, in the third Galdidur, in the fourth Rabbifor. These are the names of the West part. In the first season Mahanahym. In the second Sugor. In the third Zarzir, in the fourth Rabiur. These are the names of the South part. In the first season Naufor, in the second Alparon, in the third Machniel, in the fourth Thaumy.

These are the names [of the main angels] in the 4 parts of the world:
In the part of the East these have might or power: Gabriel, Raphael, Uriel.[1]

---

[1] Normally listed as three of the four main Archangels. The fourth, Michael, is attributed to the South.

Liber Salomonis

In the part of the North these: Adriel, Yamiel, Zabdiel.
In the part of the West these: Adtriel, Samael, Joel.
And in the part of the South these: Corabiel, Sariel, Michael.

And name them above all things that you do in the 4 parts of the world and you shall profit.

The Proper Names of the Planets in the 4 Seasons

Ista sunt nomina stellarum qui sunt et vadunt &c.

These are the names of the seven planets that [45ʳ] fly in the 7 Heavens, Sabaday, Zedek, Madyn, Hanina, Nogah, Cocab, Labana. And which of these has its own proper name ruling over the four seasons of the year we shall show in this chapter following.

And Solomon said in explanation of this place, that every planet, and each thing before mentioned, changes its name in each season, [just as] from the same tree comes to us four things [according to the season]. Of these four things the first is when it burgeons, the second is the flower. The third is the fruit, and the fourth is the seed. Therefore the Sun is called in the first season hot and moist. In the second [season] hot and dry. In the third cold & dry, and in the fourth cold and moist. These are the workings of the Sun, and these properties [are conferred] over all things, which is another reason the names of things abovesaid are changed in the four parts of the year, for [each] time has its [own] nature and its [own] complexion, as we have said of water which is in the first season temperate, and in the second hot, and in the third rotten, and in the fourth congealed [as ice]. And so other things of the world. This example [shows] why Raziel put these names to each thing. In every thing are the 4 lords that have power over each thing, and every one in his season. And it is said that there are 4 Elements, whereof one is fire that has might in the first season, and so on.

Wherefore know that every thing changes its name. [45ᵛ] As first we say a man is a child, and then a youngling, and then a middle [aged] man, and in the fourth season an old man. And so [all] things change their names, who will call them a leader, and this is [the same way] in [the life of] a man. And so understand [the same] of metal and of all things that grow and live.

And Solomon said, and all others [agreed], that it was more inst[ructive] if each thing should have 7 names [rather] than 4, for all things might descend from 4 bodies, and to them is given all the might. Truly they put 4 names to every thing, and [so] it was more easy to work, [just as] 4 names were assigned over the city of David, my fathers and mine, which had many

Sepher Raziel

names. Truly Isaac the wise man said that the first name [of that city] was Remusale, and then Jebusale, Jeroboam, Jerusalem. And these are the names this City received from the 4 Lords that were in it. And everyone gave it his proper name. And these things of this world receive 4 names in themselves, or 7 or more after God has ordered it. And therefore [let] no man marvel at the [changing] names of things in the 4 seasons.

In the highest Heaven, that is the first [heaven] from the outer part, and it is [also] the seventh [heaven] from the lowest, it serves Sabaday [Saturn] and his angel is Capciel. In the first season Sabaday is called Cuerues. In the second Palicos. In the third Quirtipos, in the fourth Panpotes.

In the sixth [Heaven] serves Zedek and his angel is Satquiel and his is name Jupiter. In the first season it is Amonor. In the [46ʳ] second Sahibor. In the third Sayin. In the fourth Eanynyel.

In the fifth Heaven serves Madin and his angel is Balquiel. And the name of Mars in the first season is called Aaryn. In the second Daron. In the third Bearon. In the fourth Pantefos.

In the fourth Heaven serves Hamina [the Sun] and his angel is Dandaniel. In the first season the name of the Sun is called Halyom, in the second Adocham, in the third Cantopos. In the fourth Pantasus.

In the third Heaven serves Nogah and his angel is Adzdiel. In the first season the name of Venus is called Aporodicy. In the second Calizo, in the third Niniptz. In the fourth Pontos.

In the second Heaven serves Cocab and his angel is Satquiel. In the first season Mercury is called Armis. In the second Angocus. In the third Tholos. In the fourth Ancholos.

In the first Heaven serves Labana and his angel is Anael. In the first [season] the Moon is called Salmi in the second Sarico. In the third Naspilij. In the fourth Afriqnym. And know that you shall name the names in their four seasons, and you shall profit when you shall know anything of them.

[Here ends the Fourth Book & here begins the Fifth Book]

[The Fifth Book]

[Treatise of Purity and of Abstinence]

Here begins the fifth book that treats of purity

Dixit Solomon revelatum fuit nitri de isto libro &c.

Solomon said, "this book of Raziel was showed to me, and many angels thereafter, that I had the book, and of those which nourished powers, [46ᵛ] virtues, matters and strength of the *potestates* [Powers] above, and that [was done] by the commandment of, and obedience to, the Creator or maker of the world." And they said that Solomon asked for understanding, and wisdom, and fairness, and strength in will, all complete, and [so he was] named great for always over the earth. And know that all kings, and lesser men, who shall come after you, should speak of you, should love you, and worship you, and should set you in high esteem, and should praise and keep this book, and work with it with reverence and purity.

And Solomon said to the benign angel Natanael, which has power in the air, and which was always associated with Solomon, which are the same 7 bodies [planets] which we see above, bright, fair, pure, and clear, which cease never to go [in their orbit], nor are their ways void, nor did they ever fail, but always endure going on their way. And [the planet whose orbit] is farthest [out, Saturn] fulfilled [its orbit] in 30 years.[1] And then they [the planets] appear [in the same position in the sky] as they were before. And thus it is said that their [orbit] should be however long God [desired]. And thus I say: in a hundred years, and [even] in a 1000 [years], that they never will be changed [in their course], but we have found them [in the same place] as the Prophets and other men of old found them. And the angel Natanael said this to Solomon.

The 7 bright bodies [the planets] which you see above [47ʳ] are put [active] beneath. And in going upwards they hold in balance, or in rulership, the 4 Elements beneath. And therefore their movment ceases not, for such power the Creator gave to them. And know that their matter is simple and pure, without corruption and always durable. And their state is like to the Lord that formed [them], and they obey him in all things. And Natanael said furthermore to Solomon, "know that in the heavens of the 7 bright bodies [planets] there are angels without number, mighty in all things, and every

---

[1] Saturn's period of orbital rotation is actually 29.47 years.

one of them has his proper power, his strength and his virtue. And they are as unlike [each other], among themselves, as men [are unlike each other], or as other beasts are. And everyone serves his office for the Creator that formed him, or made them."

And Solomon said to Nathaniel, "what is the life, or the service, that these angels do?" And Nathaniel said, "their life is [one] of purity, of orison [prayers], and of trust, and their might is of suffumigations *holocausti et sacrificii*.[1] And their service is when the Creator wills them to go from place to place, [in response to] any pure man who has prayed to the Creator, as it seems. And then they do good, or evil, as the Creator wills them, for in them is power, science & will complete." And Solomon said, "which are these 7 bright bodies [planets], and how are they named, and of what [purpose] does every one serve?"

And Nathaniel said the same that Raziel said to Adam, the higher of these that goes slower is called Sabaday [Saturn] and all the realms of his heaven are [47ᵛ] full of ice, snow and hail, and wroth, rancour and coldness. And all the angels that have been there are clothed with darkness, very dark. And their greatness is very high and very long, and [they have power] over the earth, over devils, over darkness, and [over] coldness and dryness. And they have power over winds of this nature. And they have power of doing good and evil. And the angel of it is Beel, crowned over all others.

In the second heaven stands Zedek [Jupiter] and all his realms.

Dixit Solomon rex filius regis David &c.

Solomon the king, called the son of David, that was king of Jerusalem of Jury [Jewry], and Damaske [Damascus], of Egypt, Lord of Babylon,[2] prince of science, covetous of purity, searcher of privities [secrets], keeper of good true men, avoider of lying, [keeper] of poor men, of virtues, desire over virtues, speedy with words, busily thinking, most subtle in mind, and in searching. I have enquired, and know, that in words of power [lie] virtue and effect, and of all humours whole and healthy, there may be sufficient fulfilling. And he

---

[1] The original meaning of *holocausti* or 'holocaust' was "a Jewish sacrificial offering burnt on an altar" [OED], which is precisely what it means here. There are a number of ancient references to angels standing around and enjoying the savour of sacrifices in the temple, as strange as that sounds to us today. Solomon probably holds the world record for massive sacrifices which he instigated to sanctify the original Temple which he built in Jerusalem (see *I Kings* 8:62-64). Of course 'holocaust' went on to mean 'destruction or slaughter on a mass scale', and then more recently to refer specifically to the mass murder of Jews under the Nazi regime, a strange recycling of the meaning of this ancient word.

[2] The text gives a much wider geographical remit and rulership to Solomon than he ever had.

said, I see that the most famous are wise men and prophets, [made famous] by words and books which they have left as their testimony. And I see that the sons of Adam, and of Hermes, and of Noah, and their sons, and many other prophets, have left books at their death by which they clarify their fame and [so] amongst men [48ʳ] [their] glory should remain.

And I see that my father, King David, compounded or made some book in which are contained all the orisons [prayers] which he knew and found, which truly Latin men, that is Romances,[1] call the *Psalter* which truly is prayers alone, and of the holy names of the Creator, it is names that head the Orisons.[2] In the same book, King David wrote all things that ever he knew, of patriarchs, and of old wise men, to the praise of the Creator. And I, King Solomon, truly have long studied holy words with [their] virtues, and the miracles I found to be therein fulfilled, with each thing working, and I saw this in the books in which I studied long, and found. And know that Adam, Hermes, Noah and Moses, and many other most wise men, had great secrets & virtues in their books.

Cum ergo veteres et antiquos Sapientes &c.

When therefore I understood the old wise men to have made books, how or with what understanding, or with what art, that I might know the sciences of all the aforesaid, I enquired, and there answered unto me an old man of good mind and understanding who was called Zebraymayl. And I said, "Adam had a maker and a master, that is to say the Lord his maker, and Gabriel [his] master furthermore. Hermes, that discreet and most wise man, and Moses, had a master and a friend, which is Cretus. Also Aaron truly had a friend which therefore assisted him. That a wise man may not be without a master, however attested by you, that two may be wise without one master: but [for] you to be wise, these [things] I know to be [48ᵛ] necessary to you: a wise master, and discrete, long and continual study of many old books of great wise men, often read, profited by & amended, happy and continual health of your body, long life without cares and travails, and quiet."

---

[1] Speakers of the Romance languages, that is languages descended from Latin, i.e. most of Western Europe.

[2] "It is names that head the Orisons" means it is the names (of god and the angels) that make the prayers effective. The *Psalter* is a volume containing the *Book of Psalms*. Some of the Psalms were composed by David, Solomon's father, and some by Solomon, and so it is no surprise that a number of Psalms have been used for magical purposes. For a listing of these see Table J7 in Stephen Skinner, *Complete Magician's Tables*, Singapore: Golden Hoard and St Paul: Llewellyn, 2006. For the use of Psalms in magic see David Rankine & Harry Barron, *The Book of Gold: a 17th Century Magical Grimoire...using the Biblical Psalms of King David*, London: Avalonia, 2010.

Then Solomon said to the wise man "Is not this possible to be done by a shorter way than that you have said above?" Zebraymayl answered the king "a lighter & shorter way than this is unknown, nor may it be done." To whom Solomon said, "How therefore," to which the wise man answered again saying "Open privately and fully the Ark of the Testament, no man knows or understands all its secrets, and old wisdoms, and the words of great power and virtue that you shall find [therein]. By which not only shall you know things passed, but also these that are present, and likewise those that are to come." Solomon answered again saying, "for this that you have answered to me I give thanks to that high and blessed Creator, who reigns as it pleases him, all things, with words alone, he formed or made."

[The Ark of the Covenant]

And there is not any more noble or mightier then he, without whom there is no virtue or power, who gives wisdom to wise men, he is of all things the first time, he is without beginning, and of all things the last time, there is no end. He is of all things [49ʳ] the maker, and nothing was made [without him], of whom the reign or reigning is, and shall be, and of whom all work is good, and of whom his will is over all, is truly free, and there is none that may gainsay him. Whereupon Solomon, trusting to Zebraymayl, had the Ark of the Testament brought before him. And he sought all the books of Moses, of Aaron, of Adam, and of Noah, and of their sons, and of Hermes, and of other prophets, and of others in which he might find the miracle of words and their virtues.

And he sought all the old idols of heathen men & images of many tongues, having writings, and all things engraved which are found in all the parts of the world. And he caused them to be gathered together into his palace, and he brought forth Masters of every one of the 72 [letters of the Name], who should expound to him privately the letters, or hidden Y. C. M. in Hebrew, Chaldean, Syriac, and Greek writing, that they should expound to him that which was hidden. And when the letters were expounded, he saw the most part accorded with it, in [regard to] the virtues of words.

Rex ergo Solomon fecit arcam nocte quadam aperiri &c.

Therefore King Solomon caused the Ark to be opened privately, [hoping to find] in the Ark, with [good] reason, afterwards what [he desired] to learn. And Solomon said "After the sovereign and Almighty Creator had infused that grace of his spirit in me, I opened the Ark of the Testament, in which I found all [49ᵛ] things which I had sought long and studiously before. Among which I found the book which is called Raziel, which the Creator sent to

Liber Salomonis

Adam by the angel Raziel, when upon the banks of the rivers of paradise, weeping, [to his] Creator he prayed, and he besought forgiveness of his sins.

And I found the book which the Creator gave to Moses in the hill of Sinai, when he made him partner to his privities [secrets]. In which three books, three orisons [prayers or invocations] I found. The first [book] the prophets call Semiforas, which the Creator gave to Adam in Paradise. The second book is that which the Creator gave to Adam in paradise in the hour of his necessity or need. The third [book] is that which the Creator gave to Moses in the hill of Sinai, after he had fulfilled the fasting. And Solomon said "I found in the Ark a pot full of manna, and the staff of Moses which was changed into a serpent, and afterwards from a serpent into a staff. And the Tables of the Law, and pieces of the first letters, which Moses for the sins of the people (in his wroth) broke upon the ground. Truly in the Ark I found some golden tables, quadrate or four-cornered, in which were [set] 15 [12?] precious stones, likened to the twelve tribes or lineages of Israel. And in every stone was written the high holy names of the Creator of the book Semiforas."[1]

And I found a box of marble having a green colour as Jasper. [50ʳ] And in this box were 7 figures, and in each figure [were] 7 great and virtuous names of the Creator as told to Moses, and the [other] 7 [names] which the Creator taught Adam in paradise. And this is a secret of secrets which is very learned, and ought to be kept reverently covered. I found also in the extremities of the Ark, 24 virtuous rings with names and figures of the Creator written in Semiforas, with many colours written or figured. And I, Solomon, had one of the same rings, having a mind to the same, in which I have found such virtue that when I said make it to rain, it rained. And when I said again, as you have made it to rain, so make the same rain to cease again, and it ceased. And beside Jerusalem, the same realm as well, of tempests and rains it made.

And Solomon said "I found Semiforas with which Moses made the plagues in Egypt, and with which he dried the Red Sea, and with which also he drew water out of the stone, and with which also he knew all the purity of his people, and with which he also overcame princes and kings and mighty men, and with which whatever he wished to do, he did, and that which he would destroy, he destroyed. And with these [rings] he fulfilled his own wishes."

---

[1] See *Hebrews* ix, 4 for the details of what was inside the Ark of the Covenant: "the golden pot having the manna, and Aaron's rod that budded, and the tables of the covenant." Although *I Kings*, viii, 9 states that "there was nothing in the Ark save the two tablets of stone, which Moses put there at [Mount] Horeb."

Sepher Raziel

Capitulum explanationis hujus nomina Semiforas &c.

The chapter of explanation of this name Semiforas. And it is that all devils and winds, and men living as well as dead, and all spirits, and all bodies, regard it with awe it. Wherefore truly Semiforas is called the first secret of secrets, and of great old and much [desired], and hidden, and of great virtue and power to get whatever he wanted. Semiforas is a word [50ᵛ] which ought not to be shown to all men, neither by it ought any man to work (except with great necessity or anguish). And then in awe of the Creator, he ought to purely, meekly and devoutly name it. Also Semiforas is the root and beginning, fundamental to orison, an exemplar of good life, the trust of man's body, the orison or prayer of a just man, the same dread Creator.

And Solomon said about Semiforas, "These are necessary with meekness, fasting, with orison [prayer], belief, clarity, purity, patience, meekness and constancy of a man, without which you might work nothing. And with [these qualities] you shall get whatever you wish. The virtues [necessary] in working by Semiforas ought nevertheless to be these seven: that is meekness, truth, patience, abstinence, belief, charity, and mercy, which ought in him principally to be had, or to abound.

Si ergo per Semiforas operari volumus oportet quod simus &c.

If therefore we wish to work by Semiforas, it is well that we are bright or pure of body, and in trust steadfast, and from falseness and lying fully departed. It is well also to [regard] the Creator and his creatures [with awe], amongst which we ought to most hold the Sun in awe, which gives to us light, and darkness, cold and hot, which is the cause of the changing of the seasons, and of the temperament of the air, and of herbs. We ought also to know the aspects of the Moon, and the months by which it is 12 [lunar months] and [sometimes] 13 [months] are counted, which are called Nyssan, Yar, Tina, &c.[1]

And we ought to know the waxing [51ʳ] and decreasing of the Moon, when it [causes] all creatures of the sea, floods, and wells, and all the nether bodies to wax and decrease, take blood in the veins, and marrow in the head and their bones. After the Moon waxes & decreases, they are nourished in the same [way]. Also [there is] no doubt that the virtue of the Moon works [in] the infusing, or melting, of metals.

We ought also to know Sabaday or Saturn by whom hunger and dearth and

---

[1] The first three Hebrew months, Nisan, Iyyar, and Sivan. Sometimes there will be a 13th lunar month added, to keep the lunar months roughly aligned with the solar year.

Liber Salomonis

all anguish in lands befall. We ought also to know & regard with awe Zedek or Jupiter, by whom honour, and health and righteousness, and all good is had. We should also know and regard with awe Madim or Mars of whom choler & strife, and hate and battles, and lying, and all evils comes. We ought also to know and regard with awe Hanina or the Sun by whom we have light, and darkness & clearness, and by whom [through the changing] seasons, evil into good, [and good] into evil is transmuted or changed.

We ought also to regard with awe and know Nogah or Venus, by whom we have meat and drink, and all necessaries, or things that are needful, by whom peace and love and affection among men is made fast and stable. We ought also to regard with awe Cocab or Mercury, for he is closer to us than all [planets] except the Moon, by whom merchandise and vending or selling, and all secular things, are exercised. Therefore observe those that are said and the spirits abovesaid, and thus you shall profit. And whatever you shall ask of the Creator rightfully, you shall have it.

[Here ends the Fifth Book & here begins the Sixth Book]

[The Sixth Book]

[*Samaim* which Names all the Heavens and their Angels][1]

[51ᵛ] Here begins the Sixth book that treats of the names of the Heavens

Dixit Solomon omnes coiter horas et malas &c.

Solomon said "All men commonly affirm [the existence of] good hours and evil, and good days and evil, and good signs and evil." And this with many reasons they confirmed. And I, Solomon, have tested the days and hours of Madim [Mars] & Sabaday [Saturn] which I found very grievous for work. I have tested also the hours of Zedek [Jupiter] and Nogah [Venus]. And I saw that whenever I would work with them lightly I wrought [successfully]. The hours of Cocab [Mercury] and Labana [Moon], I have tested [and found] some grievous [bad], and others good. And I saw proved that in that day, and in the hour, nothing of my wishes might I fulfill. And know that the spirits abovesaid [in the opinion of] many men are named for the first [planet] in Hebrew which is Sabaday, in Arabic *zoal*, in Greek *orgrue fenes* [?], in Latin it is called Saturn. And I say therefore that the first hour of the day of Sabaday is [also] called Sabaday, the second [hour] Zedek, the third Madim, the fourth Hanina, and the fifth Nogah. The sixth Cocab, the seventh Labana. And the hours of the night ought to [be similarly] named by you. And know that by the planets abovesaid, and the days and hours, whatever you wish [to do] you shall understand. And you shall know the hidden and secret wiles of men.

Cumque per Semiforas operari voluerat &c. [52ʳ]

When he wants to work by Semiforas first, or whenever he begins any thing, it is well to name the 7 names of Angels, for some angels are rulers over the seven Heavens, [some] rulers over the 7 planets, [some] rulers over the 7 days of the week, [some] rulers over the 7 metals, [some] rulers over the 7 colours, and [some] rulers over the 7 words having power, the names of the which are these: Raphael, Gabriel, Samael, Michael, Saquiel, Anael, Capciel.

And these are arranged so that we ought to name and to call them during the 7 days, early [in the morning] in this manner.

---

[1] In Hebrew, Samaim שׁמים, refers to the 7 Heavens. The fact that the chapter heading is a transliterated Hebrew word points to probable Hebrew roots for this text, transmitted via Latin, although it is obvious that the scribe who actually wrote this particular manuscript knew no Hebrew.

Liber Salomonis

Nota orationem o angeli supradicti sitis meae quominis quam volo quaerere auditores et misri in oibus adintores &c.

That is to say, oh angels abovesaid are the hearers of my question which I will enquire, and for me in all things, are my helpers. These truly, which we ought to name, rule over the 7 Heavens, and rule over the 7 planets are these: Capciel, Saquiel, Samael, Raphael, Anael, Michael, Gabriel. And in all things in calling these angels you shall profit. There are 7 Heavens that is: Samaym [Shamayim], Raaqu [Raqia], Saaquin [Shechaqim], Maon [Ma'on], Mahon [Makon], Zebul, and Araboth.[1] And there are 4 parts of the world, that is East, West, North and South, with Angels in every Heaven, and we say in what part [each] serves.

These are the Angels of the First Heaven:[2]

In primo caelo qui vocatur Samaym in quatuor protibus &c.

In the first Heaven which is called Samaym [Shamayim], in the four parts of Heaven, serve these. From the part of the North: Alael, Hiaeyel, Urallim, Veallum, Baliel, Basy, Unascaiel. From the part of the [52ᵛ] South these are: Duraniel, Darbiel, Darquiel, Hanin, Anael, Nahymel, Alscini, Soquiel, Zamel, Hubayel, Bactanael, Carpariel, from the part of the East are these: Gabriel, Gabrael, Odrael, Modiel, Raamyel, Janael. From the part of the West are these: Abson, Soquiel.

Angels of the Second Heaven:

In secundo caelo quod vocatur Roaquya a part Septentrionis &c.

In the second Heaven that is called Roaquya [Raqia] from the part of the North serve these angels: Tyel, Jarael, Yanael, Nenael, Nenel, Quian, Uetamuel. From the part of the South are these: Mylba, Nelia, Balyer, Calloyel, Cyoly, Batriel. From the part of the East are these: Maachin, another [source] has Carmiel, Carcoyel, Betabaat. From the part of the West is Anulus, Yesararye, in which is written the names of Macareton and in many ways explained.

Angels of the Third Heaven:

In tertio caelo quod vocatur Saaquin a part Septentrionis &c.

In the third Heaven that is called Saaquin [Schechaqim] from the part of the North serve these: Poniel, Penael, Penat, Raphael, Carmiel, Doranel. From the part of the South are these: Parna, Sadiel, Lyenyel, Vastamel, Sanael, Samyel.

---

[1] For full details of the seven Hebrew Heavens see Stephen Skinner, *Complete Magician's Tables*, Golden Hoard, Singapore, and Llewellyn, St. Paul, 2006, Tables K69-K76, M10.
[2] Compare the following list of angels of the seven Heavens with the list in Peter de Abano's *Heptameron*. These are listed in Table M10 of Skinner, *Complete Magician's Tables*.

From the part of the East are these: Satquiel, Quadissa, Taramel, Taryestorat, Amael, Hufrbria, another [source] has here the last Hifaliel. [West is missing].

Angels of the Fourth Heaven:

In quarto caelo quod dicitur Maon serviunt isti a part Septentrionis &c.

In the fourth Heaven that is called Maon [Ma'on] these serve from the part of the North: [53ʳ] Rahumiel, Haynynael, Bacyel, Serapiel, Matiel, Serael. In the part of the South are these: Saoriel, Mahamel, Gadiel, Hosael, Vaanyel, Verascyer. In the part of the East are these: Capiel, Braliel, Braaliel, Raguel, Gael, Daemael, Calcas, Atragon. In the part of the West are these: Lacana, Astagna, Nobquin, Sonatas, Yael, Yas, Yael, Lael, Yyel.

Angels of the Fifth Heaven:

In quinto caelo isti sunt quod dicitur Mahon.

In the [fifth Heaven, Makon, from] the part of the North serve these Hayel, Hanyel, Veal, Quiel, Margabiel, Saeprel, Mamyel. In the part of the East are these: Lanifiel, another [source] has Barquiel, Zaquiel, Sanficiel, Zoaziel, Aciel, Farbiel, Uranacha. [The part of the South is missing]. In the part of the West are these: Anhael, Pabliel, Uslael, Bortaz, Suncacer, Zupa, Faly, Paly.

Angels of the Sixth Heaven:[1]

In sexto caelo quod vocatur cebul dices a part Septentrionalis &c.

In the sixth Heaven that is called Cebul [Zebul] you shall say from the North part "*Est Deus fortis et potens sine fine,*" that is to say "God is mighty and strong without end." From the part of the South you shall say "*Deus sanctus patiens et misericors,*" that is to say "God holy patient and merciful." From the part of the East you shall say "*Deus magne excelse et honorate per saecula,*" that is to say "great god high and worshipped by the world." From the part of the West you shall say "*Deus sapiens clare et juste. Deus tuam clementiam et sititatem exoro qua quaestionem meam et opus meum et laborem meum hodie* [53ᵛ] *complete et integre verficere digneris qui vivis et regnas Deus per o. s. s. Amen,*" that is to say "God wise clear and righteous. God your meekness and your holiness I beseech, that question and my work do daily fulfill and hallow, you vouchsafe to fulfill that [which] lives and reigns, God by all world of worlds, so mote it be. Amen."

---

[1] There are no angels listed for the two highest Heavens, as these are occupied by god, not the angels, hence the prayers to be said are listed here instead. Peter de Abano follows the same pattern, even if his angel names do not fully agree with *Sepher Raziel*.

Liber Salomonis

Angels of the seventh Heaven:

In septimo caelo est Semiforas scriptum in libro vitae &c.

In the seventh Heaven [Araboth] the Semiforas is written in the *Book of Life*. In the name of the meek and merciful god of Israel, and of paradise, and of heaven, and of earth, and of the seas, and of hills, and of creatures.[1]

[Here ends the Sixth Book & here begins the Seventh Book]

---

[1] Traditionally, the highest two Heavens, Makon and Araboth, do not have any angels associated with them.

[The Seventh Book]
[Book of Virtues and Miracles]

Here begins the Seventh Book that treats of names and of their virtues

Incipiunt sraem et verba et nomina Semiforas &c.

Here begins the words and names of Semiforas, which god the Creator gave to Adam in paradise. In which are four letters [IHVH] which [correspond] to the 4 parts of the world, to the 4 Elements, to the 4 complexions, and to the 4 natures of the beasts, they are likened such they are יהוה הוהי.[1] And these are letters piteously, devoutly, and meekly named [so] that petitions [prayers] for all things [may be] fulfilled. Solomon said there are 7 Semiforas.

And the first is the [54r] Semiforas of Adam, in which are contained 4 chapters. The first is when Adam spoke with the Creator in paradise. The second is when he spoke with the angels. The third is when he spoke with the devils. The fourth is when he spoke with men, with fowls & fish, beasts, reptiles and wild beasts. The fifth is when he spoke with seeds, herbs, trees, and all growing things. The sixth is when he spoke with the winds, and with the 4 Elements. The seventh is when he spoke with the Sun and the Moon, and the planets. And by the 7 virtues of Semiforas whatever he wished to do, he did, and whatever he wished to destroy, he destroyed. And this Semiforas Adam had when the Creator inspired grace into him.

[*The Seven Semiforas*]

The First Semiforas

Primum Semiforas est quando Creator Adam formavit &c.

The first Semiforas is when the Creator formed Adam, and putting him in paradise named גגגג יהוה הוהי,[2] that is to say *Yana*, the natures and virtues of which above we have declared. If in great necessity, or need, name this name meekly and devoutly, before the Creator, and doubt not that you will find grace and help.

---

[1] The Hebrew is very badly written, but this is very likely to be IHVH, Tetragrammaton, the name of god plus its mirror image.

[2] The first block of IHVH and its mirror image HVHI is crossed out. It is followed by גגגג. GGGG, which adds numerically to 4 x 3 = 12. This might have been Eleazar's famous דדדד. None of these reads as *yana*, unless you mistake the ו [Vav] for a נ [Nun] and transliterate יהוה YHVH as יהנה YHNH, or *yanah*, which is what has probably happened here.

Liber Salomonis

The Second Semiforas

Secundum Semiforas est quando Adam locutus fuit &c.

The second Semiforas is when Adam spoke with the Angel which brought to him these letters, a written example of which is such אשר אהיה, that is *yeseraye*.[1] And this name you shall name when you will speak with angels. And then your question and your [54ᵛ] work shall, without doubt, be fulfilled.

The Third Semiforas

Tertium Semiforas est quando locutus est cum daemonibus &c.

The third Semiforas is when he spoke with devils, and with dead men, and of them [asked] counsel, and they sufficiently answered [him]. And all this he did with these names of which this is the explanation: Adona[i], Sabaoth, Adonay, Cados [Kadosh], Addona, Annora. And these names you shall name when you wish to gather together winds or devils or serpents.

The Fourth Semiforas

Quartum Semiforas est quando animalia et spiritus &c.

The fourth Semiforas is when he bound and loosed beasts and spirits with these 7 names: Lagume, Lamizirm, Lanagzlayn, Lagri, Lanagala, Lanatozin, Laifyalasyn. And when you wish to bind or loose beasts you shall name the names abovesaid.

The Fifth Semiforas

Quintum Semiforas est quando arbores et sementa &c.

The fifth Semiforas is when he called or named the 7 natures with which he bound seeds and trees. And these are: Lihaham, Lialgana, Liafar, Vialurab, Lelara, Lebaron, Laasasilas. And when you wish to bind seeds, or trees, you shall name the names abovesaid. And you shall bind [them with these].

The Sixth Semiforas

Sextum Semiforas est magnae virtutis &c.

The sixth Semiforas is of great virtue and power, of which these are the names: Letamynyn, Letaglogen, Letafiryn, Babaganaritin, Letarimitin, Letagelogin, [55ʳ] Letafalazin, these names you shall name when you want the elements and winds to fulfill your wishes in all things.

---

[1] The Hebrew is totally corrupt, and virtually unrecognizable. It was probably meant to be אשר אהיה AShR AHIH, 'Asher Eheieh.'

Sepher Raziel

The Seventh Semiforas

Septinum Semiforas est magnum et virtuosum &c.

The seventh Semiforas is great and virtuous, for they are names of the Creator which you ought to name [when doing] each thing, and in all your works call. And they are these: Eliaon, Yaena, Adonay, Cados, Ebreel, Eloy, Ela, Egiel, Ayom, Sath, Adon, Sulela, Eloym, Deliom, Yacy, Elim, Delis, Yacy, Zazael, Pabiel, Man, Myel, Enola, Dylatan, Saday, Alina, Papym, another [source gives] Saena, Alym, Catinal, Uza, Yarast, Calpi, Calsas, Safna, Nycam, Saday, Aglataon, Sya, Emanuel, Joth, Lalaph, Om, Via, Than, Domyfrael, Nimel, Lalialens, Alla, Phenox, Agsata, Tiel, Piel, Patriceion, Chepheron, Baryon, Yael. And these you should name in each season that you work, ruling over the 4 Elements, and whenever you wish do [destruction] by them, it shall be destroyed.

[The Semiforas of Moses]

Here begins the Semiforas of Moses

Incipit Semiforas qui dominus dedit Moisi et &c.

Here begins Semiforas that our Lord gave to Moses, and it is divided into 7 Chapters, of which the first [chapter] is when Moses ascended the hill [Mt Sinai] and spoke with the flames that surrounded the bush, and the bush seemed to burn, but nevertheless it burned not. The second [chapter] is when he spoke with the Creator on the hill. The third was when he divided the Red Sea and passed through it. [55ᵛ] The fourth was when his staff was changed into a serpent and the serpent devoured another [serpent]. The fifth is the name that was written on the forehead of Aaron. The sixth is when he made the brazen adder and the Calf in brass, and smote the Egyptians with the plagues. The seventh is when he rained manna in the desert, and drew out water from the stone, and let out the children of Israel from captivity.

Cap[itulum] Primum [First Chapter]

Haec sunt nomina quae dixit Moises quando est &c.

These are the names that Moses [heard] when he ascended the hill and spoke with the flames: Maya, Afi, Zye, Yaremye, Une, Bace, Sare, Binoe, Maa, Yasame, Roy, Lyly, Leoy, Yle, Yre, Cyloy, Zalye, Lee, Or, See, Loace, Cadeloy, Ule, Meha, Ramechi, Ry, Hy, Fossa, Tu, Mimi, Sehie, Nice, Yelo, Habe, Uele, Hele, Ede, Quego, Ramaye, Habe. And when you name these names devoutly, know your work will without doubt be fulfilled.

Liber Salomonis

Capitulum Secundum [Second Chapter]

Haec sunt nomina quae dixit Creator &c.

These are the names which the Creator said to Moses when he ascended the hill and spoke with him: Abgincam, Loaraceram, Naodicras, Pecaccecas, Acaptena, Yeger, Podayg, Saccosicum. These are the names with which the temple of Bozale was founded. These are the names of the prophets, and the Angels with which the 4 parts of the world were sealed, with which you may do many miracles. And beware least you name them, but be chaste and pure, from three days [56r] fasting, and whatever you wish do by them you shall do.

Capitulum Tertium [Third Chapter]

Haec sunt nomina quae Moses dixit &c.

These are the names that Moses said when he divided the Red Sea: Ena, Elaye, Sayec, Helame, Maace, Lehahu, Lehahu, Alielie, Qore, Azaye, Boene, Hyeha, Ysale, Mabeha, Arayha, Arameloena, Qleye, Lieneno, Feyane, Ye, Ye, Malece, Habona, Nechee, Hicers. And when you want to have grace from any man, these names you shall name devoutly and meekly, and you shall have it.

Capitulum Quartum [Fourth Chapter]

Haec sunt nomina quae dixit Moses &c.

These are the names that Moses said when his rod staff was changed into a serpent, of the enchanters and the Prophets: Micraton, Piston, Yeymor, Higaron, Ygniron, Tenigaron, Mycon, Mycondasnos, Castas, Laceas, Astas, Yecon, Cuia, Tablinst, Tabla, Nac, Yacuf. And these aforesaid names you shall name when you wish to fulfill your question.

Capitulum Quintum [Fifth Chapter]

Haec sunt nomina quae scripta erant in populus Aron &c.

These are the names that were written by the people of Aaron when he spoke with the Creator: Saday, Haleyos, Loez, Elacy, Citonij, Hazyhaya, Yeynimeysey, Accidasbaruc, Huadonenu, Eya, Hyebu, Ueu, Uaha, Oyaha, Eye, Ha, Hia, Zalia, Haliha, Eyey, Yaia, El, Ebehel, Ua, Ua. Keep well these names abovesaid for they are holy and virtuous, and these you shall name so you may get what you ask of the Creator. [56v]

Sepher Raziel

Capitulum Sextum [Sixth Chapter]

Haec sunt nomina quae scripta erant in virga Moysi &c.

These are the names that were written on the staff of Moses when he made the brazen serpent and destroyed the golden calf, when all that drunk in the well had a beard [were men]: Yana, Yane, Sia, Abibhu, Uanoia, Accenol, Tiogas, Yena, Eloym, Ya, Uehu, Yane, Hayya, Uehu, Ahiacmed. And these names contain in themselves many virtues, for with them you shall destroy evil and all enchantments. And presume not to name them in the 7 works.

Capitulum Septimum [Seventh Chapter]

Haec sunt nomina quae Moses dixit qua pluit &c.

These are the names that Moses said when manna rained in the desert, and he drew out water from the rock, and led out from captivity the children of Israel: Saday, Samora, Ebon, Pheneton, Eloy, Eneiobceel, Messias, Jahe, Yana or Eolyen. When you wish to do any marvels, or if you were in any anguish, these names you shall name.

And in all things you shall feel their help and the virtue. And when you have done this, rehearse these words by which the names aforesaid are explained:

"Deus vive verax, magne, fortis, poleus, prio, sancte, munde, omni, bonifate, plene, benedicte dominus benedictum nomen sum tua, completer nostram compleas questione tu factor fac nos ad fine urim operis provenire tu largitor nobis integrum complementum urim operis elargire tu sancta et misericors nobis misereres nomen tuam Yeseraye, sit per secula benedictum. Amen."

That is to say, "living true God, great, [57ʳ] strong, mighty, meek, holy, pure, full of all goodness, blessed Lord be your name, fulfill our questions, you make us to come to the end of our work. You holy and merciful, have mercy on us. Your name, Yeseraye, be it blessed by the worlds, Amen."

In the name of the sovereign almighty Creator I begin the explanation of his name Yeseraye,[1] that is to say God without beginning and without end. Angilae is the name of a prophet and properly written on a golden plate by living men. And whoever bears it, and however long he has it with him, so he shall not dread sudden death.

Here ends the *Book of Raziel* of the Seven Treatises.

---

[1] Corrupt Hebrew godname.

Appendix 1 – Incense Nomenclature [1]

	N20. Perfumes and their Plant Source.	
Name in *Sepher Raziel*	**Perfume/Incense**	**Botanical Source**
Algalia	Algalia *see* Civet	
Almabum / Acil almalie	Almabum = Rosemary	*Rosmarinus officinalis*
Aloes	Aloes resin	Resin of *Aquillaria agallocha*
Lignum Aloes	Aloes wood (Oud)	Wood of *Aquillaria agallocha*
Apinum	Apinum	Maybe *Eryngium apinum*
Apium / Apii	Apium *see* Celeriac, Parsley	
Ambra / Ambram	Ambergris	A substance regurgitated by the sperm whale
Arzolla / Arzolle	Arzolla *see* Lady's thistle	
Asafoetida / Assa	Assafoetida	*Ferula assafoetida*
Auricular muris	Auricular muris *see* Hawkweed	
Balsamus / Balsamo	Balsam	Sap of *Commiphora opobalsamum*
Lignum balsami	Balsam wood	Wood of *Commiphora opobalsamum*
Benzoin	Benzoin	Resin from *Styrax Benzoin*
Cancer mastum	Camphor	*Cinnamomum Camphora*
Cardamom	Cardamom	*Eliettaria Cardamomum*
Cassia	Cassia / Kasia [Classical Mercury incense]	*Cinnamomum Cassia*
Apium / Apii	Celeriac, Parsley	*Apii graveolentis rapaceum*
Cera alba	Cera alba = white wax	Bee hives
Scicorda	Chicory, succory [wild chicory]	*Cichorium intybus*
Cicorea		
Cicuta	Cicuta *see* Hemlock, water	
Cinamomus / Cinamomo	Cinnamon	Bark of the *Cinnamomum verum* or *Cinnamomum zeylanicum*

---

[1] Taken from Table N20 of Stephen Skinner, *Complete Magician's Tables*, Singapore: Golden Hoard Press, and St. Paul: Llewellyn, 2006, with amplifications.

Name in *Sepher Raziel*	Perfume/Incense	Botanical Source
Pentaphyllon / Pentaphylon	Cinquefoil	*Potentilla reptans*
Citron	Citron / lemon or orange	*Citrus medica*
Algalia	Civet (from Spanish)	From the odorous sacs of the civets, animals of the family *Viverridae*
Classen	Classen *see* Sandalwood oil	
Gariophylli / Garyophillo / Gariofilum	Cloves	*Eugenia caryphyllata*, or *Syzygium aromaticum*
Colofoniam / Pix Graecum	Colophony / Greek pitch	*Pine oleoresin*, distilled from pine trees
Dragantium / Dragantia	Columbrina gum [Maybe Adderwort]	Genus *Colubrina* [Maybe the fern *Ophioglossum vulgatum*]
Costum / Costo	Costus / kostos [Classical Mars incense]	Root of *Costus Arabicus*, *Costus Speciosus* or *Saussurea lappa*
Crocum	Crocus (or saffron from its stamens)	*Crocus sativus*
Cipressum	Cypress	*Cupressaceae* family
Eringo	Eryngo, Sea-holly	Genus *Eryngium*, such as *Eryngium maritimum*
Euphorbium	Euphorbium	Sap of various species of *Euphorbia*
Folia lauri	Folia lauri *see* Laurel	
Thur /Thure	Frankincense [Classical Sun incense]	Gum resin from several species of *Boswellia* mainly *Boswellia cartierii* and *Boswellia thurifera* (hence the name '*thur*')
Thus / Thuris	Frankincense oil (Olibanum)	
Galbanum	Galbanum	Sap from *Ferula galbaniflua*
Gariophylli / Garyophillo / Gariofilum	Gariophylli *see* Clove	
Auricular muris	Hawkweed, mouse-ear	*Hieracium pilosella*
Cicuta	Hemlock (Northern Water Hemlock), Cowbane (highly poisonous)	*Cicuta virosa*
Insqrmo = Jusquiami	Henbane, Stinking nightshade [psychoactive and highly poisonous]	*Hyoscamus niger*
Marrubio albo	Horehound, white	*Marrubium vulgare*
Arzolla / Arzolle	Lady's thistle, Holy histle	*Silybum marianum*
Folia lauri	Laurel	*Laurus nobilis*
Masticem / Mastice / Mastiche	Mastic	Gum resin from *Pistacia lentiscus*
Menta	Mint	Various species of *Mentha* such as *Mentha viridis*
Muscum / Muscus / Muscu / Musco	Musk	Odoriferous substance from the glands of the male musk deer

N20. Perfumes and their Plant Source.

Liber Salomonis

Name in *Sepher Raziel*	Perfume/Incense	Botanical Source
	N20. Perfumes and their Plant Source.	
Myrrh	Myrrh [Classical Lunar incense]	Gum from *Balsamodendron myrrha*, *Commiphora myrrha*
Musthalazeratis / Muculazarat / Muschullaroth [see also Tejpatra]	Mukul = Myrrh from Zafar, Yemen Muql = Bdellium [both speculative]	Myrrh = *Commiphora myrrha* Bdellium = *Commiphora wightii*
Mirtal / Folius myrti / Mirtum	Myrtle	*Myrtus communis*
Nucem muscata / Nux muscata	Nutmeg	*Myristica fragans*
Oleo olivrarum	Olive oil	Oil of the olive tree Family *Oleaceae*
Olibanum	Olibanum *see* Frankincense oil	
Opopanaces	Opoponax	Sap of *Opopanax orientalis*
Pulegium	Pennyroyal	*Menta pulegium*
Pentaphyllon	Pentaphyllon *see* Cinquefoil	
Piperum Nigrum / Piper Negrum / Piperis Nigri	Pepper, black	*Piper nigrum*
Piper longum	Pepper (Long Pepper)	*Piper longum*
Papavere nigro	Poppy, black	*Papaver nigrum*, related to *Papaver somniferum*
Reubarbarum	Rhubarb	*Rheum rhabarbarum*
Salvia	Sage	*Salvia officinalis*, or maybe *Salvia divinorum*
Sanders / Sandalos / sandalus	Sandalwood	Wood of *Santalum album*
Sandalum niger	Sandalwood, black	*Santalum nigrum* related to *Santalum album*
Sandalum rubrum	Sandalwood, red	Wood of *Pterocarpus santalinus*
Sandalum album	Sandalwood, white	Wood of *Santalum album*
Classen	Sandalwood oil	Oil of *Santalum album*
Satureia	Savory	*Satureia hortensis*
Scicordia	Scicordia *see* Chicory	
Storax	Storax / Styrax [Classical Saturn incense]	Gum resin from *Styrax officinalis* (from Liquid amber orientalis tree)
Malabathron / Malabatrum [not specifically mentioned in *Sepher Raziel*]	Tejpatra / Tamaalpatra / Indian Bay leaves [Classical Jupiter incense]	*Cinnamomum tamala*
Thur / Thure / Thus / Thuris	Thur *see* Frankincense	
Thymiama	Thyme	*Thymus vulgaris*
Thymiamata	Thymiamata = Sacred incense in general	-

Appendix 2 – Selected Table of Angels in *Sepher Raziel* [1]

		A45. The Angels of the 12 Hebrew Months in *Sepher Raziel*.	
		Hebrew Month	Angels
♈	1	Nisan	Oriel, Malaquiran, Acia, Yaziel, Paltifus, Yesmactria, Yariel, Araton, Robica, Sephatia, Anaya, Quesupale, Semquiel, Sereriel, Malgas, Ancason, Pacyta, Abedel, Ram, Asdon, Casiel, Nastiafori, Sugni, Aszre, Sornadaf, Adniel, Necamia, Caisaat, Benit, Quor, Adziriel.
♉	2	Iyar	Safuel, Saton, Cartemat, Aryel, Palthia, Bargar, Galms, Nocpis, Aaron, Manit, Aadon, Qwenael, Quemon, Abragin, Yehoc, Adnibia, Parciot, Marinoc, Galus, Gabmion, Resegar, Affry, Absamon, Sarsaf, Alxim, Carbiol, Regnia, Achlas, Nadib, Absafyabitan, Pliset.
♊	3	Sivan	Amariel, Tatgiel, Casmuch, Nuscifa, Almux, Naamab, Mamiazicaras, Samysarach, Naasien, Andas, Paltamus, Abris, Borhai, Salor, Hac, Yayac, Dalia, Azigor, Mabsuf, Abnisor, Zenam, Dersam, Cefania, Maccafor, Naboon, Adiel, Maasiel, Szarhyr, Cartalion, Adi, Ysar.
♋	4	Tammuz	Moriel, Safida, Asaf, Mazica, Sarsac, Adnyam, Nagrow, Galuf, Galgall, Danroc, Saracus, Remafidda, Luliaraf, Nediter / Delgna, Maadon, Saamyel, Amrael, Lezaidi, Elisafan, Paschania, Maday.
♌	5	Ab	Byny, Madrat, Amantuliel, Cassurafarttis, Nactif, Necif, Pdgnar, Tablic, Mamirot, Amacia, Qnatiel, Reycat, Qnynzi, Paliel, Gadaf, Nesquiraf, Abrac, Amyter, Camb, Nachal, Cabach, Loch, Macria, Safe, Essaf.
♍	6	Elul	Magnyny, Arabyel, Hanyel, Nacery, Yassar, Rassy, Boel, Mattriel, Naccamarif, Zacdon, Nafac, Rapion, Sapsi, Salttri, Raseroph, Malgel, Samtiel, Yoas, Qualabye, Danpi, Yamla, Golid, Rasziel, Satpach, Nassa, Myssa, Macracif, Dadiel, Carciel, Effignax.
♎	7	Tishri	Suriel, Sarican, Gnabriza, Szucariel, Sababiel, Ytrut, Cullia, Dadiel, Marhum, Abecaisdon, Sacdon, Pagulan, Arsabon, Aspiramo, Aquyel, Safcy, Racynas, Altim, Masulaef, Vtisaryaya, Abri.
♏	8	Marchesvan	Karbiel, Tiszodiel, Raamyel, Nebubael, Alisaf, Baliel, Arzaf, Rasliel, Alson, Naspiel, Becar, Paliel, Elisuaig, Nap, Naxas, Sansani, Aesal, Maarim, Sasci, Yalsenac, Iabynx, Magdiel, Sarmas, Maaliel, Arsaferal, Manistiorar, Veaboluf, Nadibael, Suciel, Nabuel, Sariel, Sodiel, Marcuel, Palitam.
♐	9	Kislev	Adoniel, Radiel, Naduch, Racyno, Hyzy, Mariel, Azday, Mandiel, Gamiel, Seriel, Kery, Sahaman, Osmyn, Sachiel, Pazehemy, Calchihay, Hehudael, Nerad, Minael, Arac, Arariqniel, Galnel, Gimon, Satuel, Elynzy, Baqwylaguel.
♑	10	Tebet	Anael, Aniyel, Aryor, Naflia, Rapinis, Raaciel, Pacuel, Hahon, Guanrinasuch, Aslaqwy, Naspaya, Negri, Somahi, Hasasisgafon, Gasca, Szif, Alzamy, Maint, Xatinas, Sargnamuf, Oliab, Sariel, Canyel, Rahyeziel, Pansa, Insquen, Sarman, Malisan, Asirac, Marmoc.
♒	11	Shebet	Gabriel, Israel, Natriel, Gazril, Nassam, Abrisaf, Zefael, Zamiel, Mamiel, Tabiel, Miriel, Sahumiel, Guriel, Samhiel, Dariel, Banorsasti, Satyn, Nasyel, Ranfiel, Talgnaf, Libral, Luel, Daliel, Guadriel, Sahuhaf, Myschiel.
♓	12	Adar	Romiel, Patiel, Guriel, Laabiel, Addriel, Cardiel, Aguel, Malquiel, Samiel, Sariel, Azriel, Paamiel, Carcyelel, Amaluch, Parhaya, Ytael, Beryel, Cael, Tenebiel, Pantan, Panteron, Fanyel, Falafon, Masiel, Pantaron, Labiel, Ragael, Cetabiel, Nyahpatuel.
	13	Adar *bis* / Bisertillis	Lantiel, Ardiel, Nasmyel, Celidoal, Amyel, Magel, Gabgel, Sasuagos, Barilagni, Yabtasyper, Magossangos, Dragos, Yayel, Yoel, Yasmyel, Stelmel, Garasyn, Ceyabos, Sacadiel, Guracap, Gabanael, Tamtiel.

---

[1] Taken from Stephen Skinner, *Complete Magician's Tables*, Singapore: Golden Hoard Press, forthcoming third edition.

Liber Salomonis

	Day	Angels
☾	Monday	Semhahylyn, Stemehilyn, Jasyozyn, Agrasinden, Aymeylyn, Cathneylyn, Abrasachysyn, Abrasasyn, Layzaiosyn, Langhasin, Anayenyn, Nangareryn, Aczonyn, Montagin, Labelas, Mafatyn, Feylarachin, Candanagyn, Laccudonyn, Casfrubyn, Bacharachyn, Bathaylyn, Anmanineylyn, Hacoylyn, Balganarichyn, Aryelyn, Badeilyn, Abranocyn, Tarmanydyn, Amdalycyn, Sahgragynyn, Adiamenyn, Sacstoyeyn, Latebaifanysyn, Caybemynyn, Nabyalni, Cyzamanyn, Abramacyn, Lariagathyn, Bifealyqnyn, Baiedalin, Gasoryn, Asaphin, Dariculin, Marneyelin, Gemraorin, Madarilyn, Yebiryn, Arylin, Farielin, Nepenielin, Branielin, Asrieylin, Ceradadyn.
☿	Tuesday	Michael, Zamirel, Beerel, Dufuel, Aribiriel, Boel, Bariel, Meriol, Amiol, Aol, Semeol, Aaon, Berion, Farionon, Kemerion, Feyn, Ameinyn, Zemeinyn, Cananyn, Aal, Merigal, Pegal, Gabal, Leal, Amneal, Farnnial, Gebyn, Caribifin, Ancarilyn, Metorilin, Nabiafilyn, Fisfilin, Barsfilin, Camfilin, Aaniturla, Feniturla, Geniniturla, Elmia, Calnamia, Rabmia, Rasfia, Miaga, Tiogra, Bee, Ylaraorynil, Benenil.
♀	Friday	Hasneyeyl, Barnayeyl, Uardayheil, Alzeyeil, Szeyyeil, Uachayel, Zesfaieil, Morayeil, Borayeyl, Apheieyl, Arobolyn, Canesylyn, Anrylin, Zarialin, Marilin, Batoraielyn, Kelfeielyn, Azraieylin, Ambayerin, Ayayeylin, Cadneirin, Alserin, Afneirin, Abneyrin, Nonanrin, Eazerin, Orinyn, Gedulin, Hareryn, Nanylin, Halilin, Himeilin, Resfilin, Noraraabilin, Hayeylin, Laudulin, Et, Effilin, Thesfealin, Patnilin, Keialin, Lebraieil, Ablaieil, Talrailanrain, Barcalin, Bahoraelin.
☉	Sunday	Daniel, Elieyl, Saffeyeyl, Dargoyeyl, Yelbrayeyl, Comaguele, Gebarbayea, Faceyeyl, Caran, Neyeyl, Talgylnenyl, Bethaz, Rancyl, Falha, Hyeyl, Armaqnieyeyl, Roncayl, Gibryl, Zamayl, Mycahe, Zarfaieil, Ameyl, Torayeil, Ronmeyeyl, Remcatheyel, Barhil, Marhil, Barhil, Mehil, Zarafil, Azrageyl, Anebynnyl, Denmerzym, Yeocyn, Necyl, Hadzbeyeyl, Zarseyeyl, Zarael, Anqnihim, Ceytatynyn, Ezuiah, Vehichdunedzineylyn, Yedmeyeyl, Esmaadyn, Albedagryn, Yamaanyl, Yecaleme, Detriel, Arieil, Armayel, Veremedyn, Unaraxxydin.
♂	Wednesday	Samayelyn, Tartalyn, Dexxeyl, Racyeylyn, Farabyn, Cabyn, Asymeylyn, Mabareylyn, Tralyelyn, Rulbelyn, Marmanyn, Tarfanyelyn, Fuheylyn, Ruffaraneylyn, Rabfilyn, Eralyn, Enplyn, Pirtophin, Brofilyn, Cacitilyn, Naffrynyn, Impuryn, Raffeylyn, Nyrysin, Memolyn, Nybirin, Celabel, Tubeylyn, Haayn, Reyn, Paafiryn, Cethenoylyn, Letityelyn, Rorafeyl, Cannyel, Bastelyn, Costiryn, Monteylyn, Albeylyn, Parachbeylyn, Alyel, Uaceyl, Zalcycyl, Amadyeyl, Usaryeyel, Emcodeneyl, Dasfripyel, Unleylyn, Carszeneyl, Gromeyl, Gabrynyn, Narbell.
♃	Thursday	Sachquiel, Pachayel, Tutiel, Osfleel, Labiel, Raliel, Beniel, Tarael, Snynyel, Ahiel, Yebel, Ancuyel, Jauiel, Juniel, Amyel, Faniel, Ramnel, Sanfael, Sacciniel, Galbiet, Lafiel, Maziel, Gunfiel, Ymrael, Memieil, Pariel, Panhiniel, Toripiel, Abinel, Omiel, Orfiel, Ael, Bearel, Ymel, Syymelyel, Traacyel, [42ʳ] Mefeniel, Antquiel, Quisiel, Cunnyryel, Rofiniel, Rubycyel, Jebrayel, Peciel, Carbiel, Tymel, Affarfytyriel, Rartudel, Cabrifiel, Beel, Briel, Cherudiel.
♄	Saturday	Micraton, Pacryton, Pepilon, Capeiel, Themiton, Alsfiton, Chenyon, Sandalson, Panion, Almyon, Expion, Papon, Calipon, Horrion, Melifon, Aurion, Temelion, Refacbilion, Ononiteon, Boxoraylon, Paxilon, Lelalion, Onoxion, Quilon, Quiron, Vixalimon, Relion, Cassilon, Titomon, Murion, Dedion, Dapsion, Leuainon, Foylylon, Monichion, Gabion, Paxonion, Xysuylion, Lepiron, Belon, Memitilon, Saron, Salion, Pion, Macgron, Acciriron, Felyypon, Ymnybron, Raconeal, Zalibron.

Sepher Raziel

A47. Names of the Planets by the Elements, with their Angels in *Sepher Raziel*.

	Planet	Fire	Air	Water	Earth
☽	Levanah	Claron	Becyla	Tasfit	Pantours
	Angels:	Gabriel, Paticael, Daliel	Barasiel, Ztaziel	Caziel, Memyiel, Pazicaton	Simyllyel, Lafaqnael, Toniel
☿	Kokab	Piztal	Cabran	Facayl	Tarzon
	Angels:	Paradiel, Darifiel, Dameyel	Ramatiel, Loriqniel, Bengariel	Rinafonel, Mellifiel, Alatiel	Alapion, Beriel, Rabiel
♀	Nogah	Dusuyon	Clarifon	Narubni	Cabras
	Angels:	Capciel, Debitael, Deparael	Camirael, Cakaziel, Neraziel	Saloniel, Emyel, Expaoniel	Paziael, Amurael, Salainel
☼	Hamina	Yeye,	Don	Agla	On
	Angels:	Dandaniel, Saddaniel, Ellalyel	Karason, Berriel, Oliel	Muracafel, Pecyrael, Michael	Homycabel, Lucifel, Locariel
♂	Madim	Roqnyel	Pyryel	Tasfien	Ignofon
	Angels:	Kaliel, Cabryel, Raloyl	Pyroyinel, Flatoniel, Carbiel	Cazabriel, Pasaliel, Zebaliel	???
♃	Zedek	Pheon	Fidon	Calidon	Mydon
	Angels:	Tinsyel, Necanynael, Fonyel	???	Meon, Ykiel, Yryniel	Palriel, Tufiel, Quyel
♄	Sabaday	Campton	Srynongoa	Synyn	Onion [sic]
	Angels:	Libiel, Nybiel, Phynitiel	Arfigyel, Gael, Nephyel	Almemel, Hoquiel, Fulitiel	Lariel, Tepyel, Esyel

A48. Names of the 4 Elements and the Lowlands [Underworld] in the 4 Seasons in *Sepher Raziel*.

	Spring	Summer	Autumn	Winter
F	Quoyzil	Enlubra	Mezayn	Aybedyn
A	Ystana	Furayl	Oadion	Gulynon
W	Angustiz	Theon	Maddrylk	Sebillgradon
E	Ingnedon	Yabassa	Coliel	Aradon
UW	Hahan *Angel*: ?	Cipaon *Angel*: Jacyel	Meresac *Angel*: Ababaot	Aycyhambabo *Angel*: Caaniel

Liber Salomonis

A49. The 7 Heavens and the Angels ruling in each of their Directions in *Sepher Raziel*.

Heaven		North	East	West	South
Shamayim	1	Alael, Hiaeyel, Urallim, Veallum, Baliel, Basy, Unascaiel	Gabriel, Gabrael, Odrael, Modiel, Raamyel, Janael	Abson, Soquiel	Duraniel, Darbiel, Darquiel, Hanin, Anael, Nahymel, Alscini, Soquiel, Zamel, Hubayel, Bactanael, Carpariel
Raqia	2	Tyel, Jarael, Yanael, Nenael, Nenel, Quian, Uetamuel	Maachin or Carmiel, Carcoyel, Betabaat	Anulus, Yesararye [corrupt godname], in which is written the name Macareton	Mylba, Nelia, Balyer, Calloyel, Cyoly, Batriel
Shechaqim	3	Poniel, Penael, Penat, Raphael, Carmiel, Doranel	Satquiel, Quadissa, Taramel, Taryestorat, Amael, Hufrbria or Hifaliel	???	Parna, Sadiel, Lyenyel, Vastamel, Sanael, Samyel
Ma'on	4	Rahumiel, Haynynael, Bacyel, Serapiel, Matiel, Serael	Capiel, Braliel, Braaliel, Raguel, Gael, Daemael, Calcas, Atragon	Lacana, Astagna, Nobquin, Sonatas, Yael, Yas, Yael, Lael, Yyel	Saoriel, Mahamel, Gadiel, Hosael, Vanyel, Verascyer
Makon	5	Hayel, Hanyel, Veal, Quiel, Margabiel, Saeprel, Mamyel	Lanifiel or Barquiel, Zaquiel, Sanficiel, Zoaziel, Aciel, Farbiel, Uranacha	Anhael, Pabliel, Uslael, Bortaz, Suncacer, Zupa, Faly, Paly	???
Zebul	6	[no angels]			
Araboth	7	[no angels]			

A50. Names of Heavens, and the names of the Directions, distributed over the 4 Seasons from *Sepher Raziel*.

	Spring	Summer	Autumn	Winter
Names of the Heavens	Hacibor	Rumcaqnia	Mesfisnogna	Saaemaho
Names of the East	Acbedan	Cardrenac	Abrthel	Acritael
Names of the North	Henniyna	Abodich	Galdidur	Rabbifor
Names of the West	Mahanahym	Sugor	Zarzir	Rabiur
Names of the South	Naufor	Alparon	Machniel	Thaumy

Sepher Raziel

		A51. Angel Names for the Semiforas from *Sepher Raziel*.	
Heaven	Chapters [Capitulum]	Moses' Semiforas	Ordinary Semiforas
Shamayim	1	Maya, Afi, Zye, Yaremye, Une, Bace, Sare, Binoe, Maa, Yasame, Roy, Lyly, Leoy, Yle, Yre, Cyloy, Zalye, Lee, Or, See, Loace, Cadeloy, Ule, Meha, Ramechi, Ry, Hy, Fossa, Tu, Mimi, Sehie, Nice, Yelo, Habe, Uele, Hele, Ede, Quego, Ramaye, Habe.	בגבג יהוה הוהי [no angel names]
Raqia	2	Abgincam, Loaraceram, Naodicras, Pecaccecas, Acaptena, Yeger, Podayg, Saccosicum.	אשר אהיה. [no angel names]
Shechaqim	3	Ena, Elaye, Sayec, Helame, Maace, Lehahu, Lehahu, Alielie, Qore, Azaye, Boene, Hyeha, Ysale, Mabeha, Arayha, Arameloena, Qleye, Lieneno, Feyane, Ye, Ye, Malece, Habona, Nechee, Hicers.	Adona[i], Sabaoth, Adonay, Cados [Kadosh], Addona, Annora.
Ma'on	4	Micraton, Piston, Yeymor, Higaron, Ygniron, Tenigaron, Mycon, Mycondasnos, Castas, Laceas, Astas, Yecon, Cuia, Tablinst, Tabla, Nac, Yacuf.	Lagume, Lamizirm, Lanagzlayn, Lagri, Lanagala, Lanatozin, Laifyalasyn.
Makon	5	Saday, Haleyos, Loez, Elacy, Citonij, Hazyhaya, Yeynimeysey, Accidasbaruc, Huadonenu, Eya, Hyebu, Ueu, Uaha, Oyaha, Eye, Ha, Hia, Zalia, Haliha, Eyey, Yaia, El, Ebehel, Ua, Ua.	Lihaham, Lialgana, Liafar, Vialurab, Lelara, Lebaron, Laasasilas.
Zebul	6	Yana, Yane, Sia, Abibhu, Uanoia, Accenol, Tiogas, Yena, Eloym, Ya, Uehu, Yane, Hayya, Uehu, Ahiacmed.	Letamynyn, Letaglogen, Letafiryn, Babaganaritin, Letarimitin, Letagelogin, Letafalazin.
Araboth	7	Saday, Samora, Ebon, Pheneton, Eloy, Eneiobceel, Messias, Jahe, Yana or Eolyen.	Eliaon, Yaena, Adonay, Cados, Ebreel, Eloy, Ela, Egiel, Ayom, Sath, Adon, Sulela, Eloym, Deliom, Yacy, Elim, Delis, Yacy, Zazael, Pabiel, Man, Myel, Enola, Dylatan, Saday, Alina, Papym, another [source gives] Saena, Alym, Catinal, Uza, Yarast, Calpi, Calsas, Safna, Nycam, Saday, Aglataon, Sya, Emanuel, Joth, Lalaph, Om, Via, Than, Domyfrael, Nimel, Lalialens, Alla, Phenox, Agsata, Tiel, Piel, Patriceion, Chepheron, Baryon, Yael.

Liber Salomonis

A52. Names of the Angels ruling over the 4 Elements in *Sepher Raziel*.	
	Angel
F	Michael, Rafael, Rasoiel, Acdiel, Roqniel, Myriel, Indam, Malqniel, Gazriel, Amynyel, Cariel, Yafrael.
A	Rafael, Quabriel, Michael, Cherubyn, Ceraphin, Orychyn, Pantaceren, Micraton, Sandalfon, Barachiel, Ragehyel, Tobiel.
W	Urpeniel, Armariel, Yyamnel, Abrastos, Sapiel, Uiotan, Oriel, Bachmyel, Porackmiel, Acceriel, Galliel, Zsmayel.
E	Samael, Yatayel, Baraniel, Oriel, Arfaniel, Latgriel, Daniel, Affariel, Partriel, Bael, Byeniel.

A53. Name of the Planets, and their Angels, in the 4 Seasons, in *Sepher Raziel*.					
	Angel	Spring	Summer	Autumn	Winter
☽	Anael	Salmi	Sarico	Naspilii	Afriqnym
☿	Satquiel	Armis	Angocus	Tholos	Ancholos
♀	Adzdiel	Aporodicy	Calizo	Niniptz	Pontos
☉	Dandaniel	Halyom	Adocham	Cantopos	Pantasus
♂	Balquiel	Aaryn	Daron	Bearon	Pantefos
♃	Satquiel	Amonor	Sahibor	Sayin	Eanynyel
♄	Capciel	Cuerues	Palicos	Quirtipos	Panpotes

A54. Angels ruling over 7 Heavens in *Sepher Raziel*.		
	Heaven	Angel
☽	Shamayim	Capciel
☿	Raqia	Saquiel
♀	Shechaqim	Samael
☉	Ma'on	Raphael
♂	Makon	Anael
♃	Zebul	Michael
♄	Araboth	Gabriel

A55. Names of Angels having power in each Direction in *Sepher Raziel*.	
Direction	Angels
Names of the East	Gabriel, Raphael, Uriel
Names of the North	Adriel, Yamiel, Zabdiel
Names of the West	Adtriel, Samael, Joel
Names of the South	Corabiel, Sariel, Michael

Bibliography

Manuscripts

British Library Sloane MS 3826
Paper. Quarto. 101 folios. 16th Century. English. [the present text]

Printed notices of this manuscript (see also pages 63-65):

- *Alchemy Web Site*, "organised by Adam McLean." "Sepher Raziel Manuscripts," on-line at www.alchemywebsite.com/raziel.html; this list of manuscripts is also in print as an appendix to Steve Savedow's *Sepher Rezial Hemelach: The Book of the Angel Rezial*, York Beach: Samuel Weiser, Inc., 2000.

- Cresswell, Julia. *The Watkins Dictionary of Angels*, London: Watkins Publishing, 2006; Cresswell uses British Library Sloane MS 3826 as her "base text" in compiling this grand list of "angels and angelic beings."

- Klaassen, Frank F. Religion, Science, And The Transformations Of Magic: Manuscripts Of Magic 1300-1600. Ph.D. dissertation: Toronto: University of Toronto, 1999: p. 133 (ref. *Liber sacer* i.e., Honorius material), p. 207 (as an example of a seventeenth-century collection combining ritual and scholastic image magic), p. 259 (listed under "Seventeenth Century [MSS]").

- Mathiesen, Robert. "A Thirteenth-Century Ritual to Attain the Beatific Vision from the *Sworn Book* of Honorius of Thebes," in *Conjuring Spirits: Texts and Traditions of Medieval Ritual Magic*, edited by Claire Fanger. University Park: Pennsylvania State University Press, 1998: p. 145 (Sloane MS 3826 ff. 58-83 is listed as a MS of the *Sworn Book of Honorius*).

- Plessner, M, article on 'Balinus' in *Encyclopedia of Islam* (new edn.1959) I, p. 995. (This entry appears on the British Library reference form which accompanies the MS from which the current transcription has been done.)

- Shah, Idries. *Oriental Magic*. New York: E.P. Dutton & Co., 1956; rpt 1973: page 191, *Bibliography*, Grimoire References, *Chaldea*: "The following 'Black Books' of the sorcerers have traces of Chaldean magical rituals or processes attributed to Chaldean origin: Sefer Raziel (The Book of Raziel). B.M. Sloane MS 3826."

- Shah, Idries. *The Secret Lore of Magic*. Secaucus: Citadel Press Inc., 1958: pp. 288, 289, 290, and 310; ref. abbreviation (SR).

- Thorndike, Lynn. *History of Magic and Experimental Sciences*, volume II: THE FIRST THIRTEEN CENTURIES. New York: Columbia University Press 1923: p. 281.

- Waite, Arthur Edward. *Book of Black Magic and of Pacts*. London: Redway, 1898; reprinted New York: Samuel Weiser, Inc., 1972: pp. 33-4 of the Weiser edition.

- Waite, Arthur Edward. *The Book of Ceremonial Magic*. London: Rider, 1911; reprinted New York: Bell Publishing Company, 1969: pp. 20-21 and 22 of the Bell edition. (*The Book of Ceremonial Magic* is a revised version of *Book of Black Magic and of Pacts*.)

Manuscripts of *Sepher Raziel* grouped according to their content

a) *Manuscripts of Cephar Raziel: Liber Salomonis (arranged in Seven Treatises):*

British Library Sloane MS 3826
Paper. Quarto. 101 folios. 16th Century (1564?). English. [The present MS.]

ff.1-57. *Cephar Raziel: Liber Salomonis.*

British Library Sloane MS 3846
Paper. Quarto. 186 folios. 1564. English.
[The text in English is very similar to Sloane MS 3826 with minor differences].

ff.129-157. *Liber Salomonis*, called *Cephar Raziel*, containing seven treatises, written by William Parry of Clifford's Inn in November 1564.

British Library Sloane MS 3847
Paper. Quarto. 188 folios. 16th Century. Latin.

[The Latin text parallels the English of Sloane MS 3826 and MS 3846, but breaks off incomplete in Chapter Three.]

ff.161-188. *Praefatio in Librum Razielis J.V. in nomine Dei omnipotentis vivi et veri, et eterni, et sine omni Fine qui dicitur Adonay - Saday - Assereye - Jucipio - scribere istum librum qui dicitur Cephar Raziel cum omnibus suis Pertinentiis, in quo sunt septem Tractatus completi, et septem libri.*

1. Introductio Libris.
2. Clavis Libris. Liber Primus de Astronomia.
3. De Lapidibus. Liber Secundus.
4. De Herbis.

[The introduction lists the *incomplete* Seven Treatises as:]
1. Clavis de Astromonia et de Stellis. [Astronomy]
2. Ala de virtutibus quorundam Lapidum, Herbarum, Animalia.
3. Thimiamatum de Suffumigationis [Incenses].
4. Temporum Anni [Times of the Year].
5. Munditio de Abstinentia [Purity and Abstinence].
6. Samahym [Heavens. Names of God and Angels of the 7 Heavens].
7. Virtutum quod ubi determinatur… [Virtues of the art of magic].

Sepher Raziel

British Library Sloane MS 3853
Paper. Quarto. 268 folios. 16th/17th Century, Latin & English.

1. Tractatus cui titulus, Thesaurus Spiritum, secundum Robertum Furconem et Rogerum Bacon, cum tabula contentorum et prologo praemissis. ff.3-45.
2. Liber qui vocature *Sephar Rasiel* [Latin - incomplete]. ff.46-49v.
   Circle diagrams [probably not related to *Sephar Rasiel*] ff.50-53v.
3. Experimenta plurima magica. ff.54-63, ff. 70-120.
4. The book of consecration. ff.64-69.
5. De spiritibus, solaribus, in figuris delineatis. ff.120v-127.
6. The divine Seal of Solomon. ff.127v.
7. Invocationes, orationes, etc. ff.129-137.
8. Tractatus qui vocatur, Speculum quatuor Regum. ff.138-141.
9. Processus magici, excitationes spirituum, etc. ff.142-174.
10. A magical book called the Dannet, containing various magical experiments. ff.176-219.
11. The book of the science of 'nygromancie.' ff.219v-241.
12. De sigillis planetarum, etc. f.243.
13. Conjurations, etc. ff.245v-252, 253-256.
14. Of the Offices of Spirits. ff.257-264.
15. Experimenta quaedeam magica. f.266.

Yale University - Beinecke Rare Books Library Osborn MS fa.7
Paper. 303 x 205 mm. 33 folios. Late sixteenth century. English.

The text claims to be the *Book of Virtue* which the Angel Raphiel [*sic*] gave to Adam, with Solomon's Hebrew additions. Incipit: "In the name of allmyghtie God livinge trewe & everlasting and without all end, wch ys said Adonay Saday ... I begin to write this booke wch ys said *Cephar razyell* with all his portenaunce in wch be 7 treatises complete." The seven treatises are listed as:

1. Clavis,
2. Virtues of stones, herbs and beasts,
3. Tractatus thimiamatum,
4. Treatise of time,
5. Treatise of cleanness,
6. Samaym,
7. Book of Virtue.

Bodleian Ashmole MS 1790
Paper. Quarto. 1564. English and Latin.

f.116-116v. A fragmentary copy of the first few pages of *Cephar Raziel*.

Liber Salomonis

Bodleian Ashmole MS 1730
Paper. Quarto. Circa 1600. English and Latin.

ff.168-168v. A one folio letter from Sir Richard Napier to his uncle referring to his projected transcription of *Cephar Raziel,* undated, but circa 1600.

Prague, National Museum Library MS XVII F25
1595. Czech.
Sepher Raziel in 7 Treatises.
Translated by Joannes Polenarius, a courtier in the court of Rudolph II. This manuscript may have a Dr John Dee connection, as the translation was made just after the time Dee was in touch with Rudolph II's court.

Bibliotheca Vaticana MS Reg. Latin 1300
13th century? Latin.

Liber Secretorum de Raziel
Queen Christina of Sweden's Latin *Sepher Raziel* manuscript, given to her in 1650 from the collection of Rabbi Menasseh ben Israel (1604-1657), via Michel Le Blon. This manuscript possibly dates from the 13th century, as it is dedicated to Alfonso the Wise of Castile (d. 1284) who caused a translation to be made from a Latin *Sepher Raziel* (probably this manuscript) into Castilian. This manuscript probably belongs in this first category, with other *Sepher Raziels* divided into 7 Treatises, and may be the root of the other Latin manuscripts.

Sepher Raziel

b) Manuscripts of Sepher Raziel arranged according to the Seven Heavens

These may be a fuller expansion of *Liber Samaim*, Treatise 6 of the present text, and are similar in structure to *Sepher Razim*.

Alnwick MS 596
18th century, Italian, Latin, and English.
Liber Sameyn [Book of the Heavens] pp. 1-96.

The following work is a Book of great fame among the Magi and Cabalists called *Sepher Raziel* or the *Book of the Angel of the Secret*.

p. 1   For the Account of this Book see the *Zohar* of the Jews in Genesis. When Adam was in the garden of Eden J.H.V.H. sent him a Book of the Angel Raziel in which were engraved characters of the highest wisdom...

p. 3   Compendium of the Book called *Sepher Raziel* or the *Angel of the Great Secret*...

p. 8   [a recipe for cabalistic ink].

p. 11 Operation of the First Heaven.

p. 20 Operation of the 2nd Army ... and attributed to Mercury.

p. 25 Operationi del 2do Exercito.

p. 35 Operationi del 3^{zo} Exercito.

p. 47 Operazioni del 4to Exercito.

p. 56 Operations of the 5th Army.

p. 62 Operations of the 6th Army.

p. 69 Operazioni de 7mo Cielo.

p. 75 [Lists of qualities of the seven Heavens].
       [List of various Angel names].

p. 88 Oratio.

p. 90 l'Orazioni.

p. 92 Tavola [Contents of the manuscript in Italian].

p. 93 Haec sunt 72 nomina Dei [List of 72 names of God, with their qualities and powers].

Alnwick MS 585
18th Century. Italian.

f. ii "This Book was bought at Naples from the Jesuit's College when that Order was suppressed and all their goods seized upon by the King and confiscated [1773]. It was brought from there by a Gentleman in a publick Employment in the English service and at his death was purchased in London with other MSS of the Jesuits College."

[Four short tracts bound together, of which only the first is relevant].

p. 1-43. *Cephar Raziel*.

Liber Salomonis

p. 1   Erudition hujus Libri. *Zoar* [*Zohar*]: Sectione in principio Genesi I.
p. 1   Comprendio de Libro dello *Cephar Raziel*, id est *Angelus Magni Secreti* Communicato ad Adamo, ed esposto da Salomonie in Ebreao [Hebrew]...
p. 2   Incomincia.
p. 3   Disse Salomone in guest libro guello che disse l'Angelo Raziele a Adamo.
p. 6   Operazione de primo Cielo.
p. 8   Seguone l'operazione del i° cielo.
p. 11 Operazioni del 2° esercito, qual'e nel Cielo di Labana, ed attribuiscon a Mercurio.
p. 12 Operazioni del 2° Esercito.
p. 14 Opperazioni del terzo esercito.
p. 17 Le operazioni de IV esercito, il quale sta' nel Cielo di Labana, ma' é attribuito al Sole.
p. 18 Operazioni del IV Esercito.
p. 21 Operazioni del IV Esercito, il quale ben che stia nel Cielo di Labana, non di meno e' attribuito a'Marte.
p. 22 Operazioni del quinto [V] esercito.
p. 25 Operazioni del VI esercito, il quale ben che stia ne Cielo di Labana, non di meno, e' attribuito à [Jupiter].
p. 26 Dell' operazioni del VII esercito.
p. 29 Operazioni del VII Cielo. ill 7° Cielo si chiama Araboth.
p. 37 Il Complimento.
p. 40 Questae l'orazione.
p. 41 Siegrie il Nome Magno.

Sepher Raziel

c) Manuscripts of the 13th century Rabbinical Sepher Raziel

British Library Additional MS 15299
Parchment. 153 folios. 13th century, maybe 1235.[1] Hebrew.

[Notes written on the first pages of the MS.]
"Presented to His Royal Highness the Duke of Sussex by W Webb, Esq.
[Coat of Arms with motto] 'Si Deus Pro Nobis Quis Contra Nos.'
Purchased at the Duke of Sussex Sale 3 August 1844 Lot 466."[2]

[In another hand] "Ce Manuscript est un traitè Cabalistique de la fin du dousieme Siècle [end of the 12th century]. Mon cousin le cardinal me la donnè a don retour après le Conclave de Mil sept cent septante quatre [1774]. Il lavoit achete d'un juif de Maguse[?] durant son embassade a Venise pour quatre cents livres de notre argent. Les notes aux marges sont du quinzieme siècle."

[In another hand] "I suppose that the Book is the *Sepher Raziel*; the author is unknown, but Wolff's *Bibliotheca Rabbinica* contains some notice about the matter. It contains high mysteries of Cabbala."

[In another hand] "*The Book Raziel* (*The Hidden Things of God*) the Angel Raziel delivered this Book to Adam after 130 years of his Repentance, which Book contains Cabbala, by which they can cause Angels, according to his month and his day, to perform miracles, and cast out the evil spirits which occasionally enter into men; & it also contains the knowledge of conversing concerning the sun, the moon, the stars, the cause to be sick, & to heal again; & it speaks of many other powers of the vegetable world, precious stones, fishes, fowls, wild beasts; also to be inabled to foretell by the means of the stars, & to explain the rod of Moses, wherewith he performed wonders.
Vide *Labia Dormientium*, letter ד [Daleth] No. 31."

"This MS contains the book *Jetzirah* [*Sepher Yetzirah*] with the Commentary apparently of R[abbi] Eleasar [Eleazar of Worms] ben Juda de Garmiza, who lived in the middle of the 13th century. There are various other Cabalistic treatises in it. See the note at fol. 132b. J.M.   See Wolfius, tom[e] i.p.23."[3]

ff. 1-132v *Sepher Raziel*
ff. 133-153 a commentary on the *Sepher Yetzirah*.

---

[1] There is a marginal calculation of the Hebrew year 4995 in the margin, which equals 1235.
[2] Prince Frederick Augustus, Duke of Sussex (1812/13-1843) was one of the early Grand Masters of the United Grand Masonic Lodge of England and son of King George III.
[3] Wolff's *Bibliotheca Rabbinica,* Vol. I, 23. Also see Vol. II, iii; Vol. IV, 771, 1033, or according to Goldmerstein: Vol I, 111 (cf. III, 69; IV, 711).

Liber Salomonis

d) Other Sepher Raziel manuscripts not examined

Bibliotheque Nationale Fonds Latin MS 3666
Latin.

British Library Additional MS 16,390
Paper. Small quarto. 17th Century. Two tracts in Hebrew plus some Italian.

(i) The Seven Names.
(ii) The eight chapters of Maimonides, or introduction to *Aboth* [imperfect].
At the end is an extract from a Hebrew cabalistic work, entitled *Raziel*, in Italian.

Dresden MS N. 36
18th Century. German.

Dresden MS N. 96
Quarto. 187 and 175 folios. 18th Century. German. With figures.

Cabala Alba. "Dieses ist das Buch Adam, oder Razielis, durch welches du wissen und verstehen kannst, alles mit einander, alle Wunder Dinge, welche geschehen sind, und noch gemachet werden konnen... Dieses Buch hat der Engel Raziel den Adam ubergeben. - Fortsetzung des Buches Adae seu Razielis."

Leipzig Senate Library Codex Latinus 745
Liber Razielis Angeli

Briefly referred to by Margalioth when he was establishing the Hebrew text of *Sepher ha-Razim*.

Lübeck, Bibliothek der Hansestadt, MS Math. 4° 10
Quarto. 16th/17th Century. German.

Lyon MS 970
17th/18th Century. French.

New York Jewish Theological Seminary Library
German rabbinical script.

Sepher Raziel.

Printed Sources on Solomonic Magic
& Works of Related Interest

Abraham von Worms, AKA Abraham of Wurzburg, Abraham the Jew.

- *The Book of Sacred Magic of Abramelin* [*Abra-Melin*] or *Abramelin the Mage*.

- Translated and edited by S. L. MacGregor Mathers (London: Watkins, 1898; 2nd edition 1900; rpt. New York: Causeway Books, 1974; New York: Dover Publications, Inc., 1975).
- A SHORTER VERSION IN SEVEN CHAPTERS, translated by S. L. MacGregor Mathers, edited by Adrian Axworthy [KABBALISTIC GRIMOIRE SERIES VI] (Edmunds: Holmes Publishing Group, 2001; 2nd revised edition, Sequim: Holmes Publishing Group, 2008).
- A NEW TRANSLATION, compiled and edited by Georg Dehn, translated by Steven Guth (Lake Worth: Ibis Press, 2006).

In a lecture from 1975[1], Gershom Scholem says of the Abramelin text that

> [it] is not a Jewish book. No Jew would call his son "Lamech," you can believe me. "Lamech" in Jewish parlance is a *goylim*, is a fool. [...] It is obviously a non-Jewish text written in the beginning of the sixteenth century by somebody who knew about the *kabbalah* from the writings of Pico della Mirandola, which can be proved in my opinion.
>
> There was a time that I thought it might be a Jewish text. If it would be a Jewish text, it's very interesting. [*laughter from the audience*] I no longer believe it to be a Jewish text. You know, philology works against your own inclinations. [...] It was certainly written by a man who knew Hebrew quite well—better than other Christians of this age, I would say. I have studied the book quite often and it concerns the conjuration of your own personal angel—exactly what Eleazar [in the *Zohar*, son of Rabbi Shimon bar Yohai] says cannot be done, he does it, as a Jew, but I don't believe it. I think he took

---

[1] "Conception of *Tselem*, the Astral Body, in Jewish Mysticism," A PANARION CONFERENCE, Los Angeles, 1975 (Los Angeles: C.G. Jung Institute of Los Angeles, 2012)—2 audio CDs.

Note Scholem's statements in *Kabbalah* (Jerusalem: Keter Publishing House Ltd., 1974):

> By the same token, *The Book of Sacred Magic of Abra-Melin* (London, 1898), which purported to be an English translation of a Hebrew work written in the 15th century by a certain "Abraham the Jew of Worms" and was widely regarded in modern European occultist circles as being a classical text of practical Kabbalah, was not in fact written by a Jew, although its anonymous author has an uncommon command of Hebrew. The book was originally written in German and the Hebrew manuscript of it found in Oxford (Neubauer 2051) is simply a bad translation. Indeed, the book circulated in vaious editions in several languages. It shows the partial influence of Jewish ideas but does not have any strict parallel in kabbalistic literature. (—*Kabbalah*, page 186)

it from some Neoplatonic [source]. He took it, not from Jewish sources but from other ones, although it has a long autobiographical introduction about the feats he has done, the tremendous feats he has done in his magical career among the gentiles.

The book is a very curious one anyway.

- *Abraham the Jew on Magic Talismans to be engraven on Seals of Rings made of various metals under the influence of the Fixed Stars and the Twenty-eight Mansions of the Moon*, from a manuscript by Frederick Hockley, edited and introduced by Silens Manus (York Beach: Teitan Press, 2011).

> "There is no doubt that the text is to a large degree a compilation made from earlier sources, notably Cornelius Agrippa's *Three Books of Occult Philosophy*" —INTRODUCTION, page ix.

Agrippa, [Henry] Cornelius. *The Fourth Book of Occult Philosophy*, edited, with commentary, by Stephen Skinner (London: Askin Publishers, 1978; rpt Berwick [ME]: Ibis Press, 2005).

> This translation (London: 1655) includes *all* of the items in Robert Turner's collection rather than just *The Fourth Book* and *Heptameron* (see below).
>
> - OF OCCULT PHILOSOPHY, OR OF MAGICAL CEREMONIES: THE FOURTH BOOK—Agrippa
> - HEPTAMERON, OR MAGICAL ELEMENTS—Peter de Abano
> - ISOGOGE: AN INTRODUCTORY DISCOURSE ON THE NATURE OF SUCH SPIRITS—Georg Pictorius Villinganus
> - ARBATEL OF MAGICK: OF THE MAGICK OF THE ANCIENTS
> - OF GEOMANCY—Agrippa
> - OF ASTRONOMICAL GEOMANCY—Gerard Cremonensis

_____. *The Fourth Book of Occult Philosophy: The Companion to the Three Books of Occult Philosophy*, edited and annotated by Donald Tyson (Woodbury: Llewellyn Publications, 2009).

> Again, Robert Turner's translation of the six-book collection, following Stephen Skinner's edition (listed immediately above). Tyson's edition includes an "analysis" of each book containing both historical and practical support material.

_____. *Of Occult Philosophy, Book Four*, edited and translated by Robert Turner. Originally published, Antwerp: 1531; Turner's translation, 1655 (Gillette: Heptangle Books, 1985).

> Includes the pseudo-Agrippan *Fourth Book* and the *Heptameron* or *Magical Elements* of Peter de Abano.

_____. *Three Books of Occult Philosophy*, edited and annotated by Donald Tyson (original English translation 1651; Tyson's edition, St. Paul: Llewellyn Publications, 1993).

> The support material which Tyson provides makes this edition a valuable reference source.

Åkerman, Susanna. "Queen Christina's Latin *Sefer-ha-Raziel* Manuscript," in *Judeo-Christian Intellectual Culture in the Seventeenth Century: A Celebration of the Library of Narcissus Marsh (1638-1713)*, [INTERNATIONAL ARCHIVES, 163] edited by Allison P. Coudert, Sarah Hutton, Richard H. Popkin, and Gordon M. Weiner (Dordrecht: Kluwer Academic Publishers, 1999).

> "The Latin copies of *Sefer-ha-Raziel* in particular shows (*sic*) a continuation of interest in Hebrew angelology among Christian readers well after the great blooming of such concerns among Rosicrucian authors in 1614-1620" (page 13).

> "The angelic doctrine of *liber Raziel* is taken up by a group of texts called *Claves Salomonis*, magical texts that in conjunction with al-Magriti's book of Arabic magic, *Picatrix*, influenced Cornelius Agrippa" (page 18).

(anon.) *The Black Pullet: Science of Magical Talisman*, translated from the French: *La Poule Noire* (New York: Samuel Weiser, Inc., 1972; rpt. edited by Darcy Kuntz [KABBALISTIC GRIMOIRE SERIES II] Edmonds: Holmes Publishing Group, 1998).

> On *The Black Pullet*, see Waite, *Ceremonial Magic*, pages 113-132.

(anon.) *The History of Dr. John Faustus, Showing How He Sold Himself to the Devil, to Have Twenty-Four Years to Do Whatsoever He Pleased*, edited by Darcy Kuntz [KABBALISTIC GRIMOIRE SERIES VII] (Edmonds: Holmes Publishing Group, 2001; 2nd revised edition, Sequim: Holmes Publishing Group, 2008).

Bailey, Michael D. *Battling Demons: Witchcraft, Heresy, and Reform in the Late Middle Ages* [MAGIC IN HISTORY SERIES] (University Park: Pennsylvania State University Press, 2003).

Barrett, Francis. *The Magus. A Complete System of Occult Philosophy* (London: 1801; rpt. New Hyde Park: University Books, 1967; rpt. York Beach: Samuel Weiser Inc., 2000).

> Most of the contents were copied from Agrippa and other sources. See the defense of Barrett in Alison L. Butler, THE REVIVAL OF THE OCCULT PHILOSOPHY: CABALISTIC MAGIC AND THE HERMETIC ORDER OF THE GOLDEN DAWN (M.A. thesis, St. John's: Memorial University of Newfoundland, 2000): CHAPTER TWO: "Beyond Attribution: The Importance of Barrett's *Magus*."

Best, Michael; and Brightman, Frank H. (eds) *The Book of Secrets of Albertus Magnus. Of the Virtues of Herbs, Stones, and Certain Beasts, Also of the Marvels of the World* (13th century) (Oxford: Oxford University Press, 1973; rpt. York Beach: Samuel Weiser Inc., 1999).

> The Weiser edition is far preferable to the reprint from Kessinger (Kila, Montana) entitled *Egyptian Secrets or White and Black Art for Man and Beast* of Albertus Magnus (copied from the Egyptian Publishing Co. [Chicago] edition).

Betz, Hans Dieter (ed). *The Greek Magical Papyri in Translation, Including the Demotic Spells*, Volume One: Texts (2nd edition, Chicago: University of Chicago Press, 1992).

Black, Laurelei; Black, Natalie; and Birkel, John. *The Witches' Key to the Legion: A Guide to Solomonic Sorcery* ([US]: Asteria Books, 2013).

> The "Solomonic Sorcery" addressed here is *Goetia*.
>> "I have two main reasons for targeting this book to Witches and not, say, Ceremonial Magicians. The first is that every other book available on the Goetia is aimed at Ceremonial Magicians. ... I especially recommend Lon Milo DuQuette's *Illustrated Goetia*. Our biggest complaint with these books is that they continue to advocate spirit torture.
>>
>> "My second reason for marketing this 'new key' to Witches specifically is that Natalie and I both firmly believe that it has been the role of the Witch to summon and stir spirits as allies in magic since Witches first started practicing the Craft." (from § "Why Create a Key for Witches?")

The book recommended is *Aleister Crowley's Illustrated Goetia*, by Lon Milo DuQuette and Christopher Hyatt, illustrated by David P. Wilson (Tempe: New Falcon Publications, 1992). See above, note 25.

Black, S. Jason; and Hyatt, Christopher S. *Pacts with the Devil. A Chronicle of Sex, Blasphemy & Liberation* (Tempe: New Falcon Publications, 1993 and 1997).

Pacts includes versions of *Grimoirum Verum, Grand Grimoire* and *Honorius*, edited and adapted to render them "doable." May I suggest "doabolic"?

Bodin, Jean. *On the Demon-Mania of Witches*, translated by Randy Scott with an Introduction by Jonathan L. Pearl (Toronto: Centre for Reformation and Renaissance Studies, 1995).

A translation of Bodin's *De la démonomanie des sorciers* (1580), "a lengthy and complex discussion of many aspects of magic and witchcraft" (— page 22).

Budge, E. A. Wallis. *Amulets and Talismans* (originally published Oxford/Cambridge: 1930, as AMULETS AND SUPERSTITIONS; rpt. New York: Collier Books, 1970).

See especially chapter XXIII: "The Kabbalistic Names and Signs, and Magical Figures, and Squares of the Seven Astrological Stars or Planets."

Burnett, Charles. *Magic and Divination in the Middle Ages. Texts and Techniques in the Islamic and Christian Worlds* [COLLECTED STUDIES SERIES: CS557] (Aldershot: Variorum/Ashgate Publishing, Brookfield, 1996).

Cauzons, Th. de. *Magic and Sorcery in France, I.* (French original: LA MAGIE ET LA SORCERIE EN FRANCE, vol. 1 [of 4], Paris: Dorbon-aine, 1910-12; Palm Springs: I.G.O.S., 1994).

Christian, Paul. *The History and Practice of Magic*, translated from the French by James Kirkup and Julian Shaw; edited and revised by Ross Nichols (French original: 1870; New York: Citadel Press, Inc., 1963).

A Wicked Pack of Cards (see below under Decker) treats this 18th-century occultist in CHAPTER 9, "From Ghost Writer to Magus: Paul Christian."

Copenhaver, Brian (trans.) *The Book of Magic from Antiquity to the Enlightenment* (USA | UK, etc.: Penguin Books, 2015).

"A strange blend of mumbo-jumbo, fear, fraud and deeply serious study, magic was at the heart of the European Renaissance, fascinating many of its greatest leaders." (quote on the endpaper) A 643-page compendium, from Deuteronomy to Dee, Moses to Milton, Ptolemy to Paracelsus.

Cresswell, Julia. *The Watkins Dictionary of Angels: Over 2,000 Entries on Angels & Angelic Beings* (London: Watkins Publishing, 2006).

As her "base text," Cresswell used British Library Sloane 3826, *Liber Salomonis: Sepher Raziel*—the original online edition at *Esoterica*, Volume V, edited by Arthur Versluis (East Lansing: Michigan State University, 2003) > "Archives" >
(1) http://www.esoteric.msu.edu/VolumeV/Raziel1.html
(2) http://www.esoteric.msu.edu/VolumeV/Raziel2.html

Davidson, Gustav. *A Dictionary of Angels, Including the Fallen Angels* (New York: The Free Press [A Division of the Macmillan Company], 1967).

Davies, Owen. *Grimoires: A History of Magic Books* (Oxford: Oxford University Press, 2009).

Davies' broad summary of magic books through history in the first few chapters is may be useful, but it is awfully rapid. *Grimoires* gets most interesting—and original—in its chapters on more recent times: "Grimoires USA," "Pulp Magic," and "Lovecraft, Satan, and Shadows."

Decker, Ronald; Depaulis, Thierry; and Dummett, Michael. *A Wicked Pack of Cards: The Origins of the Occult Tarot* (New York: St. Martin's Press, 1996).

Wicked Pack is a well-written and well-researched treatment of how Tarot came to be positioned at the core of the Western occult, focusing on its assumption by the French occultists J.-B. Alliette (= Etteilla), Eliphas Levi, Gerard Encausse (= Papus), and, important in the present context, Paul Christian.

Dee, John. (various titles)

See my references to Dee in *Study of Christian Cabala in English*, Part 1, pages 35-39, at http://www.digital-brilliance.com/contributed/Karr/Biblios/ccinea.pdf, and the reference list at University of St. Andrews, http://www-groups.dcs.st-and.ac.uk/~history/References/Dee.html

de Givry, Emile Grillot. *Picture Museum of Sorcery, Magic, and Alchemy*, translated from the French by J. Courtney Locke (French original, Paris: 1929: *LE MUSEE DES SORCIERS, MAGES ET ALCHEMISTES*; New Hyde Park: University Books, 1963).

Dictionary of Deities and Demons in the Bible (DDD), editors: Karel van der Toorn, Bob Becking, and Pieter W. van der Horst (Leiden: E. J. Brill, 1995; second edition, extensively revised, 1999).

Dictionary of Gnosis & Western Esotericism, two volumes, edited by Wouter Hanegraaff in collaboration with Antoine Faivre, Roelof van den Broek, and Jean-Pierre Brach (Leiden/Boston: Brill, 2005).

> This superb collaboration contains entries on AGRIPPA, ALBERTUS MAGNUS, ALCHEMY, AMULETS, ASTROLOGY, FRANCIS BARRETT, JOHN DEE, INTERMEDIARY BEINGS, MAGIC, MAGICAL INSTRUMENTS, MICHAEL SCOT, PETER OF ABANO, SATANISM, and many more.

Ennemoser, Joseph. *The History of Magic*, 2 vols. translated from the German by William Howitt, "To which is added an appendix... selected by Mary Howitt" (London: Henry G. Bohn, 1854; rpt. New Hyde Park: University Books, 1970).

Fanger, Claire. "Virgin Territory: Purity and Divine Knowledge in Late Medieval Catoptromantic Texts," in *Aries*, NEW SERIES, vol. 5, no. 2 (Leiden: Koninklijke Brill, 2005).

Flint, Valerie I. J. *The Rise of Magic in Early Medieval Europe* (Princeton: Princeton University Press, 1991).

Frazer, Sir James G. *The Golden Bough: A Study in Magic and Religion* (one-volume abridged edition, New York: Macmillan, 1922; rpt. 1942, 1951, and subsequently).

_____. *The New Golden Bough. A New Abridgement*, revised in the light of recent scholarship by Theodor H. Gaster (New York: Mentor Books, 1959; rpt. 1964).

Gardner, F. L.; Hockley, Frederick; and Redgrove, H. S. *Hebrew Talismanic Magic*, edited by Darcy Kuntz [KABBALISTIC GRIMOIRE SERIES V] (Edmunds: Holmes Publishing Group, 2001).

Gollancz, Hermann (trans.) *The Book of Protection: Syrian Magic and Charms*, Being Codex A of a Syrian Magical Manuscript (Edmonds – Sequim: Holmes Publishing Group, 2001).

Goodrick-Clarke, Nicholas. *The Western Esoteric Traditions: A Historical Introduction* (Oxford: Oxford University Press, 2008).

See in particular, CHAPTER 2, "Italian Renaissance Magic and Cabala," CHAPTER 3, "Planetary and Angel Magic in the Renaissance," and CHAPTER 10, "Ritual Magic from 1850 to the Present."

Greene, Thomas M. "Language, Signs and Magic," in *Envisioning Magic: A Princeton Seminar & Symposium*, edited by Peter Schäfer and Hans G. Kippenberg (Leiden – New York – Köln: Brill, 1997).

> Greene opens his discussion comparing the attitudes of sixteenth-century "country gentleman Reginald Scot" and his contemporary "English theologian William Perkins" toward witchcraft, concluding that "the perception of these two authors was generally correct, that witchcraft—and more broadly magic— does indeed threaten a conventionalist disjunctive linguistics. Both Scot and Perkins understood that a belief in magic required an alternate linguistic theory which would give substance and energy to the word…" (– page 256).

Griffith, F. L.; and Thompson, Herbert. *The Leyden Papyrus. An Egyptian Magical Book* (originally published 1904 as THE DEMOTIC MAGICAL PAPYRUS OF LONDON AND LEYDEN; rpt. New York: Dover Publications, 1974).

Guazzo, Francesco Maria. *Compendium Maleficarum*. Milan: 1608. Translated by E. A. Ashwin and edited by Montague Summers (London: John Rodker, 1929; rpt. New York: Dover Publications, Inc., 1988).

> "Collected in 3 Books from many Sources … showing the iniquitous and execrable operations of witches against the human race, and the divine remedies by which they may be frustrated" (from the 1929 title page).

Harms, Daniel. "Grimoires in the Conjure Tradition," in *Journal for the Academic Study of Magic*, Issue 5, edited by Susan Johnson Graf and Amy Hale (Oxford: Mandrake of Oxford, 2009).

Harms, Daniel; Clark, James R.; and Peterson, Joseph H. *The Book of Oberon: A Sourcebook of Elizabethan Magic* (Llewellyn Publications, 2015).

> An illustrated grimoire for summoning fairies and goetic demons, along with "one of the oldest known copies of" *The Enchiridion*.

Henson, Mitch and Gail. "Magical Notebooks: A Survey of the Grimoires in the Golden Dawn," in *The Golden Dawn Journal*, Book III: THE ART OF HERMES. [LLEWELLYN'S GOLDEN DAWN SERIES] (St. Paul: Llewellyn Publications, 1995).

Hockley, Frederick. (Alan Thorogood, ed.) *Clavis Arcana Magica ... compiled by Frederick Hockley* (York Beach: Teitan Press, 2012).

_____. (Dietrich Bergman, ed.) *A Complete Book of Magic Science ... transcribed from an Ancient Manuscript Grimoire by Frederick Hockley* (York Beach: Teitan Press, 2008).

Bergman describes *A Complete Book of Magic Science* as "a lengthier version of the text that had been published as 'The Secret Grimoire of Turiel.'" See below under "Malchus."

A Complete Book... is also included in Joseph Peterson's *Clavis or Key of the Magic of Solomon* (Lake Worth: Ibis Press, 2009).

_____. (Alan Thorogood, ed.) *Dr. Rudd's Nine Hierarchies ... transcribed by Frederick Hockley* (York Beach: Teitan Press, 2013).

Includes English translations of John Dee's "angelic keys" and invocations of the angels concerned with the Table of the Earth.

_____. *Invocating by Magic Crystals and Mirrors*, introduction by R. A. Gilbert (York Beach: Teitan Press, 2010).

_____. (Silens Manus, ed.) *Occult Spells: A Nineteenth Century Grimoire ... compiled by Frederick Hockley* (York Beach: Teitan Press, 2009).

_____. (John Hamill, ed.) *The Rosicrucian Seer: Magical Writings of Frederick Hockley* (Wellingborough: Aquarian Press, 1986; revised edition with a chapter on Hockley's Manuscripts and a Note on Hockley as an Astrologer by R. A. Gilbert (York Beach: Teitan Press, 2009).

For other Hockley manuscripts/transcriptions:
- see above, page 4, note 10.
- see above, at the end of § 1. a. on *The Clavis or Key to the Magic of Solomon*.
- see above, toward the end of 1. b. "*Lemegeton*, or LESSER KEY OF SOLOMON," *A Book of the Office of the Spirits*.
- see above within this bibliography, the listing for the Hockley MS of *Abraham the Jew on Magic Talismans...*, edited and introduced by Silens Manus (York Beach: Teitan Press, 2011).

On Hockley, see Joscelyn Godwin, *The Theosophical Enlightenment* (Albany: State University of New York Press, 1994), CHAPTER NINE.

Idel, Moshe. "Hermeticism and Judaism," in *Hermeticism and the Renaissance: Intellectual History and the Occult in the Early Modern*

Europe, edited by Ingrid Merkel and Allen G. Debus (Washington: Folger Books, 1988).

_____. "The Magical and Neoplatonic Interpretations of the Kabbalah in the Renaissance," in *Jewish Thought in the Sixteenth Century*, edited by Bernard Dov Cooperman (Cambridge/London: Harvard University Press, 1983).

Izmirlieva, Valentina. *All the Names of the Lord: Lists, Mysticism, and Magic* (Chicago – London: University of Chicago Press, 2008).

> In the first section of her book, Izmirlieva analyzes *The Divine Names* of (pseudo-) Dionysius the Areopagite (1st century); in the second section, she studies the (Slavonic) amulet known as *The 72 Names of the Lord* (13th century). Izmirlieva "demonstrate[s], over a large body of textual traces, that *The 72 Names of the Lord* has its roots in the Gnostic Kabbalah and originates from a Kabbalo-Christian exchange that most probably took place in Provence in the twelfth century" (—page 12).

Janowitz, Naomi. *Magic in the Roman World: Pagans, Jews and Christians* [RELIGION IN THE FIRST CHRISTIAN CENTURIES] (London/New York: Routledge, 2001).

Kahane, Henry; Kahane, Renee; and Pietrangeli, Angelina. "*Picatrix* and the Talismans," in *Romance Philology* 19:4 (Berkeley: University of California, 1966), pages 574-593.

Kieckhefer, Richard. *Forbidden Rites: A Necromancer's Manual of the Fifteenth Century* [MAGIC IN HISTORY SERIES] (University Park: Pennsylvania State University Press, 1998).

_____. *Magic in the Middle Ages* [CAMBRIDGE MEDIEVAL TEXTBOOKS] (Cambridge: Cambridge University Press, 1989; rpt. 1995).

Kiesel, William. *Magic Circles in the Grimoire Tradition* [THREE HANDS PRESS OCCULT MONOGRAPH 3] (Richmond Vista: Three Hands Press, 2012).

King, Francis. *The Rites of Modern Occult Magic* [= RITUAL MAGIC IN ENGLAND] (New York: The Macmillan Company, 1970): Appendix B. "Mathers' Versions of the Grimoires."

King, Francis, and Sutherland, Isabel. *The Rebirth of Magic* (London: Corgi Books, 1982): Chapter 3. "Grimoires and Sorcerers"

Klaassen, Frank. "English Manuscripts of Magic, 1300-1500: A Preliminary Survey," in *Conjuring Spirits: Texts and Traditions of Medieval Ritual Magic*, edited by Claire Fanger (University Park: The Pennsylvania State University Press, 1998).

_____. "Medieval Ritual Magic in the Renaissance," in *Aries*, NEW SERIES, vol. 3, no. 2 (Leiden: Koninklijke Brill, 2003).

_____. "Subjective Experience and the Practice of Medieval Ritual Magic," in *Magic, Ritual, and Witchcraft*, Volume 7, Number 1 (Philadelphia: University of Pennsylvania Press, Summer 2012), pages 19-51.

_____. *The Transformations of Magic: Illicit Learned Magic in the Later Middle Ages and Renaissance* [MAGIC IN HISTORY SERIES] (University Park: Pennsylvania State University Press, 2012).

Kramer, Heinrich; and Sprenger James. *The Malleus Maleficarum* (Rome: 1484. Translated by Montague Summers, London: John Rodker, 1928; rpt. New York: Dover Publications, Inc., 1971).

Láng, Benedek. *Unlocked Books: Manuscripts of Learned Magic in the Medieval Libraries of Central Europe* [MAGIC IN HISTORY SERIES] (University Park: The Pennsylvania State University Press, 2008).

> Not the libraries of Spain, Italy, or Greece, but rather Poland, Hungary, and Bohemia.

Lisiewsky, Joseph C. *Howlings from the Pit: A Practical Handbook of Medieval Magic, Goetia & Theurgy*, introduction and commentary by Mark Stavish, afterword by David Rankine (Tempe: The Original Falcon Press, 2011).

Luck, Georg. *Arcana Mundi. Magic and the Occult in the Greek and Roman Worlds, A Collection of Texts* (Baltimore: Johns Hopkins University Press, 1985; SECOND EDITION 2006).

Malinowski, Bronislaw. MAGIC, SCIENCE AND RELIGION *and Other Essays* (Garden City: Doubleday [Anchor Books A23], 1948; rpt. 1954).

Malchus, Marius. *The Secret Grimoire of Turiel, Being a System of Magic of the Sixteenth Century* (London: Aquarian Press, 1960; rpt. edition edited by Darcy Kuntz [KABBALISTIC GRIMOIRE SERIES I] Edmunds: Sure Fire Press, 1994).

> See the note on Hockley's MS of *Complete Book of Magic Science*, listed above.

Magic in the Biblical World: From the Rod of Aaron to the Ring of Solomon, edited by Todd Klutz JOURNAL FOR THE STUDY OF THE NEW TESTAMENT SUPPLEMENT SERIES, 245] (London – New York: T&T Clark, 2003).

> Of particular interest: Philip S. Alexander, "*Sefer ha-Razim* and the Problem of Black Magic in Early Judaism" (pages 170-190), and Todd E. Klutz, "The Archer and the Cross: Chorographic Astrology and Literary Design in the *Testament of Solomon*" (pages 219-244).

Man, Myth & Magic: An Illustrated Encyclopedia of the Supernatural, edited by Richard Cavendish (New York: Marshall Cavendish Corporation, 1970).

> Though this over-sized set of twenty-four books looks like something one might buy a volume per week at the supermarket, one has to be impressed with the names which appear on the list of contributors and the editorial advisory board: Mircea Eliade, R. J. Zwi Werblowsky, R. C. Zaehner, to name a few.
>
> Topics include ABERDEEN WITCHES, ABRACADABRA, [H.C.] AGRIPPA, ALPHABET, FRANCIS BARRETT, BLACK MAGIC AND WITCHCRAFT, BLACK MASS, MAGIC AND MYSTICISM, CORRESPONDENCES, JOHN DEE, DIVINATION, EUROPEAN WITCH PERSECUTIONS, EXORCISM, FAUST, FINDING OF WITCHES, FRENCH WITCHCRAFT, GERMAN WITCHCRAFT, GRIMOIRE, ITALIAN WITCHCRAFT, LOVE MAGIC, MAGIC, MAGIC PAPYRI, MAGIC SQUARES, MODERN WITCHCRAFT, NORTH BERWICK WITCHES, OLD AGE AND WITCHCRAFT, PENTAGRAM, PICATRIX, RITUAL, RITUAL MAGIC, ROOTS OF RITUAL MAGIC, SACRED MAGIC OF ABRA-MELIN, SALEM WITCHES, SATANISM, SOMERSET WITCHES, THEURGY, THOMAS WEIR, WHITE MAGIC, and WITCHCRAFT.

Massello, Robert. *Raising Hell: A Concise History of the Black Arts – and Those Who Dared to Practice Them* (New York: Perigree Books, 1996).

> See especially Chapter 1. "Black Magic and Sorcery," which includes sections on "The Great Grimoires" and "Conjurations from the *True Grimoire*."

Mastrocinque, Attilio. *From Jewish Magic to Gnosticism* [STUDIEN UND TEXTE ZU ANTIKE UND CHRISTENTUM 24] (Tübingen: Mohr Siebeck, 2005).

McIntosh, Christopher. *The Devil's Bookshelf: A History of the Written Word in Western Magic from Ancient Egypt to the Present Day* (Wellingborough: The Aquarian Press, 1985).

McIntosh has written two of the best "popular" books on their respective subjects: *The Rosicrucians: The History, Mythology, and Rituals of an Esoterica Order* (London: Aquarian Press, 1980; rpt York Beach: Samuel Weiser, Inc., 1997) and *The Devil's Bookshelf*. These treatments are readable and reliable, being distillations of the long and careful research of a first-rate scholar.

McLean, Adam (ed). *A Treatise on Angel Magic, Being a Complete Transcription of MS. Harley 6482 in the British Library* [MAGNUM OPUS HERMETIC SOURCEWORKS #15] (Edinburgh: Magnum Opus Sourceworks, 1982; rpt Grand Rapids: Phanes Press, 1990; rpt York Beach: Weiser Books, 2006).

The second of six volumes collectively called "The Treatises of Dr. Rudd" (MSS Harley 6181-6486). *Angel Magic* gathers material from several sources, including Agrippa, Dee, Reginald Scott, *Lemegeton*, and *Arbatel*.

Meyer, Marvin; and Mirecki, Paul (eds). *Ancient Magic and Ritual Power* [RELIGIONS IN THE GRÆCO-ROMAN WORLD, volume 129] (Leiden – New York – London: E. J. Brill, 1995).

Meyer, Marvin; and Smith, Richard (eds). *Ancient Christian Magic. Coptic Texts of Ritual Power* (San Francisco: HarperSanFrancisco, 1994).

Monod, Paul Kléber. *Solomon's Secret Arts: The Occult in the Age of Enlightenment* ([New Haven]: Yale University Press, 2013).

"The winding, muddy and often submerged paths of occult thinking in the eighteenth century may not be as familiar to British historians as its more visible public byways in the late seventeenth century, but they were well travelled nonetheless. Adherents of the occult kept up a lively interaction with conventional intellectual trends, reconfiguring Hermeticism and Neoplatonism to suit the age of steam engines and revolutionary politics. As in the past, they eagerly absorbed heterodox religious ideas and maintained a keen interest in popular magic." (*Solomon's Secret Arts* – pages 18-19)

Necronomicon. A Sumerian High Magical Grimoire, edited and introduced by Simon (New York: Avon Books, 1975; 1980).

A search of NECRONOMICON on the Internet yields all kinds of entertaining and curious stuff, including shreds of the debate over whether the mysterious text ever actually existed. Adding to the scholarship, confusion, or hoax — as you wish — surrounding this work are

- *The Necronomicon: The Book of Dead Names*, edited by George Hay, introduced by Colin Wilson. London: Neville Spearman Ltd, 1978; rpt. London: Skoob Books, 1992.
- *The R'lyeh Text: Hidden Leaves from the Necronomicon*, edited by George Hay, researched, transcribed and annotated by Robert Turner, introduced by Colin Wilson. London: Skoob Books, 1995.
- Tyson, Donald. *Necronomicon: The Wanderings of Alhazred*. St. Paul: Llewellyn Publications, 2004.

For a brief account, refer to Owen Davies' *Grimoires: A History of Magic Books* (Oxford: Oxford University Press, 2009), pages 262-8.

Neusner, Jacob; Frerichs, Ernest S; and Flesher, Paul V. Mc. (eds). *Religion, Science, and Magic: In Concert and in Conflict* (Oxford – New York: Oxford University Press, 1989).

Page, Sophie. *Magic in Medieval Manuscripts* (Toronto: University of Toronto Press, 2004).

_____. *Magic in the Cloister: Pious Motives, Illicit Interests, and Occult Approaches to the Medieval Universe* (University Park: The Pennsylvania State University Press, 2012).

Paracelsus. *Archidoxes of Magic: Of Supreme Mysteries of Nature, or the Spirits of the Plants, of Occult Philosophy*, etc., translated by Robert Turner, 1655, introduction by Stephen Skinner (London: Askin Publishers Ltd, 1975; rpt Berwick: Ibis Press, 2004. Published as *The Archidoxes of Magic*, Kila: Kessinger Publishing, n.d.)

Petit Albert: The Marvelous Secrets of Natural & Cabalistic Magic – 1752, translated by Tarl Warwick, introduced by Willam Kiesel (Emerald City: Ouroboros Press, 2016).

This grimoire used by "rural folk magic practitioners" is perhaps best known for "the glorious hand" or "hand of glory," namely the talismanic use of the severed hand of a hanged man.

Picatrix: The Classic Medieval Handbook of Astrological Magic, translated [from the Latin] by John Michael Greer and Christopher Warnock (Iowa City: Adocentyn Press, 2010).

Picatrix OR *Ghalat al-Hakim* [THE GOAL OF THE WISE – the first English edition].

- VOLUME ONE, translated from the Arabic by Hashem Atallah; edited by William Kiesel (Seattle: Ouroboros Press, 2002)
- VOLUME TWO, translated by Hashem Atallah and Geylan Holmquest; edited by William Kiesel (Seattle: Ouroboros Press, 2008).

> Published earlier were *"Picatrix": Das Ziel des Weisen von Pseudo-Magriti*, translated into German from the Arabic by Helmut Ritter and Martin Plessner (The Warburg Institute/University of London, 1962)—a summary in English appears on pages lix-lxxv; and *Picatrix: The Latin Version of the GHAYAT AL-HAKIM*, edited by David Pingree (The Warburg Institute, 1986).

Raphael. *Raphael's Ancient Manuscript of Talismanic Magic* (Chicago: The de Laurence Co., 1916).

> "The Art of *Talismanic Magic:* Being Selections from the *Works of* Rabbi Solomon, Agrippa, F. Barrett, etc. *by* Raphael"—all in hand script.

Redgrove, H. Stanley. *Magic and Mysticism: Studies in Bygone Beliefs* (London: Rider, 1920; rpt. Secaucus: Citadel Press, 1972).

Rollo, David. *Glamorous Sorcery: Magic and Literacy in the High Middle Ages* [MEDIEVAL CULTURES, Volume 25] (Minneapolis - London: University of Minnesota Press, 2000).

Runyon. Carroll "Poke." *The Book of Solomon's Magick* (Pasadena: Church of the Hermetic Science, Inc.,1996).

Ryan, W. F. *The Bathhouse at Midnight. An Historical Survey of Magic and Divination in Russia* [MAGIC IN HISTORY SERIES] (University Park: Pennsylvania State University Press, 1999).

Savedow, Steve (ed/tr). *Sepher Rezial Hemelach. The Book of the Angel Rezial* (York Beach: Samuel Weiser, Inc., 2000).

> *Sepher Reziel Hamelach* (≈ *Sefer Raziel*) is primarily a production of Jewish folk magic. It is discussed by Joshua Trachtenberg in *Jewish Magic and Superstition* (New York: Behrman's Jewish Book House, 1939; subsequently reprinted), a rare academic treatment of Jewish magic, considered something of a classic, though in sore need of updating.
>
> Savedow's work seems to attempt two things: (1) to provide a reliable English edition of the text, and (2) to provide practicing magicians with yet another *grimoire*.
>
> An appendix to this book (pages 280-286) gives a list of *Sefer Raziel* texts in manuscript compiled by Adam McLean. The first MS listed is British

Library MS. Sloane 3826, which is discussed in the present paper above as *Liber Salomonis*. McLean's list is posted on the Internet at the *Alchemy Web Site*: "Sepher Raziel Manuscripts," www.levity.com/alchemy/raziel.html.

Schäfer, Peter; and Kippenberg, Hans G. (eds). *Envisioning Magic: A Princeton Seminar and Symposium* [STUDIES IN THE HISTORY OF RELIGIONS (*Numen* BOOK SERIES), vol. LXXV] (Leiden – New York – Köln: Brill, 1997).

Scot, Reginald. *The Discovery of Witchcraft* (1584 edition published by John Rodker, 1930; rpt., New York: Dover Publications, Inc.)

Scott, Sir Walter. *Demonology and Witchcraft: Letters Addressed to J. G. Lockhart, Esq* (1830; rpt. New York: Bell Publishing Company, 1970).

Seligmann, Kurt. *The History of Magic* (New York: Pantheon Books, Inc., 1948).

Shah, Sayed Idries. *Oriental Magic* (New York: Philosophical Library, 1957).
- Chapter 2. "Jewish Magic"
- Chapter 3. "Solomon: King and Magician"
- Bibliography, "Grimoire References"

Shores, Travis W. THE CONJUROR'S TOOLKIT 1400-1800: CIPHERS, IMAGES, AND MAGICAL CULTURES OF POWER WITHIN THE SOLOMONIC GRIMOIRES (MA Thesis, Hanover: Dartmouth College, 2014).

Shumacher, Wayne. *Natural Magic and Modern Science: Four Treatises, 1590-1657* [MEDIEVAL AND RENAISSANCE TEXTS & STUDIES, volume 63] (State University of New York at Binghamton, 1989).

The treatises discussed are
(i) Bruno's *De Magia, Theses de magia, De magia mathematica*
(ii) Martin Delrio's *Disquisitionum magicarum libri sex*
(iii) Campanella's *De sensu rerum et magia*; (iv) Gaspar Schott's *Magia universalis*

_____. *The Occult Sciences in the Renaissance* (Berkeley: University of California Press, 1972; 2nd printing 1973).

Shumaker's study gives full accounts of astrology, witchcraft, magic, alchemy, hermetic doctrine.

Skemer, Don C. *Binding Words: Textual Amulets in the Middle Ages* [MAGIC IN HISTORY SERIES] (University Park: Pennsylvania State University Press, 2006).

Skinner, Stephan. *Techniques of Graeco-Egyptian Magic* (Singapore: Golden Hoard Press, 2014)

Skinner, Stephan. *Techniques of Solomonic Magic* (Singapore: Golden Hoard Press, 2015)

Sullivan, Lawrence E. (ed). *Hidden Truths: Magic, Alchemy, and the Occult*. [RELIGION, HISTORY AND CULTURE: Selections from THE ENCYCLOPEDIA OF RELIGION, edited by Mircea Eliade] (New York: Macmillan Publishing Company, 1989).

>Encyclopedia entries in four categories: 1. OCCULTISM, 2. MAGIC, 3. MAGICAL OBJECTS TECHNIQUES, AND POWERS, and 4. ALCHEMY.

Thomas, Keith. *Religions and the Decline of Magic* (Oxford – New York: Oxford University Press, 1971; rpt. 1997).

Thompson, R. Campbell. *Semitic Magic: Its Origins and Development* (London: Luzac & Company, 1908; rpt New York: Ktav Publishing House, 1971; New York: AMS Press, 1976; York Beach: Red Wheel/Weiser Books, 2000).

Tomlinson, Gary. *Music in Renaissance Magic. Toward a Historiography of Others* (Chicago – London: University of Chicago Press, 1993).

Tyson, Donald. *The Demonology of King James I: Includes the Original Text of Daemonologie and News from Scotland* (Woodbury: Llewellyn Publications, 2011).

_____. *Enochian Magic for Beginners. The Original System of Angel Magic*. St. Paul: Llewellyn Publications, 1997.

_____. *Ritual Magic. What It Is and How to Do It* (St. Paul: Llewellyn Publications, 1992).

Walker, D. P. *Spiritual and Demonic Magic. From Ficino to Campanella* (London: University of Notre Dame Press, 1958; rpt. 1975).

_____. *Unclean Spirits. Possession and Exorcism in France and England in the Late Sixteenth and Early Seventeenth Centuries* (Philadelphia: University of Pennsylvania Press, 1981).

Weyer, Johann (= Jean Wier, John Wier, Ioannes Wierus). *Witches, Devils, and Doctors in the Renaissance* (DE PRÆSTIGIIS DÆMONUM, 1583), introduction and notes by George Mora; translation by John Shea; preface by John Weber [MEDIEVAL AND RENAISSANCE TEXTS & STUDIES, volume 73] (Binghamton: State University of New York at Binghamton, 1991; rpt. Tempe: Arizona State University, 1998).

> Of particular interest are two sections of Book Two: Chapter II, "A DESCRIPTION OF THE INFAMOUS *magician and of GOETEIA and THEOURGIA*"; and Chapter V, "CONCERNING CERTAIN *books of magic*," which discusses "books passed down by Raziel and Raphael," *Book Four on Occult Philosophy* attributed to Agrippa, but appraised by Weyer as "falsely ascribed to his hand," and "the pestilential little book of Pietro d'Abano entitled *Heptameron or Elements of Magic*." Chapter VI goes on to discuss Trithemius and his book *Steganographia*.

> Unfortunately, this volume excludes the Appendix, *Pseudomonarchia Daemonum*. However, Joseph Peterson includes *Pseudomonarchia Daemonum* in both Latin and English as Appendix 2 in his edition of *The Lesser Key of Solomon* (York Beach: Weiser Books, 2001), pages 227-259. Appendix 3 gives a chart comparing the spirits of the *Goetia* with those of Weyer.

Whitcomb, Bill. *The Magician's Companion: A Practical and Encyclopedic Guide to Magical and Religious Symbolism* [LLEWELLYN'S SOURCEBOOK] (Woodbury: Llewellyn Publications: 1993).

Wilkinson, Robert J. "The Tetragrammaton in Private Devotion and Magic in the Middle Ages," = CHAPTER 7 of *Tetragrammaton: Western Christians and the Hebrew Name of God – From the Beginnings to the Seventeenth Century* [STUDIES IN THE HISTORY OF CHRISTIAN TRADITIONS, 179] (Leiden – Boston: Brill, 2015), pages 266-279.

Winters, Dana. "Hermetic/Cabalist Ritual in Christopher Marlowe's *Doctor Faustus*," in *Journal for the Academic Study of Magic*, Issue 5, edited by Susan Johnson Graf and Amy Hale (Oxford: Mandrake of Oxford, 2009).

Solomonic Magic on the Internet

Some Solomonic texts seem to be everywhere on the Internet, while others are not represented at all. Anything touched by one of the founders of the Golden Dawn is, for better or worse, reproduced, pirated, and linked over and over, as, for example, W. W. Westcott's ubiquitous *Sefer Yezirah* or S. L. MacGregor Mathers' *Key of Solomon* and *Lemegeton*.

Many sites offering magic texts carry viruses and other sorts of e-vermin which can plague those unfortunate enough to enter. Thus, for safety and, fortunately, a wide array of reliably presented texts, refer to the following sites:

- ALCHEMY WEBSITE AND VIRTUAL LIBRARY: http://www.alchemywebsite.com/

- INTERNET SACRED TEXTS ARCHIVE: www.sacred-texts.com

- TWILIT GROTTO: www.esotericarchives.com

On *Liber Salomonis* and other portions of Sloane MS 3826:

- A full transcription of British Library Sloane MS 3826 appears at HERMETIC KABBALAH: *Don Karr's Solomonic Magic*: http://www.digital-brilliance.com/contributed/Karr/Solomon/index.php

- The transcription of a closely related text, Sloane MS 3846: *Book of the Angel Raziel*, also in English, can be viewed at TWILIT GROTTO: http://www.esotericarchives.com/raziel/raziel.htm

Index

The dozens of angel names in *Sepher Raziel* have not been indexed, as they appear in a much more readable form in the tables of Appendix 2. The modern text of *Sepher Raziel* has been indexed, but only a few key words in the transcription have been indexed, as it is much more likely that readers will search the index under the familiar modern spellings of words rather than the contracted, older or obsolete forms found in the transcription. The names of animals and birds listed in the four *Ala* have not been indexed. Selected authors from the bibliographic sections have been indexed.

Abano, Peter de, 14, 241, 242, 267, 268, 272, 283
Abramelin, 30, 40, 266
Adderwort, 187, 193, 250
Additional MS 15299, 15, 264
Adelard of Bath, 18
Agrippa, Henry Cornelius, 17, 28, 30, 39, 43, 50, 60, 267-269, 272, 278, 280, 283
Åkerman, Susanna, 20, 63, 268
Ala, the four, 9, 10, 22, 68, 74, 89, 111, 167, 183, 184, 190, 197, 204, 259
Albafortum, 192
Alfonso X, 21, 69, 70, 261, 285, 291
Algalia, 123, 249, 250
Almabum. See Rosemary
Almadel, 40, 45, 48, 54
Almalie. See Rosemary
Alnwick MS 585, 15, 262
Alnwick MS 596, 15
Aloes, 17, 114, 249, 262
Alphonso X of Spain, 23
Ambergris, 249
Ambra. See Ambergris
Amethyst, 188
Angelus Magnus Secreti Creatoris, 20, 167
Angilae, 160, 248

Aniseed, 191
Apinum, 195, 249
Apium. See Parsley
Araboth, seventh Heaven, 218, 241, 243, 255, 256, 257, 263
Arbatel of Magick, 267, 278
Ark of the Covenant, 10, 168, 236, 237
Ars Almadel, 40, 45, 48, 54
Ars Notoria, 45, 49-52, 54, 58, 60
Ars Nova, 45, 52
Ars Paulina, 40
Artemisia, 96, 190
Arzolla, 249, 250
Ashmole MS 1730, 261
Ashmole MS 1790, 260
Ashmole, Elias, 17, 18, 20
Assafoetida, 249
Auricular muris, 249, 250
Babylon, 166, 234
Bacon, Roger, 22, 260
Balsam, 170, 211, 249
Bdellium, 170
Beleemus De imaginibus, 68
Benzoin, 249
Beryl, 183, 185, 188, 194
Bibliotheca Vaticana, 21, 261
Bilgal, 68

Bodleian Library, 18, 19, 20, 260, 261
Book of Enoch, 30
Book of Mysteries, See *Sepher ha-Razim*
Booke of Vertues, 68
British Museum, 15, 21
Butler, Alison, 269
Butler, E M, 26, 27, 28, 31, 40, 42, 46, 55, 57, 61
Byzantium, 39
Calamint, 195
Camphor, 191, 215, 216, 221, 222
Cancer mastum, 215, 249
Cannabis, 96, 191
Cannaferula, 195
Caput Draconis, 76, 170, 180, 181
Carbuncle, 183
Cardamom, 191, 209, 215, 249
Carnelian, 185, 186
Cassia, 101, 114, 121, 122, 195, 208, 215, 216, 249
Celeriac, 187, 192, 194
Celonites, 94, 188
Centaurea, 193
Cephar Raziel, 20, 261. See also *Sepher Raziel*
Cera alba, 249
Cecchetelli, Michael, 55
Cherubim, 13, 196
Chicory, 193, 195, 200, 249, 251
Cicorea. See Chicory
Cicuta, 191, 192, 249, 250
Cinamomus. See Cinnamon
Cinquefoil, 195, 250, 251
Citron, 250
Civet, 249, 250
Clarifaton, 74, 168
Classen. See Sandalwood oil
Claves Salomonis, 268

Clavicula Salomonis, 38- 41, 49, 53
Clifford's Inn, 18
Clove, 250
Codex Latinus Monacensis, 40
Colophony, 250
Columbrina, 187, 193, 250
Complete Magician's Tables, 40, 215, 235, 241, 249, 252
Constitution of Honorius, 57
Coral, 187
Coriander, 191, 192
Costum. See Costus
Costus, 17, 192, 250
Crocum. See Crocus
Crocus, 17, 114, 169, 187, 191, 192, 194, 200, 201, 208, 211, 215, 221, 222, 250
Crowley, Aleister, 27, 31, 40, 45, 46
Crystal, 17, 185, 186, 187, 188
Cypress, 250
Das Kloster, 27, 58, 60
Davies, Owen, 268
Decans, 214, 215
Dee, Dr John, 2, 17, 19, 20, 261, 271-274, 277, 278
Dehn, Georg, 266
Diamond, 183, 188
Dragantia, 193, 250
Dragantium, 187, 250
Driscoll, Daniel, 58
Duke of Sussex, Prince Augustus Frederick, 15, 264
Eleazar, Rabbi of Worms, 13, 14, 15, 16, 244, 264, 266
Elizabeth I, Queen, 18
Emerald, 13, 171, 183, 184
Enochian, 2
Eringo, 250
Euphorbium, 250
Faguncia. See Hyacinth

Fanger, Claire, 23, 27, 31, 42, 50, 51, 59, 64, 65, 69, 258, 272, 276
Fennel, 191
Flint, Valerie, 272
Folia lauri, 250
Forman, Simon, 17, 20
Frankincense, 187, 192, 195, 200, 210, 211, 215, 222, 250, 251
Frankincense oil, 250, 251
Freemasonry, 15
Fumigiis, 122, 123, 215, 216
Galbanum, 250
Gariofilum. See Cloves
Gaster, Moses, 272
Ginzberg, Rabbi Louis, 16
Gioin, John, 19
Godwin, Joscelyn, 44
Goetia, 28, 32-34, 40, 45-49, 52-54, 269, 270, 276, 283
Golden Dawn, Hermetic Order of, 31, 267, 273, 284
Gollancz, Hermann, 272
Goodrick-Clarke, Nicholas, 272
Gower, John, 22
Grand Grimoire, 270
Greene, Thomas, 273
Grillot de Givry, 27, 271
Grimoire of Pope Honorius, 57, 58
Grimorium Verum, 28, 40, 54, 55, 270
Guth, Steven, 266
Gwyne, John, 18, 19
Hanegraaff, Wouter, 272
Harms, Daniel, 271
Hedegård, Gösta, 32, 60
Heliotrope, 186
Hemlock, 249, 250
Henbane, 250
Heptameron, 30, 40, 241, 267, 268, 283

Hermes, 13, 68, 83, 87, 99, 103, 108, 114, 115, 117, 119, 120, 122, 145, 146, 171, 178, 181, 193, 194, 196, 198, 201, 208-210, 212, 213, 215, 235, 236, 273
Hockley, Frederick, 267, 272, 274, 277
Holocaust, meaning of, 234
Honorius, 23, 29, 41, 52, 56-61, 63, 65, 175, 259, 270
Horehound, 250
Hyacinth, 183, 184
Hygromanteia, 25, 29, 37-39
Hypericon, 191, 195
Idel, Moshe, 274
Insqrmo. See Jusquiami
Iris, 93, 187
Jasper, 186
Jekyll, Sir Joseph, 21
Jerusalem, 70, 141, 144, 148, 209, 232, 234, 237, 266
Johnson, Sarah Iles, 26
Jusquiami, 191, 192, 195
Kalonymus, Rabbi Judah ben, 16
Kamazan, 73, 167
Karr, Don, 28, 62, 64, 70, 71, 271, 284
Kieckhefer, Richard, 31, 59, 275
Kippenberg, Hans, 273, 281
Klaassen, Frank, 27, 31, 51, 59, 64, 258, 276
Kuntz, Darcy, 50, 56, 268, 272, 277
Láng, Benedek, 64, 276
Leitch, Aaron, 30-32, 40
Lemegeton, 28, 33, 34, 38-40, 45, 46, 48-50, 52, 53, 274, 278, 284
Lesser Key of Solomon, 28, 38, 45, 46, 49, 50, 52. See also *Lemegeton*
Levita, Elias, 21
Libavius, Andreas, 19

Liber Clavis, 9, 88, 172, 182
Liber Hermetis, 22, 193
Liber Imaginum, 22
Liber Juratus/Liber Iuratus, 29, 41, 59-61
Liber Lunae, 18, 68
Liber/Librum Razielis, 21- 23, 65, 66, 69, 70, 169, 259, 265
Liber Salomonis, 1, 2, 5, 7, 9, 18, 68, 70, 71, 163, 165, 259, 271, 281, 284
Liber Sameyn, 69, 262
Liber Virtutum, 168
Liber Visionum/Liber Visionem, 22, 59, 202, 203
Lignum aloes, 170, 192, 195, 201, 202, 208, 210, 214, 215, 216, 221, 222
Lilly, William, 33
Linum, 100, 194
Llanidloes, 18, 19
Luck, Georg, 276
Ma'on, fourth Heaven, 218, 241, 242, 255, 256, 257
Magnetite, 188
Makon, fifth Heaven, 218, 241, 242, 243, 255, 256, 257
Malachim, 14, 15
Marathakis, Ioannis, 25, 29, 37
Margalioth, Mordecai, 265
Marjoram, 193, 194
Marrubio albo, 250
Martagon, 101, 195
Mastic, 17, 169, 170, 187, 195, 200, 208, 212, 214, 215, 221, 250
Mathers, S L MacGregor, 266, 275, 284
Mathiesen, Robert, 31, 59, 64, 258
McLean, Adam, 29, 49, 50, 65, 258, 278, 280, 281

Merkavah/ Merkabah, 4, 14, 30, 31, 270
Metatron, 13, 50
Meyer, Marvin, 31, 278
Micraton, 136, 196, 206, 227, 230, 247, 253, 256, 257
Mint, 250
Morgan, Michael, 15, 274
Morigny, John of, 22, 202, 203
Mortagon, 98, 192
Moses, 60, 61, 158, 159, 169, 170, 205, 207, 235- 237, 246-248, 256, 264, 271
Mucraton, 112, 196, 206
Muculazarat, 170, 251
Muschullaroth, 212, 251
Muscum. See Musk
Musk, 98, 129, 170, 192, 193, 195, 201, 202, 208, 211, 215, 216, 222, 250
Musthalazeratis, 121, 251
Myrrh, 170, 211, 212, 251
Myrtle, 251
Napier, Richard, 20, 261
Nasturtium, 195
Necronomicon, 278, 279
Nepita, 99, 194
Nightshade, stinking, 250
Notary Art, See *Ars Notoria*
Nottingham, Gary, 32-36, 40, 42, 44, 47
Nutmeg, 114, 208, 215, 216, 251
Nucem muscata. See Nutmeg
Nux muscata. See Nutmeg
Oberion, 18, 68
Occulta Philosophia, 30
Olibanum. See Frankincense oil
Onyx, 91, 185
Opoponax, 251
Osborn MS fa. 7, 260

Page, Sophie, 27, 51, 69
Pantaseron, 112, 196, 206
Parry, William, 18, 19, 259
Parsley, 191, 192
Pentaphyllon, 250, 251
Pepper, 251
Peterson, Joseph, 25, 29, 38, 44, 46, 48, 52-56, 58, 59, 61, 62, 273, 274, 283
Picatrix, 20, 27, 30, 63, 268, 275, 277, 279, 280
Piper Nigrum, 17
Pirkei Hekhalot, 30
Poppy, 251
Postel, Guillaume, 173
Prasius, 187
Psalter (*Psalms*), 235
Pseudomonarchia daemonum, 46
Psyllium, 99, 193
Quatuor Annulus Solomonis, 22
Rankine, David, 19, 28, 33, 43, 52-54, 58, 192, 235, 276
Raqia, second Heaven, 218, 241, 255, 256, 257
Red Dragon, 28, 55, 56
Rhubarb, 251
Rosemary, 190, 249
Rosicrucian, 19, 268, 274, 278
Rudd, Dr Thomas, 28, 29, 52-54, 274, 278
Runyon, 'Poke', 32
Sacrifice, 14, 16, 113, 120, 124, 207, 209, 210, 213, 217
Sage, 194, 251
Salvia, 100, 194, 251
Samaim, 9, 10, 16, 68, 74, 168, 240
Sameton, 73, 167
Sandalon, 112, 196, 206
Sandalus, 208, 216, 251
Sandalwood, 17, 195, 208, 212, 214, 222, 250, 251
Sandalwood oil, 250, 251
Sandaton, 196, 206
Sapphire, 13, 171, 183, 185
Savedow, Steve, 7, 14, 15, 222, 229, 258, 280
Savory, 192, 251
Schäfer, Peter, 273, 281
Schechaqim, third Heaven, 241
Scheible/Scheibel, Johann, 27, 58, 60
Scholem, Gershom, 266
Scicordia, 251
Season, names & angels, 14, 168, 215, 216, 219, 220, 229, 230, 231, 232, 246
Secret Lore of Magic, 42, 65, 258
Semiforas, 10, 15, 75, 77, 89, 95, 102, 112, 147, 148, 149, 151, 154-157, 167, 168, 171, 183, 189, 196, 205, 237, 238, 240, 243-246, 256
Semiforax. See Semiforas
Sepher ha-Malbosh, 222, 229
Sepher ha-Malbush, 14
Sepher ha-Mazloth, 15
Sepher ha-Razim, 13, 14, 15, 262, 265, 277
Sepher ha-Shem, 13, 14, 16
Sepher Maphteah Shelomoh, 41
Sephar Rasiel, 11, 22, 67, 260
Sepher Raziel, 7, 14, 16, 20, 68, 71, *et seq.*
Sepher Raziel ha-Melakh, 7, 11, 13-16, 161, 162
Sepher Razim, See *Sepher ha-Razim*
Sepher Sodei Razya, 16
Sepher Yetzirah, 14, 16, 264
Shah, Idries, 25, 42, 46, 48, 54, 56, 57, 61, 65, 258, 281

Shakespeare, 17, 18
Shamayim, first Heaven, 218, 241, 255, 256, 257
Shechaqim, third Heaven, 218, 241, 255, 256, 257
Shem ha-Mephorash, 14, 167
Shemhamphoras Salomonis Regis, 29, 60
Shi'ur Qomah, 15
Shimmush Tehillim, 60
Shumacher, Wayne, 281
Sibley/Sibly, Ebenezer, 43, 44
Skemer, Don, 27, 281
Skinner, Stephen, 23, 34, 36-41, 43, 44, 52-54, 62, 64, 70, 163, 267, 279, 282
Sloane, Hans, 21
Sloane MS 313, 58
Sloane MS 2731, 48-50, 52
Sloane MS 3648, 48-50
Sloane MS 3826, 11, 12, 16, 18, 20, 21, 23, 61-65, 68-70, 71-160, 258, 259, 284
Sloane MS 3846, 7, 11, 17-21, 23, 24, 69, 167, 169, 178, 187, 193, 194, 197, 259, 284
Sloane MS 3847, 7, 11, 21, 23, 66, 165, 166, 167, 168, 169, 172, 173, 174, 184, 192, 193, 212, 259
Sloane MS 3853, 7, 11, 22, 23, 67, 260
Solomon, King, 2, 13, 22, 23, 68, 69, 165, 166, 168, 169, 171-178, 182-184, 190, 193, 196, 197, 204, 207, 209, 210, 211-216, 220, 221, 231, 233, 234-238, 240, 244, 260, 274, 277, 278, 280, 281, 283, 284
Somers, Baron, 20, 21
Spirits, 82, 92, 95-97, 99, 101, 105, 106, 108, 110, 113, 114, 116-120, 148, 150, 151, 156, 171, 176, 186, 189, 190-195, 197, 199-203, 207, 208, 210-214, 238-240, 245, 264, 266
Stamonea, 215
Storax, 251
Stratton-Kent, Jake, 54
Succo, 98, 99, 192, 193
Succum, 193, 215, 216
Swedenborg, Emanuel, 20
Sworn Book of Honorius, 22, 28, 40, 51, 57-60, 64, 258
Techniques of Graeco-Egyptian Magic, 25, 36, 282
Techniques of Solomonic Magic, 25, 36-40, 44, 282
Temporum Anni, 167, 217, 259
Testament of Solomon, 25, 40
Theurgia-Goetia, 32-36, 40, 45, 47, 48, 54
Thorndike, Lynn, 31, 50, 58, 61, 65, 258
Thur/Thure/Thuris. See Frankincense
Thyme, 75, 169, 170, 193, 214, 251
Thymiamata, 10, 113-115, 117, 170, 206-209, 212, 215, 251
Topaz, 171, 183, 184, 185, 194
Torijano, Pablo, 25, 26
Trachtenberg, Joshua, 15, 16, 31, 280
Tractatus Munditia, 168
Tractatus Thymiamatus, 9, 10, 68, 74, 207
Tragacanth, gum, 169
Treatise of Cleanesse, 68, 74
True Black Magic, 28, 55, 56
Turner, Robert, 31, 49-51, 53, 267, 268, 279

Twilit Grotto, 25, 29, 32, 48, 56, 60, 284
Tyson, Donald, 267, 268, 279, 282
Vat. MS Reg. Latin 1300, 21, 261
Vazebelil, 98, 192
Veenstra, Jan, 48
Veritable Key of Solomon, 28, 34, 37, 43
Veronèse, Julien, 51
Verus Jesuitarum Libellus, 60
Viterbo, Cardinal Egidio, 21
Waite, A E, 26, 27, 31, 42, 46, 48, 54-57, 59-62, 65, 258, 268
Walmesbury, William, 19
Warnock, Christopher, 44
Wierus, See Weyer
Wellcome MS 3203, 53
Wellcome MS 4666, 43, 58
Wellcome MS 4669, 43
Wellcome MS 4670, 43
Weyer, Johann, 46, 52, 282, 283
Worcester, 19
Zauberbibliothek, 27
Zazont, 73, 167
Zebraymayl, 145, 146, 235, 236
Zebul, sixth Heaven, 125, 152, 218, 241, 242, 255, 256, 257
Zodiac, Perfumes of, 10, 214
Zohar, 262, 263

www.ingramcontent.com/pod-product-compliance
Lightning Source LLC
Chambersburg PA
CBHW081802300426
44116CB00014B/2208